Shakespeare,
IN FACT

IRVIN LEIGH MATUS

Shakespeare, IN FACT

➤ ◄

CONTINUUM · NEW YORK

1994
The Continuun Publishing Company
370 Lexington Avenue, New York, NY 10017

Copyright © 1994 by Irvin Leigh Matus

Printed in the United States of America

Library of Congress Cataloging-in-Publication Data.

Matus, Irvin Leigh.
Shakespeare, in fact / Irvin Leigh Matus.
p.   cm.
Includes bibliographical references (p.) and index.
ISBN 0-8264-0624-6 (alk. paper)
1. Shakespeare, William, 1564–1616—Authorship.   2. Dramatists,
English—Early modern, 1500–1700—Biography.   I. Title.
PR2939.M36   1994
822.3′3—dc20

[B]

93-16327
CIP

To Sam and Marilyn Schoenbaum
With affection and gratitude

Contents

Author's Preface

Although I was living in Washington, D. C. in September 1987, I was only vaguely aware of the "trial" there of the case of the *Earl of Oxford v. William Shakespeare* regarding their respective claims to the authorship of the most famous and popular plays in world literature. To put it frankly, I was not very much interested. Besides, I was busy at the time with the research and writing of a book about the surviving buildings and monuments of England that hold stories of Shakespeare, his drama and his theater, and had little time to spare for anything, no less something I considered of no real importance.

However, when I read James Lardner's excellent article about the trial in the April 11, 1988, *New Yorker,* my interest in the authorship was awakened. And so it was that, when I received an invitation to speak on the subject from Carol Sue Lipman, the president of the Shakespeare Authorship Roundtable in Los Angeles, I gladly accepted. My talk was scheduled for September 30, 1989, but I went there several weeks in advance and in that time spent many hours in the company of members of the Roundtable. I wish to report those who hold to this cause aright.

I did not find them to be, as I have heard them called, "kooks" or "loonies" (except insofar as Oxford's supporters adhere to a cause founded by a J. Thomas Looney). In my time amidst the Roundtablers, and in my contacts with the many Oxfordians I have come to know since, I have found those who dispute the authorship to be intelligent and thoughtful people, many of whom are interested in aspects of the English Renaissance and its theater beyond the confines of the authorship question, reflected in the range of topics presented by invited speakers before its membership. What is more, despite our differences on a certain subject, my contacts with the anti-Stratfordians have been, with few exceptions, cordial and congenial, and, from time to time, can even resemble real friendship (such is the case with Joe Sobran, whom I owe thanks for many a kindness).

Not that even my friendly opponents can resist getting in an occasional dig—such as the one who just barely exempted me from the worst by calling me "almost an academic." Indeed, my years of research at the Folger Shakespeare Library may raise questions about how much of the influence of the academics I know is felt in this book, and it is therefore important for you, the reader, to know precisely who contributed to it—and how.

I must first say that I come honestly by the opinion that will be heard throughout this book, which is that Shakespeare is but one of the great dramatists in the age of English Renaissance theater. If there are among his plays a number that the others do not approach, there are also a number that they have surpassed. I have taken advantage of those rare opportunities to see the plays of his contemporaries and I will confess that my most memorable evening of theater was at an Off-Broadway production of Marlowe's *Dr. Faustus*. I must agree with my dear friend, Roy Kendall, that if this play had Shakespeare's name on it, it would be one of the most performed of classical dramas. But it does not, and so it is not—and that is unfortunate.

I have not approached the authorship question with the intention of confirming Shakespearean scholarship nor refuting Oxfordian scholarship merely. It is, instead, informed by the questions raised by the Oxfordians and the opportunity they afford to view Shakespeare from a different perspective. "Orthodox scholarship" (as the Oxfordians term it) has long inclined toward viewing Shakespeare as the central fact of Renaissance theater—which the Oxfordians would remedy by viewing Shakespeare in the person of Oxford as the central figure of the age. How did Shakespeare, in fact, stand in relation to his contemporaries, both as a man and a man of the theater? This is the central question in the authorship controversy.

Let it be plainly stated that nowhere in this book is there an unsolicited contribution from, or the exploration of any line of inquiry that was initiated by an academic. To the contrary, it was such as the challenge of a certain prominent Oxfordian regarding the dating of a Folger manuscript in which "Shakespeare ye Player by Garter" appears beneath a sketch of the Shakespeare arms that spurred my personal study of the item that appears in the Afterwords to chapter 3. Similarly, it was a question about why Shakespeare was not one of the authors of the King James Bible I was asked by Kim Marshall Alston (whose connection with the Folger is solely as an employee in its gift shop) that allowed me to discover facts about this great work that are fascinating in themselves as well as pertinent to certain authorship issues. I have, however, taken full advantage of my contact with academic scholars and I cannot be too grateful to the many who listened patiently and offered invaluable guidance as I made my way through the muddle of conflicting opinion regarding Shakespeare, the theater and the age. Thank you, one and all.

But on occasion I specifically solicited the knowledge of others and I here wish to express specific thanks for the special attention of these scholars. I am most expecially indebted to Steven W. May for sharing his singular expertise about Oxford's poetry. Similarly, David Cressy has few rivals in the study of literacy and education in Shakespeare's time and I am most grateful for the special information he provided to me. Thanks are owed to David Thomas of the Public Record Office in Kew, London, for his personal help in regard to the 1595 Chamber account. William J. Tighe deserves my thanks for sending portions of his dissertation on the Band of Gentlemen Pensioners regarding Brian Annesley, and was so thoughtful as to send along pertinent personal notes as well. I am doubly grateful to Geoff Chester of the National Air and Space Museum, who not only supplied the exact information on the eclipses mentioned in *King Lear,* but enlivened my day with a recital of Geoff Chaucer. My thanks too to K. R. Andrews for his important advice that aided my research on the question of Oxford's ownership of the ship *Edward Bonaventure.* I have the rather odd problem of thanking the archival scholar who so thoroughly gave of his knowledge of Elizabethan legal documents in Latin in the case of the Ostler-Heminges suit, but preferred to remain anonymous.

There are the debts of long standing I happily pay here; foremost, my thanks to Richard Dutton for allowing me to make frequent withdrawals from his fund of knowledge about Ben Jonson and the Office of the Revels, which came in letters that were no less informative than enjoyable. Similarly, Robert Bearman of the Shakespeare Birthplace Trust was unfailingly prompt and forthcoming in answering my every inquiry and he has my gratitude. Particular thanks are due those at the Folger who so often gave their help so generously—most of all, Jean Miller, J. Franklin Mowery, Elizabeth Niemyer and, as always, Laetitia Yeandle. I am no less indebted to the staff of the Folger Reading Room for so many personal attentions, and especially Betsy Walsh, who runs the Reading Room so gently that it is only relatively recently that I discovered it is she who runs it. I also thank Bruce Martin for his assistance in providing research facilities to me at the Library of Congress. It is a particular pleasure to acknowledge Shane Poteet's timely and capable help in upgrading illustrations.

I wish to give special thanks to the Virginia Center for the Creative Arts, where I revised this typescript, and to the Morris and Gwendolyn Cafritz Foundation for the fellowship that made it possible. I cannot adequately express my appreciation to the staff and to my fellow fellows for their inspiration and, of course, their good fellowship. No small contribution was made to the success of my stay by the staff of the Sweet Briar College Library, who completely met my rather specialized needs.

At last, it must be said that the way of an "independent scholar" (such as myself) is not an easy one and I am especially grateful to those whose encouragement and friendship have been invaluable. I therefore share this book with the Kleins—Rich, Julie and Bobby—who, from before the beginning, have always been at the ready with a kind word and a kinder deed. So, too, do I share this with Dan Burney and Martin Green, gentlemen and scholars both, for so much kindness and good fellowship throughout my years in Washington; as well as with newer, timely arrivals, Dan Borinsky and Phil Bufithis (with added thanks, Phil, for the "college try"). At last, words are inadequate to express the pleasure of knowing Vicki Barker; thus, to Ruth Barker go my thanks for both her daughter and her own kindness toward me. To two most accommodating friends, Rod Lawrence and Jim McConkey (who may have got it just right when he said that Shakespeare's plays would be a miracle no matter who wrote them), my thanks equally for your good cheer and your hospitality. For their contributions to this book and its author I thank Dave Kelly and Tom Mann, and certainly Jozef Topolski, whose help may be imitated but never duplicated. It is both fitting and a pleasure to remember here the warmth and caring of Sheila MacRae, a worthy descendant of the famed Sarah Siddons, the granddaughter of John Ward, whose acting company's performance of *Othello* in Stratford in 1746 was instrumental in the dispute over the Stratford church monument discussed in these pages. And I cannot forget Ben Thompson—as though anybody could.

Finally, there is the 12-year-old "Oberon," whom I met at the Folger in the summer of 1988. I must confess I have forgotten his name, but it is as Oberon he deserves to be remembered, for the magic of his experience of Shakespeare lingers still and allows me to believe the conclusion I have reached is the right one.

➔ 1 ⬅

In the Court
of Public Opinion

*Nine times out of ten, in the arts as in life,
there is actually no truth to be discovered;
there is only error to be exposed.*
—H. L. Mencken

A virtual genre of books has come into being in which the author declares that he set out to prove one thing and found the opposite to be true. This is not another. Regarding the authorship of William Shakespeare's plays, I am satisfied that a glover's son, born in a market town in the English Midlands, having had nothing more than a grammar school education, was *the* William Shakespeare who wrote a number of the world's greatest literary works. If I cannot offer incontrovertible proof of his authorship, the smoking pen if you will, I did not find either that the evidence which is supposed to undermine his authorship, any more than the evidence that alleges to show another to be the more likely author, stands up to investigation.

Shakespeare has maintained a unique position in the modern world, especially in a time when the great figures and momentous events quickly recede from the consciousness, soon to be forgotten. Thanks to his plays, he remains an always vital, lively part of the contemporary scene. And so it is not surprising that our age, with its appetite for every intimate detail of every shooting star that streaks across its firmament, expects nothing less of the fixed star of England. It is by no means unique.

The passion in earlier centuries for discovering Shakespeare, to the growing exclusion of all his contemporaries, evolved into the belief that he must have been an overpowering figure in English Renaissance theater, that great flowering of popular drama between 1590 and 1642. Generations of literary men, scholars and private "Bardolators" searched for every scrap of lore, every whisper of gossip, every allusion, some real, many imagined, to the man and his work that could be found. In the process, both man and work underwent a "sea-change," a transformation most literally into something "rich and strange."

This all began with the collections of his plays edited by some of the great literary figures of the eighteenth century. What emerged from their close studies by the time the nineteenth century rolled around was a widespread "perception of beauties" that had been "before descried as faults." Bit by bit, Shakespeare was found to possess every virtue of art, mind and spirit imaginable—and to a greater degree than had ever been possessed by any mortal. Inevitably, the image of the man had to be brought into line with his works.

The first manifestations of the transformation of his image were in the images of the man himself. His contemporaries left behind only two portraits: one, the frontispiece with its "horrible hydrocephalus development" in the 1623 folio edition of his plays; the other, his monument in the church where he was buried in Stratford-upon-Avon, which has been described as "suggestive of a man crunching a sour apple, or struck with amazement at some unpleasant spectacle." They are not pretty pictures. No matter. By the mid-1700s, these features were remodeled to show Shakespeare as he should have, *must* have been. He now took on the appearance of a man of intellect, of dignity, of, yes, a certain nobility.

However, making a life to go with these images was no mere matter of cosmetics. Embellish it though one may, the record of the man left him a stubbornly ordinary individual. Perhaps something of a rascal in his Stratford years, the mature Shakespeare remained solidly in the ranks of the Elizabethan bourgeoisie. It has been truly said of him that "In the shadowy throng of the Great he cuts an uninspiring figure." * Sooner or later, someone was bound to decide that the Immortal Bard could not possibly have been so blandly mortal. So began the search for an inspiring figure worthy of being Shakespeare.

Is It Important?

It can be said, and so it has, that who wrote the plays is not really important. Even if some miraculous document turned up that put beyond any doubt that someone else wrote the plays, the plays themselves would not change. For, as the author himself said, "the play's the thing." Not so, insist the doubters. One such, Charles Vere, Earl of Burford, went so far

---

* Alice Fairfax-Lucy, *Charlecote and the Lucys*, 14. The author is descended from one of the earliest figures in the Shakespeare mythology, Sir Thomas Lucy, famous as the man who drove Shakespeare from Stratford for poaching his deer.

as to say, "If you get Shakespeare wrong, you get the Elizabethan Age wrong."[1] In other words, to get the Elizabethan Age right, you must get the right Elizabethan—the one deserving of being the author of the plays that have become the greatest glory of that age. The search has uncovered no less than 56 such Elizabethans including virtually the entire Court of Elizabeth (not excluding the queen herself); the playwright Christopher Marlowe (whose death in 1593, it is argued, was faked); the Jesuits and the Rosicrucians, and the now deposed long-time favorite, Sir Francis Bacon. The current front-runner for the True Author laurel is Edward de Vere, the 17th Earl of Oxford, who happens to have been an ancestor of the Earl of Burford.* His sweeping proposition, therefore, might be dismissed as the statement of a man who stands to "enhance the family tree if he can convince the world he is right." However, it does reflect the popular perception of Shakespeare that has grown over the past two centuries.

Shakespeare is usually the way we come upon the Elizabethan Age. For many he is all they will ever know—ever care to know—of that era. It is viewed through his eyes, heard in his voice—a voice that has risen above the din of his time. If Shakespeare came to Queen Elizabeth's court as a mere player, it can only have been a matter of time before his gems of wit were the crown jewels of the court coterie. All's well if it ends there. For the minute we dare to test these assumptions, a very different picture emerges. His contemporaries tell us very little about the man. Most of what we hear is in routine documents: church records, tax certificates, a deposition in a lawsuit, business transactions—building stone, land, tithes. His plays were not published in dainty books; instead of flowers pressed between their pages, we find traces of scissors and spectacles. And the printed texts themselves—ill-set, punctuated by errors, and perhaps not very faithful versions of the author's work to boot. The Elizabethans cannot possibly have been as careless as all that! This demands an explanation.

The most popular way of searching for this explanation nowadays is an extension of the image of the artist that has been built up over the generations. It seeks to find the man who could create these omniscient works, and a distant market town and the theaters do not seem the places to look. Rather, it is to the universities we must go; to the societies of lawyers

---

* This is an opportune point to explain the term that will be used most often for those who question the Shakespeare authorship. The proponents of Oxford have succeeded in pushing their candidate to the forefront to no small degree by refining, amplifying, and adding to the research the supporters of other candidates have, over the years, developed against the "Stratford man." Therefore, rather than using ponderous general terms for the "anti-Stratfordians," the challengers will be referred to by the generic term *Oxfordians*, except when clearly inappropriate.

known collectively as the Inns of Court, to the court of England itself. It is there he should be found: a person of learning, of importance, of stature; of, yes, very definite nobility.

There are, however, problems with this explanation. Why should the author have wanted anonymity and allowed his plays to be printed under a pseudonym that sounded almost the same as the name of a common player? Why did he write them? Why were they published in such careless texts, some anonymously, some surreptitiously; all without any signs that their creator authorized their publication? And what about that fellow William Shakespeare, or Shakspere, or something like that, whose name appears in the records of an acting company and even in the editions of the plays? If he was not the author, who was he?

These questions and others like them touch every facet of the player and playwright in Shakespeare's time. They involve the status of the public stage and those who made it their profession; they define the functions of governmental and regulatory powers; they encompass the most powerful figures of the age. The answers call into question the reliability of documents and the authenticity of government records. They reinterpret the society and the culture, as well as the role played by a number of important figures who were in some way connected with these plays and their author. The upshot is not only an alternative Shakespeare, but an alternative version of the age in respect to him. And there is more. The self-styled heretics call into question the "orthodox" scholarship, as well as the "objectivity" of the scholars who stubbornly refuse to see things their way; the heresy has thereby given rise to an alternative scholarship as well. Thus, there are two opposing viewpoints of the author, his age, and the interpretation of the facts regarding them. Which is the right one? The answer to this question may help us to discover the impetus to his genius, and the nature of his genius itself. The answers to the authorship questions can be important indeed.

These questions take on added importance because the authorship debate has been brought before the court of public opinion—literally—in moot court trials of the claims of Shakespeare and Oxford argued before three United States Supreme Court Justices in Washington, D.C. in September 1987, and before three Lords of Appeal in London in November 1988. What is on trial to a greater degree than which of the two was actually the author is the "evidence" that shapes the public understanding of a man and his age. After all, both Shakespeare and Oxford are past caring about the verdict—only the partisans of one side or the other care about that. But, everyone else who has heard the questions and is curious about the answers is owed the best evidence by which a verdict may be reached. In the Washington trial, the acting chief, Justice William Brennan, put the burden of proof on the Oxfordians.[2] Shakespeareans, however, also bear a burden: the lore and legend, the speculation and conjecture accumulated over the centuries. Although modern scholars have discarded a good deal of this and modern studies seek to place Shakespeare in his contemporary world and among his contemporaries, the old tales die hard and the Oxfordians breathe new life into them as representative of the dubious Shakespearean record and the failings of orthodox scholars. But they have also raised numerous questions about both Shakespeare and the contemporary record that are good ones. What is at issue are their answers—and how they arrive at them.

Is the major difference between orthodox and heterodox scholarship (as Peter Jaszi, the attorney for the Oxfordians in the Washington trial, said) merely a matter of "scholarly method—footnote style, and so forth—which the Oxfordians do not understand as well aŝ the professional Shakespeare scholars"?[3] To answer this we must first define "scholarly method." In fact, it is somewhat more than a mere matter of footnote style. An excellent, concise definition was set out by Giles E. Dawson. "The scholar," he wrote, "has no axes to grind":

> He is not eager to prove his own hypotheses correct, but rather to find out whether they are correct or not. He is ever ready to reevaluate and reinterpret his evidence and to discard one hypothesis in favor of a better. When he uncovers a fact that does not square with his hypothesis he neither shuts his eyes to it nor tries to explain it away nor trims it to fit the facts.[4]

The authorship debate is evidence that "professional" scholars can fall short of the ideal. Some have been, like the Oxfordians, less than "humble in attempting to solve problems that have baffled many before," and anything but "slow to announce discoveries that will upset well established beliefs." Such studies rarely stand up to scrutiny. When we look for the reasons why they fail, we find it is most often because they set out to prove a predetermined conclusion.

It is precisely that, however, that defines much of the Oxfordian method. In this book it will be seen from time to time that the critical eye that looks so severely upon Shakespearean scholarship does not fall so critically upon opinion and conjecture that has only the virtue of supporting or agreeing with the Oxfordian point of view. In some cases, their friendly facts come from the works of "orthodox" scholars. Here the critical eye winks, untroubled by any suspicion that such kindred spirits in the Shakespearean ranks may be no more, maybe a lot less, reliable than those whose views do not conform to theirs. But it is most evident in their most perplexing task: how to get rid of that persistent fellow from Stratford. For, in the words of Charlton Ogburn, the American champion of Oxford's authorship claim, "you can't get anywhere with Oxford unless you dispose of the Stratford man."[5] In the course of the next five chapters, the Oxfordian attempt to interpret the Shakespeare record in order to do just that will be investigated in depth. This will concentrate on materials of which there is some verifiable means of testing their facts. Very little attention will be given therefore to refuting their interpretations of contemporary allusions to Shakespeare.

Allusion and Illusion

Shakespeare's contemporaries were intoxicated with language and, when off on a binge, saw no reason to use one word or one sentence when three came to mind. It was very much as the Shakespearean actor Charles Dance remarked: "if you bump your head you probably say 'damn'; an Elizabethan would curse the door, curse the wood, curse the tree the wood came from, curse the acorn."[6] Just as this prolixity can allow an actor great latitude in interpreting a line, a speech or a character in a play, it also allows the scholar and the authorship partisan alike great freedom in reading anything into these same things, or any of the writings of the period.

Whereas Oxfordians say that concealing the author's identity was something of a state affair, by their account it does seem an awful lot of people outside of court—literary figures, printers and booksellers, even college students—were in on the secret, and dropping hints about his real identity in puns and anagrams was a pastime in literary circles. Thus, in what appear to be straightforward references to a Shakespeare who was a common actor and popular playwright, they discern clues that he was actually something, and someone, else. Unfortunately, this power of discovering that telltale word or phrase seems to come and go. Two neighboring items in Charlton Ogburn's massive opus, *The Mysterious William Shakespeare*, may serve to illustrate this, as well as demonstrate that literary interpretation is not quite the exact science he might have you believe.

The first example, on pages 104–5, is the epigram "To our English Terence, Mr Will: Shake-speare," which Ogburn anoints "the only truly informative reference to Shakespeare as an actor" in contemporary sources. It is the handiwork of John Davies of Hereford, a master of penmanship who took his poetical talents very seriously. The verse in question was published in the collection of his poems entitled *The Scourge of Folly*, and reads:

> Some say (good Will), which I, in sport, do sing,
>> Hadst thou not played some kingly parts in sport,
> Thou hadst been a companion for a king,
> And been a king among the meaner sort.

> Some others raile; but rail as they think fit,
> Thou hast no railing, but a reigning wit:
> And honesty thou sow'st, which they do reap:
> So, to increase their stock which they do keep.

Here the clue, according to Ogburn, is the phrase "a companion for a king." The title of count, it seems, is derived from the Latin word *comes,* which took on the meaning of a "companion to the Emperor," and as the English equivalent to a count is an earl, the equivalent to emperor a king, Davies struck upon an ingenious way of telling the world that the subject of his rhyme was a nobleman—a nobleman so stagestruck that he threw caution to the winds to play the king on the stage *in sport,* though it cost him his place as "a companion for a king" at court.

However, within a few pages, Ogburn's etymological powers fail him in his discussion of the three plays collectively known as the Parnassus Plays, performed and presumably written by the students of Cambridge University between 1598 and 1602. The students, Ogburn notes, do not sort Shakespeare with his supposed fellow actors, Richard Burbage and Will Kemp who, along with their profession, are derided in the third of the plays, the Second Part of *The Return from Parnassus.* Indeed, how could he be classed with those "leaden spouts" when the students revere him as a poet? This is to be found in the First Part of *The Return,* where the student Ingenioso and a courtier named Gullio speak with "marked respect" of "Sweet Mr. Shakespeare." Or so says Ogburn.

Somehow, he has missed the obvious derivation of the courtier's name from the word *gull,* familiar to anyone versed in the literature of the time as signifying, according to the *Oxford English Dictionary,* "A credulous person; one easily imposed upon; a dupe, simpleton, fool." We know it nowadays as the root of *gullible.* But we need no dictionary to know this is exactly what Gullio represents, for this is how he is introduced by Ingenioso: "Now, gentlemen, you may laugh if you will, for here comes a gull."[7] We soon hear Gullio's favorite poet, "Sweet Mr. Shakespeare," like everything else about the courtier, is held in contempt by the student, who humors him only because he is desperate and needs the courtier's patronage:

> Why, who could endure this post put into a satin suit, this haberdasher of lies, this Braggadocio, this lady monger, this mere rapier and dagger, this cringer, this foretop, but a man that's ordained to misery?[8]

In fact, fully three-quarters of the last three acts of the First *Return* are given over to the courtier and the student. It does not take a close reading of the play to learn that Gullio is a ridiculous figure and, like the foppish courtier Osric in *Hamlet,* " 'tis a vice to know him." How anyone could find confirmation of Shakespeare's exalted reputation in this play and in the approbation of this character is but one of the unintended mysteries in *The Mysterious William Shakespeare.*

Even if there is no substance to Ogburn's argument concerning the *Parnassus Plays,* what about the Davies epigram? It is, in fact, one of 292 such poems in the section of the book that gave its name to the whole, "The Scourge of Folly." After a lengthy 293rd epigram ("Upon English Proverbs") the author begins a new set of epigrams addressed "To Worthy Persons." Here we find poems to King James and nearly all the nobility of the realm, as well as several associated with the popular stage, including Francis Beaumont and George Chapman, "Father of Our English Poets." He also reveals the author of the play *Mustapha,* printed anonymously in 1609, to have been the famous courtier Sir Fulke Greville, without any detriment to his standing in court. It is in this elite company that we find one of the longest epigrams, written to Shakespeare's fellow, "honest-gamesome Robert Armin, That tickles the spleen like a harmless vermin."[9]

Armin had probably replaced Kemp in 1599 as the leading clown of the Lord Chamberlain's Men—the company for which Shakespeare acted and wrote from 1594 on—and was named on the patent by which he, Shakespeare, and six other player-shareholders in the Chamberlain's company, were taken into the service of King James on May 19, 1603. Davies' epigram to Armin begins and ends as follows:

> Armin, what shall I say of thee, but this,
> Thou art a fool and a knave? Both? fie, I miss:
> And wrong thee much, sith thou in deed art neither,
> Although in shew, thou playest both together.
> We all (that's king and all) but players are
> Upon this earthly stage . . .
> .   .   .   .   .   .
> So, play thy part, be honest still with mirth;
> Then when th[ou] art in the tiring-house of earth,
> Thou being his servant whom all kings do serve,
> May'st for thy part well played like praise deserve;
> For in that tiring-house when either be,
> Y'are one man's men and equal in degree.
> So thou, in sport, the happiest men dost school—
> To do as thou dost—wisely play the fool.

Here we can see that Armin played the fool's part—as Shakespeare did kingly parts—*in sport.* After all, anyone who is not actually a king or a fool, who only plays the part, does so "in sport." Davies' puns on the word *king* in his epigrams to the two actors is doubly appropriate, both for the roles they played (Armin is presumed to have played the role of King Lear's Fool) and because both were indeed in the King's company— of players. This word-play leads one to suspect that in Davies' lines on Shakespeare—as in all his epigrams—the most important secret he wanted to reveal was that he was himself a pretty clever fellow.

For that matter, in scrutinizing the Shakespeare epigram for obscure word clues, the title itself bears attention. *The Scourge of Folly* was published in 1611, seven years after Oxford's death, while the address "To our English Terence" certainly seems to be to one who is among the quick. What is more curious is why Shakespeare, who would by then have been renowned for his great tragedies, should be likened to a Roman comic poet. It was not dramatic skill, for Terence's comedies were not regarded as especially successful examples of the genre. Rather, it was his "command of words" which, wrote Cicero in tribute, "put Menander in our midst, translated and set out in the Latin tongue, in your quiet tone; whose speech can charm, whose every word delights." [10] Terence appealed to Elizabethans for much the same reason. He was in the curriculum of Westminster School, one of the great schools of the day, "for the better learning [of] the pure Roman style." Shakespeare, in turn, was most often praised by his contemporaries for the charm and delight he brought to the English tongue. This is the most probable reason that Davies likened his countryman to Terence.

Another and more significant source for interpretative tastes that will not be found in these pages is Shakespeare's Sonnets. One need not be a Shakespeare scholar or a heterodox detective to join the hunt for the identity of the Beloved Youth, the Dark Lady, the Rival Poet, or The Poet himself. Not a few who simply fell under the charm of the poetry have been drawn into the search for the intimate details and inmost soul of a man of whose outward life so little is known. The results are, on occasion, compelling reading and can be quite convincing. Nor are there other sources for comparison that can positively refute the conjecture of one who is truly knowledgeable and most skillful—except those others who are similarly knowledgeable and skillful, and have an utterly different and equally persuasive argument.

If even the most persuasive were introduced into this book it would, like the rest of the interpretive exercises, drive out the attention that should be given to those sources that offer the means of discovering and uncovering the age and the milieu in which Shakespeare lived as a man among men. This requires that we go beneath the cloistered circles of court life and its literary pastimes and into the world of the working playwright and the miscellany of humanity who crowded into playhouses to approve his work.

It is there that we may learn most about the time of Shakespeare—and about the substantive questions raised regarding the authorship of the plays.

This Book and Its Sources

One product of the Oxfordian search for hidden clues is that it makes the commonplace mysterious and, all put together, reads like a mystery novel. This points to one respect in which the Shakespearean scholar is at a disadvantage to his Oxfordian counterpart. The trail of clues he follows holds mysteries, but nothing mysterious; just information that must be pried from them and from their time, which often left behind only scant, stubborn means for decoding them, and which lead relentlessly to the theater, depositing an uninspiring Shakespeare squarely on its workaday doorstep. Hardly a match for the hunt for secret messages that lead to a melancholy nobleman, resigned to the offspring of his genius being stepfathered by a bumpkin, roaming through a romantically ruined castle. It is therefore unlikely anyone will ever say of a book on Shakespeare's authorship that it is the greatest detective story he has ever read, as John Galsworthy said of J. Thomas Looney's *Shakespeare Identified in Edward de Vere*, the seminal work on Oxford's claim. But then, detective stories are works of fiction.

In fact, the documentary record of English Renaissance theater and its denizen is not the stuff of stories of any kind. On the other hand, it is enlivened by contemporary literature; by the words of those who lived by or loved the vitality of the playhouse, as well as those who reviled it. But rarely is there a voice that hints of any suspicion that this was an age that would be best remembered for the creative force nurtured in its common theaters. Nowhere is this more evident than in the remains of the theater itself, which consist of little more than business entries punctuated by occasional letters from desperate playwrights that make it plain it was a precarious life for most. Posterity had to wait upon the day's dinner that, even for such luminaries as Ben Jonson and George Chapman, might be served in a jail cell where they languished for debt, mayhem or official displeasure. To know Shakespeare we must also know the contemporary theater and literary world in all its aspects.

Ultimately, the authorship question is made up of a swarm of small questions. But there are several basic questions that are at the heart of the debate and, therefore, this book. The first is whether the contemporary record of and about Shakespeare, the man and the dramatist alike, is so suspiciously lacking as the host of controversialists have posed it as being? Second, are the contemporary materials that associate Shakespeare with popular theater ambiguous, even suspect, especially in comparison with what we have of the others in the theater of his day? Which leads to the third question: was his reputation in his own time such that we should expect to find references to him that we would not expect of others? Finally, what about the current favorite, the Earl of Oxford? Are his "qualifications" so compelling, the "circumstantial evidence" so authentic, as his partisans would have us believe?

In seeking the answers to questions large and small, modern studies will play an important role. Modern literary and theater scholars especially view the great age of English drama in its entirety; their observations and conclusions, if not necessarily the last word, are invaluable to the study of the world of which Shakespeare was a part. At the same time, virtually all the documents of Shakespeare, his colleagues and of English Renaissance theater are available in modern transcriptions; all the surviving published books available in facsimile, microfilm and modern editions. Therefore, the first source in this book will always be these materials to the greatest extent possible, and the voices of his contemporaries will be the first heard wherever appropriate. After all, the surest way to find Shakespeare is to view him in the perspective and perceptions of his own age—not ours.

→ 2 ←

Shakespeare of Stratford,
His Record and Remains

Shakespeare—or "Shakspere"?

T hose who challenge the authorship of the plays and poems by William Shakespeare of Stratford-upon-Avon allege that, from his own time onward, evidence was systematically suppressed that revealed them to be the creations of another—let's say the Earl of Oxford. The scenario goes something like this: headstrong and eccentric though he was, however unable to control his compulsion to write plays of unsurpassed genius, he recognized the disgrace this would bring to his ancient title and honorable name and agreed to suppress his authorship. Thus did he accept the attribution of his works to a not very nice, not very literate, not very good actor in a London acting company. Accordingly, any record of this actor that might alert anyone to the fact he was an unlettered provincial were destroyed or altered so he would henceforth get the credit for being the author of the plays and poems. However, this deception was discovered, owing in no small part to the fact that what Charlton Ogburn calls "Operation Clean Sweep" was far from thorough.

For instance, the operatives failed to seize a large number of the documents in Stratford, which reveal that the first syllable of the name of the imposter and his family was most often spelled to produce a short *a* pronunciation: *Shack*-speare. Variable though spelling might be during the Elizabethan Age, Ogburn contends that those familiar with the bearer of a name would spell it as it was pronounced. But in the records of the Corporation of Stratford, he notes, only once was it spelled to produce the long *a* pronunciation of Shakespeare.[1] This example in the minutes and accounts of Stratford is interesting, for it was how it was spelled some dozen times by Henry Rogers after he became the borough steward and clerk in 1570. From his first entry of the name of Shakespeare's father,

John, on January 24, 1571, until the record of April 2, 1572, Rogers spelled the name "Shakespere" exclusively.[2] But, exactly one week later, he entered it as "Shaxpere" for the first time and continued to do so as long as the minutes and accounts of Stratford are identified as being in his handwriting (at least until January 1577).

But was this in fact the only time such a spelling is found? In the very same year that Rogers took on his secretarial duties, John Shakespeare was accused of lending money at interest to a John Musshem, in violation of the usury laws. In the document of this charge, we find William's father identified as "John Shappere alias Shakespere de Stratford upon Haven."[3] It appears the elder Shakespeare may have preferred this pronunciation for a time.

However, is Ogburn right that, however inconsistent the spellings might be, Elizabethans would spell a familiar name something like it was pronounced? The name of Quiney was definitely a familiar one in Stratford, for several of this family served the corporation. Nevertheless, among the thirteen different spellings of Quiney in the Stratford records, several are rendered exactly as or to be pronounced Queeney and Quinny.

In fact, a variety of spellings of names and words is the rule rather than the exception, even in the case of formal documents. One such is the deed of partnership between "Phillippe Hinshley, citizen and dyer of London . . . and John Cholmley," made on January 10, 1587, which prepared the way for the erection of the Rose, the first playhouse in Southwark.[4] However, in this same document the first name of the former is also rendered as Phillype, Phillip and Philip; his last name as Henslow and Hinshleye, as well as Hinshley. Today we know the man only as Philip Henslowe, whose accounts and papers supply virtually all the information we have of the business of theater in the great age of English drama. In these records are found many of the players and playwrights of the day who had dealings with him at one time or another; certainly they were familiar with Henslowe and certainly they could read and write. Nevertheless, when putting his name on paper, they did so in no less than twenty-six spellings with an array of pronunciations, Hinchlow and Henslaw, Hentchloe and Inclow among them.[5] But then, Henslowe suffered some indecision in the matter himself. Writing to his son-in-law and business partner, the actor Edward Alleyn, he signed his letter of July 5, 1593, Phillipe Henslow; the next, about one month later, Phillipe Hensley.

In fact, many of Shakespeare's contemporaries in theater were subject to a similar diversity in spellings and pronunciation, the oddest case being Christopher Marlowe's. He appears in both the Birth Register of the Church of St. George the Martyr, Canterbury, and the Burial Register of St. Nicholas, Deptford, as "Marlow." In between, however, his name is spelled to be pronounced everything but: in the records of the King's School of

Canterbury (Marley); of Cambridge University (Marley, Marlin, Merling, among others); in a letter from the Privy Council (Morley). In the one signature accepted as being in his hand, as a witness to the will of Katherine Benchkin, he signed as Marley, as did his father, John.[6] Nevertheless, no question has been raised as to whether this cobbler's son is the same man who is found on title pages as Christopher Marlowe.

One final bit of evidence in the telltale long *a*–short *a* hypothesis involves the playwright, poet and soldier who happens to have been named Shakerley Marmion. Or was it Shackerley? His three works published with his cooperation offer no conclusive answer. The title page and author's dedication in the first, *Hollands Leaguer* (1632), agree that it is Shackerley. However, in the next year, his name on the title page of *A Fine Companion* is spelled Shakerley, though his dedication to Sir Ralph Dutton is signed "Shack: Marmyon." Similarly, it is Shakerly on the engraved title page of the poem *Cupid and Psyche* (1637), but on the typeset title page, as well as in his dedicatory epistle and the commendatory verses to him, it is Shackerley.

Ultimately, nothing displays the complete lack of substance in this matter more than the writings of the Oxfordians. According to their argument, there is no contemporary document that links the native of Stratford with the plays nor specifically identifies the player in the Globe company as being one and the same as the playwright of the Globe company. However, as it is necessary to their case for both Shakespeare and Shakspere to be associated with this troupe, they claim a special gift for knowing when a reference to Shakespeare is really to Shakspere. After June 4, 1604, the day Oxford died, it is obviously Shakspere, although the name is always rendered *Shakespeare* except for the title page of *King Lear* (1608), where the author is named as "Shak-speare." On the other hand, except for three of the four documents in which he is listed as a tax defaulter in the Bishopsgate ward, all the artifacts before that date also render the name as *Shakespeare*. These include the draft of the patent by which a coat of arms was granted to John Shakespeare, and the royal patent of May 19, 1603, which made William and eight fellow players the servants of King James. Plainly stated, while his surname would most often be rendered to produce a short *a* in Stratford, the man, the player, the playwright and the Globe shareholder was nearly always Shakespeare.

It may not be coincidental that the tax documents in which he is recorded as "Shakspere" or "Shackspere" (in the other it is Shakespeare) are in regard to Privy Council levies where a "legal" name might be required. Otherwise, it appears that he had adopted a stage name that would become his pen name as well, and that he was known as Shakespeare in the city, Shakspere in the country.

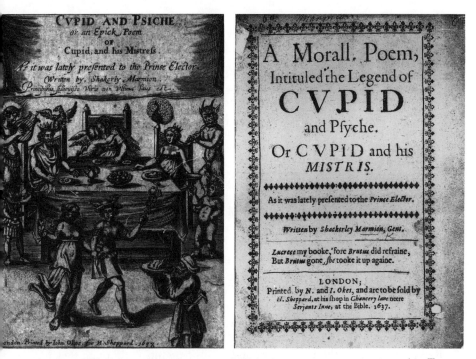

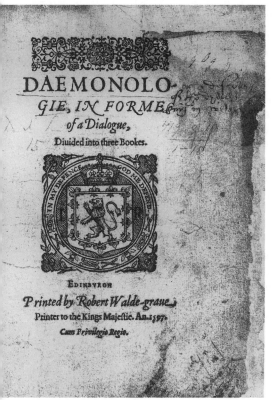

The engraved and typeset title pages of Shakerley Marmion's *Cupid and Psyche* (1637). (By permission of the British Library)

The imprint of Robert "Walde-Grave" on the title page of *Daemonologie*, its author, James VI of Scotland (later James I of England), represented by his coat of arms. (By permission of the British Library)

Hyphenated Shakespeare

The author's name on the title page of *King Lear* is a curiosity not only because of its spelling, but because it supposedly holds the answer to the Oxfordian question of "What's in a name?" When what is in the name is a hyphen and the name hyphenated is "Shake-speare," the Oxfordians assert that this was the way his contemporaries chose to let the world in on the secret that Shakespeare was a pseudonym.[7] This is why, we are told, the author's name is hyphenated on the title pages of fifteen of the 32 quarto editions of individual plays published before the First Folio of 1623. What we are not told is that thirteen are in editions of just three plays— *Richard II, Richard III* and *Henry IV, Part One*—all published by Andrew Wise and, after 1603, his assignee Matthew Law. (The other two are the 1603 "Bad Quarto" of *Hamlet* and the *Lear*.) This repetition is of no significance, for it was a common practice in the printing trade for title-page information to be repeated from one edition to the next and even outdated references would survive one printing or more. For instance, the 1605 quarto of *Richard III* stated this play "hath been lately acted by the Right Honourable the Lord Chamberlain his Servants," although they had been under the patronage of King James for two years at the time. It was not until the next quarto in 1612 that James was finally acknowledged as their patron. Most remarkable, though, is the 1655 *King Lear,* which repeated the title-page announcement from the 1608 quarto that the tragedy was "played before the King's Majesty at Whitehall upon St. Stephen's night in Christmas holidays," despite the fact that the king referred to, James, had been dead nearly thirty years and, since the execution of his son Charles I by the Parliamentarians, England had not had a monarch on its soil for six years.[8]

At last, if Wise was indeed privy to special knowledge about the author, it must be asked why he omitted the hyphen from the playwright's name when he published *Henry IV, Part Two* and *Much Ado About Nothing* in partnership with William Aspley in 1600?[9]

Be that as it may, it is a fact that Shakespeare's name was hyphenated in these quartos and elsewhere, and Ogburn notes that "Orthodox professors have been unable to come up with a single case of a genuine English name similarly hyphenated in common usage."[10] If a non-professor's response will do, it is not as unknown as he would have you believe.

There is Sir Thomas Campbell's name for one. On October 29, 1609, he was installed as the Lord Mayor of London, and for the occasion, Anthony Munday wrote a pageant. Only four leaves of the printed pageant survive—the title page is not one of them, but the "running title" (the titles at the top of the page above the text) render his name as "Camp-bell."[11] It has never been suggested Dunstan was the pseudonym of the sainted tenth-century Archbishop of Canterbury, but the imprint of Thomas Creede, the printer of George Chapman's comedy, *Monsieur D'Olive,* advertised that the book was to be sold by William Holmes "at his Shop in Saint Dun-stons Church-yard in Fleete-streete." As we can see, either Creede or Holmes was especially fond of hyphens.

Another printer, Robert Waldegrave, was so enamored of hyphens that he had to have one of his own. But it had nothing to do with a pseu-donym—and if ever a man was in need of one it was Waldegrave. As the printer of Puritan tracts, he was in constant trouble. In 1584, his workmen and presses were seized, and he was imprisoned for six weeks.[12] When in 1588 he again incurred official wrath, Waldegrave fled London, setting up presses in one town after another until he finally crossed the border into Scotland in 1589, where he would be appointed the printer to King James VI, the future James I of Great Britain.

For all his notoriety, there was no agreement on the spelling of his name. Whereas his name was invariably entered as Walgrave in the register of the Stationers' Company (the guild of printers and booksellers), he always used Waldegrave in his imprints. However, from his earliest work, *A Cas-tle for the Soul* in 1578, until *Certain Short Questions and Answers* in 1582, he printed his name as one word. In two other books he printed in that year he adopted a hyphen, and in every book thereafter his name appears as Walde-grave.

Another example, one of particular interest to Shakespeareans, is the hyphenation of the name of the Protestant martyr Sir John Oldcastle. This was the man whom Shakespeare originally cast as Prince Hal's "villainous abominable misleader of youth . . . that old white-bearded Satan" in *Henry IV, Part One.* This aroused the ire of the Brookes, a family descended from Oldcastle. The elder of this family, William, 7th Lord Cobham, would be appointed Lord Chamberlain when Henry Carey Lord Hunsdon, the patron of Shakespeare's company, died on July 23, 1596. It was probably during this period that it was thought politic to change the name of Hal's tutor in riots to Sir John Falstaff. Indeed, even the epilogue of *Henry IV, Part Two* contains a disclaimer that promises to despatch the character to oblivion, perhaps from a sweat, "unless already a' be kill'd with your hard opinions; for Oldcastle died a martyr, and this is not the man." In the one and only quarto edition of this play (1600), the martyr's name is spelled "Old-castle."

Despite Shakespeare's submission, the playwrights Anthony Munday, Michael Drayton, Richard Hathway and Robert Wilson decided to capi-talize on his embarrassment. In the autumn of 1599 they collaborated on a play extolling Oldcastle for the Lord Admiral's players and, in the pro-logue, recalled the embarrassment of the rival company's dramatist: "It is no pampered glutton we present, / Nor aged counselor to youthful sin . . .

let fair Truth be graced, / Since forged invention former time defaced."
This play was entered for printing with the Stationers Company on August
11, 1600, twelve days before Shakespeare's play. The title page names the
play, *The first part of the true and honorable historie, of the life of Sir
John Old-Castle, the good Lord Cobham,* and all the running titles read
"The first part of Sir John Old-castle."[13] Nevertheless, the title on the first
page spells his name without the hyphen.

As the foregoing indicates, there was no uniform style manual for printers in this period. Furthermore, whether in printed works or holographs,
punctuation in this period could be as arbitrary and as irregular as spelling. Finally, it must be commented that if all the sources in which Shakespeare's name was hyphenated were added up, it would appear the
knowledge that the name was a pseudonym was one of the worst-kept
secrets of the age.

Literacy and the Shakespeares

Among the "disqualifications" of Shakespeare as the author of the plays is
what might be best called hereditary illiteracy. No letters written by John
Shakespeare have come down to us and when he had to sign a document,
he is not known to have made anything but marks—a cross or renderings
of a glover's compass, which he as a glover used to cut ornaments on
gloves. Some biographers, appalled by the thought that the poet's father
was unable to write, have argued that it was not that he couldn't, but
preferred a mark because it held some religious or allegorical significance.
Professor David Cressy, whose specialty is literacy in Tudor-Stuart England, doubts this. He directs attention to a 1559 Leet court record wit-
nessed by John Shakespeare as one of Stratford's five affeerors (adjudicators
of fines). The elder Shakespeare signed with a mark, as did two others,
while two used signatures. Of this he comments, "We are not told why
the other affeerors and associates of John Shakespeare irreverently signed
their names, but a good guess would be that they were the only ones who
could write."[14] On the other hand, John Shakespeare's friend and col-
league Adrian Quiney also would use a mark—an inverted capital Q—but
there are also surviving letters in his handwriting. No similar remains of
John Shakespeare, however, have come to light.

Oxfordians find further evidence that illiteracy was a Shakespeare family
tradition in the fact that the daughters of this supposed master wordsmith
could not even sign their own names. However, this was hardly excep-
tional for women, and especially rural women, in that time—and for some
time thereafter. "Most women did not need to be able to write," wrote
Cressy; "The domestic routine of cooking and sewing and child-rearing
had little need for reading, and it scarcely afforded the time":

The mark of John Shakespeare.
Affixed to an order in a Stratford
Council Book. (Courtesy of the
Shakespeare Birthplace Trust)

Only in London did women break away from their massive illiteracy. Elizabethan and Stuart women in the capital city were no more able to sign their names than women anywhere else, but their condition was transformed in the last quarter of the seventeenth century.[15]

Beyond keeping women usefully employed at home, illiteracy also kept them in their place, which outraged Mrs. Bathusa Makin. At the threshold of the transformation, Mrs. Makin publicized her private academy for young ladies with an essay published in 1673, containing the observation that:

A learned woman is thought to be a comet, that bodes mischief wherever it appears. To offer to the world the liberal education of women is to deface the image of God in man, it will make women so high and men so low, like fire in the house top it will set the whole world in flame.[16]

This attitude, she allowed, was prevalent "especially among a sort of debauched sots" and such language undoubtedly did little to allay their fears (and may have sent a shudder through the upright sober as well). But Shakespeare's time was untroubled by the likes of the formidable Mrs. Makin, and the illiteracy of his daughters is in keeping with the custom of the day.

Be that as it may, Oxfordians are satisfied that the illiteracy of the father was visited upon the son and that, contrary to the speculation of Shakespeareans, he did not attend the King Edward grammar school in Stratford. Indexed under the "eradication of his traces," Ogburn gives voice to his suspicion that the school records disappeared because they would have revealed William's name did not appear among those who attended it.[17] However, Robert Bearman, the senior archivist of the Shakespeare Birthplace Trust in Stratford, states:

> The surviving records for King Edward's school, Stratford-upon-Avon, are very meagre indeed before the nineteenth century . . . apart from papers relating to the appointments of masters and their subsequent dealings with the Corporation, virtually nothing has survived prior to 1800.[18]

Aside from the corporation papers, the only other significant source of information about the school before 1800 is in the correspondence of the Reverend Joseph Greene, the mid–eighteenth-century Stratford schoolmaster and curate. These facts alone indicate that there is no foundation for Ogburn's suspicions.

However, it should also be considered that the grammar school traces its origins to the fraternal and religious Guild of the Holy Cross founded in 1269. Among its good works was the founding of the school and as early as 1295 we learn of the hiring of a master. Thus there could have been up to 500 years of documents before those that have come down to us beginning 200 years ago. Little credence can be given to a suspicion that so extensive a record of a vital institution in the life of Stratford would have been intentionally obliterated to prevent the discovery that William Shakespeare did not attend the school for some period during the 1570s.

Even if it is granted that Shakespeare was an exception in his family and he did indeed attend the King Edward School, the Oxfordians dismiss it as a provincial institution in a not especially nice Elizabethan town. Besides, it was certainly not an Oxford or a Cambridge, where most other dramatists of the age had been educated.[19] One of these was not the dramatist who is coincidentally ranked second to Shakespeare: Ben Jonson. Jonson also had only a grammar school education, but they are quick to point out it was at Westminster School that, according to Jaszi, he "attended under the specific patronage of the great William Camden, who was his particular teacher there," and Camden was "among the greatest antiquarian and classical scholars of his day."[20] This is a typically uncritical rendition of the facts.

A little history is once again enlightening. The Westminster School was originally connected with the Benedictine monastery of which Westminster Abbey was the heart. In the Reformation Henry VIII refounded the school, which he "seems to have taken . . . under his special protection."[21] Queen Mary restored the abbey to the Benedictines; but within two years of her accession Elizabeth suppressed the order once again and refounded the school. She took a personal interest in it, coming by not only to see the Latin plays performed in the College Hall, but just to see the boys at their lessons. Scholarships were awarded by academic competition in the form of "challenges" in which a candidate tried to best his rivals in two days of examinations. Truly Westminster was "one of the elite academies of Tudor England," and, in the words of Laurence Stone, "the most fashionable school in the country."[22]

First of all, it should be noted that record keeping was of no more importance here than in Stratford. There is, therefore, no record of Ben Jonson's attendance, nor of any of the students during Elizabeth's reign but for those successfully elected to Oxford or Cambridge, whose names were engrossed in the "Buttery Book." There are records for two decades in the seventeenth century in a headmaster's account book, but the earliest books of admissions begin in 1715. "At no time in the past," wrote an editor of the Westminster School records, "do the Head Masters' Admission books appear to have been kept with any great care, and the names are omitted of several boys who should have been entered, and are known from other sources to have been at the school."[23]

In fact, the only source for our knowledge that Jonson was a Westminster scholar is William Drummond's notes of his conversations with him when the latter stayed with him at Hawthornden, Scotland, over the Christmas season of 1618, where he was told by Jonson that he was "put to school by a friend (his master Camden)."[24] It is only because Camden is known to have been a master at Westminster that Jonson can be placed as a student there. Jonson's intellectual debt to Camden is evident in his dedication to the 1616 folio version of *Every Man in His Humor*, as well as in his 14th Epigram, where he wrote:

> Camden, most reverend head, to whom I owe
> All that I am in arts, all that I know.[25]

But did he attend the school under Camden's "specific patronage"? Jonsonians do not believe that the parenthetical note "his master Camden" means that it was Camden who put Jonson to school but only that his master at school *was* Camden. Which leads to the question of just how much schooling did Jonson have? Camden, who became headmaster in 1593, was the second master at the time Jonson would have been at Westminster and thus would have "taught the whole lower school to the Fourth inclusive"—students fourteen to sixteen years of age—according to his biographers Herford and Simpson, all of which "favours the view that Jonson's language in the epigram means simply that Camden had been his sole or principal teacher."[26]

Jonson's interest in theories of versification and his facility in Greek suggest to some that he might have continued on to the sixth form. It is also possible this reflects his determination to be recognized as a scholar, which was enhanced by his continuing association with Camden. This is the conclusion suggested by Rosalind Miles's observation that most of the classical sources of his "new creative materials he found by himself; of the writers he praised to Drummond (Pliny, Quintilian, Horace, Tacitus, Juvenal, Martial and Hippocrates) only Martial and Horace had been on the syllabus of Westminster School."[27]

However much the Oxfordians may understandably wish to inflate the benefits of his education at Westminster School and his relationship with Camden, the fact remains that they cannot account for Jonson's achievements. He would be the pattern for playwrights throughout the seventeenth century and was awarded a pension by King James in 1616 that allowed him to advertise himself as the Britain's Poet Laureate. In the front rank of classical scholars, he would become a "Master of Arts in the Universities [Oxford and Cambridge] by their favor not his study."[28] (There is no record of the award of an honorary degree from Cambridge). Thus, in popular esteem and in royal favor, in intellectual attainments and in honors, few in the annals of Jacobean-Carolinian literature who did have a university education equaled Jonson in any one area, no less in all. Ultimately, the attributes that make a Jonson—or a Shakespeare—cannot be taught.

The Stratford Grammar School

The Stratford grammar school, of course, could not attract the likes of a Camden. But the education of its children was of the greatest importance to the Elizabethan town fathers. Several years after the Holy Cross Guild was dissolved in 1547 (along with all such religious foundations in England), Stratford petitioned for borough status to restore the customs and privileges they had enjoyed from the guild. The charter of incorporation was granted on June 28, 1553, and the lands and properties of the guild were given over to the borough to meet the annual payments that became the responsibility of the corporation, including maintaining the school (now renamed The King's New School for the reigning monarch, Edward VI) and paying its schoolmaster. On December 20, 1554, the corporation engaged its first master, William Smart, charging him "during his natural life, diligently to employ himself with such godly wisdom and learning as God hath and shall endow him with: to learn and teach in the said grammar school all such scholars and children as shall fortune to come to learn godly learning and wisdom being set for the grammar school or at least-wise entered or ready to enter into their accidence and principles of grammar.[29]

As the Oxfordians contend that Shakespeare had to have had some Latin to be admitted to the school in the first place, it is noteworthy that the charter allows three levels of preparedness: those "set for the grammar school" or at least "entered or *ready* to enter into their accidence" (that is, rudiments). The last indicates that would-be scholars need be nothing more than of age to enter into studies.

Even if this is so, the Oxfordians, attempting to cover all possibilities, do not concede that the town necessarily would have admitted him when he reached the age of admission in 1571, simply because his father had served the corporation in a wide array of positions since his earliest appointment in September 1556 as an ale-taster. David Cressy, whose doubts about John Shakespeare's literacy were quoted above, does not share the Oxfordians' doubts regarding his son's eligibility to attend the grammar school:

> given the period of his upbringing (early Elizabethan), his location (a small market town with a grammar school), and his parentage (urban craftsman/sub-elite), [he] could be expected to attend the grammar school. . . . Quite apart from his subsequent history and achievement, someone with his social background would normally move into the literate world and certainly surpass the educational level of his father.[30]

But the Oxfordians raise still another doubt. Stratford, in their book, indelibly remains a place where the glories of Renaissance England had not penetrated—hardly the place to receive an education consonant to the lofty erudition they perceive in Shakespeare's writings. In fact, Stratford did actively seek and employ excellent scholars to teach their young, among whom John Brownswerd is of particular interest. He had been the student of John Bretchgirdle, the schoolmaster and curate of Witton in Cheshire. Bretchgirdle had been enticed to Stratford, where he became vicar in 1561, and likely played a role in the hiring of his former pupil in 1565. Coincidentally, John Shakespeare was the chamberlain at the time, and it was his duty to bring Brownswerd, his wife and goods from Warwick, and put the house provided to him in order.

Additional interest attaches to Brownswerd because he is likely to have been influenced as a pedagogue by Bretchgirdle, who had set down a curriculum for the grammar school scholar in his Witton days; which was:

I will the children learn the Catechism and then the *Accidence and Grammar* set out by Henry VIII, or some other, if any can be better, to induce children more speedily to Latin speech; and then *Institutum Christiani Hominis,* that learned Erasmus made; and then *Copia* of the same Erasmus, *Colloquia Erasmi, Ovidius Metamorphoses,* Terence, Mantuan, Tully, Horace, Salust, Virgil, and such other as shall be thought convenient.[31]

It is probable that Brownswerd followed a similar course, for these works are typical of what is generally found in grammar school curricula of the time. If this reflects what the young Shakespeare had been taught to any degree, he would definitely have the advantage over many who doubt his authorship.

Brownswerd, coincidentally, would later be honored as both a teacher and a poet by his friend Thomas Newton who, in 1589, collected and published his Latin poems, entitled *Progymnasmata quaedam Poetica.* This helped him to a mention in Francis Meres's famous *Palladis Tamia; Wits Treasury* (1598), where he happens to share a page with the son of the Stratford chamberlain. On page 280 we find Brownswerd among those "English men being Latin poets"; in the very next paragraph we find Shakespeare amidst those by whom "the English tongue is mightily enriched and gorgeously invested in rare ornaments and resplendent habiliments."

Evidence that teachers such as Brownswerd gave Stratford's scholars a solid grounding in Latin may be found in a letter written by 11-year-old Richard Quiney, Jr., to his father, Richard, Sr., in October 1598. The lad asked that his father "provideres fratri meo et mihi duos chartaceos libellos" (provide my brother and me two copybooks). The boy goes on:

gratias tibi ago quia a teneris, quod aiunt, unguiculis, educasti me in sacrae doctrinae studiis usque ad hunc diem: Absit etiam verbulis meis vana adulationis suspicio, neque enim quenquam ex meis amicis cariorem aut amantiorem mei te esse judico, et vehementer obsecro ut maneat semper egregius iste amor tuus sicut semper antehac, et quanquam ego non possum remunerare tua beneficia, omnem tamen ab intimis meis praecordiis tibi expotabo salutem: Vale.

(I give thee thanks that "from tender soft nails," as they say, unto this day thou hast instructed me in the studies of Sacred Learning. Far from my poor words be even a suspicion of flattery, for I deem not any one of my friends to be dearer or more loving of me than thou art, and earnestly I pray that that surpassing love of thine may always remain as always hitherto; and although I am not able to repay thy kindnesses, nevertheless I shall wish thee from my heart of hearts all prosperity. Farewell.)[32]

nius, Mantuanus, Philelphus, Quintianus and *Germanus Brixius* haue obtained
known and good place among the aunci-
ent Latine Poets: so also these English
men being Latine Poets, *Gualter Haddon,*
Nicholas Car, Gabriel Haruey, Christopher
Ocland, Thomas Newton with his *Leyland,*
Thomas Watson, Thomas Campion, Bruns-
werd & Willey, haue attained good report
and honorable aduancement in the Latin
Empyre.

As the Greeke tongue is made famous
and eloquent by *Homer, Hesiod, Euripedes,*
Æschilus, Sophocles, Pindarus, Phocylides
and *Aristophanes*; and the Latine tongue
by *Virgill, Ouid, Horace, Silius Italicus,*
Lucanus, Lucretius, Ausonius and *Clau-*
danus: so the English tongue is mightily
enriched, and gorgeouslie inuested in rare
ornaments and resplendent abiliments by
Philip Sidney, Spencer, Daniel, Drayton,
Warner, Shakespeare, Marlow and *Chap-*
man,

As *Xenophon,* who did imitate so excellently, as to giue vs *effigiem iusti imperij,* the
portraiture of a iust Empyre vnder y̆ name
of *Cyrus* (as *Cicero* saieth of him) made
herein an absolute heroicall Poem; and as
Heliodorus writ in prose his sugred inuentio
of that picture of Loue in *Theagines* and
Cariclea

John Brownswerd ("Brunswerd") and
Shakespeare in *Palladis Tamia.*
(Courtesy of the Folger Shakespeare Library)

The phrase "from tender soft nails" is taken from Cicero's *Epistolae ad Familiares.* It is noteworthy that the boy retained Cicero's structure—"a teneris, ut Graeci dicunt, unguiculis"—but in a burst of originality replaced "ut Graeci dicunt" (as the Greeks say) with "quod aiunt" (as they say).[33] At any rate, young Quiney's letter suggests that the grammar school could turn out students well versed in Latin and who could write fluently in the language.

Sad to report, young Richard's wish may not have been granted, for his father was in London seeking tax relief for Stratford, only to find himself in need of relief. This occasioned the only surviving letter to Shakespeare, to whom the elder Quiney wrote for help in getting a loan of £30—which suggests he was under the impression his "loving good friend and countryman" could read. But then, for some reason, the letter apparently was not delivered. We may anticipate the Oxfordian explanation for this: at the last moment, Quiney discovered his good friend could not read after all.

The last word on the issue of schooling, taken from his *Literacy and the Social Order,* belongs to David Cressy. In the course of this thorough survey of literacy in England he observed, "the bulk of the evidence, strengthened by the literacy figures, points to the first two decades of Elizabeth's reign [1558–78] as a period of unusual educational excitement and achievement. It may be no coincidence that Shakespeare and his talented literary contemporaries were of school age at this time and that part of his audience was uniquely well-educated."[34]

Shakespeare: The Heel, and His "Achilles' Heel"

It appears that the reason Richard Quiney's letter was not delivered is because he had a meeting with his townsman. Later in the same day that he penned the letter, October 25, he wrote to Abraham Sturley that Shakespeare had promised to help secure the loan. Sturley replied guardedly on November 4, saying of the arrangement that "I will like of as I shall hear when, and where, and how." Perhaps Shakespeare already had developed a reputation in Stratford as a hard-nosed businessman, one he would not relinquish. This is, in Oxfordian reckonings, another of his "disqualifications."

One of their prime exhibits is "The note of corn and malt. Taken the 4th of February 1598." This survey was made by justices of the peace upon the order of the Privy Council to seek out those who were hoarding grains. Hoarding drove up the price of wheat and barley (called corn and malt respectively in Elizabethan times) and the shortages led to brawls and open revolt, and the hoarders were condemned as "wicked people in conditions more like to wolves or cormorants than to natural men." Among these people in Stratford we find the name of Shakespeare, who possessed ten quarters of corn (a quarter was ten bushels).[35] This set Charles Champlin, the *Los Angeles Times* art critic, to wonder:

> Did the man who hoarded grain at a time of famine also write, "What a piece of work is man! How noble in reason! How infinite in faculty, in form and moving! How express and admirable in action! How like an angel in apprehension! How like a god!"? *

There will be no attempt here to excuse Shakespeare, but his actions may be put into perspective. The list of Stratford's engrossers included both Richard Quiney and the pious Abraham Sturley mentioned above, as well as Alexander Aspinall, the parish priest and schoolmaster. In addition, such Warwickshire notables as Sir Thomas Lucy (as well as one of Lucy's servants) and Sir Fulke Greville, the great friend of Sir Philip Sidney and himself a poet and playwright of some standing in his time, entrusted the storage of their corn to various Stratford householders. In all, grains were found in the dwellings of some 120 of Stratford's citizens—there could

---

* Charles Champlin, "The Great Shakespeare Mystery Caper," 133. The unfamiliar punctuation of this passage from act two, scene two of *Hamlet* is based on the second quarto text published in 1604 and accepted as being from Shakespeare's own manuscript.

not have been many more houses in the town. Evidently hoarding was so commonplace that few were troubled by the legal and moral burdens.

That there were few fine feelings in business dealings in Shakespeare's time is illustrated by another document: the suit brought by Thomasina Ostler, the widow of William Ostler, an actor in the King's Men, against John Heminges—her own father—regarding her late husband's shares in the company. But to the Oxfordian Ruth Loyd Miller, this legal document written in Latin is something more than a family feud—nay, it is nothing less than "the Achilles' heel of the Stratfordian case." [36] According to Mrs. Miller, a passage in it reveals that the William Shakespeare who was a shareholder in the Globe and Blackfriars theaters and the fellow of John Heminges, was dead when the suit was drawn up in early October 1615— months before the death of the purported poet was recorded in the burial register of Holy Trinity Church in Stratford, on April 25, 1616. Or so it would, she asserts, had Stratfordians not tampered with it.

Such is the case in the books by E. K. Chambers and B. Roland Lewis, where the passage in question is rendered:

> pro Consideracionibus in eadam Indentura tripartita mencionatis & expressatis, dimisisset, Concessisset & ad firmam tradidisset quibusdam Cuthberto Burbadge & Ricardo Burbadge de londonia generosis, *prefato Willelmo Shakespeare, & Augustino Philipps & Thomae Pope de londonia generosis defunctis*.[37]

It is the portion italicized here that is in dispute. With the comma inserted after Shakespeare's name by Chambers and Lewis, it reads in translation: "the aforesaid William Shakespeare, and Augustine Phillips and Thomas Pope of London gentlemen deceased," thereby separating Shakespeare from his departed colleagues, Phillips and Pope, who died in 1605 and 1604 respectively.

Mrs. Miller's case against the Chambers/Lewis rendition was amplified in a multiple letter by her husband, retired Judge Minos D. Miller:

> The *Ostler* case was transcribed but not translated in Chambers two volume *Life of Shakespeare*. Chambers added punctuation to fit his mold; but his added punctuation does not appear in the original document. A translation of the legal latin, as originally written, will not support Chamber's transcription. . . . The Chamber's added punctuation was adopted by B. Roland Lewis in his two volume work *The Shakespeare Documents*.[38]

The conclusion of the Latin scholars engaged by Mrs. Miller was that the offending comma altered the meaning. Without it, it would appear that Shakespeare had joined Phillips and Pope and thus, "The William Shakespeare who was a shareholder at the Globe *was dead* (by 1615)." Appearances can be deceiving—in this matter they definitely are.

First of all (though it may be dismissed as a mere matter of scholarly style), it should be noted that there is no work by Chambers entitled *Life of Shakespeare* and we can only assume that Judge Miller is referring to the extract in volume two of Chambers' *William Shakespeare; A Study of Facts and Problems,* pages 58–64. More to the point, the absence of punctuation marks in the original is typical of the style of English legal documents dating back to the end of the fourteenth century, and *Ostler v. Heminges* in the original rolls along for pages uninterrupted except for a rare slash. Chambers and Lewis added punctuation for (in Lewis' word) "clearness," rather than to fit a mold. Of greater consequence is the style of the original itself, which the Millers apparently knew of. It was printed in transcription by Charles William Wallace as *Advance Sheets from Shakespeare, The Globe, and Blackfriars.* Not only is this transcript without added punctuation but, no less importantly, it has 72 lines that precede the text in the extracts and contains essential material that sheds light on the disputed passage.

It is not clear whether the Millers' "Latinists" had the Wallace text at their disposal or if they were competent in the legal Latin of the day (which is something quite apart from classical Latin); for a person experienced in the translation of legal documents might have recognized the importance of the phrase, "the aforesaid William Shakespeare." I am here indebted to an archival scholar who has just that experience and did at once recognize that this indicated an earlier reference to Shakespeare not included in the Chambers/Lewis extract, and that in it Shakespeare would be found amongst the living. And, indeed, in Wallace's *Advance Sheets* we find:

> praedicto Ricardo Burbadge praefato Johanni hemynges & quibusdam Willelmo Shakespeare Cuthberto Burbadge henrico Condell Thomae Evans de londonia praedicta generosis.[39]

> (to the aforementioned Richard Burbage, the aforesaid John Heminges and to a certain William Shakespeare, Cuthbert Burbage, Henry Condell, Thomas Evans, of London, aforementioned, gentlemen.)

Therefore, according to this same scholar, the correct interpretation of the passage questioned by the Millers is:

> for the considerations mentioned and expressed in the same tripartite indenture [1599] did lease, concede and set to farm to a certain Cuthbert Burbage and Richard Burbage of London, gentlemen, [to] the aforesaid William Shakespeare, and [to] Augustine Phillips and Thomas Pope of London, gentlemen, deceased.

Shakespeare's Autograph

However reassuring it may be to find Shakespeare was still among the living after all, it would be refreshing to find him in livelier situations. Unfortunately, such as the census of grain hoarders and the Ostler suit are typical of what may be expected of people of Shakespeare's status. Apart from the mighty, only the most contentious left a revealing paper trail of their lives, albeit unenviably ones. Such a one was Ralph Brooke, the York Herald in the College of Arms. The comments regarding him by Sir Anthony Wagner, one of the most esteemed experts on heraldry and genealogy in this century, are enlightening as well as pertinent:

> Because of the intense feeling aroused and the constant strife and litigation he provoked we possess a series of complaints, petitions and depositions throwing light upon the detail of his life and character which one may seek for in vain for so eminent a contemporary as Shakespeare.[40]

In fact, this tumultuous figure would cross paths, though indirectly, with Shakespeare, as will be seen. For the moment, Wagner's comment is significant because it bears on one of the most important issues regarding the contemporary record of Shakespeare: the virtual absence of papers in the writer's own hand.

Of all the suspicions raised about Shakespeare, nothing is made to seem quite so suspicious by the Oxfordians as the scant remains of the author. Surely the great man's letters would have been treasured; his signature on any document, no matter how routine, preserved for posterity. His autograph should survive in abundance; his manuscripts the prize of every library. Instead, there are only six rather scratchy Shakespeare signatures, all on documents. The earliest, dated May 11, 1612, is on his deposition in the suit of Stephen Belott against his father-in-law Christopher Mountjoy (in whose house Shakespeare lodged in 1604); two more on deeds connected with his purchase of a house in Blackfriars in 1613; another three, only two legible, on his will made in 1616, with the addition of the words "By me" before his last signature. Whether each of these six specimens is from his pen is questioned—and not only by Oxfordians.

In his *Shakespeare in the Public Records*, David Thomas of the Public Record Office states that it "is obvious at a glance that these signatures, with the exception of [the two on the will], are not in the same hand," but disputes the Oxfordian argument "that Shakespeare did not sign the documents himself because he was illiterate or that he did sign them but, because he was not used to writing, each time the signature and the spelling was different."[41] Thomas proffers Sir Hilary Jenkinson's explanation that clerks would sign a deponent's name "using a different hand from

The Shakespeare signatures: (a) On deposition in Bellott-Mountjoy suit, 1612; (b) on vendor's copy of Blackfriars property deed, 1613; (c) on mortgage deed for Blackfriars property, March 11, 1613; (d and e) on the second and last pages of his will, 1616. (In David Thomas, *Shakespeare in the Public Records* [1985], p. 33)

"Hand D" in *Sir Thomas More*. (By permission of the British Library, Harleian MS 7368, folio 9.)

that which they used for the body of the text to give it 'an air of verisimilitude.' " He further notes that "there was no necessity for a will to bear the testator's signature at all" until the Statute of Frauds of 1667, though a clerk might nevertheless have taken it upon himself to "forge" the signatures onto his will—which would account for the dissimilarities in letter forms and spellings in the Shakespeare signatures. The eminent Shakespearean biographer S. Schoenbaum offers a more prosaic explanation for "such latitude as exists among the Shakespeare signatures":

> Firstly, abnormal conditions affect five of the six signatures. Two [on the Blackfriars conveyance] were constrained by the narrow dimensions of the parchment tags inserted through the slots at the foot of legal documents for the attachment of seals; three were set down by a man shortly to die.[42]

It is doubtful that either explanation will shake the Oxfordian certainty that the hand that wrote the signatures belonged to an illiterate who needed a helping hand in order to make them. However, there is a growing conviction that an extensive example of Shakespeare's handwriting is to be found in one of the great treasures of English Renaissance theater: the manuscript of the play *Sir Thomas More*.

This manuscript survived because it was among the papers preserved by Edward Alleyn in the library of his charitable foundation, the College of God's Gift, now Dulwich College. (The manuscript has since been removed to the British Museum.) There is speculation that the play was abandoned because either it encountered official censorship or so many had a hand in it that it was an artistic failure. The handwritings of Henry Chettle, Thomas Dekker and Anthony Munday, perhaps Thomas Heywood's too, have been identified in it. However, it is "Hand D," the author of "Addition II.D" in the play, that is the subject of great curiosity, for the evidence points to that hand being Shakespeare's. ("Addition III," although in a scribal hand, is also attributed to Shakespeare on stylistic grounds.)

One thing is certain: the contribution of Hand D, in which More calms a May Day uprising against foreigners, is the working manuscript of an accomplished dramatist—one for which no comparable handwriting sample has come to light. The major reasons for the Shakespeare attribution—handwriting and style—may be found in two recent studies, one by Dr. Giles E. Dawson, "Shakespeare's Handwriting" in *Shakespeare Survey 42;* the other, Professor Charles R. Forker's "Webster or Shakespeare?" in *Shakespeare and Sir Thomas More*. According to Dr. Dawson, there are four similarities between the manuscript hand and Shakespeare's signatures that are uncommon or rare, plus that Hand D, like Shakespeare, frequently uses the "dialectical 'a' " for "he," otherwise employed by only five of 42 playwrights, and then only sparingly. It is highly unlikely, he concludes, "that two skilled dramatists, writing simultaneously about the year 1600, would be engaging in all these unusual practices, some highly unusual."[43]

The only other serious contender for Hand D is John Webster, for whom no autograph of any kind is known. Forker, a self-described "longtime student of Webster's style and canon," doubted the attribution to Webster from the first, "for the style seemed to me eminently Shakespearean." His study of Hand D reinforced that suspicion. He found that the comparisons of vocabulary and spelling inconclusive because there are far fewer plays by Webster and because printed texts may not necessarily reflect the author's original spelling. However, of the 60 words, out of a total of 545 in the manuscript, that are not common to both playwrights, 50 appear in other Shakespeare plays but never in Webster, whereas only one *(transportation)* is exclusive to Webster. "The vocabulary test," Forker concludes, "however hesitant we may be to use it as evidence in Shakespeare's favour, would seem to be overwhelmingly negative as evidence for Webster." The only other possibility would be another dramatist "otherwise unknown to us," which he dismisses, for "given the number of gifted poets writing for the stage during the period we are considering, this hypothesis seems unlikely."[44]*

The Survival of Manuscripts

The chance survival of *Sir Thomas More* may make it seem stranger still that fortune has not delivered us some greater work of Shakespeare's.

---

*During production of this book, the autograph expert Charles Hamilton announced his discovery that a manuscript in the British Library, Lansdowne 807, is the play of *Cardenio*, which was written by Shakespeare in collaboration with John Fletcher and presumed to be lost. If this was not surprise enough, he declared the manuscript to be entirely in Shakespeare's handwriting. (For the history of this play, see pp. 163–64.)

I do not concur. The play is identified in the manuscript as *The Second Maiden's Tragedy*, attributed by scholars to Thomas Middleton. The manuscript itself is a fair copy of the play annotated for performance, and the handwriting bears a strong resemblance to that of Ralph Crane, a scrivener periodically employed by the King's Men.

The major objections to the Shakespeare attribution are these. First, Fletcher is accepted as having collaborated with Shakespeare in the play of *Cardenio*, but there is only one handwriting throughout. It is highly doubtful that Shakespeare would have performed the service of a playhouse scribe. Second, the play in question bears no resemblance to the story of Cardenio as it appears in its source, Cerventes's *Don Quixote*. Third, and most conclusive, *Don Quixote* was not translated into English until 1612. The promptbook, however, bears the license of Master of the Revels George Buck, which is dated October 31, 1611 (some months before the translation of *Don Quixote*). Shakespeare may have known of the story in the original, but there are no grounds for this assumption subject to proof.

(I wish to thank Dr. A. J. Prescott of the Department of Manuscripts, British Library, for his help in gaining access to this document.)

Without a nod to Hand D, Charles Champlin employs the Oxfordians' best friend, the analogy, in voicing his doubts.

> The authorship of Shakespeare's poems and plays is history's most teasing literary mystery because no manuscript in the author's hand is known to exist, although much earlier documents, like the Dead Sea Scrolls and the Magna Carta have survived the ravages of time.[45]

On the face of it, it seems reasonable to ask why manuscripts twice and four times as distant as Shakespeare's have survived whereas his have not. But is it?

It should be obvious that the survival of the Dead Sea Scrolls, like similar millennia-old works that have been discovered in the Middle East (such as the late first century or early second AD copies of Aristotle's *Constitution of Athens*), is attributable in good measure to the very dry climate of the region, quite unlike England's. The effect of its climate on manuscripts was noted upon the discovery of the office book of Sir Henry Herbert, the Master of the Revels from 1623 until 1673. The industrious scholar Edmond Malone received permission to transcribe material from it and in 1790 described the condition of the book: "This valuable manuscript having lain for a considerable time in a damp place, is unfortunately damaged, and in a very mouldering condition."[46] Though Malone evidently recognized its value, it appears it could not be saved. Nothing more is heard of the book itself and it is presumed lost.

But, then, it may be objected, Herbert's office book is not in the same class with a Shakespeare document. Nor, for that matter, would a Shakespeare document be in the same class with the Magna Carta—the most revered state document in English history. Tracing the history of the surviving copies of the great charter is quite revealing of the attitude that prevailed for centuries toward documents of every kind.

There can be no question of the importance of this paper from the moment King John affixed his signature to it in 1215. When he almost immediately showed that his commitment to it was somewhat less than wholehearted, the barons promptly took up arms and even invited Louis, the dauphin of France, to replace him on the English throne. Although they failed, John died sixteen months after the signing and his opponents made sure his nine-year-old heir, Henry III, would comply with it. During Henry's minority, Magna Carta was revised three times, the last in 1225, when the contractual nature of the document was emphasized. Its symbolic as well as legal importance to the nobility is evident, for throughout the Middle Ages English kings were called upon to confirm their adherence to it.

Shakespeare, however, did not make specific mention of Magna Carta in *King John*. There is a reason for this. The modern perception of it as a broader declaration of rights and liberties (especially in the United States where it is regarded a precursor of the Constitution) was just beginning when Shakespeare's career in theater was ending. It wasn't until 1610 that it was first cited in a case in common law, when it was used to challenge duties imposed by the Crown without the consent of Parliament. In the 1620s, under the guidance of Sir Edward Coke, it was invoked in a challenge to royal prerogative in Parliament. It may not be coincidental that it was at the end of that decade that the modern history of the original copies of the Magna Carta begins.

The earliest record of a copy of the charter since its issue in 1215 is the one given to Sir Robert Cotton on January 1, 1629, by Humphrey Wyems; nothing is known of its earlier history. In the next year another copy was presented to Cotton by Sir Edward Dering; found in the archives of Dover Castle, it is presumed to be the one delivered to the barons of the Cinque Ports.* (Both are now in the British Museum.) Nothing is heard of the Lincoln Cathedral charter, one of the first copies distributed and the finest surviving, until the year 1800, when it is mentioned as being in the Chapter archive. The fourth and last of the known copies is in Salisbury Cathedral, the discovery of which was played out over 55 years. The Salisbury charter was first mentioned in James Tyrell's *History of England* (1697–1704); in April 1759 Sir William Blackstone went to Salisbury in search of it, only to be told that it had been lost thirty years before during repairs to the cathedral library. It was still not to be found some forty years later when the report of a royal commission seeking the national records was issued in 1800.[47] However, fourteen years later, the cathedral historian William Dodsworth casually wrote: "A copy of this celebrated document . . . is still preserved among the Records of the Chapter. . . . Search was made for it by order of the commissioners for examining the Public Records, but it was then overlooked."[48]

While it might seem that four surviving copies of so ancient a document are a lot, charter scholars are puzzled that there are so few. As many as 35 copies were made according to a distribution list issued upon the signing of the compact.[49] "The basis of distribution is uncertain," wrote G. R. C. Davis of this dilemma,

> but it has been plausibly suggested by Professor C. R. Cheney that acquisition of them was dependent, as with other royal grants, upon payment of the prescribed fees. Sheriffs and bishops are referred to by contemporary chroniclers as being among those who received them, but the issue is

---

*Dering is familiar to Shakespeareans as the editor of a *Henry IV* in manuscript that was intended for private performance.

actually recorded of only thirteen of them, three of which were handed to two bishops, and ten to the steward of the archbishop of Canterbury for onward transmission.[50]

If the great monasteries were indeed where most of the copies of the Magna Carta were kept, it is probable that they were hunted down for destruction by Henry VIII's commissioners upon their dissolution during the Reformation. Not only did it have articles confirming the supremacy of the Catholic church, but imposed restrictions upon royal power, upon which great Harry recognized no bounds. If this is indeed the case, the survival of the two church copies is possibly owed to the cunning of the monks of Lincoln and Salisbury, who hid the charters so well that it would be 250 years before they would be seen again.

There is a curious parallel in the survival of the principal records of English Renaissance theater: the papers and account book of Philip Henslowe, known as *Henslowe's Diary*. His son-in-law Edward Alleyn, had removed Henslowe's theatrical cache to the College of God's Gift in Dulwich. When the Parliamentarians gained control over the government in 1642, the playhouses assumed the role in Oliver Cromwell's regard that the monasteries had in Henry VIII's. The theaters were dissolved and, though playbooks were apparently spirited away by the actors, the records of the companies were lost—save for the materials Alleyn had fortuitously taken to Dulwich years before. When the college was occupied by the soldiers of the Commonwealth they "committed great havoc," sparing neither its chapel nor the black marble slab that covered Alleyn's remains, which was severely damaged. They certainly would not have shown so much respect to the relics of the outlawed playhouses. However, whether because the Puritans never expected to find such profane things in a house of pious purpose, or because the documents were safely hidden away, Henslowe's crude treasures escaped their zealotry.

There were other, more mundane dangers that documents of all kinds could not escape. At the other pole of the damp that probably claimed Herbert's Revels account book was the ever-present danger of fire, which bears on the mysterious disappearance of the accounts of the highest immediate authority over theater in Shakespeare's age, the Lord Chamberlains of the Household. Ogburn imagines that these records, like those of the Stratford grammar school, might have been deliberately eradicated "because they would have showed how little consequential a figure Shakspere cut in the company."[51] The truth is somewhat more prosaic: they were probably lost, along with the records of the offices of the Signet, Privy Seal, and Council Chamber (of far greater importance at the time), when Whitehall Palace banqueting house and the chamber below where they were kept were destroyed by fire on January 12, 1619. However, the

Edward Alleyn. (By
permission of the Folger
Shakespeare Library)

Chamberlain's accounts for the years after the fire have survived and they
are for the most part routine entries—authorizations, preparation, and
payments for court performances, the disbursement of properties and apparel, and the like. They are not in the least concerned with the hierarchies
of the acting companies.[52]

That literary manuscripts were little esteemed is seen in the unexpectedly
lighthearted poem Ben Jonson wrote when his library was devastated by
fire in 1623. In "An Execration upon Vulcan," he chides the god for greed-
ily devouring his writings all at once, when his contemporaries would have
allowed him to savor them:

> Thou mightst have had me perish, piece, by piece,
> To light tobacco, or save roasted geese,

Singe capons, or poor pigs, dropping their eyes;
Condemn'd me to the ovens with the pies;
And so, have kept me dying a whole age,
Nor ravish'd all hence in a minute's rage.[53]

Jonson's reference to his papers "Condemn'd . . . to the ovens with the pies," is an allusion to the custom of putting paper under the bottom of pies during baking, seemingly a particular peril to literary holographs. In *Naps Upon Parnassus* (1658), a collection of "voluntary and jovial verses [by] some of the wits of universities," its editor related his pains in reclaiming them from the keeper of an alehouse where an author had left them: "Much ado I had to recover them out of the good woman's hands, who left the bottoms of her pies (that baking) in very great jeopardy for want of them: yet at last I did get them, as many as you see there are of them."

John Warburton, the eighteenth-century Somerset Herald of the College of Arms, was apparently unaware of this culinary use for paper, for he claimed to have entrusted the manuscripts of more than fifty Renaissance plays to his cook, the notorious "Betsy Baker." When he discovered his loss, he noted at the end of his inventory of the plays: "After I had been many years collecting these manuscript plays, through my own carelessness and the ignorance of my servant, in whose hands I lodged them, they was unluckily burnt or put under pie bottoms."[54] Warburton claimed that only three of his plays survived Betsy's blaze. Among those listed as lost were a number by Shakespeare and other great playwrights of his age. W. W. Greg doubts that Warburton actually had all the plays that he named, but sees no reason to doubt that those he had and left "within reach of the parsimonious fingers of Betsy the baker of pies," did indeed enrich the flavor of many a savoury.

Another of the many uses for old paper was employed by bookbinders, who used unwanted sheets to stiffen the covers of books. What was unwanted covered a great range and resulted in an astonishing discovery. J. Franklin Mowery, the conservator of the Folger Shakespeare Library, routinely investigates the composition of covers when preserving and restoring antique books. In October 1984 he removed the paper wrapping on the covers of two medical texts printed in 1578 and discovered that it concealed two vellum leaves of text in handsome Irish half-uncial characters.* These turned out to be leaves from a translation of the *Historia Ecclesiastica* of Eusebius, the third-century "Father of Church History." Dated from the early to middle seventh century, this is the oldest known

---

* The obscure medical texts are *An Hospital for the Diseased,* and *Orders Thought Meete by Her Majestie . . . in Such Townes . . . Infected with the Plague.*

manuscript written in English. Furthermore, as it is possibly among the works that had been brought to Durham by the monks of Wearmouth and Jarrow, who fled there in 1022 with relics of the Venerable Bede, this may have been the actual text used by the Bede in the composition of the most important of his works, *Historia ecclesiastica gentis Anglorum* (The ecclesiastical history of the English nation).[55] It was probably amongst the plunder when the monastery at Durham was dissolved in the Reformation.

It could be said that those who would destroy the glorious architecture and obliterate the gorgeous images associated with the Roman church could not be expected to respect the contents of its libraries. But what about the manuscript of the greatest undertaking of the new religious order, which turned out to be a masterpiece of world literature: the King James Bible? What became of the working papers and the final manuscript produced by the six companies of Greek, Latin and Hebrew scholars, divided equally between Westminster, Oxford and Cambridge?

Work was begun by King James's order in 1604 and a draft, completed in 1607, was then gathered to be "circulated amongst learned men and returned" for emendation. This was done in 1608 and the revised text was ready in the next year. In 1610, three copies of the whole Bible were sent by each location to London where, depending upon the source, either six or twelve of the scholars reviewed and revised the entire work to put it into final form. At last, in 1611, the Authorized Version, popularly known as the King James Bible, came off the presses of the King's Printer, Robert Barker, who, "groan[ing] under the burden of this book," had taken two cousins and John Bill into partnership in its printing.[56] What became of this manuscript?

After numerous printings of this Bible by Barker, Bill, and their successors, during the Commonwealth the rights settled on Oliver Cromwell's favored printer, John Field, who published an edition in 1648, later joined by Henry Hills, one of the printers to the Council of State and the Parliament, in subsequent editions. The restoration of the monarchy in 1660 did not shake their exclusive hold on the Bible, an intolerable situation as far as London's printers were concerned, no less because of their past loyalties than because the James was extremely profitable. This outrage was made public in *The London Printers Lamentation,* in which the anonymous pamphleteer asks:

Have they not obtained (and now keep in their actual possession), the manuscript of the last translation of the *Holy Bible* in English (attested with the hands of the venerable and learned translators in King James his time) ever since 6 March 165[6]?[57]

The divine work surrendered to the care of printers? Although the writer is unusually precise about the event, scholars are not certain that it can be taken as gospel. Under any circumstances, this is the last time the manuscript is heard of.

Indeed, of this great undertaking—the first draft and the commentary upon it by the learned men; the revised text of 1609, the three copies sent to London in 1610, and all the working papers—what survives? The only autograph remains of the translators are an annotated Bishops' Bible, now in the Bodleian Library, Oxford, and a translation of the Epistles, at Lambeth Palace (the London residence of the archbishops of Canterbury). One translator, John Bois, a member of the second Cambridge company and one of the twelve that met in London to make the final revisions on the text, made 39 pages of notes of the meetings.[58] These, too, survive, but only in copies made later in the seventeenth century by one William Fulman, at the end of which he noted: "Transcribed out of a copy taken by some unskillful hand, very confused and faulty, especially in the Greek."[59] In other words, Fulman's copy is a copy of a copy. These are all that have come to light of the most important work in the English language.

⇥ 3 ⇤

On the Paper Trail of the Player and the Playwright

The Records of the Player

According to Charlton Ogburn, *all* the famous playwrights, as well as many prominent actors of the time, are to be found in *Henslowe's Diary*—except William Shakespeare. Putting aside the mention of playwrights for the moment, let's consider the case of the actor. Referring to the illusive "Shakspere," he asserts that if certain prominent Shakespearean scholars knew of any other actor of his "alleged prominence" who is not named in the *Diary*, certainly they would have told us so. That they did not allows Ogburn to come to the firm conclusion that this figure's "alleged career on the stage is illusory."[1]

The *Diary* is extant (though hardly written in very choice English) and is available in a transcription by W. W. Greg, originally published in 1904 and reprinted in 1976, as well as in an edition by R. A. Foakes and R. T. Rickert issued in 1961. Therefore, one needn't be a prominent Shakespearean to discover that the list of famous actors not to be found is impressive. Among the missing are Richard Burbage, Augustine Phillips, John Heminges and the rest of Lord Strange's players when they were the resident company at Henslowe's Rose playhouse during 1592–93. These were the players who, with the addition of William Shakespeare, would shortly become the Lord Chamberlain's company that was destined to be the most famous theatrical ensemble in history. For the record, several do appear in the *Diary* later on—but not in connection with the stage. For example, on October 11, 1594, we find William Sly, because he purchased a jewel from Henslowe for a down payment of twelve pence and the remainder in eight easy weekly installments.[2] Thomas Pope is mentioned on August 30, 1598, but only because Henslowe loaned his associate William Birde ten shillings to pursue a lawsuit against this Chamberlain's man.[3]

The famous clown Will Kemp is also in the *Diary,* but not at the height of his renown in the companies of Strange and the Lord Chamberlain in the 1590s. Kemp, one of the charter members of the Globe syndicate in 1599, ended his association with the Chamberlain's Men later in that year or early in the next (some contend this was because Shakespeare wanted a more serious clown, but the actual reason is unknown). Shortly thereafter he added luster to his reputation by performing his fabled 125-mile morris dance from London to Norwich. But his fame plummeted and in 1602 he joined the Earl of Worcester's company, which was affiliated with Henslowe. His reduced circumstances are reflected in a *Diary* entry at this time, for Henslowe loaned him twenty shillings "for his necessary uses."[4]

Edward Alleyn, the first renowned tragedian of the age, is in the *Diary* in the early years—but never as an actor. Henslowe records the marriage of Alleyn to his stepdaughter on October 22, 1592, and from time to time we hear of him, but only as the recipient of Henslowe's generosity, especially for work on his son-in-law's house. It was not until Henslowe itemized loans "unto my son Edward Alleyn as followeth for the company" (the Lord Admiral's Men) between May 2 and July 8, 1596, that the most renowned actor of the day is mentioned in connection with theater.[5]

In fact, 1596 is the first year that Henslowe kept itemized accounts of theatrical transactions in the *Diary.* By this time, Shakespeare and the rest of the Chamberlain's Men had been plying their trade at the Shoreditch theaters of James Burbage for about two years.

Ogburn makes similar allegations about the absence of notice of Shakespeare as a player in the records of provincial cities and towns, as well as the absence of scholarly comment on his non-appearance.[6] The reason for both is easily explained: anyone who has the least familiarity with these records would not expect to find Shakespeare named in them, any more than he would expect to find any other actor. Rarely is even so routine a matter as the name of an actor who received payment for his company noted. In the relatively thorough records of Canterbury, for example, a payee was named on only two occasions, once in 1602–3 and again in 1621–22. However, when a presentment was made to a grand jury against one Mr. ffoscew for "breaking the peace and drawing a blade upon one of the Queen's players," the secretary did not bother recording the player's name.[7]

It is only when players themselves ran afoul of the town government, most often because they defied an order denying them permission to perform, that we may find the names of individuals. Probably the best-known case of this occurred in the city of Leicester in 1583, when the Earl of Worcester's players were merely asked to put off playing until another day and given money toward their dinner. Not satisfied, they accosted the mayor about two hours later to request permission to play at the inn where they were lodging. When he refused, the players said they would play anyway, "with other evil and contemptuous words," and preceded to march about the town playing the trumpet and drum that signaled a performance. Ultimately they were restrained and apologized to his honor, pleading that he not inform their patron of what had happened. Among the records of this incident are the names of eight players in Worcester's company—including that of 17-year-old Edward Alleyn.[8] However, such occurrences were infrequent.

Normally, notices of players in a provincial town appear only because they were paid for a performance by the corporation or for leaving the town quietly upon being denied permission to play. In these cases, the entry was almost always a simple one: the name of the company, the date they were paid and how much, perhaps the building where they played or who authorized the payment, sometimes (not often) the date of the performance. Simply, these were bookkeeping entries, solely to keep track of how the town's money was spent. However, "If a company of players came to a town," Giles Dawson observed, "performed, and departed without cost to the corporation, their presence would not be shown in the accounts and we should have no knowledge of it."[9] Of Shakespeare's company there are notices of only 38 performances in only nineteen provincial venues from 1594 to 1611. No member of the troupe is mentioned by name in any of them at all.

The Lord Chamberlain's Man

If, as we have been told, "Shakspere" the player was at best insignificant, it is then surprising to find a William Shakespeare in the company of Kemp and Burbage in the accounts of the Treasurer of the Chamber, whose duties included making payment for entertainments at court. It reads:

> To Willam Kempe, Willam Shakespeare & Richard Burbage, servants to the Lord Chamberlain, upon the Council's warrant dated at Whitehall 15th March 1595, for two several comedies or interludes showed by them before her Majesty in Christmas time last past, viz, upon St. Stephens Day & Innocents Day . . . [£20].[10]

Finding Shakespeare so suddenly in such fast company aroused Oxfordian suspicions. Furthermore, the discovery that "contemporary records" showed the Lord Admiral's Men were also reported to have performed before the Queen on Innocent's Day (December 28) 1594, deepened the doubts. To top it off, when it is considered that there is an account of a performance of Shakespeare's *Comedy of Errors* at Gray's Inn on this very same date, their suspicions seem to be confirmed.[11] Obviously, argue the Oxfordians, the Chamberlain's Men couldn't have performed at the same time as the Admiral's at Greenwich Palace, no less at Gray's Inn on the same day as well. Clearly, the Chamber account must be in error—or, worse, fraudulent. The Oxfordians believe they have evidence that makes the latter possibility the more likely.

The culprit, it turns out, is none other than Mary, the dowager Countess of Southampton and mother of Henry, the 3rd Earl of Southampton, to whom Shakespeare dedicated his poems *Venus and Adonis* and *The Rape of Lucrece*.[12] She had taken Sir Thomas Heneage, the Treasurer of the Chamber, for her second husband on May 2, 1594. They were married only a year and a half when Heneage died on October 17, 1595, leaving his widow an inheritance of three years of his unaudited Chamber accounts. The telltale clue for what is posed as the countess' deliberate deception was discovered in Charlotte Carmichael Stopes's biography of her son. Stopes refers to a letter from Queen Elizabeth, supposedly dated December 16, 1596, in which the countess is reminded that at her husband's death "he had £1314 15s 4d in hand as Treasurer of the Chamber" and, according to the monarch's accounting,

You as executrix have paid £401. 6s. 10d. and £394. 9s. 11d. to the Guard. We require immediate payment of the balance of £528. 18s. 7d. to the treasury of the Chamber, on which you shall receive acquittance for the whole sum.[13]

Ogburn suggests that the £528 was some unaccounted-for sum and deduces that the desperate widow began concocting receipts to explain it. The payment of £20 to Kemp, Shakespeare and Burbage for a fictitious court performance was one such. However, in the first place, the queen's letter does not demand an accounting; rather, it plainly demands the return of funds in the Chamber treasury at the time of Heneage's death, of which all but £528 had been returned when Elizabeth wrote to his widow. More to the point, at the time the countess made up the accounts she did not owe the Crown anything, for the dating of the letter in Stopes is wrong.

David Thomas of the Public Record Office, London, correctly deduced that Stopes got her information from a document in the *Calendar of State Papers Domestic, Elizabeth I, 1595–97,* in which no year was given and was assigned to the 39th year of her reign (1596). "In fact," he states,

the text of the warrant is given in E 351/542 and it is clearly dated 16 December 38 Elizabeth (1595). The account shows that the sum was received on 17 December 1595.[14]

Therefore, the debt had then been liquidated well before the countess submitted the Chamber accounts for 1592–95, which were formally audited between January and March 1597.

And it should be noted that Ogburn omitted a slight detail in his rendering of the payment to Kemp, Shakespeare and Burbage: that that payment was made "upon the Council's warrant." This means the payment had formal written authorization from the Privy Council—something not even the most desperate person was likely to falsify. Thomas has supplied the following information on the Chamber accounts and those submitted by Heneage's widow in particular:

> The account is a formal Exchequer document, part of the complex machinery for preventing fraud and ensuring the collection of revenue which had developed since the middle ages. . . . having been checked by an auditor, it was signed by Lord Treasurer Burghley [William Cecil, Lord Burghley] and Chancellor [of the Exchequer, Sir John] Fortescue.[15]

There is a great deal of material somewhat more accessible that reveals there is no substance whatever to the suspicions about this Chamber account.

First of all, it should be noted the evidence that revealed it was actually the Admiral's Men who appeared at court on Innocent's Day is to be found in only one contemporary record—singular, not plural, as Ogburn states—and that trustworthy document happens to be the very same page of the very same Chamber account in which the performance of the Chamberlain's Men was recorded. Nor was it uncommon for two companies to perform at court on the same day. In fact, on Twelfth Night (January 6), 1601, at least three troupes performed before the queen—the Chamberlain's, Admiral's and the Children of the Chapel, who gave "a show with music and special songs." The Earl of Derby's players may have been a fourth; there was a payment to one of his actors, Robert Browne, though the company is not mentioned by name.[16]

What is more, the Chamber accounts always connoted an evening performance by adding the phrase "at night" after the date, which was most often rendered as the name of a holiday or feast day. As the 1595 entry does not have this notation for either the Chamberlain's or Admiral's Men, the companies must then have performed at Greenwich during the day. The players would have had little trouble covering the several miles from Greenwich Palace to Gray's Inn in time to play *Comedy of Errors* on "Innocent's Day at Night"—as it is even noted in the record of that performance. This same record reveals that they would have had plenty of time to cover that distance.

That record is, by name, the *Gesta Grayorum*, the mock-formal account of the Christmastime revels of the lawyers of Gray's Inn, presided over by my Lord of Misrule, "The Prince of Purpool." The play was scheduled to be the last of the entertainments for the "Ambassador" of "Frederick Templarius," the "Emperor" of the society of lawyers of the Inner Temple, who came "very gallantly appointed, and attended by a great number of brave gentlemen, which arrived at our court about *nine of the clock at night*" (emphasis added).[17] Upon his arrival speeches were given, followed by "dancing and reveling with gentlewomen" and it was not until "after such sports" that the long night ended when "a Comedy of Errors (like to *Plautus* his *Menechmus*) was played by the players."

It is interesting to note that the *Gesta Grayorum* account adds to the likelihood that it was indeed the Chamberlain's company that played Gray's Inn Hall. *The Comedy of Errors* turned out to be the climax of a "night [that] was begun, and continued to the end, in nothing but Confusion and Errors; whereupon it was ever afterwards called, *The Night of Errors*." The next evening's proceedings included a commission of oyer and terminer that directed the court of His Majesty of the Revels to find out the party guilty of causing, by "great witchcraft," the previous night's "great disorders and misdemeanours," by no means the least of which was foisting upon the austere gathering "a company of base and common fellows to make a play of Errors or Confusions." As this was how players were commonly viewed at the time, it does appear that the reference is indeed to Shakespeare and his now-legendary company.

Ogburn also asserts that this Chamber account is not merely the only document that associates Shakespeare with the Chamberlain's company, but the only one that associates him "with acting at all" during the reign of Elizabeth.[18] Is it indeed? One other document clearly puts Shakespeare in that company: the indenture drawn up on February 21, 1599, for the Southwark property on which the Globe playhouse was erected. Though the land was owned by Sir Thomas Brend, his son Nicholas was the agent in the transaction by which seven of the Chamberlain's Men became shareholders in the playhouse itself. Half of the shares were divided among Shakespeare, Kemp, Heminges, Phillips and Pope, while the other half went to the brothers Richard and Cuthbert Burbage.[19] The Burbages got the lion's share because the Globe was built from the timber of the Theatre, the playhouse their father James erected in Shoreditch in 1576, and they bore the brunt of a protracted dispute with the owner of the property on which it stood. Ultimately, they had it dismantled under the cover of darkness on December 28, 1598, and its wooden bones hauled across the Thames to Bankside, where it was rebuilt and named the Globe. Considering the Burbages' principal personal and financial interest in this enterprise, the next document is curious.

Sir Thomas died not long after the indenture and the post-mortem inventory of his property made on May 16, 1599, includes his Bankside plot on which was "Una domo de novo edificata . . . in occupacione Willielmi Shakespeare et aliorum" (a house newly built . . . in the occupation of William Shakespeare and others).[20] It is interesting to note that Shakespeare, although only a one-tenth shareholder, seems to have had the greatest name recognition among its occupants to those who drew up the inventory.[21] Perhaps he was not quite so illusory a figure after all.

And is the 1595 Chamber account actually the only document that associates Shakespeare with acting in the period? It so happens it is the only one that does so for Kemp and Burbage. Not so Shakespeare—though he probably would have preferred to have been left out of this other document, for it injected him (among numerous others) into a feud in which he was a hapless bystander.

In 1596 John Shakespeare was granted a coat of arms, of which there remains an original draft and a revised draft of the patent in a badly damaged state.[22] Also extant is the draft of 1599 authorizing the arms of his wife's family, the Ardens (one of the three oldest families in England), to be displayed beside those of Shakespeare (such display is known as impalement).[23] The arms granted to Shakespeare were one of many that became ammunition for fiery Ralph Brooke, the York Herald mentioned earlier, in his ongoing battle with the no-less-incendiary Garter King of Arms, William Dethick.[24]

Brooke and Dethick were well matched—both were combative, jealous of their standing and foul-tempered. Naturally, as is often the case with like-minded people, they especially enjoyed turning their social skills on each other. A notable confrontation began at court on Easter Day, 1594, when Brooke launched a verbal assault on Dethick and three days later received a "rappe" from Garter in reply. York, in turn, "sued Mr. Garter upon that brabble and prosecuted at law most extremely against him in the Court of the Exchequer."[25] But trouble in the College of Arms was not limited to this pair. Dissension among all its officers, though not as pronounced, was widespread and, in February 1596, Sir Edward Hoby (Lord Chamberlain Hunsdon's son-in-law) and Sir George Carew requested their attendance to present "such articles . . . for the reformation of the disorders" between them. Brooke would be singled out as the target of disaffection in a joint petition drawn up by a majority of the heralds and pursuivants.[26] It might have been for this occasion that Brooke created a manuscript that is as beautiful as it was meant to be damning: his "Attack on Dethick," consisting of splendidly executed colored illustrations of coats of arms with brief, occasionally scathing objections to each grant.[27]

If this was indeed the occasion for this manuscript, it was made months before the grant of arms to John Shakespeare on October 20, 1596 (no

Shakespeare in York Herald's "Attack on Dethick." The Shakespeare name is the fourth written onto the flyleaf. (Courtesy of the Folger Shakespeare Library)

The answer of the Kings of Arms regarding the Shakespeare grant. (Courtesy of the College of Arms London. MS WZ. 276b.)

coat of arms in the Attack is dated after 1594). His grant, however, did not escape Brooke's attention when he renewed his assault on Dethick in 1601 or early 1602, which he expanded to include grants by William Camden and William Segar, who in 1597 had been made Clarenceux and Norroy Kings of Arms respectively, bypassing the smoldering York Herald.

In preparation for this new attack, Brooke annotated his old one, adding a little list of the 23 grants on its flyleaf that he intended to challenge. The fourth named was Shakespeare. Most of the Flyleaf 23 were indeed incorporated in an enlarged version of the Attack, which he called "A note of some coats & Crests lately come to my hands given by William Dethick when he was York and since he hath executed the Office of Garter King of Arms." Similar in format to the earlier Attack, it survives in a copy made about 100 years later (see Afterwords, pp. 79–82).

The document detailing Brooke's charges is lost, but his grounds for challenging the Shakespeare arms can be adduced from the reply to the charges in "The answer of Garter & Clarenceux Kings of Arms to a Libelous Scroll against certain Arms supposed to be wrongly given." This survives in a perfect copy in the College of Arms and a draft in the Ashmolean Library, Oxford, dated March 21, 1602, in both of which the Shakespeare coat is in the left margin and the coats of Mauley, Harley, and Ferrers in the right. Between them is the Kings of Arms' justification for the grant, which in the College of Arms scroll reads:

> It may as well be said that Harley who beareth gold on a bend between two cotizes sables [black], and all other or [gold] and Argent [silver] a bend sables charged in like manner, usurp the coat of the Lord Mauley. As for the spear on the bend is a patible difference. And the person to whom it was granted hath born magistracy and was Justice of peace at Stratford-upon-Avon; he married the daughter and heir of Arden and able to maintain that estate.[28] (See Afterwords, p. 82)

In plain language, Brooke evidently charged that the Shakespeare arms was too similar to others and, besides, the Shakespeares were unworthy of bearing arms in the first place. A device he apparently used to support the latter charge may be found in Brooke's second manuscript where beneath the drawing of the Shakespeare arms he had written, "Shakespeare ye Player by Garter." As William Shakespeare is nowhere named in the three drafts for the Shakespeare arms, it does appear that it was common knowledge who, and what, John Shakespeare's son was.

Was there any substance to York Herald's questioning of the eligibility of Shakespeare, as well as numerous others who are identified by Brooke as too humble by occupation to bear arms at all? The last word on this matter belongs to Sir Anthony Wagner, now Clarenceux King of Arms and the dean of modern heraldists and genealogists:

"Shakespeare ye Player by Garter."
(Courtesy of the Folger Shakespeare Library)

Shakespeare and fellow King's Men in Sir George Hume's wardrobe account book. (Crown copyright. Public Record Office, London; by permission of Her Britannic Majesty's Stationery Office. LC 2/4[5].)

Will of Augustine Phillips May 4, 1605. (Crown copyright. Public Record Office, London; by permission of Her Britannic Majesty's Stationery Office. PROB 11/1055.31.)

These particular charges against Dethick seem to have had little substance and were dropped at the Queen's death. The accusation of granting arms to base persons was, in fact, an old one, brought out of store whenever a stick was wanted to beat a King of Arms with. . . . As everyone knew, one of the chief purposes of granting arms was to establish the gentility of persons whose status was doubtful. Discretion in the matter was essential, but not easy. Dethick seems in this matter to have been at least as discreet as his colleagues.[29]

The King's Man

Queen Elizabeth died on March 24, 1603, and on May 17 the new sovereign, James I, issued a Royal Warrant for a patent to make the shareholders in the Chamberlain's Men the servants of the king. Sir Robert Cecil, the Keeper of the Privy Seal, executed the order and on the 19th the letters patent were issued. Shakespeare is the second named, after a new addition to the company, one Lawrence Fletcher, who had performed before James in Scotland and appears to have been his favorite. (The story is told that when James in the company of another heard from an English agent in Edinburgh that Fletcher had been hanged, the Scots' king "in merry words, not believing it, [replied] very pleasantly that if it were true he would hang them also.")[30]

As the plague raged in London during much of 1603, James was crowned at Westminster Abbey on July 25, but the traditional triumphal procession from the Tower of London to Whitehall Palace was postponed until "the pest" abated. It was at last scheduled for March 15, 1604, and for the occasion 4½ yards of scarlet red cloth for suits were issued to the King's servants. These grants were entered in the account book of Sir George Hume, Master of the Wardrobe, in which the nine players on the king's patent are named, Shakespeare now at the head of the list. Ogburn tells us nothing more specific about the place of Shakespeare and his fellows in this book other than they were recipients of "a grant to 'diverse persons.' "[31] Meanwhile, Ruth Loyd Miller asserts, "Overlooked by most commentators is the fact that the clothe [sic] was issued to them not as 'actors' but as men of 'The Chamber.' "[32] Let us see.

Shakespeare and company *are* sorted in Hume's records with the monarch's household servants in the section headed "The Chamber." And it is true that they are not called *actors*. But, as Gerald Eades Bentley has shown, whereas " 'actor' is sometimes used by the printers and occasionally in the texts of plays, in the profession itself 'player' was the normal term." It was also the term used almost exclusively in any form of document or account of that time.* Accordingly, written beside their names in Hume's account, in unavoidably large, elegant letters is the word *Players*. The reasons for the Oxfordian evasiveness about Shakespeare's precise place in this document will be seen.

Ogburn's treatment of the next document that identifies Shakespeare as an actor is especially resourceful, for references to Shakespeare's theatrical associations after the Earl of Oxford's death in June 1604 can be awkward. Thus the problem of Augustine Phillips' will, dated May 4, 1605. On page 31 of *The Mysterious William Shakespeare*, only the first item relating to Phillips' bequest to theatrical associates is printed, and that in a very abridged version: "unto and amongst the hired men of the Company which I am of . . . the sum of five pounds . . . to be equally distributed amongst them," to which Ogburn adds: "First of those to be named was 'my fellow William Shakespeare.' " From this, one might think that Shakespeare was a hired man; that is, an actor who was not a shareholder and would then have been paid weekly by the acting company. Then, on page 111, having determined that it is a reference to "Shakspere"—although the name in the will is unmistakably spelled Shakespeare—we are told only that Phillips (oddly identified here by Ogburn as nothing other than one of the Lord Chamberlain's Men although he is named in the patent of the King's Men) had made a bequest to his "fellow" William Shakespeare—"whatever construction may be put upon that." Perhaps reconstructing this part of the document whole will help. It reads:

> Item, I give and bequeath unto and amongst the hired men of the company of which I am of which shall be at the time of my decease the sum of five pounds of lawful money of England to be equally distributed amongst them. Item, I give and bequeath to my fellow William Shakespeare a 30 shilling piece in gold. To my fellow Henry Condell one other 30 shilling piece in gold.

Others whom Phillips called his fellows and gave twenty shillings in gold a piece were Lawrence Fletcher, Robert Armin, Richard Cowley, Alexander Cooke, and Nicholas Toole.[33] Also mentioned in the will is Samuel Gilburne, "my late apprentice," who was bequeathed forty shillings and "my mouse coloured velvet hose, and a white taffety doublet; a black taffety suit, my purple cloak, sword and dagger, and my base viol." Hem-

---

* See Gerald Eades Bentley, *The Profession of Player in Shakespeare's Time, 1590–1642*. Bentley's entire discussion of the comparative use of "player" and "actor" on pp. x–xii is most informative.

inges, Burbage, and Sly, as overseers of the will, were each to receive "a bowl of silver of the value of five pounds."[34]

As we can see, Shakespeare was not named among the hired men—who were not named at all. Rather, he is first among the specific bequests to seven members of the King's Men, of whom a total of eleven are named in the will. The evident construction to be put upon Shakespeare's inclusion in this company is that he belonged to it and in it.

There is a later document that confirms Shakespeare's association with the King's company well after Oxford's death. In 1635 three King's players petitioned to purchase shares in the Globe and Blackfriars playhouses, which was addressed to then Lord Chamberlain Philip Herbert, Earl of Pembroke and Montgomery. In the reply of Cuthbert Burbage, the brother of Richard; Cuthbert's son William, and Richard Burbage's remarried widow Winifred Robinson, the history of the syndicate is traced, from James Burbage's building of the Theatre and its demolition and re-erection by Cuthbert and Richard on Bankside as the Globe. Of this event the document states that the brothers "to ourselves . . . joined those deserving men, Shakespeare, Heminges, Condell, Phillips and others partners." Of particular interest, however, is the portion concerning the Blackfriars:

> Now for the Blackfriars, that is our inheritance; our father purchased it at extreme rates and made it into a playhouse with great charge and trouble; which after was leased out to one Evans that first set up the boys commonly called the Queen's Majesty's Children of the Chapel. . . . the boys daily wearing out, it was considered that house would be as fit for ourselves, and so purchased the lease remaining from Evans with our money and placed men players, which were Heminges, Condell, Shakespeare, &c.[35]

The Burbages reclaimed the Blackfriars in August 1608 and this document leaves no doubt that Shakespeare was still an active member of the company at the time and specifically names him as a player. Coincidentally, along with four of his fellows, Shakespeare also joined the Burbages as a shareholder in the Blackfriars.

Early Notices of the Playwright

This chapter began with the introduction of Charlton Ogburn's observation concerning the absence of Shakespeare as a playwright as well as a player in *Henslowe's Diary*—including his assertion that *all* the playwrights but Shakespeare are to be found in it. Whereas the absence of Shakespeare the actor in the *Diary* suggests to Ogburn that his acting career was "illusory," he finds his non-appearance as a dramatist explicable, "if the author were a nobleman writing under a pseudonym."[36] It is true enough that the literary arts, especially common plays, were not an approved occupation for aristocrats, but if all the playwrights not named in the *Diary* were noblemen writing pseudonymously, then all the playwrights of the early 1590s must also have been noblemen. For Christopher Marlowe, Thomas Kyd, Robert Greene, Thomas Lodge and others now unknown whose plays were put on at the Rose prior to 1596, are not mentioned in it either.

A look at the *Diary* shows that Henslowe's entire notice of plays in this period is limited to spare ledger entries giving the name of the work and the take for its performance on a particular date. For example, the first record anywhere of the staging of a play by Shakespeare is in the diary—amidst dozens of like entries under the heading "In the name of God. Amen. . . . my Lord Strange's Men as followeth/1592"—where it appears as nothing more earthshaking than:

R[eceived] at harey the vi the 3 of March . . . £3 16s 8p.[37]

The name of the playwright is never mentioned in these line entries, nor is there any record of a payment to one until 1596 when among the loans to the Lord Admiral's Men after October 14th was thirty shillings for "Hawodes bocke," presumed to be the book of an unidentified play by Thomas Heywood.[38] By this time Shakespeare had been for about two years the resident dramatist of the Lord Chamberlain's Men, which had no connection with Henslowe or his playhouse.

A little more than six months after Henslowe entered the first record of a Shakespeare play came the first distinct allusion to Shakespeare as a playwright, albeit an unflattering one. It is found in a *Groatsworth of Wit,* which bears the name of Robert Greene on the title page. Just how much of a hand he had in it is a matter of debate. Of the "longstanding suspicion that both *Greenes Groats-Worth of Witte* (1592) and *The Repentance of Robert Greene* are virtually pure forgeries," wrote Daniel Kinney, "it is hard to rule out the conjecture that both works are editors' compilations largely based on known facts and Greene's notes."[39]

One of the "university wits," Greene squandered both his talents and eventually his life. In early August 1592, in the company of Thomas Nashe and other cronies, he dined on Rhenish wine and pickled herring, fell ill and died on September 3, aged 34. Seventeen days later, *Groatsworth* was entered for publication in the Stationers' Register. Toward the end of this pamphlet, the author addresses three men "that spend their wits in making plays," generally thought to be Christopher Marlowe, perhaps George Peele and (doubtfully) Thomas Nashe. It is here that we find:

Base-minded men all three of you, if by my misery ye be not warned; for unto none of you (like me) sought those burrs to cleave: those puppets (I

Performance of "Harey the VI" at the Rose Playhouse on March 3, 1592, in *Henslowe's Diary*. (Courtesy of the Governors of Dulwich College)

Edward Alleyn's emendations in a fair copy of Greene's *Orlando Furioso*. (Dulwich College, MS I, item 138, folio 267. Courtesy of the Governors of Dulwich College)

John Fletcher's letter to the Countess of Huntingdon. (Courtesy of the Huntington Library, San Marino, California. MS HA 1333.)

mean) that spake from our mouths, those antics garnished in our colours. Is it not strange that I, to whom they all have been beholding; is it not like that you, to whom they all have been beholding, shall (were ye in that case as I am now) be both at once of them forsaken? Yes, trust them not: for there is an upstart crow, beautified with our feathers, that with his "Tiger's heart wrapt in a player's hide," supposes he is as well able to bombast out a blank verse as the best of you; and being an absolute *Johannes fac totum,* is in his own conceit the only Shake-scene in a country.[40]

This has every appearance of being a pretty straightforward reference to Shakespeare—in the roundabout language of such verbal assaults in that time. In plain words, it says that a presumptuous player, beautified as such with the plumage (the words) of these playwrights, now imagines that he can write with the best of them. Who might this "upstart crow" be? Greene chastises him with a parody of the line in Shakespeare's *Henry VI, Part Three,* "O tiger's heart wrapped in a woman's hide," and caps it off with a play on his name in calling him a "Shake-scene." It all fits the orthodox Shakespeare to a T. To those who question his authorship, this obvious meaning must be dispelled and there has been no end to their contortions of language and logic as they try to make it say anything but what it appears to say or to refer to anyone but whom it apparently refers to.

In the case of the Oxfordians, they contrive to show that the object of the author's ire was not at all the great playwright, but a mere *Shak*-scene. Charlton Ogburn's interpretation is unexceptional but for his reading of the phrase in which the offending actor "supposes he is as well able to bombast out a blank verse as the rest of you."[41] Here we are given a Shakespeare who is a bit-actor of the kind Hamlet cautioned the tragedians against—"let those that play your clowns speak no more than is set down for them"—and the bombast in question is the kind used to pad clothes. In other words, according to Ogburn the offending player was padding out his parts. If this was indeed the provocation for the *Groatsworth* tirade, it seems a rather extreme reaction to what Hamlet suggests would hardly have been unusual. It is, under any circumstances, surprising to hear that so much passion could have been aroused by someone whose acting career, the same source tells us, was "illusory."

In fact, there is no reason to believe that the meaning of bombast here is anything but inflated, high-flown language—of which the parodied line from *Henry VI* is an example. Furthermore, it is interesting to discover that the earliest use of the word in this sense according to the *Oxford English Dictionary* is in Thomas Nashe's introduction to Greene's *Menaphon* (1589). What is more, in inveighing against authors who, in "servile imitation of vain-glorious tragedians . . . embowel the couds in a speech of comparison," Nashe's words have a very familiar ring:

But here I cannot so fully bequeath them to folly as their idiot art-masters that intrude themselves to our ears as the alchemists of eloquence; who (mounted on the stage of arrogance) think to outbrave better pens with the swelling bombast of a bragging blank verse.[42]

It is not surprising that Nashe was accused of having been the author of *Groatsworth,* wringing an outraged reply from him in his *Pierce Penniless:*

Other news I am advertised of, that a scald, trivial, lying pamphlet, called *Greene's Groatsworth of Wit,* is given out as being my doing. God never have any care of my soul, but utterly renounce me, if the least word or syllable in it proceeded from my pen, or if I were any way privy to the writing or printing of it.

Another accused of being Greene's ghost was Henry Chettle, the publisher of *Groatsworth,* who no less vehemently denied any blame for its content. Oxfordians do not believe him, which has given rise to the latest effort, by Tom Bethell, to explain away the passage in *Groatsworth.* In this version, Chettle inadvertently unmasked Shakspere, revealing that he was "passing himself off in the 'feathers' of a playwright." Informed that he had instead revealed a closely guarded state secret, Chettle "swiftly backtracked" in his book *Kind-Hearts Dream.* According to Bethell:

Two people took offense [to *Groatsworth*], apparently. Chettle was acquainted with neither of them, "and with one of them I care not if I ever be." (Shakspere, I surmise.) Chettle apologized to the other. "Divers of worship have reported his uprightness of dealing, which argues his honesty, and his facetious [polished] grace in writing. . . ." Possibly then, Chettle found out that the upstart Shakspere, relatively new in town, was putting on airs as a "playmaker" (that is, fronting for Oxford). Not realizing that a nobleman had arranged it, Chettle imprudently blew the whistle. He soon found out that divers of worship could do without investigative journalism Elizabethan style, and he duly groveled.[43]

Some investigative scholarship is in order. It is curious how the "divers of worship" who reported the playwright's "uprightness of dealing," are magically transformed into censors shutting off "investigative journalism." Bethell does not mention that Shakespeareans believe that the playwright apologized to was Shakespeare, and on reasonable grounds, if Chettle's apology is given more fully:

With neither of them that take offense was I acquainted, and with one of them I care not if I never be. The other, whom at that time I did not so much spare, as since I wish I had . . . I am as sorry as if the original fault

had been my fault, because myself have seen his demeanor no less civil
than he [is] excellent in the quality he professes. Besides, divers of worship
have reported his uprightness of dealing, which argues his honesty, and
his facetious grace in writing that approves his art.[44]

The reason that Shakespeare is assumed to be the latter is the mention of
his excellence in "the quality he professes." Turning once again to the
Oxford English Dictionary, we find the contemporary meaning of quality
was: "Profession, occupation, business, *esp.* that of an actor." Of the four
men alluded to in the Groatsworth passage, only one professed the quality
of player, and that one is William Shakespeare.

Greene, along with Marlowe, Kyd, Peele and the "upstart crow," formed
the first corps of what may be categorized as professional playwrights.
There is no indication at this time that any had a permanent arrangement
with an acting company or theater owner. Rather, it appears that they
acted as their own agents, selling their plays to whichever company wanted
them. Greene may have taken advantage of this free-lance status, for which
he would be castigated in print.

Greene's attack on the player turned playwright is in keeping with his
attitude toward the popular stage and those who populated it, if we may
give credit to the accusation leveled against him by the pseudonymous
Cuthbert Cony-Catcher in The Defence of Cony-catching, published after
late April 1592. One of his plays was a dramatization of Ariosto's Orlando Furioso and, according to "Cony-Catcher," he tried to double his
income from it:

> Ask the Queen's players if you sold them not Orlando Furioso for twenty
> nobles, and when they were in the country sold the same play to the Lord
> Admiral's Men for as many more. . . . I hear, when this was objected,
> that you made this excuse; that there was no more faith to be held with
> players than with them that valued faith at the price of a feather . . . that
> they were uncertain, variable, time-pleasers that measured honesty by profit,
> and that regarded their authors not by dessert but by necessity of time.*

This shady transaction would have taken place some time before a play
called Orlando appears in the Diary (only once, on February 22, 1592, as
the third offering at the newly opened remodeled Rose), where it is listed

---

* See Edmund Kerchever Chambers, The Elizabethan Stage, 3:325. This pamphlet is sometimes attributed to Greene himself although the subtitle, A Confutation of Those Two Injurious Pamphlets Published by R. G., suggests otherwise. Greene had indeed previously written
two pamphlets on "coney-catching," literally a rabbit-catcher, but then a popular phrase for
a cheat or swindler.

among the plays performed by Strange's Men. However, this company was led by Edward Alleyn, who was himself in the service of the Lord Admiral at this time, and it is probably through him it came into the possession of Strange's players. Alleyn's connection with *Orlando* is confirmed by a scribal copy that has emendations in his handwriting.

Shakespeare fits into the pattern of the free-lance playwright according to his earliest quartos. The title page of the first of his published plays, *Titus Andronicus* (1594), states that it found its way into the repertory of three acting companies—those of the Earls of Derby, Pembroke and Sussex. But there is no suggestion that Shakespeare went Greene one better and it was apparently sold by one troupe to the next. The title page of the quarto of *Henry VI, Part Three* (1595) attributes it to the Earl of Pembroke's Men, as does the title page of *The Taming of a Shrew* (1594), a precursor to Shakespeare's play that is found in *Henslowe's Diary* in a single performance by the combined Admiral's-Chamberlain's Men on June 13, 1594. *Henry VI, Part Two* was printed in 1594 without the mention of any company whatever. We can only speculate whether this was the play Strange's Men put on at the Rose. Clearly, Shakespeare got around until he began his association with the Chamberlain's Men some time in 1594 and thus became the first playwright known to be affiliated exclusively with one acting company.

The "Missing" Manuscripts

Besides *Henslowe's Diary,* another area where Shakespeare is supposedly suspiciously, singularly among the missing is in autograph manuscripts. Ogburn notes his absence in W. W. Greg's compilation of facsimiles entitled *English Literary Autographs, 1550–1650,* where he counts the hands of 35 dramatists, 36 prose writers and 42 poets, but Shakespeare's is not among them.[45] Ogburn makes no further comment, leaving one to assume that the estimable scholar did not think a single Shakespeare autograph authentic. However, on the first page of his editorial note to "Part I—Dramatists," Greg explained the absence of a Shakespeare facsimile: "I have avoided the controversial subject of Shakespeare's hand, everything bearing on it having been reproduced within the last few years."

Also overlooked was Greg's observation a few lines before: "Unfortunately of several of the most important of the regular playwrights no writing appears to be known, and the hands of Marlowe, Greene, Beaumont, Fletcher, Webster, Ford and Shirley among others will be sought in vain in this collection." Scattered autographs of several Greg named have been discovered since.

Apart from Marlowe's signature mentioned earlier, John Fletcher and James Shirley may also be taken off the list. Theirs are of particular interest because these two men, like Shakespeare, were attached play-wrights of the King's Men. Shirley's association was brief, 1640 to 1642, but he was a prolific playmaker for other companies. Nevertheless, all that has survived in what appears to be his handwriting is a manuscript volume of poems and a draft of his will. Fletcher, on the other hand, had a long association, beginning several years before he became their house drama-tist no later than 1616. His one surviving autograph document is a curious one. He composed a verse poem to the Countess of Huntingdon that in-cluded a prose note at the bottom—all in the hand of a scribe except for his signature, the address on the verso, and the insertion of the single word *Maddame* in the note. Furthermore, among the numerous plays he wrote for the King's Men before he began his formal connection with them, sev-eral were in collaboration with Francis Beaumont, who is still among the totally missing. Therefore, in the 48-year history of the Chamberlain's/ King's Men, only Philip Massinger, their playwright from 1626 to 1640, has left behind any significant autograph remains. Though they too are relatively few, among them is the most extraordinary single document that has come down to us, which will be discussed shortly.

A playwright who is not numbered among the missing in Greg's com-pilation is the unusually prolific Thomas Heywood. In his address "To the Reader" in his *English Traveller* (1633), Heywood says of the play that it is but "one reserved amongst two hundred and twenty, in which I have had either an entire hand, or at the least a main finger." However, of this incredible output only 56 plays—"including collaborations and lost plays known only by title"—have even been so much as identified.[46] The two manuscripts that are accepted as being in his autograph hand, *The Cap-tives* and *The Escapes of Jupiter,* were attributed entirely on internal evi-dence.[47] These are very slight remains for so prolific an author.

A more telling case at point is rare Ben Jonson. He was rare indeed among his contemporaries in seeing his plays into print, beginning with his very first published work, *Every Man Out of His Humour,* in the year 1600. He did not view his plays as mere dramatic entertainments and, about 1612, set to work on a collection of his works that was not to be, in the words of Professor Richard Dutton, "simply a record of his career to date, but a deliberate and selective account of his career, emphasising those elements which the eminent man-of-letters wished to commemorate and quietly expunging those he did not."[48] He called the folio volume that was published in 1616, *The Workes of Benjamin Jonson;* three-quarters of its bulk is fastidiously edited plays. He underscored that his plays were the workings of a conscious artist by rewriting the first in the folio, *Every Man In His Humour,* originally written in 1598, creating a play "self-consciously new in style and format, with a clear ancestry in Roman com-edy." The singularity Jonson proclaimed by this volume was captured by Bentley:

The pretentiousness of the volume, the elaborate engraved title page with its theatrical and symbolic figures, the Latin motto, the numerous sets of commendatory verses, several of them in the language of learning [that is, Latin], the formal table of contents, the inclusion of eighteen masques and entertainments prepared for the nobility and royalty with plays from the commercial theatres—all this constituted a direct claim to status and permanence unprecedented in the English theatre world and quite foreign to the practices of the attached professional dramatists.[49]

The folio succeeded in his "promotion of the image of himself as a serious poet—something very different from a mere playwright."[50] There can then be no doubt that Jonson saw his plays as being of great literary worth and if any dramatist would be expected to have recognized the value of his manuscripts to posterity it would be he. Furthermore, he clearly retained control over them to a degree unprecedented up to that date. Nevertheless, whereas holographs exist of his poems, epigrams, and letters, even a presentation copy of the *Masque of Queens* in his own hand that he made for King James's son Prince Henry, not a single autograph manuscript of a play has come to light.

That his self-promoted image worked is evident in his appointment as Britain's poet laureate in the year of his folio, which also happens to be the year of Shakespeare's death. If his vision of the dramatist as a conscious artist came too late to influence Shakespeare, what about those who followed? In fact, there was not a dramatic change. No other playwrights engineered their own folio collections of their works and it was not until the last ten years or so of this age that any showed a marked interest in bringing their plays to press in quarto editions. Even then they labored under a well-established restraint: the acting companies' insistence on maintaining control over the plays in their repertories. Thomas Heywood stated this explicitly in his address to the readers of his *English Traveller* (1633), where he says that one of the reasons why his plays had not been collected and "exposed to the world in volumes, to bear the title of works," was because some "are still retained in the hands of some actors, who think it against their peculiar profit to have them come into print."

Author's Rights and the "True Originall Copies"

The Oxfordians reject utterly any suggestion that Shakespeare could not keep his manuscripts and do with them whatever he saw fit. They have not presented any evidence from contemporary sources that this was not the case, only for the reason perhaps that all the evidence points to the fact that he could not. As we have just heard from Heywood, as long as a company felt there was some "profit" in a play it owned, such as the common practice of staging a revival, its author had no right to it.

Shakespeare's company in particular, held on tightly to its play texts, whether or not there was any profit left in them. For instance, Thomas Middleton's play, *The Witch,* cannot have had any lasting value to the King's Men, for it was unsuccessful when they put it on as a new play around 1614. Nevertheless, when Middleton asked the company for the text of the play in order to have a scribal copy made at the request of one Thomas Holmes some ten years later, in his dedication to Holmes he reveals that it was "recovered into my hands—(though not without much difficulty)," even though the actors had "made her lie so long in an imprisoned obscurity." The words of Heywood and Middleton reflect what is evident from the records of the theater: playwrights did not keep copies of their plays, whether their own manuscripts, known as foul papers, or the "fair" copies made from them.

When Shakespeare's fellows John Heminges and Henry Condell assisted in the texts printed in the First Folio of 1623, precisely what sources did they have at hand? The title page of the collection claims that the plays within were "Published according to the True Original Copies." The actors lend support to this in their epistle "To the great Variety of Readers," when they compare the folio texts with those previously printed in quarto editions

> where you were abused with divers stolen and surreptitious copies, maimed and deformed by the frauds and stealths of injurious imposters that exposed them: even those are now offered to your view cured, and perfect of their limbs; and all the rest absolute in their numbers as he conceived them.

However, in his exhaustive two volume work on the folio published in 1961, Charlton Hinman took issue with Heminges and Condell's declaration:

> Some of the plays in the Folio apparently do reproduce Shakespeare's own "foul papers"; but others are mere reprints of earlier quartos, and a number were set into type from combinations, part manuscript and part printed, of materials variously related to Shakespeare's original papers. . . . Some of the copy supplied to the Folio printers, on the other hand, must have been very different both from Shakespeare's original text and from anything that can be thought to reflect accurately his final intentions or even his acquiescence—though notably inferior copy was commonly mended by copy of higher authority.[51]

The second part of Hinman's statement reflects the established critical viewpoint that informed modern textual scholarship for decades. It is true that the plays first published in the folio were of playhouse origins (though perhaps only half), and even when a quarto was the primary source for a folio text it was not merely reprinted, but instead emended to some degree by performance texts, although the majority of the earlier versions give evidence of having been from Shakespeare's foul papers or something close to them. (This will get further examination in the next chapter.)

That playhouse versions were the ones proffered to publishers, even when the author's originals (or something closer to them) might have been extant, is not unique to the Shakespeare folio. This is clearly seen in the third great folio collection of plays from this period: the Beaumont and Fletcher Folio of 1647. The shareholders of the dormant King's Men cooperated in its publication and were given the honor accorded Heminges and Condell in the First Folio, which was to write its dedicatory epistle to Philip Herbert, Earl of Pembroke and Montgomery, the surviving brother of the "incomparable pair of brethren" to whom the Shakespeare folio was dedicated. Unlike its predecessor, this collection is made up exclusively of never-before-published plays—34 in all. There are not, therefore, earlier printed texts to complicate matters; all the sources for these texts were manuscripts of some kind. But of what kind?

The answer we are given parallels the claim of Heminges and Condell in the Shakespeare folio. The Beaumont and Fletcher preface was written by the folio's publisher, Humphrey Moseley, in which he notes the ravages of acting companies upon dramatists' originals:

> When these comedies and tragedies were presented on the stage, the actors omitted some scenes and passages (with the authors' consent) as occasion led them, and when private friends desired a copy, they then (and justly too) transcribed what they acted.

He is at pains to reassure the reader that such debased texts would not be found in his folio, declaring unequivocally that "now you have all that was acted, and all that was not, even the perfect originals without the least mutilation." Were the texts Moseley printed indeed from the "perfect originals"? In fact, there are five existing manuscripts of plays in the folio, and they show not only that Moseley did not often have the authors' manuscripts, but that he didn't even necessarily have the best texts extant.

Both the manuscript copies and folio texts of *The Honest Man's Fortune* (the manuscript of which is a promptbook with the license of Master of the Revels Sir Henry Herbert), *The Humorous Lieutenant* and *The Woman's Prize, or The Tamer Tamed*, are from playhouse sources, but in each case the manuscript version is considered superior to the folio's.[52] *Beggars Bush* is the only one of the five plays for which the folio text was taken from what appears to have been the authors' original text. Whereas the manuscript copy was made from a promptbook, "the various examples of common errors" it shares with the folio version indicate it was "made up directly from the very manuscript (conjecturally the authors' working papers) that was later to serve as the printer's copy for the 1647 Folio."[53]

The fifth play, *Bonduca*, offers a most revealing glimpse at the state of the playhouse archives. The copy of this play, Fletcher's first solo effort for the King's Men (dated to 1611), was made by the King's Men's bookkeeper and part-time scribe, Edward Knight for a private collector.[54] The first four acts proceed smoothly, but at the beginning of act five the scribe gives a summary of the first two scenes that were lost, and of the 36½ lines missing from scene three. In their place, Knight noted:

> The beginning of this following scene between Petillius and Junius is wanting. The occasion, why these are wanting here [is] the book whereby it was first acted from is lost: and this hath been transcribed from the foul papers of the author's which were found.

In other words, at the time Knight made this transcript, believed to be some time between 1625 and 1635, "the book whereby it was first acted" (the promptbook) was not to be found, and Knight made his copy from Fletcher's own manuscript, of which a portion was missing. Curiously, though the fact that Fletcher's foul papers for this play were extant before the printing of the folio and were still presumably when the folio texts were assembled, when the promptbook was recovered it was apparently chosen for the printed text in preference to the author's manuscript.

All told, of these five plays, only *Beggars Bush* seems to be what Moseley claimed for them all—a perfect original "without the least mutilation"—the only one with "all that was acted and all that was not." However, from this play and the scribal copy of *Bonduca*—as well as the Shakespeare folio, where foul papers or transcripts were the only source for at least seven plays and for emending two corrupt quarto texts—we learn that the King's Men did have physical possession of the authors' manuscripts. The most likely reason for this is that they were worthless to the author, for the acting company owned all rights to the plays. It also suggests that, as far as the King's Men (both in 1623 and in 1647) were concerned, the "true originals" were possibly considered to be the texts that were altered for performance. After all, it is logical that players should believe that a play achieved its state of perfection when it was emended for the stage—the idea of a play as something merely to be read or studied may have been incomprehensible, if not preposterous, to them.

Believe as You List

It is only by purest chance that any playscripts, or any of the vast store of documents generated by the theater during this legendary half-century, have

The engraved title page of *The Works of Benjamin Jonson*. (Courtesy of the Folger Shakespeare Library)

Edward Knight's note of missing scenes in Fletcher's *Bonduca*. (Courtesy of the British Library. MS Add 36758.)

The last page of the autograph manuscript of *Believe as You List* with the autograph license of Master of the Revels Sir Henry Herbert. (Courtesy of the British Library. MS Egerton 2828.)

come down to us at all. Once past the contemporary hazards and the depredations of the English Civil War, there were still snares that awaited the survivors for generations to come. While the growing Cult of Shakespeare in the late eighteenth century set people scrambling for any souvenir of the Bard, his once-famous colleagues were reduced to bit-parts, if not crowded off the stage altogether. Among the latter was Philip Massinger, one of his successors as the attached playwright of the King's Men. Thus, it was only by incredible chance that one of the great treasures of English Renaissance theater was saved from oblivion: the licensed promptbook of the play *Believe As You List,* in Massinger's own handwriting.

On January 11, 1631, Sir Henry Herbert wrote in his office book that he had refused to give his license to this play because "it did contain dangerous matter, as the deposing of Sebastian King of Portugal by Philip the [Second of Spain] and there being a peace sworn twixt the kings of England and Spain." Massinger's solution was to substitute the story of Sebastian, whose death led to Spain's annexation of Portugal, with an analogous story from antiquity, the defeat of Antiochus the Great of Syria by Rome. Massinger's reformed manuscript was submitted to Herbert who, satisfied, licensed the play on May 6, 1631. It so satisfied the King's Men that they did not bother to have a fair copy made, but instead transformed the manuscript into a promptbook: the actors' names, the stage directions and the prompts were written directly onto it by bookkeeper Edward Knight. It has led a precarious, charmed life ever since.[55]

A manuscript of this play was on Warburton's list of those done to a turn by "Betsy the Baker," but rumors of its existence persisted. It was mentioned in the fourth edition of the actor Colley Cibber's autobiographical *Apology* of 1756 and, in September 1808, a writer to the *Monthly Mirror* thought the manuscript might still exist. Rumor at last became fact when, on April 26, 1844, one Samuel Beltz sent the manuscript, which had been the property of his late brother George, to T. Crofton Croker of the Percy Society. In a letter dated June 6, Beltz revealed that he found it "concealed in a vast mass of rubbish which was submitted to my inspection by a member of my family previous to its intended destruction."

The manuscript was acclaimed at once as a rarity. "This is one of the few play-house copies of any English plays before the Suppression of Theatres known to exist," wrote J. O. Halliwell (later known as Halliwell-Phillips), the foremost theater scholar of the day, "& the present is a peculiarly interesting one, being a play of Massinger's long supposed to be lost, not included in any edition of his works, & known only be name until Mr. Croker resuscitated it for the Percy Society." Nevertheless, so indifferent had even foremost-theater scholars become to everyone but Shakespeare that it was not until this century that the manuscript was recognized as being in Massinger's own hand. For that matter, Halliwell's declaration of its importance notwithstanding, the troubled career of the promptbook continued on. It was allowed to pass into private hands and was often lost sight of until 1900, when it was purchased at auction for the British Museum at a mere £69. The manuscript that so barely escaped extinction has been accorded the same distinction as a leaf from *Sir Thomas Moore* in Shakespeare's hand: display in a British Library showcase.[56]

The precarious history of the *Believe As You List* manuscript reflects the indifference that manuscripts of every kind had to survive if they were to survive at all. In his *English Literary Hands from Chaucer to Dryden*, Anthony Petti explained the low survival rate of early literary manuscripts, of which the following observations are especially pertinent. First, of the regard in which manuscripts in general were held, he wrote:

> Even literary figures preoccupied with posthumous fame did not apparently place value on preserving their holograph manuscripts after publication, much less their earlier drafts, and neither, generally speaking, did anyone else, other than close friends, for the cult of collecting literary autographs did not begin in earnest until the end of the 18th century. . . . It should therefore be understandable why there is a dearth of literary holographs even of major English authors from earliest times to the end of the Renaissance period and beyond.[57]

And of plays specifically:

> A particularly heavy toll has been taken of drama. It is obvious that not only single plays of the medieval period have disappeared but also complete cycles. The manuscript holdings for Renaissance drama are in a poorer state: there are references to over three thousand plays in the Elizabethan and Jacobean period, but only a handful of manuscript copies survive.[58]

The difference between how Shakespeare's century and ours judged the worth of things can be seen in the most desirable of Shakespeare artifacts, the First Folio. The book was put in circulation shortly after November 8, 1623, when the printer Issac Jaggard and the bookseller Edward Blount entered sixteen Shakespeare plays thought not previously licensed for publication with the Stationers. One copy was automatically sent to the Bodleian Library of Oxford University under the agreement made by its founder, Sir Thomas Bodley, with the London Company of Stationers whereby a copy of every book licensed by the guild and printed would be given to the library.

Because the Bodleian required a special binding for its books, the folio was among the volumes the library sent to the binder William Wildgoose, who returned the bound copy on February 17, 1624. The Second Folio of 1632 was bypassed, probably as a mere reprint of the First. But the second issue of the Third Folio of 1664 had seven new plays added that, with the exception of *Pericles*, were wrongly attributed to Shakespeare. As this appeared to be a more complete edition, it was presumably at this time that the Bodleian's First Folio was removed from its collection and is supposed to have been among the "superfluous library books sold by order of the Curators" to the Oxford bookseller Richard Davis, who paid a total of £24 for the lot.[59] This folio made its way into the library of the Turbutts, a Derbyshire family, perhaps bought as early as the first half of the eighteenth century by Richard Turbutt. He was a great lover of plays, purchasing individual editions that he then had bound together, amassing a total of some sixty volumes of ten to twelve plays each.

On January 23, 1905, his descendant G. M. R. Turbutt brought this copy of the First Folio to the university, where its binding was recognized as a Bodleian—one of the few known to be in its original binding. The folio was purchased from Turbutt in the next year for £3000.[60] Eighty years later the library of Paul Francis Webster, which included copies of each of the four folios of Shakespeare's plays, was put up for auction. The First Folio was knocked down at $580,000 (plus a 10 percent buyer's premium)—the Third a mere $25,000.* Shakespeare's century and our own are clearly worlds apart.

Afterwords

"Shakespeare ye Player by Garter"

"A note of some coats & Crests" (Folger Shakespeare Library MS V.a.350) was dated c 1700; however, there is no documentation for the ascription of this date to the manuscript. To ascertain the date of this manuscript, I made freehand drawings of the two distinct types of watermarks in the paper of V.a.350, which are:

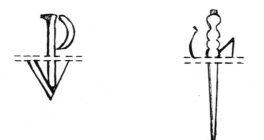

[Drawing of watermarks in Folger MS V.a. 350.]

---

* In a subsequent Sotheby's auction, November 10, 1989, the four folios as a set commanded $2,090,000 (including the buyer's premium), of which the later three folios can account for $250,000 at best.

Both figures are to be found in the papers of Thomas Bowrey relating to his ship, *Mary Galley*, which are dated 1704. They are here reproduced from Edward Heawood's *Watermarks, Mainly of the 17th and 18th Centuries* (Plate 519, illustrations 3922 and 3923):

[Watermarks, from Heawood, plate 519, nos. 3922 and 3923.]

The c. 1700 date of V.a.350 does appear to be well-founded. But does this undermine the authenticity of the Shakespeare arms—and especially the notation "Shakespeare ye Player by Garter"—in MS V.a.350?

It is one of several manuscripts bound together from the library of Peter Le Neve. (It was rebound separately by the Folger in 1978.) Le Neve was an officer of the College of Arms, beginning as Rouge Croix pursuivant in 1690. He was advanced to Richmond Herald in April 1704 and to Norroy King of Arms one month later, a position he held until his death in 1729. Who drew the coats of arms and crests and transcribed the comments that accompany them is not known, but the annotations and notation of colors on the coats and crests are identified as being in Le Neve's hand. It should be here noted that the manuscript from which V.a.350 was made might have included additional folios and documents, for beneath the drawings of the Shakespeare and West arms on page 28 are handwritten notes by Le Neve that suggest there were illustrations of other arms, as well as patents and a document, presumably by Brooke, of "A pedigree made by Garter [Dethick] of 18 descents with many coats, all forged." It may be conjectured that Brooke's exception to the Shakespeare arms were made in a separate document that was included with the original manuscript.

There is little room for doubt that the Attack on Dethick (Folger MS V.a.156) was the precursor to the manuscript of which Le Neve's manuscript was a copy. The correlation of V.a.350 to V.a.156 is as follows:

Pages 1–6. Six coats of arms, five dated 1595 to 1600, one undated. Three are among the 23 grants on the flyleaf of V.a.156. They are: Thwaite

(p. 1); Morecatret [Macatret] (p. 2); and Cowley (p. 3). (The Clarke on page 6 is not the same as the one on Brooke's list.)

Pages 7–25. Coats of arms and crests in the identical order to the colored renditions in V.a.156. Ten are on the flyleaf list.

Page 26. Arms of Austin, drawn on last folio of V.a.156.

Page 27. Four coats, including Hall and Pettous (Pethouse) on the list of 23 on the flyleaf of V.a.156.

Page 28. Arms of Shakespeare and notations of other coats, crests and patents, including Peake and, possibly Heyward (Haward of Surrey) of the 23 listed in V.a.156, as well as of Norton and Elkyn, who are also mentioned in a notation on folio 15 verso of V.a.156.

Page 29. Arms of Hickman, a colored version of which is included with V.a.156 on a loose folio of smaller dimensions.

Page 30. Arms of Calvert; not mentioned in V.a.156.

Thus, of the 23 names on the flyleaf of V.a.156, all but Lound and Clarke are found in some form in V.a.350. In a draft of the document Dethick and Camden made in reply to Brooke that is in the Ashmolean Library, Oxford (MS 846, folio 50), entitled "The answer of Garter & Clarenceux Kings of Arms to Scroll exhibited by Raffe Brokesmouth called York Herald," it is noteworthy that manuscript begins by stating it is in regard to "The exceptions in the scroll of xxiii arms." Also of interest is that the reply to the first five challenged grants is in the same order as on flyleaf of V.a.156 except for the transposition of Shakespeare and Clarke.

It does therefore appear that York Herald Brooke annotated V.a.156 in preparing a renewed attack on Dethick in 1601 or early 1602, adding to his challenge the arms given by the erudite Camden, who went from the headmastership of Westminster School to Richmond Herald on October 22, 1597, prior to his advancement on the next day to Clarenceux King of Arms (a position Brooke felt should have been his). For good measure, Brooke added grants by William Segar, for he was made Norroy King of Arms in that same year. It was this manuscript that came to Le Neve's hands and of which he had a copy made at some time during his forty-year association with the College of Arms.

Le Neve, called "the virtuous Norroy" by Sir Anthony Wagner, was a distinguished antiquary who, at age 26, was elected the first president of the Society of Antiquaries when it was revived in 1687. Among his papers were the Paston letters, the most thorough and revealing private documents of England during the turbulent mid–fifteenth century. When but a portion of his books and manuscripts were sold at auction after his death, among them were 584 heraldic manuscripts, 63 copies of visitations, 72 pedigree rolls, 22 portfolios of pedigrees and 28 boxes of charters.[61]

Given Le Neve's personal and professional dedication, it is not in the least surprising that a document of the foment in the College of Arms during the time of Dethick and Brooke (for so much of which they were responsible) should have been of particular interest and that he would want a copy of it. It is not credible that Le Neve would have wanted anything for his own collection but a faithful rendition of a document in the muniments of the College of Arms, just as it not credible that a document from the college had been altered.

That Brooke should have noted John Shakespeare's son was a common player is consistent with his challenges to others arms. For example, the crest of the sun rising above the Earth given to William Sanderson, a fishmonger, provoked the outraged comment, "This crest is not fit for so mean a person but rather for one who possesseth the whole world." So did he question the eligibility of such as Smyth the innkeeper, Parr the embroiderer, Laurence the goldsmith, Wythens the vintner, Whitmore the haberdasher, Molesworth the stocking-seller, and so on. It must have been with particular pleasure that he could call attention to a grant of arms to Robert Young, a soapmaker, "being the father to the said Garter's wife." However humble these professions, all were honorable ways to make a living. Not so the player, and it is entirely in keeping with Brooke's tactics to have had it made known that the newly armigerous Shakespeares had so tainted a scion.

"A Bend between Two Cotizes"

A bend is the band that runs diagonally across a coat of arms. A cotize (modern spelling, *cottice* or *cottise*) is the "diminutive" that is one-quarter of the width of the bend. The Shakespeare arms, however, does not have a cottice.

[Coat of arms illustrating the "bend" and "cottises."]

⇥ 4 ⇤

The Publication
of Shakespeare's Plays

M any have taken John Heminges and Henry Condell at their word
about the quarto editions of Shakespeare's plays, which they alleged were, without exception, "stolen and surreptitious copies." Whereas
Shakespeareans agree that any unauthorized publication of his works was
enabled by the absence of authorial copyright laws at the time, Oxfordians
have their own explanation. For example, although Peter Jaszi acknowledged this fact, he told the moot court in Washington that the

> extensive piracy of the plays and poems, according to authorities on the
> publishing practices of the day, marks them out as likely to have been the
> works of a nobleman. A nobleman could not complain of piracy. A com-
> mon person, such as Shakspere of Stratford, with a good business head
> and a strongly developed self-interest, not only could but almost certainly
> would have complained.[1]

Their usual source for the notion that authors had some form of legal
recourse is Sir George Greenwood, who claimed that authors had common-law protection. However, he supported this with opinion in cases
brought in the eighteenth century, after the first English copyright law was
enacted in 1709, and he acknowledged that there were not any records
"showing that authors in those old days had successfully appealed to the
courts in vindication of their common-law right to prevent the unauthor-
ised publication of their works." Nor, for that matter, is there a record of
any who tried to do so unsuccessfully. Ultimately, Sir George decided that
the Elizabethan author must have been protected by the laws of common
decency, for:

> I think we may confidently assert that English law would never have sanc-
> tioned a proceeding so entirely iniquitous as that in which . . . a pub-

lisher might, without let or hindrance, publish a stolen manuscript if only he had obtained the license of the Stationers' Company.[2]

On the other hand, even if recourse in common law did exist "to provide a remedy for the violation of so elementary a right" as an author's ownership of his own work, Greenwood conceded that "it may well have been that, in practice, it was found difficult and troublesome for an author to enforce such a right":

> The offending publisher would, of course, be a member of the powerful Stationers' Company, and the poor author might constantly find that it was better to "take it lying down" than endeavour to obtain justice by litigation.

Greenwood's use of the word *troublesome* is especially interesting, for that was precisely the word used by Sir Francis Bacon when he wanted to prevent the unauthorized publication of his *Essays,* as we will hear shortly.

Jaszi, on the other hand, moved the venue of an author's recourse from the courts of law to the court of the Company of Stationers, asserting that

> there were procedures in existence, under the Company of Stationers, to which all the printers of the day, both those authorized and those unauthorized, subscribed, by which an author who believed that a member-stationer had taken his work without authorization could appeal and get relief—injunctive relief or damage relief. . . . And there are instances, from the time of the plays and poems in question, of authors who have been abused by publishers doing just that. No one did that on behalf of Shakespeare or Shakspere.

Greenwood and Jaszi agree that the Stationers Company was at the very heart of publication in the time of Shakespeare, but their stories disagree about author's rights under this powerful guild. It is therefore essential to know just what it was and what it did. At the same time, it is also important to clarify two commonly used—and misused—words as they are applied to the publication of printed works during this time, which are *copyright* and *piracy*.

The Worshipful Company of Stationers

The Stationers was a guild of printers and booksellers that received its charter from the Crown in May 1557. It came under the immediate jurisdiction of the Archbishop of Canterbury and the Bishop of London—though the Crown, through the Privy Council, would have something to say about its operation from time to time. R. C. Bald defined its functions during the Shakespearean era, when it was at the height of its power, as follows:

> (1) it regulated conditions of production and labor within the trade; (2) it protected the rights of its members in their property; and (3) it acted as the intermediary by which the government controlled the press.[3]

However incredible it might seem to Sir George Greenwood, and wherever Peter Jaszi may have gotten his information, there is no evidence there was in Shakespeare's lifetime any concept of author's rights. How a stationer came by the work he was entering, whether or not his copy was corrupt, whether or not the author wished it to be published, had been compensated for it, or could in any way be damaged by its publication, were *not* questions asked by the wardens of the company when licensing a work. What Greenwood found impossible to believe—"that a publisher might, without let or hindrance, publish a stolen manuscript if only he had obtained the license of the Stationers Company for such publication"— turns out to be precisely the case, as we hear from the poet and pamphleteer George Wither, in his *Schollers Purgatory* (1624):

> Yea, by the laws and orders of their corporation, they can and do settle upon the particular members thereof a perpetual interest in such books as are registered by them at their Hall, in their [the printers and booksellers] several names: and are secured in taking the full benefit of those books, better than any author can be by virtue of the King's grant, notwithstanding their first copies were purloined from the true owner, or imprinted without his leave.[4]

While it may seem Wither's claim that the stationer's right was stronger than even an author's right "by virtue of the King's grant" is merely the hyperbole of an outraged author, there is evidence that it is not much of an exaggeration.

On April 24, 1626, King Charles I issued letters patent to George Sandys, granting him exclusive rights for 21 years to his translation of the fifteen books of Ovid's *Metamorphosis*, "the better to encourage him and others to employ their labors and studies in good literature." On May 7, a standard entry for this work was made to William Stansby in the register of the Stationers, and it was published with the title-page announcement that it was printed *"Cum Privilegio"*—with royal permission. Nevertheless, in 1628 the printer Robert Young put out an edition that imitated Stansby's.[5] Why did Young dare to fly in the face of a royal warrant and a formal entry to another stationer?

It seems that in 1621, Sandys had sold his translation of *five* books of the *Metamorphosis* to printer Matthew Lownes and bookseller W. Barrett, who entered the book on April 27 and published an edition in that year. Eventually rights to this work, duly registered with the Stationers, were assigned to Young. For this reason, he apparently felt that the book entered to Stansby was merely an enlarged version of the work he had the rights to and so printed all fifteen books in the Stansby edition in his own. Sandys complained to the Stationers and on April 8, 1628, an order was openly read in their hall that he had "patent for the sole printing" of his translation and that all entries to others, the assignment to Young included, "shall be crossed out of the Register Book of the Company, for that no man shall lay any claim to the printing of the same or any part thereof." Here it was the stationer who would not "take it lying down."

By early 1632, Young was ready to print another edition, to be sold by John Haviland, which incited Sandys to lodge another complaint with the Stationers. On January 26, 1632, Young and Haviland were called before the wardens and assistants of the guild, who ruled

> that the said Robert Young & John Haviland (at the time of their imprinting of the said books) did know that Mr. Sandys had before obtained his Majesty's letters patents for the sole printing of the said Translation. And that they printed the books now in question by a copy printed with this addition (cum privilegio), which induceth the court to conceive that they could not be ignorant that the sole printing of the same books belonged to the said Mr. Sandys. Whereupon the Court again ordered that the printing of the said book is to remain solely in the disposition of the said Mr. Sandys and his assigns.

There is no record of what Young said in his defense, but it is apparent he felt that he had been unfairly deprived of his copyright. It is important to note that there is no mention of any punishment meted out to Young or Haviland, and that Sandys initiated this action on the strength of his patent and the earlier enforcement of it by the Stationers' Court. Equally noteworthy is the fact that Young, playing by the old rules, believed his "perpetual interest" remained, the patent and the order of the court notwithstanding.

Young's 1628 edition of Sandys's Ovid was, by modern standards, a textbook example of "piracy": he almost exactly reproduced the text, and even had made a crude imitation of the engraved title page of the authorized 1626 edition. However, the type of piracy at issue here—a text obtained and printed without the author's involvement—was far more prevalent. Authors often had no one to blame for this but themselves.

It was a common practice of the time to allow scribal copies to be made

The title pages of George Sandys's *Ovid*—the authorized edition published by Stansby (1626) and Young's "Piracy" (1628). (RIGHT: Courtesy of the Folger Shakespeare Library; LEFT: By permission of the British Library)

of "private" writings. Interesting evidence of how out of hand this could get is provided by Thomas Nashe, who sold his *Terrors of the Night* (1594) to a printer to stem the flood of copies of this work. How he came to that pass was explained in his dedicatory epistle to Elizabeth Carey (the daughter of the future patron of Shakespeare's company, Sir George Carey);

> the urgent importunity of a kind friend of mine (to whom I was sundry ways beholding) wrested a copy from me. That copy progressed from one scrivener's shop to another, & at length grew so common, that it was ready to be hung out for one of their signs, like a pair of indentures. Whereupon I thought it as good for me to reap the fruit of my own labors, as let some unskillful pen-man or Noverint-maker [literally, a writ-

maker] starch his ruff & new spade his beard with the benefit he made of them.

In other words, Nashe's proclaimed purpose was to prevent scriveners from making any further profit off him. For in taking his work to the printer, he would thus "reap the fruit of my own labors"—that is, he got the fee for selling it for publication. Thus, not only did he forestall the scriveners from further profit but, potentially, the owner of a scribal copy as well, who otherwise could have collected the fee from the stationer he sold it to. This was indeed the fate of many a scribal copy and is how a play in the King's Men's repertory, *A King and No King* by Beaumont and Fletcher, came to be printed—and it appears that the actors are the likeliest source of this text.

This play was entered in the Stationers' Register in 1618 and published in the next year. Its publisher, Thomas Walkley, prefaced the play with a dedicatory letter to Sir Henry Neville that leaves no doubt he was the source of the copy: "Worthy Sir, I present, or rather return unto your view, that which formerly hath been received from you, hereby effecting what you did desire." Neville apparently felt this play deserved the recognition of publication and handed it over to Walkley with his "approbation and patronage, to the commendation of the authors, and encouragement of their further labors." (It is not likely to have given much encouragement to Beaumont—he died in 1616.) The text itself is a good one and the likely source for it was the King's Men, which may have allowed him a "favor copy"—a scribal copy made at his request. (This may explain why Middleton had such difficulty in getting the text of *The Witch* from them when he wanted to have a copy made for Thomas Holmes five years later.)

Scribal copies were by no means the only way a play could come into print without authorization. In fact, plays were subject to surreptitious transcription from which other forms of writing were largely immune. One way was memorial reconstruction, presumably by actors in most cases. The most famous (and infamous) example unquestionably is the first *Hamlet* quarto of 1603, the botched text of which is held to be the work of two players who had small roles in the play. The quarto of the first part of Thomas Heywood's *If You Know Not Me You Know Nobody* (1605) is also flagrantly corrupt and when the play was revived in the 1630s, he wrote a prologue to be spoken by an actor that reveals another way to get the text of a desirable play. According to Heywood, the multitude that

> Did throng the seats, the boxes, and the stage
> So much that some by Stenography drew
> The plot, put it in print (scarce one word true)
> And in that lameness it hath limped so long,

The author now, to vindicate that wrong
Hath took the pains, upright upon its feet
To teach it walk, so please you sit and see't.[6]

If Heywood's allegation is true, this would seem blatantly illegal. But there is no record of a formal protest by either Queen Anne's players or Heywood and seven editions appeared before the good text was published in 1639.

Such unauthorized publication of a play that was in the repertory of an acting company was a serious matter. In the first place, the shareholders had paid the author for his work and keenly felt the injustice of seeing it put into print without any compensation whatever. Perhaps even more appalling to them was that, once in print, there were no statutory means to prevent another acting company from performing it—which did not prevent the King's Men from trying to do so and, presumably, succeeding. Some three years after Shakespeare's plays were published in folio with the active involvement of the players, the company at the Red Bull began putting on his plays from the now-convenient texts. Heminges paid £5 to Master of the Revels Herbert to forbid the playing of these plays by this company, which he so ordered on April 11, 1627.[7] However, this was by no means the first time (and definitely not the last) that this acting company tried to protect their plays and it will be shown shortly that, contrary to Jaszi's assertion that no one tried to prevent Shakespeare's plays from being published, this is precisely what the players did, beginning nearly thirty years earlier.

For the moment, there is one other assertion by Jaszi's that needs to be tested, which is whether a "nobleman could not complain of piracy" whereas a "common person, such as Shakspere of Stratford . . . not only could but almost certainly would have complained." The evidence points to precisely the opposite. Whereas the Chamberlain's/King's company had only indifferent success in protecting their common plays despite their powerful patrons, the literary works of the well-born stood a better chance of successful suppression. But even then success was not guaranteed.

Perhaps the best example of this is the case Sir Philip Sidney's *Arcadia*, which had somehow fallen into the hands of an anonymous printer. In November 1586, a month after his death, Sidney's worshiping friend Fulke Greville wrote to Secretary of State Sir Francis Walsingham, to say

this day one Ponsonby, a book-binder in Paul's Churchyard, came to me and told me that there was one in hand to print Sir Philip Sidney's old *Arcadia*, asking me if it were done with your honour's voice or any other of his friends. I told me to my knowledge, no; then he advised me to give warning of it, either to the archbishop [of Canterbury, John Whitgift] or

Doctor Cousin [Richard Cosin, an associate of Whitgift's], who have, as he says, a copy to peruse to that end.

This tip from "Ponsonby" (William Ponsonby that is, who has been called the most important publisher in Elizabethan England), enabled the Sidney circle to head off unauthorized publication of this work by the unnamed printer, who had not yet either registered the work with the Stationers or printed it, and thus had not established any right to it. Whether or not the archbishop played an active part in forestalling the printing of the old *Arcadia,* his was the licensing hand when the authorized edition of the "New" *Arcadia* was entered in the Stationers' Register on August 23, 1588.[8] The publisher was Ponsonby, who apparently was thus rewarded for his part in the affair by becoming the "authorized" publisher of the hallowed Sir Philip's literary remains, as well as the works of his sister Mary, Countess of Pembroke, the wife of the 2nd Earl and the mother of that "incomparable pair of brethren," William and Philip, to whom the First Folio of Shakespeare would be dedicated in 1623.

Suppressing a work already in print was another, more difficult matter—even for the Sidney circle, even if they went to the highest level of the government and even if the work in question was not duly registered with the Stationers. Such was the case in the publication of Sidney's *Astrophel and Stella* by Thomas Newman. In 1591, Newman happened "to light upon" this collection of sonnets, to which he added "sundry other rare sonnets of divers noblemen and gentlemen." One, which begins "Faction that ever dwells, in Court where wit excels," is signed "E. O." Newman seemingly wished to give the impression it was by the Earl of Oxford, but it is actually by Greville, the 29th sonnet in his *Caelica.*[9]

A greater impression Newman wanted to make was that his text of Sidney's sonnets was a good one, unlike those "being spread abroad in written copies, [which] had gathered much corruption from ill-writers." It was not in fact a good text at all. Into the bargain, he did not enter his volume with the Stationers. On September 18, 1591, we find in the guild's records that the unsold copies were confiscated and taken to Stationers' Hall; two entries later we learn that Lord Burghley had a part in the seizure, fifteen shillings having been paid to John Wolfe "when he rid with an answer to my Lord Treasurer, being with her majesty in progress, for the taking in of books entitled *Sir P: S: Astrophel and Stella.*"[10]

Burghley's personal interest and the drastic action of the Stationers point to the likelihood that this was undertaken at the request of the Pembrokes—evidence that the nobility could complain, would complain, and could get action at the highest level of the government. The little good it did. For, despite the fact that Newman did not register the book with the Stationers, despite the fact that the publication was not authorized by Sidney's relations, despite the intervention of high government officials, New-man was able to publish a quarto from a good manuscript before the year was out without any sign of hindrance. Except in the doubtful possibility the *Astophel and Stella* furor concerned nothing more than the inclusion of the sonnets of "divers noblemen and gentlemen" with the work of the revered Sir Philip (these were removed in the second quarto) it appears the Stationers were able to protect Newman's copyright against a challenge by the most powerful and influential people in the realm.* In fact, in these circumstances, the Pembroke clan could do nothing more than a "common person, such as Shakspere of Stratford," which was to provide the printer with a good text to replace a bad one. We have evidence of this in the words of playwrights themselves.

For example, Thomas Heywood in his epistle to the reader of his play *The Rape of Lucrece* (1608), explains that he cooperated in the publica-tion of this work because, in the past,

> some of my plays have (unknown to me, and without any of my direction) accidentally came into the printers' hands, and therefore so corrupt and mangled (copied only by ear), that I have been as unable to know them as ashamed to challenge them.[11]

Thirty years later, the situation was the same for the reluctant play-wright Jasper Mayne. His comedy, *The City Match,* was performed by the King's Men at court, where the critic-in-chief, Charles I, enjoyed it so much that he commanded it be given public performance. Such good notices from on high were bound to make the play attractive to a stationer. And so it was. In his address "To the Reader" of the play, Mayne details his grudging participation in its publication:

> The author of this poem, knowing how hardly the best things protect themselves from censure, had no ambition to make it this way pub-

---

*The most likely instigator of the action against Newman is Ponsonby, but the only clear winner appears to have been the poet-dramatist Samuel Daniel. Twenty-eight of his sonnets were among the sundry sonnets and were printed in the next year among the fifty sonnets in his *Delia*. These were published not by Newman, but Simon Waterson, who entered them as his copy in the Stationers' Register on February 4, 1592 (Arber, 2:603). Newman is not known to have challenged Waterson's entry and thus, according to Kirschbaum, *Delia* has the distinction of being "the only definite example I have been able to discover of an Eliza-bethan stationer's being deprived of copyright in a work which he had printed without the author's or assigns' consent" (Leo Kirschbaum, *Shakespeare and the Stationers,* 132).

There is no evidence the action was taken on Daniel's behalf. Although he dedicated *Delia* to the Countess of Pembroke, he is not known to have had any connection with her prior to the publication of his sonnets in the *Astrophel and Stella* and he may have been in Italy at the time of its publication. (John Rees, *Samuel Daniel: A Critical and Biographical Study,* 8).

lic. . . . Yet he hath at length consented it should pass the press, not with an aim to purchase a new reputation, but to keep that which he hath already from growing worse. For understanding that some in London, without his approbation or allowance, were ready to print a false, imperfect copy, he was loath to be libelled by his own work, or that his play should appear to the world with more than its own faults.

There is one example of an author who did not accept that possession of a text was ten-tenths of the right to publish it. On January 24, 1597, Richard Sergier entered the *Essays of M. F. B. with the Prayers of His Sovereign*.[12] Unfortunately, he did not have the blessings of M. F. B.— Master Francis Bacon. Certain that the texts Sergier had were "untrue copies," Bacon did not content himself with offering the printer true texts in their stead, but rather set about wresting the work from him altogether. Sergier had given Bacon an opening: his edition was not yet published and the Register entry had the license of no one but Thomas Dawson, a junior warden of the Stationers. Engaging Humphrey Hooper as his publisher, Bacon rapidly assembled perfect copies of his essays and additional writings, which were ready for the press one week later. On February 5 Dawson was presented a copy of Bacon's *Essays, Religious Meditations, Places of Persuasion, and Dissuation* to be entered to Hooper under the hands of Edward Stanhope, the Archbishop of Canterbury's vicar-general; "Master Barlowe" (probably William Barlowe, a protégé of Richard Cosin), warden Dawson and, for good measure, Bacon himself. Two days later, the cancellation of Sergier's copyright was noted beside his entry. In his dedication of the *Essays* to his brother Anthony, Bacon wrote: "I do now like some that have an orchard ill-neighbored, that gather their fruit before it is ripe to prevent stealing. These fragments of my conceits were going to print; to labour the stay of them had been troublesome." Leo Kirschbaum said of this last statement that these words, "coming from the pen of one of the greatest lawyers of his day, are highly significant."[13] It is equally significant that this great lawyer did not seek remedy in law courts, but by taking advantage of the Stationers' procedures and getting the support of their overseer, the Archbishop of Canterbury. There is no record of anyone else taking this strenuous course to control publication of his own work.

Acting companies did not have the services of a Bacon, and there is an instance of a resort to cruder means to prevent the publication of a play. From October 16 to December 19, 1599, five loans were received of Henslowe by the Admiral's Men for payments to Thomas Dekker, Henry Chettle and William Haughton for their play *Patient Grissel*.[14] As the play neared production, another twenty shillings was borrowed on January 26, 1600, to "give unto the tailor to buy a grey gown for Grissel." There cannot have been many performances of this popular play when the actors caught wind of Cuthbert Burby's intention to publish it and decided that the surest, easiest way to prevent him from doing so was to buy him off. Thus, one of the players, Robert Shaw, borrowed forty shillings from Henslowe on March 18 "to give unto the printer to stay the printing of *Patient Grissel*." Although Burby entered the play in Stationers' Hall ten days later, apparently he did so to establish his right to it. The play would not be printed until 1603 by Burby's former apprentice, Henry Rocket.[15]

All told, the records of the Stationers Company show that once a work had been entered in their register or had actually been published (with or without entry), the copyright in Shakespeare's day was the privilege of the printer or publisher. Furthermore, in the absence of any explicit prohibition against unauthorized publication, as well as of any explicit acknowledgment of the rights of an author, the word *piracy* to describe the practices of publication in the time of Shakespeare is an entirely modern notion.

The Acting Companies and Publication

Oxfordians dismiss the idea that playwrights could not maintain control over their works from the companies of players and point to Ben Jonson as an example of one who did. Indeed he did—but here Jonson is, as ever, an exception, not the rule. Like most playwrights of the time, he had no affiliation with an acting company, but he alone seems to have considered retaining publication rights to his plays. It was not until the last decade of English Renaissance theater that other dramatists showed a similar interest in bringing their plays to press. However, even then, there is no question that they had to be free of any contractual obligation to the acting company for which they wrote them before they could do so.

The publication record of dramatists and, on occasion, their own statements in published works (such as the remarks of Heywood and Middleton quoted earlier) constitute most of what we know about the control of plays by acting companies. But there are two explicit pieces of evidence—which, as usual, come to us through lawsuits—that reflect the determination of the companies to control the wares they purchased. The first is the prohibition in the sharers' agreement of the Whitefriars theater syndicate, dated March 10, 1608, which was introduced in a suit involving the theater in the following year. The pertinent article states:

> *Item* it is also covenanted, granted, concluded and fully agreed between the said parties . . . that no man of the said company shall at any time hereafter put into print, or cause to be put in print, any manner of play book now in use, or that hereafter shall be sold unto them, upon the penalty and forfeiture of forty pounds Sterling, or the loss of his place and share of all things amongst them. Except the book of Torrismount

and that play not to be printed by any before twelve months be fully expired.[16]

This article in the Whitefriars contract gives firm evidence of what is otherwise apparent from the patterns of play publication: acting companies wanted to prevent their plays in use from being published. It is interesting to note that even though *Torrismount* had seemingly just about run its course at the time of the contract, the syndicate determined that its time for the press was fully one year away. There is no reason to believe that the Chamberlain's/King' Men shareholders, of which Shakespeare was one, were not similarly protective. If anything, as we shall see, they appear to have been more so.

It is fitting that one of the "Tribe of Ben," Richard Brome, was a party in the only contract that has come down to us in which publication rights between a dramatist and the company to which he was attached are specifically mentioned. On July 20, 1635, Brome signed a contract with Queen Henrietta's players at the Salisbury Court theater, which was renewed for seven years in August 1638. In the next year, however, Brome was lured away by William Beeston, the manager of the King and Queen's Young Players at the Phoenix theater, popularly known as the Cockpit. The abandoned company brought suit against Brome, and a portion of the contract offered in evidence reveals that he had been forbidden to

> suffer any play made or to be made or composed by him for your subjects or their successors in the said company in Salisbury Court to be printed by his consent or knowledge, privity, or direction without the license from the said company or the major part of them.[17]

We may recall Heywood's remarks in *The English Traveller*, which give further evidence of the control over publication exercised by acting companies. The reason he gave for why his plays had not been "exposed to the world in volumes, to bear the title of *Works*," was that some number "are still retained in the hands of some actors, who think it against their peculiar profit to have them come in print." And though this play was but one "amongst two hundred and twenty, in which I have had either an entire hand, or at the least a main finger," only about twenty were published during his lifetime. Of the plays for which he wrote prefatory material, in only two does he not protest that they had gone to the printer without his prior knowledge.[18]

Heywood, incidentally, is the only dramatist whose experience as a player, playwright and sharer is comparable to Shakespeare's. He served in these roles, beginning in 1602, for the Earl of Worcester's Men, which soon came under the patronage of James's Queen Anne, and continued to do so until the company broke up after her death in 1619. His attitude toward the publication of his plays may well be typical of the attached playwright in Shakespeare's active years. It is heard clearly in his epistle in *The Rape of Lucrece,* where he said:

> It hath been no custom in me of all other men (courteous readers) to commit my plays to the press . . . for though some have used a double sale of their labours, first to the stage and after to the press, for my own part I here proclaim myself ever faithful in the first, and never guilty of the last. . . . This, therefore, I was the willinger to furnish out in his native habit: first being by consent, next because the rest have been so wronged in being published in such savage and rare ornaments.

Heywood's swipe at playwrights who made "double sale of their labours" is directed especially at Ben Jonson. Under any circumstances, he leaves no doubt that his allegiance was owed to the stage and to his fellows, taking care that it be known he had a hand in the printing of *Lucrece* "by consent," that is, with the permission of the company.

It is by such prefatory material that a play is known to have been printed with its author's participation. There is, of course, no such play among the Shakespeare quartos. Ogburn introduces the testimony of G. E. Bentley, regarding this strange state of affairs, to wit: "Not one was printed just as he had written it," and "It is obvious that he did nothing about seeing them through the press." [19] Oxfordians believe that this is the very opposite of what Shakespeare the Artist would have done—had he any say in the matter, that is. Thus, Ogburn found it unnecessary to mention Bentley's following thought about what truly concerned Shakespeare the Artist: "Actually, it is simply another of many pieces of evidence that Shakespeare was primarily a man of theatre; his act of creation reached its fulfillment when his actors presented his play before an audience." [20]

In fact, numerous plays throughout this entire period were printed without the material that indicates they were published with the author's participation. But no suspicion has been heard that their authors were noblemen forced to suffer this indignity in silence. It is only the publication of Shakespeare's plays that has given rise to grave suspicions and elaborate schemes; only the circumstances of the publication of his plays are alleged to be shrouded in mystery, cloaked in intrigue. And mystery and intrigue are at the core of the Oxfordian scenario regarding Shakespearean publication, from the first quarto, *Titus Andronicus* in 1594, to the First Folio of 1623.

Give Them No Quarto

According to Ogburn, six plays were published anonymously between 1594 and 1598; they are, *Titus Andronicus,* Parts Two and Three of *Henry VI* (misidentified as Parts One and Two), *Romeo and Juliet, Richard II,* and

Richard III.[21] In fact, they were all printed between 1594 and 1597. (Omitted from his list of anonymous printings, for some reason, are *Henry IV, Part One*, which *was* published in 1598, as well as *Henry V*, in 1600.) The significance of these six quartos to Oxfordians is that it was the author himself who was anonymous. We may imagine London abuzz, wondering who the author of these masterpieces might be; whispers that it might be a nobleman, some hinting of One in Particular. The friends of Oxford realized something must be done. Before we hear their exciting conclusion, a few words about anonymous printed plays are in order.

Especially in these earlier years, plays were often published without attribution. Of the 42 popular plays published between 1590 and 1597, an author's name is found in only seven (six of which were by either Robert Greene, Thomas Lodge, or Christopher Marlowe). In fact, a substantial number of plays published during the entire period of Renaissance drama gave no author on the title page, and the authorship of numerous plays is still a matter of active critical debate. Now back to the story.

Sometime in 1598, the decision was reached that Oxford would get a pseudonym, and the one chosen was William Shakespeare—a name that the literate Londoner would presumably know to be a pseudonym and dare to ask no further, leaving those as dense as Shakspere himself to think his illiterate bumpkin persona was just a put-on. Most importantly, publishers now had a name to put on the hitherto anonymous plays. The messenger they selected to spread the word was one Francis Meres, whose only previous published work was a sermon. And so it was, in *Palladis Tamia, Wits Treasury*, the author's name was revealed in a chapter tucked deep in the book entitled, "A Comparative Discourse of our English Poets, with the Greek, Latin, and Italian Poets," where we read:

> As Plautus and Seneca are accounted the best for comedy and tragedy among the Latins, so Shakespeare among the English is the most excellent in both kinds for the stage; for comedy, witness his *Gentlemen of Verona*, his *[Comedy of] Errors*, his *Love's Labors Lost*, his *Love's Labors Won*, his *Midsummer Night's Dream*, and his *Merchant of Venice*; for tragedy, his *Richard the 2*, *Richard the 3*, *Henry the 4*, *King John*, *Titus Andronicus*, and his *Romeo and Juliet*.

Love's Labors Won? Some think this might have been another name for *The Taming of the Shrew*, others an earlier title for *Much Ado About Nothing*, but most scholars now believe it to be a lost play.

More to the point, Meres also praises Shakespeare's poetry and makes the first mention of his "sugar'd" sonnets. Although he singled out Shakespeare as the "most excellent" for both comedy and tragedy, he is also one of the seventeen named as "the best for comedy amongst us," as well as one of fourteen saluted as "our best for tragedy." It is Meres's list of Shakespeare's plays, however, that Ogburn finds remarkable. Besides Thomas Legge's *Richard III* and *The Destruction of Jerusalem,* he could discover no other playwright whose work is named, which leads him to wonder if the entire reason for the "Comparative Discourse" in the first place was to reveal the identity of the author of these plays.[22]

For the record, there is one other play named. Taking note of the theatrical scandal unleashed fourteen months earlier, Meres wrote, "As Actaeon was worried by his hounds, so is Thomas Nashe of his *Isle of Dogs.*" Of more consequence, the most likely reason that only Shakespeare's plays are so named is because he was at the moment the lone active dramatist with a large and identifiable body of plays. The rest were either at or near the beginning of their careers and most were working collaboratively.

Be that as it may, with Meres's Shakespeare catalogue Ogburn concludes that "Everything falls into place." In essence, the Oxford authorship cabal, having decided on Shakespeare as Oxford's sobriquet, put pounds in the purse of Shakspere, the "peace-threatener, tax-evader, theatrical functionary, and possible play-broker," to go back to Stratford and leave this wounded name behind for De Vere's exclusive use. Or is it, another scenario has it, that he was rewarded for being Oxford's "front man" with shares in the Chamberlain's Men, for which he functioned as a "factotum and manager"?[23] A possibility not considered in all this is that Meres may merely have reflected interest in Shakespeare that was aroused when one of his play became topical.

Palladis Tamia was entered with the Stationers on September 7th in the year Shakespeare's name appeared for the first time in published editions of his plays, one or both reprints. The title page of *Love's Labors Lost,* never entered in the Register, claims to be "Newly corrected, augmented, and amended," suggestive of an earlier edition of which no copy exists. The other, *Richard II,* first published in 1597, is extraordinary because two more editions were printed in 1598—his only play to have had three printings in two years. It is possible, just not very probable, that both 1598 editions were published after *Palladis Tamia.* What is more likely is that this play gained unexpected notoriety, which may have contributed to Shakespeare's value in the marketplace.

A work that may have both reflected and added to the notoriety of *Richard II* is noted by Meres where among "the best for satire" is the unnamed "author of *Skialetheia,*" attributed to Everard Guilpin. In his collection of satirical epigrams, one appears to be aimed at Robert Devereux, the Earl of Essex. Essex felt that he was being denied his rightful place in the queen's favor by her ambitious courtiers, which even loyal counselors had likened to the court of Richard II. The earl is said to have seen the image of his discontent in Shakespeare's play on that king's reign, while

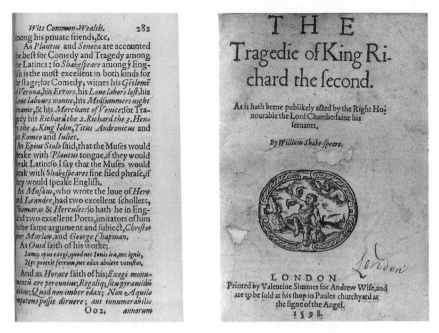

LEFT: Francis Meres proclaims Shakespeare "the most excellent" for comedy and tragedy in *Palladis Tamia*. (Courtesy of the Folger Shakespeare Library)

RIGHT: The title page of the second edition of *Richard II* (1598). (Courtesy of the Folger Shakespeare Library)

The "incomparable pair of brethren" William Herbert, the 3rd Earl of Pembroke, in a miniature by Isaac Oliver; and Philip, Earl of Montgomery. (Courtesy of the Folger Shakespeare Library)

his partisans saw him in the role of Richard's usurper, Henry Bolingbroke. Guilpin firmly linked Essex to Bolingbroke—and Shakespeare's play—in an epigram on the earl whose "puff thoughts swell, / With yeasty ambition." Dubbing him Felix, the sobriquet of the Roman general who became an emperor, Guilpin wrote:

> For when great Felix passing through the street,
> Vaileth his cap to each one he doth meet,
> And when no broom-man that will pray for him,
> Shall have less truage than his bonnet's brim,
> Who would not think him perfect courtesy?
> Or the honeysuckle of humility?

—echoing the speech in act one, scene four of *Richard II*, in which the king speaks of Bolingbroke's "courtship to the common people"—

> How he did seem to dive into their hearts
> With humble and familiar courtesy . . .
> Off goes his bonnet to an oyster-wench;
> A brace of draymen bid God speed him well,
> And had the tribute of his supple knee,
> With "Thanks, my countrymen, my loving friends"—
> As were our England in reversion his,
> And he our subjects' next degree in hope.

About two and one-half years later, Shakespeare's drama would be the prologue to Essex's downfall. A performance of *Richard II* at the Globe on February 7, 1601, commissioned by his loyalists, set in motion the events that provoked the earl into a failed rebellion. During his trial it was said he had been "so often present at the playing [of *Richard*], and with great applause giving countenance to it."

The extent to which Shakespeare's play reflected popular support for Essex and his cause, and disenchantment with the queen's court, can only be conjectured. The same may be said of how much this association stimulated sales of the quarto. Its success may be owed just as well to its good text of the earliest play that presages Shakespeare's mature command over dramatic characterization and language. Any one of these is a far more compelling reason for Shakespeare's name to have value in the book trade than that he was praised by a little-known author in the slightly regarded genre of the commonplace book.

Under any circumstances, nine additional Shakespeare quartos were issued between 1598 and 1603, all but two—the aforementioned *Henry IV, Part One* and *Henry V*—with the author's name on the title page of the first printings. Then suddenly, after the publication of the mangled *Hamlet* in 1603, the flow of new Shakespeare plays all but came to a halt—and the Oxfordian publication melodrama takes wing.

The year 1603, it so happens, was also the year that Sir George Buck got the reversion of the mastership of the Revels Office. Ogburn, giving credit to one Gwenneth Bowen for the scenario, unfolds the significance of this to the publication record of Shakespeare's plays up to the First Folio in 1623.[24] Buck, we are told, was recruited as the "chief agent" of William Herbert, 3rd Earl of Pembroke, and his brother Philip, Earl of Montgomery, to suppress publication of Shakespeare's plays for reasons Ogburn reveals in due course. The better to carry this off, in 1607, "while serving as acting Master," Buck moved the Revels Office from its posh quarters in St. John's Priory to an older accommodation near Blackfriars to have the nerve center of theater closer to the nerve center of Shakespearean affairs—Baynard's Castle, Pembroke's London residence.

Presumably this activity distracted Buck from his primary duties, for three new plays were printed in 1608 and 1609—*King Lear, Pericles* and *Troilus and Cressida*. However, except for these plays and his *Sonnets* (1609), from 1604 to 1615, Shakespearean publication was limited to reprints of some of the plays first issued between 1594 and 1603. Buck, we are given to believe, was holding the fort against piratical printers as best he could until 1615, when the Earl of Pembroke arrived with all the powers of the Lord Chamberlain's office, having spurned higher positions to get "that specific office in his hands." Can there be any doubt why? For now even the reprints ceased, except for the so-called Pavier quartos issued in 1619—*"but falsely dated as of the early 1600s"* (Ogburn's italics). This so aroused Pembroke's ire that "he stepped outside the law to forbid the Company of Stationers to publish any plays of the King's Men . . . without special consent."[25] "The design must be apparent to us," Ogburn concludes: "Pembroke, with Buck's cooperation, was clamping down on the traffic in Shakespeare's plays, anticipating publication of an authorized edition with the whole collection."

Apart from the 1619 quartos, the only rend in this splendid design, according to this story, came on October 6, 1621, when, with work well under way on the Shakespeare folio, Buck allowed *Othello* to be entered for printing in the Stationers' Register. (It would be published in quarto in the next year.) Ogburn knows the reason he sabotaged the Great Plan begun nearly two decades before: "Poor Sir George, it developed, was losing his mind." This caused such great consternation that work came to a complete halt on the folio. It would be more than two years before it was at last published.

The Publication History
of the Chamberlain's Men's Plays

That does make a good story. Unfortunately, it bears little resemblance, and even less reference to the facts. First of all, is there anything to the assertion that Buck's acquisition of the reversion of the mastership of the Revels was the beginning of the attempts to suppress publication of Shakespeare's plays? The twelve quartos published between 1597 and 1603 leave no room for doubt that there is not.

That most of these plays were not all "stolen and surreptitious copies, maimed and deformed by the frauds and stealths of injurious imposters," can be seen in the fact that the folio texts show definite reference to the quartos—some of which modern editors hold to be superior, or at least closer to the author's original. Except for the doubtful origins of several texts, such as *Henry V* and the first editions of *Romeo and Juliet* and *Hamlet,* the evidence leans toward either some form of the author's own manuscript or an authoritative playhouse script as the sources for the quarto texts. Unsatisfactory though these may be by modern standards of editing and printing, they are in keeping with the quality of most plays published in that time. And there is reason to believe that the source for many was the Lord Chamberlain's company itself.

Why should players have decided to sell their plays? One reason was that least artistic of all: they needed the money. In fact, the agents for many a nonauthorial quarto were often the acting companies. It is by no means coincidental that the number of plays published would increase dramatically when the London theaters were shut during plague years or by official inhibitions.[26] In the spring of 1593, for instance, the playhouses were shut due to plague and between the autumn of 1593 and the summer of 1594, an unusually large number of plays were entered with the Stationers. Among these were *Titus Andronicus, Henry VI, Part Two,* and *The Taming of a Shrew* (a precursor of Shakespeare's play), plays that had been in the repertoire of the Earl of Pembroke's players. We know that this company had particularly suffered because, on September 28, 1593, Henslowe wrote Alleyn, then touring the provinces with Lord Strange's Men,

> as for my Lord a Pembroke's, which you desire to know where they may be, they are all at home and have been this five or six weeks, for they cannot save their charges with travel as I hear and were fain to pawn their apparel for their charge.[27]

Actors so desperate that they would sell their costumes may reasonably be expected to part with their plays as well. There was a period when the latter might have been necessary for even so stable an outfit as the Lord Chamberlain's Men.

After the publication of *Henry VI, Part Three* in 1595, no new plays by Shakespeare were published until John Danter printed the unquestionably maimed, deformed, and surreptitious *Romeo and Juliet* in the early months of 1597, which he did not bother to enter at Stationers' Hall. This was by no means unusual for Danter; on April 10, the court of the guild ordered his presses and typefaces to be seized and defaced to make them "unserviceable for printing" as punishment for his edition of the *Jesus Psalter* and "other things without authority."[28] (A "newly corrected, augmented, and amended text" of *Romeo* was provided to Thomas Creed and Cuthbert Burby for the 1599 quarto, just as a superior text of *Hamlet* would be provided in 1604 to supersede the corrupt text printed in the preceding year.)

The flurry of publication that would put another eleven Shakespeare plays into print in about six years' time began in earnest with the entry of *Richard II* in the Stationers' Register on August 29, 1597. The major factor in the company's decision to sell the plays at this time, it appears, was owing to the failure of James Burbage's innovative scheme to make the first indoor playhouse for an adult acting company, an idea he was pushed toward due to his problems over the plot on which stood the Theatre, his Shoreditch playhouse that was the home of the Chamberlain's Men. When he erected the playhouse in 1576, he took a 21-year lease on the property from a Giles Allen, with a contract stipulation that would have allowed the lease to be renewed. As the expiration date approached the landlord put off Burbage.[29] The advantage of delay to Allen was that Burbage could pull down the building and reerect it elsewhere during the lease period, but if the lease lapsed it became Allen's property. And, indeed, the terms the landlord finally offered indicate that he did have his eye on the playhouse itself: he would extend the lease—if he could take over the building when five years had elapsed. This was unacceptable to Burbage, who cast about for an alternative and found it in a building of the dissolved Blackfriars monastery. On February 4, 1596, he took possession with the intention of making its "seven great upper rooms" into an indoor theater, which he hoped to have ready for use before the ground lease on the Theatre expired on April 13, 1597.[30]

However, his plan was thwarted when, in November 1596, 31 residents of the Blackfriars precinct successfully petitioned the Privy Council to prevent the building from being used as a theater for popular drama,

> by reason of the great resort and gathering together of all manner of vagrant and lewd persons that, under color of resorting to the plays, will come thither and work all manner of mischief, and also to the great pes-

tering and filling up of the same precinct, if it should please God to send the visitation of sickness as heretofore hath been, for that the same precinct is already grown very populous; and besides that the same playhouse is so near the church that the noise of the drums and the trumpets will greatly disturb and hinder both the ministers and parishioners in time of divine service and sermons.[31]

Although one who dwelled in Blackfriars was the Lord Chamberlain William, Lord Cobham, no friend of the theater, his name is not found on the petition. However, George Carey, 2nd Lord Hunsdon, was. The elder Burbage and the players must have been dismayed to find the company's patron on it, but it is not all that surprising. For, in addition to the seven rooms on the upper floor, Burbage also leased the Blind Room and Paved Hall in the lower story, the latter of which shared a wall with Hunsdon's house, formerly the monastic infirmary.[32] Evidently he did not want his peace disturbed, even by those who would be attracted by his own players. The petition was successful. This dispute and its resolution are thought to have hastened Burbage's death; on February 2, 1597, he was buried at St. Leonard's Church, Shoreditch.

Thus, Burbage's sons were left with a property that was useless to the players and, two months later, the lease ran out on the Theatre. The actors probably took up temporary residence in their other Shoreditch playhouse, the Curtain. Bad enough became worse when, in late July 1597, Nashe's play, *Isle of Dogs,* brought down the wrath of the Privy Council on the theater community. The play was condemned as a "lewd play . . . containing very seditious and slanderous matter," and the players condemned to tour the provinces, for the council ordered all the theaters shut in reprisal. It is probably no coincidence that in the next month, *Richard II* was entered to the bookseller Andrew Wise in the Stationers' Register; on October 20 he would add *Richard III;* four months later, *Henry IV, Part One.* Like the four plays that were published earlier, the first editions of Wise's three quartos did not have Shakespeare's name on the title page.

In this same eventful period a very important entry is to be found in the Stationers' Register. On July 22, 1598, copy was entered to the printer James Roberts,

> under the hands of both the wardens, a book of the *Merchant of Venice or otherwise called the Jew of Venice/*Provided that it be not printed by the said James Roberts or any other whatsoever without license first had from the Right Honorable the Lord Chamberlain.

This was the first of several conditional entries of the Chamberlain's Men's plays—Shakespeare's and otherwise—over the next five years.

Chronology of Shakespeare's Published Plays and Plays Entered in the Stationers' Register—1594–1603

VARIOUS COMPANIES

Play	S.R. Date	(Arber)[a]	Year	Printer/Bookseller
Titus Andronicus	Feb 6, 1594	(2:644)	1594	*Danter*[b]/E. White-Millington
"As it was played by . . . the Earl of Derby, the Earl of Pembroke, the Earl of Sussex their servants."				
Henry VI, Part Two	Mar 12, 1594	(2:646)	1594	Creed/*Millington*
Henry VI, Part Three	No entry		1595	Short/Millington
"As it was sundry times played by . . . the Earl of Pembroke his servants."				

LORD CHAMBERLAIN'S MEN

Play	S.R. Date	(Arber)[a]	Year	Printer/Bookseller
Romeo and Juliet	No entry		1597	Danter/None given
As it was "played publiquely by the . . . Lord of Hunsdon his Servants."				
			1599	Creed/Burby
"Newly corrected, augmented, and amended."				
Richard II (2)[c]	Aug 29, 1597	(3:89)	1597	Simms/*Wise*
Richard III (2)	Oct 20, 1597	(3:93)	1597	Simms/*Wise*
Love's Labor's Lost (1)	No entry		1598	W. White/Burby
"Newly corrected and augmented" edition; conjectured to have replaced an earlier corrupt edition of which no copy is known.				
Henry IV, Part One (3)	Feb 25, 1598	(3:105)	1598	Short/*Wise*
Merchant of Venice (1)	Jul 22, 1598	(3:122)	1600	Roberts/*Hayes*

Entered "provided that it not be printed . . . without license first had from the . . . Lord Chamberlain."
Transferred to Hayes October 28, 1600 (3:175).

Following three works listed on the flyleaf of Stationers' Register C, August 14, 1600, as "to be stayed" (3:37).

Play	Entry[a]		Publication	Printer/Bookseller[b]
As You Like It				
Henry V				
Much Ado about Nothing				
	Entered to Pavier, August 14, 1600, among works "formerly printed and set over" (3:169).			
Henry V	No entry		1600	Creed/Millington-Busby
Henry IV, Part 2 (1)[c]	Aug 23, 1600	(3:170)	1600	Simms/*Wise-Aspley*
Much Ado about Nothing (1)	Aug 23, 1600	(3:170)	1600	Simms/*Wise-Aspley*
Midsummer Night's Dream (1)	Oct 8, 1600	(3:174)	1600	(Braddock?)/*Fisher*
Merry Wives of Windsor (1)	Jan 18, 1602	(3:199)	1602	Creed/*Johnson*
Hamlet (1)	Jul 26, 1602	(3:212)	1603	Simms/Ling-*Trundell*
	Entered to Roberts.			
	"Newly imprinted and enlarged . . . according to the true and perfect copy."			
Troilus and Cressida	Feb 7, 1603	(3:226)	1604	*Roberts/Ling*
	Entered to Roberts to be printed "when he hath gotten sufficient authority for it."			
	No known edition. Reentered to Bonian and Walley, January 28, 1609, and published in the same year.			

[a] Volume and page number in which entry of a play is recorded in Edward Arber, *A Transcript of the Stationers' Registers*.

[b] Name in italic is the printer or bookseller to whom the play was entered in the *Stationers' Register*.

[c] Number in parentheses is of the earliest edition to have Shakespeare's name as the author.

There were no new entries for plays of the company in 1599, but the next, written on a flyleaf of Register C of the Stationers amongst other plays requiring additional authority to be licensed, again involves Roberts. "A moral of *Cloth Breeches and Velvet Hose*" and *A Larum for London* are found beneath the heading, "My Lord Chamberlain's Men's plays entered," dated May 27, 1600.[33] In the regular register for that date we find that the first play was entered to Roberts under the hands of the wardens of the Stationers, the second on May 29—each with the proviso that it was not to be printed without further authority.[34] On August 4, *As You Like It, Henry V, Every Man in His Humour* and *Much Ado about Nothing* were written immediately beneath the preceding flyleaf entry, without any publisher named (though it is assumed this was Roberts too), joined by the notation these plays also were "to be stayed." The next and last restrictive entry of a Chamberlain's play was again to Roberts; on February 7, 1603, " 'Troilus and Cressida' as it is acted by my Lord Chamberlain's Men," was entered to be printed "when he hath gotten sufficient authority for it."

Some speculate that Roberts was the instrument of the Chamberlain's Men to block publication—entering plays to himself on their behalf to prevent others from printing them. Or did he act in defiance of them?[35] All told, of the four plays conditionally entered to Roberts for certain—*The Merchant of Venice, A Larum for London, Cloth Breeches and Velvet Hose* and *Troilus and Cressida*—he would be the printer of only one, *The Merchant of Venice,* and then only after he had sold his right in it to Thomas Hayes before it was published in 1600. *A Larum for London* was also put off two years; its printer was not identified; *Cloth Breeches and Velvet Hose* is not known to have been printed at all. *Troilus and Cressida* would not be printed until 1609, after it was newly entered in the Stationers' Register to the booksellers Richard Bonian and Henry Walley. Of the four plays named on the flyleaf note of August 4, 1600, authority to print three of them—*Henry V, Much Ado About Nothing* and *Every Man in His Humour*—was granted to other stationers within weeks and all were eventually published. Only *As You Like It* would not appear in print until the First Folio. If Roberts was indeed an agent of the Chamberlain's Men, the ploy was not markedly successful.

Whatever Roberts actual role might have been, here we have evidence that Shakespeare's company was directly or indirectly trying to prevent their plays from being published—only five of which were by Shakespeare. Furthermore, this effort began nearly five years before George Buck got his long-sought-after reversion of the mastership of the Revels on June 23, 1603.

From Sir George Buck to the First Folio

Two things about Buck's position in the Revels Office are certain: when he got the reversion of the mastership, he did not have the power to suppress publication of the plays and, when he became the master and did have the power, he made no effort to do so. First of all, it must be understood precisely what having the reversion of the office meant—which was nothing more, in fact, than that he would become Master of the Revels when the office was vacated by the incumbent, Sir Edward Tilney. Until that time, Buck was never either the acting Master or deputy Master of the Revels: he had no formal title until he actually became *the* master and that was not until 1610. "It is clear from the records," W. R. Streitberger states, "that neither Buc's signature nor his name appears on any [Revels Office] document in any capacity until after Tyllney's death in 1610, although later payments suggest some kind of participation."[36] Nor was it Buck who decided to up and move the Revels Office from the buildings of the former priory of the Order of St. John of Jerusalem (the Knights Hospitallers) in Clerkenwell. Rather the Revels were removed from there by King James, who gave the properties to his cousin Esmé Stuart, Lord Aubigny, as a wedding gift. Buck was charged with finding new quarters for the Revels—which were not relocated to Blackfriars at this time but, instead, to the Priory of the Whitefriars, leased "at a high & dear rate."[37] It was probably for this reason that he did move the Revels Office to Blackfriars in 1612. However, whereas the Revels accounts show the payments of allowances to Tilney in 1608–9, and to his clerk and yeoman, and to the clerk-comptroller in 1609–10, Buck does not appear on the Revels payroll until the account of 1610–11, when he was granted money for his lodgings, which was made retroactive to November 1, 1608.[38]

On the other hand, Buck appears to have created a source of income from the Revels Office before this date. On May 13, 1606, a comedy by Edward Sharpham entitled *The Fleire* was entered to John Trundell and John Busby with the provision that it was not to be printed "till they bring good authority and license for the doing thereof." Somehow Buck's aid was enlisted and beneath the copyright finally entered on November 21 appeared the note: "This book is authorized by Sir George Buck, Master Hartwell and the wardens."[39] Licensing plays for the press would continue to provide Sir George with a source of income even after he became Master of the Revels.

As we have been told that only oncoming madness can account for Buck's breach in preventing publication when he licensed *Othello* in 1621, it is interesting to see what the Stationers' Register entries have to tell us about the Shakespeare plays licensed for printing between 1607 and 1609:

November 26, 1607, to Nathaniel Butter and John Busby:
> Entered for their copy under the hands of Sir George Buck, knight, and the wardens, a book called Master William Shakespeare his *History of King Lear* as it was lately played before the King's majesty at Whitehall upon St. Stephen's night at Christmas last past, by his Majesty's servants playing usually at the Globe on the Bankside.

May 20, 1608, to Edward Blount:
> Entered for his copy under the hands of Sir George Buck, knight, and Master Warden Seton, a book called the book of *Pericles, Prince of Tyre*.

January 28, 1609, to Richard Bonian and Henry Walley:
> Entered for their copy under the hands of Master Segar, deputy to Sir George Buck, and Master Warden Lownes, a book called *The History of Troilus and Cressida*.[40]

Rather than suppressing publication of Shakespeare's plays, we can see that Buck was actually authorizing it. There is yet more of consequence to the authorship question when one, *Troilus and Cressida*, was actually put into print.

The quarto of this play exists in two states. The title page of one reads: *"The History of Troilus and Cressida/*As it was acted by the King's Majesty's servants at the Globe"; the other: *"The Famous History of Troilus and Cressida/*Excellently expressing the beginning of their loves, with the conceited wooing of Pandarus, Prince of Licia," with the addition of an epistle, "A Never Writer, to an Ever Reader. News." What was this news? Whereas the title page of one says the King's Men had acted the play at the Globe, the epistle in the other says "you have here a new play, never staled with the stage, never clapper-clawed with the palms of the vulgar," nor "sullied with the smoky breath of the multitude."

Reconciling such conflicting information has perplexed scholars—but it is clear as day to the Oxfordian initiate. The quarto with the epistle was the "first edition" of the play and, naturally, it is replete with clues to the True Author. We are left to draw the inference that when it was realized this would blow Oxford's cover, the incriminating evidence was omitted from the second edition published that year and on its title page was the newest news: the play had been acted after all![41] Presumably the Jacobean Englishman was expected to ignore the old news, just as the modern is expected to ignore the facts, which can be found in any modern edition of the play and show the Oxfordian surmise is baseless.

It has been more than 100 years since H. P. Stopes gave bibliographic evidence in his introduction to a facsimile edition of *Troilus and Cressida* with the Globe title page that leaves no doubt that this state was the first printed. This was confirmed by Philip Williams, Jr.'s, study of the printing of these quartos, published in 1949, which also revealed that, except for the altered title page and the epistle, the type and page content are identical in both. Therefore, there were not two separate printings of the quarto at all, but rather both states were part of the same press run.[42] (This and other issues regarding this quarto will be treated in greater detail in the next chapter.)

The news that *Troilus and Cressida* was a new play in 1609 is news indeed because the Stationers' Register records the entry of "the book of *Troilus and Cressida*, as it is acted by my Lord Chamberlain's Men," on February 7, 1603, to James Roberts, which he could print "when he hath gotten sufficient authority." Apparently he never got it, for he is not known to have printed it, and presumably it was the very same play that was licensed to and published by Bonian and Walley in 1609. But there is bad news for the Oxfordians in the epistle, which says of the author: "And believe this, that when he is gone and his comedies out of sale, you will scramble for them and set up a new English Inquisition." It does appear the author was not yet gone from this mortal coil when the play was printed in 1609. But Ogburn dismisses this statement on the grounds that it would be a rather crass thing to say about one who is actually amongst the living. On the other hand, it is a rather foolish thing to say about the author if he were already dead.

Curiously, Buck's emergence as the licensing power for printed plays also coincides with an increase in new editions of previously published plays. After the bad *Hamlet* of 1603, the good second quarto of 1604 and reprints of *Henry IV, Part One* (1604) and *Richard III* (1605) were the only quartos published in the three years before Buck began licensing plays in 1606. However, in addition to the three newly licensed plays of 1607–9, four printings of old plays were also issued in this period. When Tilney died in October 1610, Buck at last became Master of the Revels; and in 1611, three more plays were reissued, as well as the old two-part *King John*, with "Written by W. Sh." added to the title-page. In 1612 *Richard III* was reprinted, followed by *Henry IV, Part One* in 1613, and *Richard II* in 1615. Buck had nothing to do with these new editions, of course, but he clearly did nothing to stem the tide either. Which brings us to December 23, 1615, when—*(flourish)*:

Enter the Earl of Pembroke, with the Lord Chamberlain's staff.

For the next eight years, we are led to believe, Pembroke successfully wielded his big stick—except for the 1619 quartos and Buck's bout of insanity that allowed the publication of *Othello* in 1622. In 1623 the First Folio was at last printed and the nearly two-decade-long adventure came to a happy ending. Unfortunately, this doesn't bear any more resemblance to the facts of the publication record after 1615 than it did to the facts before 1615. Let's begin with the 1619 quartos and Pembroke's order of about this time prohibiting further publication of King's Men's plays.

Pembroke and the 1619 Quartos

In his *Shakespeare and the Stationers*, Leo Kirschbaum states that "The chief event of 1619 from the viewpoint of the battle between the players and the stationers was the printing of the so-called '1619 quartos' by William Jaggard."[43] This assumption regarding the publication of ten plays attributed to Shakespeare in that year has gone unquestioned by Shakespearean scholars and authorship controversialists alike. As far as the Shakespearean is concerned, what else but the unauthorized publication of plays by the greatest of dramatists could have resulted in an order from the Lord Chamberlain to prohibit any further publication. From the Oxfordian point of view, this is strong evidence that Pembroke had a personal interest in the publication of Shakespeare's plays, and neatly fits their scenario of the earl's firsthand involvement in the First Folio. Before these matters are put to the test, a look at the books in question is needed.

The ten plays in nine quartos published in 1619 are usually blamed on Thomas Pavier, who had the copyright to six of the plays, including the two that are wrongly attributed to Shakespeare: *Sir John Oldcastle* (known from *Henslowe's Diary* to have been written by Anthony Munday, Michael Drayton, Richard Hathway and Robert Wilson), and *A Yorkshire Tragedy* (now ascribed to Middleton). His unscrupulous image is enhanced by his entry of the latter play with the Stationers in 1608 as "by Wylliam Shakespere," which also happens to be the only entry between 1607 and 1615 that was not licensed for publication by Buck or his deputy—either because (runs one opinion) they refused to do so because they suspected the play was not by Shakespeare, or (runs another and more likely opinion) because Pavier avoided the Revels Office altogether.[44] Nevertheless, a greater measure of culpability may rest with the man who was the printer of all the volumes, William Jaggard.

Jaggard, who would have a major role in the publication of the First Folio four years later, may have originally planned to print the quartos in imitation of Jonson's folio of 1616. Although they were published as individual books, he may have originally intended to issue the plays in a single volume, each play (like those in Jonson's folio) with a separate title page. This is suggested by the consecutive signatures of what are generally agreed to be the first two quartos: *The Whole Contention* (*Henry VI*, Parts Two and Three) and *Pericles*. (Signatures are the letters in alphabetical order, usually in the bottom margin of the righthand page, which indicate

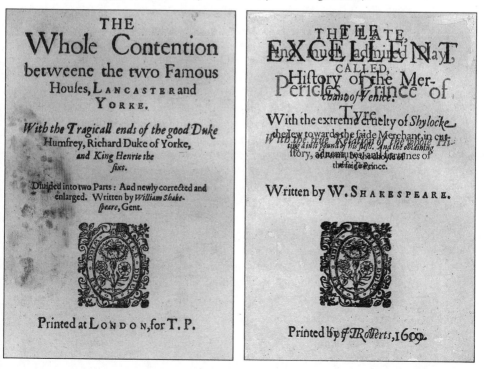

Stationers' Register entry of *King Lear* to Nathaniel Butter and John Busby, November 26, 1607. (Courtesy of the Worshipful Company of Stationers and Newspaper Makers)

LEFT: The title page of *The Whole Contention* (parts 2 and 3 of *Henry VI*), the first of the nine quartos printed by Jaggard in 1619. (Courtesy of the Folger Shakespeare Library)

RIGHT: Superimposition of the title pages of *Pericles* and *The Merchant of Venice*. "Written by W. Shakespeare" and the printer's ornament align perfectly. Note the type substituted in the imprint. (Composite photograph by John Rea Woolley, in *Modern Philology*, vol. 8. Courtesy of University of Chicago Press.)

the collation for binding. In *The Whole Contention* they run from A to Q; in *Pericles,* R-Z, Aa, Bb.) Then the consecutive signatures stop and each subsequent play is printed as a separate entity. Might this change have been occasioned by Pembroke's order to the Stationers? A closer look at the publication of these plays clearly is in order.

First of all, the title pages of the quartos refute Ogburn's assertion that *all* were dated to the early 1600s. The following is a list of the plays with the publisher and date on the title page in the order in which each was printed, according to the study by William J. Neidig:

The Whole Contention	Printed at London, for T. P. [no date].
Pericles	Printed for T. P., 1619.
A Yorkshire Tragedy	Printed for T. P., 1619.
Merchant of Venice	Printed for J. Roberts, 1600.
Merry Wives of Windsor	Printed for Arthur Johnson, 1619.
King Lear	Printed for Nathaniel Butter, 1608.
Henry V	Printed for T. P., 1608.
Sir John Oldcastle	Printed for T. P., 1600.
Midsummer Night's Dream	Printed by James Roberts, 1600.

In his meticulous measurement of these title pages, Neidig found that the title page of *Pericles* and of *A Yorkshire Tragedy* were printed on separate sheets, and that the one for the latter was printed first. He next found that only the type for the title material on the *Pericles* was removed, leaving in place "Written by W. Shakespeare," the printer's device and the imprint. It was into this setup that Jaggard placed the type for *The Merchant of Venice* title, while "J. Roberts" was tightly set in place of "T. P.," and two zeros were put in place of the "19" in the year in the imprint.[45] However, if this was done to get around the order instigated by Pembroke, why did Jaggard revert to the year 1619 when he printed *The Merry Wives of Windsor?* A possible answer may be found in the Stationers' Register, which may also give us information about when the quartos were printed.

The Merchant of Venice had been originally licensed on July 22, 1598, to James Roberts. Roberts did not print an edition of his own, but instead transferred his right to the bookseller Thomas Hayes on October 28, 1600, and an edition was printed in that year by Roberts for Hayes. Hayes died before February 6, 1604, and his widow sold some of his copyrights to other printers; the *Merchant,* however, was not among them.

Jaggard, who purchased Roberts business in 1608, may have had an honest hope that he had some right to the play. After all, it was not one of those sold by the widow and might therefore have been derelict, in which case he might claim it as Roberts' successor. Then again, he likely knew that Hayes' son Lawrence had taken up his father's trade, entering his first book with the Stationers in 1617, and in the absence of any assignment of rights to another printer, the son had a valid claim to the play. Jaggard may have tried to get around the matter by using a false imprint: "Printed by J. Roberts, 1600." If so it didn't work. On July 8, 1619, a Register entry notes that, "by consent of a full court" of the Stationers, Lawrence had the right to the *Merchant* (as well as *The Ethopian History* of Heliodorus) "which were the copies of Thomas Hayes, his father."[46] It is reasonable to suppose that Hayes learned of Jaggard's edition not long after it was in the bookstalls; if this is the case, the quarto was then printed several weeks after Pembroke's letter. Insofar as this play was the fourth of the quartos printed, that would mean five more were sent to the press afterwards, four of which Jaggard would date 1600 or 1608. Whatever his reason for this, they were published without hindrance.

Thus we return to the question of whether it was indeed the publication of these ten plays that led to Pembroke's action? In calling these quartos "the chief event" in the battle against unauthorized publication of the King's Men's plays, Kirschbaum did note that two of their plays by Beaumont and Fletcher, *A King and No King* and *A Maid's Tragedy*, were entered in the Stationers' Register in 1618 and 1619 respectively (both would be published in 1619), but gives no further attention to them. Though the very idea that these two plays by now slightly regarded playwrights could have instigated mighty Pembroke's order seems impossible, the evidence suggests it is highly probable.

The former was entered to Edward Blount on August 7, 1618, with Buck's license. (When it was issued in 1619, Blount is nowhere to be found in the book—the title page says only that it was "printed for Thomas Walkley," though there is no record that the copy had been transferred to him.) Then, on April 28, 1619, again with Buck's license, *The Maid's Tragedy* was registered at Stationers' Hall. It was just five days later, May 3rd, that notice of Pembroke's order was put into the Stationers' Court Record, which reads:

> Upon a letter from the right honorable the Lord Chamberlain: It is thought fit and so entered that no plays that his Majesty's players do play shall be printed without the consent of some of them.[47]

The letter from Pembroke that initiated this prohibition is lost but we can learn more from an authoritative version of what was in it from a source that can be considered most reliable: a letter written to the Stationers Company by his brother Philip, dated June 10, 1637.

William resigned the Chamberlain's office in 1626 to his brother (who would also add the Pembroke title to his own of Montgomery upon William's death in 1630). Philip began his letter to the Stationers with a synopsis of the one his brother sent to the guild in 1619:

> Whereas complaint was heretofore presented to my dear brother & predecessor by his Majesty's servants the Players, that some of the Company of Printers and Stationers had procured, published & printed diverse of their books of comedies, tragedies, chronicle histories, and the like, which they had (for the special service of his Majesty & for their own use) bought and provided at very dear & high rates. By means whereof not only they themselves had much prejudice, but the books much corruption to the injury and disgrace of the authors. And thereupon the Masters & Wardens of the Company of Printers & Stationers were advised by my brother to take notice thereof & to take order for the stay of any further impression of any of the plays or interludes of his Majesty's Servants without their consents.[48]

It may be first noted that Earl Philip's frank information about his brother's role in 1619 throws open to question Ogburn's assertion that Pembroke stepped outside the law in issuing his order. Secondly, precisely what law did he step outside of? As we have seen in the case of Lord Burghley's involvement in recalling Sidney's *Astrophel and Stella* and in the provision that *The Merchant of Venice* was not to be printed "without license first had from . . . the Lord Chamberlain," high government officers apparently felt they had every right to interfere in these matters. Furthermore, how can Pembroke's action be posed as something startlingly extralegal when we have been told that, by some shadowy fiat, he had been suppressing the publication of Shakespeare's plays for perhaps as many as fifteen years at that time?

More importantly, this letter contradicts the impression left by Ogburn's version of events; first, that it was William who initiated the inhibition on publication—it is plainly stated that the complaint was presented to Pembroke "by his Majesty's servants the Players"—second, that the consent required for publication was not Pembroke's but that of the King's Men, which is confirmed by the Stationers' Court Book quoted above.

Apart from the proximity between the dates when *A Maid's Tragedy* was entered in the Register and Pembroke's letter to the Stationers, there are better reasons that the Beaumont and Fletcher plays roused the King's Men to action. The players do seem to have put a lid on publication after the fifth quarto of *Richard II* was issued in 1615. Some thirty plays, masques and sundry entertainments were put into print in the next three years, but not one belonged to the King's players. If this represented some positive effort on their part, they cannot have welcomed the resumption of publication of their plays. However, it is more likely that they would have been moved to action by the printing of new plays, rather than reprints of old plays long since in circulation. What is more, the reputation of Beaumont and Fletcher was in the ascendancy; whereas it is difficult to gauge the reputation of these playwrights in comparison to Shakespeare among the playgoing public, their plays were definitely more popular at court than Shakespeare's (see chapter 7). It appears much likelier that it was the publication of their plays that resulted in the action of the King's Men.

At last, however fearsome Oxfordians imagine Pembroke's powers to have been, in reality it appears that the Stationers diplomatically gave deference to his command ("It is thought fit . . .") while, true to form, giving as little support to this intrusion in their affairs as they had to similar attempts in the past. Not only is it likely that Jaggard printed at least six of his Shakespeare quartos after the earl's order, but Walkley too went right on printing whatever of the King's Men's that came into his hands. Eight months after Pembroke's letter, he bypassed the knight in the Revels Office for the Bishop of London, whose secretary John Taverner licensed another of the King's Men's Beaumont and Fletcher plays, an especially bad text of *Philaster* (January 10, 1620); on the title page he did not hesitate to crow that this was the play "Acted at the Globe by his Majesty's Servants." Perhaps this was not wise and there was some unfavorable reaction, for his next Beaumont and Fletcher, *Thierry and Theodoret,* published in 1621, was not entered in the Register at all—which did not inhibit him from proclaiming this play was "diverse times acted at the Blackfriars by the King's Majesty's servants." Once again, Walkley seems not to have suffered in the least.

However, before the year was out, he would be following procedure to the letter. He dutifully brought the copy of his next play to Stationers' Hall, paid his six pence registration fee, and had the appropriate licensing authority—Sir George Buck.[49] In fact, of the four King's Men plays published by Walkley from 1619 to 1622, this was the only one that was both duly registered to him and had Buck's license as well. The play was, of course, by Shakespeare, his *Othello.*

Nor, for that matter, does Buck's authorization for *Othello* seem to have alerted anyone but Oxfordians to his impending madness. His licensing power was unimpeded as late as February 22, 1622, when his was the authorizing hand for *Herod and Antipater* by Gervase Markham and William Sampson. It is not until John Chamberlain's letter to Sir Dudley Carleton of March 30, 1622, that we hear definite word that "Poor Sir George Buck, Master of the Revels, is in his old age fallen stark mad, and his place executed by Sir John Ashley [Astley] that had the reversion."[50] 1622 was also the year Matthew Law was heard from again, publishing the sixth quartos of both *Richard III* and *Henry IV, Part One,* while a third quarto of the old two-part *King John* was also printed, this time spelling out the author's name: "W. Shakespeare." Therefore, the record of publication from 1619 to 1622, shows that Pembroke's order to the Stationers had been continually flouted.

Heminges and Condell versus the Noble Brethren

After all, the *Othello* panic that is supposed to have brought the printing of the First Folio to a halt turns out to be just an Oxfordian twist to a discredited assumption. In 1925, the scholar F. P. Wilson discovered a "surprising entry" in *A Catalogue of Such Bookes As Have Beene Published and (by authoritie) printed in English, Since the Last Vernall Mart, which was in Aprill, 1622, till This Present October, 1622*. What Wilson found in this catalogue was the following:

> Playes, written by *M. William Shakespeare*, all in one volume, printed by Isaack Jaggard, in fol[io].[51]

But the First Folio would not be published until more than one year later! Wilson's article began a round of speculation based on the assumption that work on the volume was expected to be completed by October 1622, but something intervened that caused the project to be put aside. There are facts aplenty that prove this was not the case.

The Vernal Mart referred to was the earlier of the book fairs held each spring and autumn in Frankfurt, Germany. For each fair an official *Mess-Katalog*, was published and, from 1617 to 1628, the King's Printer, John Bill published an English edition of the catalogue. From April 1622 until October 1626, he appended a catalogue of English books to each biannual edition. The *Mess-Katalog* was prepared at the beginning of each fair, and for a book to be listed in it, "Each dealer gave notice of the books he had for sale by presenting, usually, a copy of the title-page of each book."[52] Thus, the *Mess-Katalog* cannot have been issued until some time after the beginning of the April 1622 fair, and Bill's catalogue with the First Folio notice would then have been published some weeks later.

Therefore if, as Ogburn says, work had come to a halt on the First Folio when *Othello* was licensed for printing on October 6, 1621—and if he is right and it would be one year before work on it began again (in October 1622, that is)—how then could Jaggard have advertised that the folio would be in the bookstalls some time between April and October 1622 in Bill's catalogue? According to his timetable, no work had been done on it for months before April 1622, nor was work being done on it at the time Jaggard gave his advertisement to Bill. Therefore, there was no possibility it could be finished by October 1622—the date when Ogburn says work on it would have just resumed.

In fact, the Bill's 1622 spring catalogue includes books that had been published in 1620 and 1621, as well as at least three books besides the First Folio that would not be published in 1623. Indeed, one of the other 1623 books was also printed by Jaggard, a translation of André Favyn's *Theatre of Honour,* which was received by the Bodleian Library from the binder William Wildgoose on the same day as the First Folio, February 17, 1624. The facts agree with Charlton Hinman's conclusion in his massive study of the printing of the Shakespeare folio, "Jaggard, like other publishers, used Bill's list rather to herald his forthcoming books than to report their actual publication." Hinman's chronology of Jaggard's printing in this period has shown that work on the folio is not likely to have begun until early in 1622.[53]

Having created the fantastic Herbert scheme that was the prelude to publication of the First Folio, Oxfordians must show that the book was really a Pembroke and Montgomery Production. However, in their dedication of the work to the earls, two longtime members of the King's Men, John Heminges and Henry Condell, declare *they* collected his plays in order "to keep the memory of so worthy a friend and fellow alive as was our Shakespeare." In short, not only do they lay claim to having gathered the plays for publication, but they call Shakespeare their fellow—no great lord but, like themselves, a mere creature of the playhouse. Scholars may be fooled, but to Oxfordians the fraud is transparent. These "undistinguished stage-players" were called upon to further the myth that the plays were written by the man from Stratford. Lest there be any lingering doubt about how unlikely they were to be involved in so great an enterprise, we are told that one of them (Heminges) gave up the stage to end his days as a grocer.[54]

Of the distinction of Heminges and Condell as players we need know only that they were important members of an ensemble that required excellence in the performance of roles both great and small. Heminges was a charter member of the Lord Chamberlain's company upon its formation in 1594 and Condell had joined it no later than 1598. Nor was Heminges' role in the company limited to the stage. On December 25, 1596, we first find him performing a function he would fulfill for more than three decades, receiving payment for the company's performances at court. Indeed, he apparently became something of a business manager for the troupe and would continue to be virtually until his death in 1630, having been a payee for a court performance in April of that same year.

Where did anyone get the idea Heminges left the King's Men for cabbages? Presumably from his will, where he calls himself a "citizen and grocer of London." However, this means nothing more than Heminges at some time had been either apprenticed to a grocer and became a freeman of the Grocers' Company or that he gained his place "by patrimony." He would hardly have been the only actor with a guild association. Among others, his fellows Robert Armin and John Lowin were goldsmiths; James Burbage had been a joiner.[55] Furthermore, on the title page of *The Triumphs of Reunited Britannia*, a pageant written for the inauguration of Sir Leonard Holliday as Lord Mayor of London in 1605, its author, Anthony Munday, identified himself as "Citizen and Draper of London."[56] Munday is not known to have ever made a living as anything but the author of plays and pageants and from editing.

However, more substantive questions are raised about the role of these two players in the publication of this Shakespeare collection. For instance, they avouch the First Folio texts of previously printed plays to be "cured and perfect of their limbs," and "absolute in their numbers as he [Shakespeare] conceived them," when so many still set editors to work in search of the absolutely perfect text—which leads Ogburn to wonder how scholars can find anything Heminges and Condell say to be credible.[57] It may be they do because they know such claims of perfection are commonplace in play publication of the time, as we have seen notably in the case of Humphrey Moseley. It may be recalled that he claimed that all the plays in his Beaumont and Fletcher collection are "the perfect originals without the least mutilation." However, as we have seen, most are not from perfect originals; in fact, two plays palmed off as Fletcher's—*Wit at Several Weapons* and *The Laws of Candy*—had been so thoroughly worked over that any trace of his writing (if he had a hand in them at all) was obliterated and they are now considered to be the work of other playwrights.[58] Heminges and Condell, however, may have been on firmer ground than Moseley.

Probably the most debatable claim they made was that the quartos were "stolen and surreptitious copies," whereas only a handful are certainly corrupt and the rest are now believed to be from Shakespeare's own manuscripts or something quite close to them. Perhaps it was necessary to impugn the earlier editions because they account for nearly half of the plays in the folio and they had to offer the book-buying public a reason to purchase an expensive volume that included so many plays that had long been in circulation. More to the point, the First Folio was intended to be a collection of the works of a dramatist, which is reflected in the fact that playhouse texts were used to emend virtually every quarto text in the folio. When in 1961 Charlton Hinman wrote that some texts "must have been very different both from Shakespeare's original text and anything that can be thought to reflect accurately his final intentions or even his acquiescence," he was stating an opinion that had underlaid critical views of the texts for nearly 300 years. Over the past thirty years this has undergone considerable change. Not only do a growing number of scholars believe that the folio *Lear* is not a hack job by some presumptuous reviser, but that it is Shakespeare's reworking of his original version (represented by the 1608 quarto) to such a degree that many now accept the folio version as a separate play. In the same vein, whereas the players are blamed for the disappearance of some choice dialogue in the folio *Hamlet,* it is now thought that this is not merely Shakespeare's own doing, but that these changes may have been made before the play was ever put on the stage.[59] It might then be that the folio texts are indeed as he conceived them—as works intended for performance.

Are there any grounds for the assertion that Heminges and Condell bore the costs and were responsible for the actual production of the collection? This idea seems to be based on their statement in the epistle to the readers, where they voice the wish that the "author himself had lived to have set forth and overseen his own writings";

> But since it hath been ordained otherwise, and he by death departed from that right, we pray you do not envy his friends the office of their care and pain, to have collected & published them.

Indeed they do say they "published" the plays, which leads Ogburn to wonder where these common players got the money to finance so costly a venture. However, whereas the word *published* is nowadays associated almost exclusively with the printing and issuing of printed matter, in Shakespeare's day it had a broader and simpler meaning: to make something public—which encompassed everything from announcing an intended marriage to spreading a libel.

Conclusive proof that they did not mean that they were party to the production of the First Folio, nor that they bore any of its costs, is in the book itself. On the title page it says only that it was "Printed by Isaac Jaggard, and Ed. Blount" (though Blount, who was not a printer but a bookseller, was in effect the publisher). What makes it certain that Heminges and Condell had no financial stake in it is found in the colophon—the publication information at the end of the text—which reads:

> Printed at the Charges of W. Jaggard, Ed. Blount,
> J. Smithweeke, and W. Aspley, 1623.

Is there any basis for the suggestion that Heminges and Condell sold the texts without the consent of the other shareholders in the King's Men? If true, this would mean that they appropriated the plays for their own profit; and if they did, and boldly advertised their appropriation in the folio, it is certain that, at a minimum, their careers with the company would have been at end. To the contrary, Heminges, as shown earlier, continued to serve the King's Men as its business manager until his death, and it was

The colophon on the last page of the First Folio. (Courtesy of the Folger Shakespeare Library)

John Fletcher. Frontispiece engraving from the Beaumont and Fletcher Folio (1647). (Courtesy of the Folger Shakespeare Library)

undoubtedly in that capacity that he worked on the company's behest in providing manuscripts for the First Folio. That Condell remained in good graces with his fellows is evident from his will dated December 13, 1627, in which he left his servant Elizabeth Wheaton 40 shillings and "that place of privilege she now exerciseth and enjoyeth in the [play]houses of the Blackfriars, London, and the Globe on the Bankside"—which indicates that he maintained an active, respected position with the King's Men until the last (which came just sixteen days later). Everything considered, there are no grounds to suppose anything but that Heminges and Condell, acting on behalf of the company, became involved in the publication of the First Folio at the invitation of the four men listed in the colophon, to the profit of all the shareholders.

Why should Heminges and Condell alone have written the prefatory material to the First Folio? Most of the actors who had been with the company during Shakespeare's active years were dead by 1623 and many of the survivors were boys at that time. Heminges and Condell were the lone members of the company when it was the Lord Chamberlain's. They would thus seem a most appropriate choice to write the dedication and epistle. It is certainly less puzzling than some of the other choices for authors of prefatory material in the folio, and moreover why there is so little of it—especially evident when the Shakespeare volume is compared to the collections of Jonson, and of Beaumont and Fletcher.

Ben Jonson took great pains to insure the prefatory matter to his folio reinforced the "pretentiousness of the volume," by securing "numerous sets of commendatory verses, several of them in the language of learning." [60] The renowned jurist John Selden opens the chorus of acclaim with a two-page poem in Latin. There follows five pages more of poetical praise, with high notes hit by fellow dramatist George Chapman, as well as verses on *Volpone, Epicoene* and *Cataline* by Francis Beaumont. When it came time to celebrate Beaumont and his partner Fletcher in the 1647 folio, 41 pages were packed with laudatory verse. Knights and baronets, university scholars and poets, as well as James Shirley and Richard Brome, the leading playwrights of the day, were in the choir that lifted its pens in hosannas to the plays and their creators (to the occasional detriment of both Shakespeare and Jonson).

The Shakespeare Folio opens promisingly enough with the lengthy ode, "To the memory of my beloved, The Author, Mr. William Shakespeare," by Ben Jonson (who would have rankled at being called Pembroke's "protégé, as Ogburn has). The inclusion of a sonnet by Hugh Holland, which swims on a page of its own, is probably owed to Jonson. Holland may have been his schoolmate at Westminster and certainly was in Ben's Mermaid Inn crowd. After Holland, there is just one page of laudatory verse,

a 22-line poem by Leonard Digges, and an eight-line poem signed "J. M."—
James Mabbe. Who were these men? And why were they chosen?

Digges's only published works were a translation from the Latin of *The Rape of Prosperine* (1617), and a translation of the Spanish novel, *Gerardo, the Unfortunate Spaniard* (1622). (Oxfordian hopes may be buoyed by the knowledge that the latter work was dedicated to the Herbert brothers.) Mabbe was a Spanish scholar who published translations under the sobriquet "Don Diego Puede-Ser" (a pun on his surname—Peude-Ser translates to "May-Be"). There is nothing to link him with either Pembroke or Montgomery. In fact, the only thing both men definitely had in common was their publisher: Edward Blount. He published both books by Digges and, in 1622, the same year he published *Gerardo, the Unfortunate Spaniard*, he was also the publisher of Mabbe's most famous work, a translation of the popular Spanish novel, *The Rogue; or, the Life of Guzman de Alfarache*. Coincidentally, the commendatory verses for this book were written by Ben Jonson and Digges. It appears that the selection of Jonson, Digges and Mabbe to write commendatory verses for the Shakespeare collection is owed to their association with Edward Blount, the publisher of the First Folio.

Ultimately, what casts greatest doubt about the active involvement of the Herberts in the folio—as well as about Oxford as the author of the works in it—is the texts themselves. We have heard the questions raised by the Oxfordians about the seeming indifference of the author to his manuscripts and to the fate of his plays. The answers, we know, are entirely in keeping with what we should expect if the author was a professional playwright. But what if the author was a nobleman? Moreover, what if the author never wrote merely to "fill his pockets with contemporary pence," nor for the common stage, but instead, "always with an eye on the future and studious reader," as the nineteenth-century poet and critic Algernon Swinburne averred?[61]

Whereas we can no more ask where are Oxford's autograph manuscripts of the plays than Shakespeare's, we can ask where they are in the printed texts—especially if the Shakespeare folio was intended to be a tribute to a literary artist. We have been told that Oxford's literary affairs were being handled by a board of admiring friends, perhaps as early as 1598, when he was still alive and could see to it that perfect copies of his texts were preserved. Even if, for the sake of argument, we allow that this board didn't actually form until after Oxford's death, this still would not explain why previously published and playhouse texts should most often have been the sources for those in the First Folio.

As we have seen, scribal copies of literary works were in demand during Shakespeare's lifetime. Thomas Nashe's *Terrors of the Night* alone kept scriveners so busy that he decided to publish the work and get some of the profits for himself. Time and again, authors avouch that they cooperated in the publication of their fancy only because they got word that a scribal copy had made its way into the hands of a printer. Even Shakespeare followed this custom in one instance, for Francis Meres noted the circulation of his "sugared Sonnets among his private friends" in *Palladis Tamia,* eleven years before they were published in 1609. As far as the texts of his plays are concerned, there is no evidence that such copies were ever made for private friends, publication or posterity—but by his acting company alone.

If the Earls of Pembroke and of Montgomery were indeed involved in the publication of his plays, this is odd indeed. They were, after all, the sons of Mary, Countess of Pembroke, who was as well the sister of Sir Philip Sidney. She is given much, if not all, of the credit for the great enterprise of publishing her brother's literary remains. Her sons, therefore, should have had intimate knowledge of how to engineer the publication of great literary works. If they did indeed oversee the assembly of Shakespeare's works for perhaps as many as twenty years, they had ample time to collect the best available texts of the plays and have them worked over by the best professional scriveners. Instead, the only evidence of such care are copies that were made for the King's Men of *The Tempest, The Two Gentlemen of Verona, The Merry Wives of Windsor, Measure for Measure* and *The Winter's Tale,* all annotated, and all but the last heavily cut for performance. These are attributed to Ralph Crane, the scrivener who is known to have done a good deal of copying for the company.*

Taken on the whole, the First Folio has none of the pretentions of a serious literary work, such as we see in Sidney's or Ben Jonson's. At last, the questions raised regarding the manuscripts and published texts are a problem for Oxfordians rather than Shakespeareans.

The Publication History of the King's Men

The saga of suppressing the publication of plays ends, for the Oxfordians, when there were no more Shakespeare plays to suppress. Not so as far as the King's Men were concerned. In fact, that was the reason for the June

---

* So proud was Crane of his association with the King's Men that he commemorated it in a poem in his collection of poems, *The Workes of Mercy* (1621):

> And some employment hath my useful pen
> Had 'mongst those civil, well-deserving men,
> That grace the stage with honour and delight,
> Of whose true honesties I much could write,
> But will comprise't (as in a cask of gold)
> Under the Kingly Service they do hold.

(F. P. Wilson, "Ralph Crane, Scrivener to the King's Players," 139.)

10, 1637, letter to the Stationers Company by Philip, Earl of Pembroke and Montgomery, quoted above. Noting William's command to the guild to "stay any further impression of any of the plays or interludes of his Majesty's servants without their consents," Philip declares his brother's "caution" to have been

> grounded on such weighty reasons, both for his Majesty's service & the particular interest of the Players, and so agreeable to common justice . . . it might have been presumed that there would have needed no further order or direction in this business. Notwithstanding which I am informed that some copies of plays belonging to the King & Queen's servants the players, & purchased by them at dear rates, having lately been stolen from them or gotten by indirect means, are now attempted to be printed & that some of them are at the press & ready to be printed.

The earl then specifically ordered that no play belonging to the players of the king or queen "be printed until the assent of their Majesty's said servants be made [to] appear to the Master & wardens of the Company of Printers and Stationers by some certificate in writing" from the sharers in the acting company. Commending this order to the "special care" of the Stationers' Company, Philip concluded with the generous offer—more a courteous threat—to supply them with "any further authority or power either from his Majesty or the council table" required for the execution of the order.

Nevertheless, on August 7, 1641, Philip's successor as Lord Chamberlain, Robert Devereux, the 3d Earl of Essex (the son of the 2d Earl executed in 1601), wrote to the masters and wardens of the Stationers:

> The players which are his Majesty's servants have addressed themselves unto me, as formerly to my predecessors in office, complaining that some printers are about to print & publish some of their plays which hitherto they have been usually restrained from by the Authority of the Lord Chamberlain.[62]

Evidently neither reason nor the appeal to common justice, not the "Authority of the Lord Chamberlain" nor the implicit threat of the power of "his Majesty or the council table," could outweigh the power of the almighty six pence the Stationers collected for registering a play for publication.

However, what decisively contradicts the Oxfordian argument that there is something amiss about Shakespeare's indifference to the publication of his plays is the record of play publication by Shakespeare's successors as the attached playwrights of the King's Men, John Fletcher, Philip Massinger and James Shirley. In *The Profession of Dramatist in Shakespeare's Time, 1590–1642*, Gerald Eades Bentley has thoroughly covered the publication history of these men during their association with the troupe and I here draw upon his concise observations.[63]

Although his plays were "among the most highly reputed of the productions at Blackfriars," John Fletcher, who immediately followed Shakespeare at the Globe, did not once "in the course of his fifteen or eighteen years of exclusive work for the King's company, himself put a single one of them into the hands of the printers." In fact, of the 69 plays in which he had a hand, only nine were printed during his lifetime, four without attribution; in only one of the nine plays is there evidence of publication with Fletcher's participation. This play was *The Faithful Shepherdess* (c 1609), which had been a failure in performance. Very much as Jonson did for his failed play *Sejanus*, Fletcher tried to point out the excellences of the play that theatergoers had somehow missed (Ben, incidentally, was among those who wrote commendatory verses for this book). At any rate, the company of boy players for which he wrote the play evidently decided it would not be missed and allowed him to publish it. Bentley concluded of Fletcher that, like Shakespeare and Heywood, "he was writing for the theatre audience, and not for readers."

This is an appropriate point to note that the 1647 Beaumont and Fletcher Folio consists of thirty-four plays (as well as one masque) that the King's Men kept from the press for 22 years and more. The only reason they finally agreed to let them go to press is heard in their dedication to the Earl of Pembroke and Montgomery. It had been five years since the playhouses were closed and public theater was "withered and condemned, as we fear, to a long winter of sterility." Simply, they saw no hope that these plays would be performed in the foreseeable future and so settled for whatever profit could be had from selling them for publication.

Philip Massinger was a dramatist who definitely wanted his plays in print. He may have collaborated in plays with Fletcher and Nathan Field for the King's Men earlier, but it is not until Fletcher died in 1625 that he began his formal affiliation with the company. From 1626 until his death in 1640, Massinger was the principal dramatist for the King's Men, for which he wrote at least seventeen and perhaps as many as 25 plays in those years. He brought eleven plays to the press, three of which *were* written for this company. The timing suggests that he took advantage of the changing of the guard. In 1629, he published *The Roman Actor* with commendatory verses by John Lowin and Joseph Taylor, who had recently taken over duties long performed by Heminges. Two other of his King's plays, *The Picture* and *The Emperor of the East*, were published in 1630 and 1632 respectively, probably because neither had done well in performance.

James Shirley followed Massinger, occupying the brief period between Massinger's death and the ban on the theater passed by the Parliament on September 2, 1642. He was another playwright who had no inhibitions about seeing his work to press—in fact, he "saw to it that nearly all his plays eventually got into print." He had had a long prior association with Queen Henrietta's company, the same company with which Brome had the prohibitive contract mentioned earlier, and during this time only five of about twenty plays he had written for them were printed with his co-operation. When this relationship ended in 1636, his plays poured from the press. Including revised works, there were eighteen in the next four years, seven in 1640 alone, the year he joined the King's company. However, none of the plays he wrote for this troupe were published during his brief tenure with them, nor would any be until 1653, when the theaters had been closed for eleven years and, as in the case of Beaumont and Fletcher's plays, the ongoing "suppression had killed all hope for a revival of the old days."

Thus, in the 48-year history of the Lord Chamberlain's/King's company, Bentley found only three plays written for the company by its attached playwrights that went to press with the participation of its author. This was done with the consent of the company. Everything considered, there is absolutely nothing in the history of Shakespeare publication in this period that gives any hint the author of the plays was anything but an attached dramatist of an acting company—and of the Chamberlain's/King's Men in particular.

→5←

Questions about the Writing of the Plays

W ithout the tales from antiquity and the latest fables from contemporary continental authors; without the historical chronicles in which fact and rumor could be almost indistinguishable; without these and a host of similar sources, Elizabethan literature would have starved. The idea of inventing stories and plots, and the characters to populate them, might even have seemed wasteful to the Elizabethan author, who was supplied a bottomless source of inspiration—all there for the taking.

Shakespeare, in keeping with the time, was a great taker. He borrowed lavishly: from the histories of Plutarch and Holinshed; from ancient dramatic poets such as Plautus and such contemporary prose writers as Giraldi Cinthio. Indeed, had he drawn from Plautus and Cinthio in the original, this is, in the eyes of the Oxfordians, proof of the author's great learning. If he got his inspiration for *Hamlet* from reading the French work *Histoires Tragiques* (1576), it is (according to the Oxfordians) a confirmation of the singular erudition of our author. But what if he got the idea from an earlier play by someone whose name, like his play itself, is lost to history? The idea is appalling to Oxfordians, such as Gordon Cyr:

> I remember reading that "Hamlet" was a sort of patchwork based on something called the Ur-Hamlet, with the scenes taken in almost the same order. This was very disturbing information—that Shakespeare had done nothing more than take something from an inferior playwright and witch it up.[1]

The *ur* in *ur-Hamlet* is from the German and means original or earliest, and as early as 1589—more than a decade before the date of Shakespeare's play—there is indeed a reference to a play of *Hamlet*. Was this the *ur-Hamlet*? We cannot know. No printed version of a play of *Hamlet* exists before the garbled text published in 1603 and blamed on Shakespeare. Therefore, there is no way of knowing what the order of the scenes was in the *ur-Hamlet,* or just how much and in precisely what ways Shakespeare's play is indebted to it.

The critical point here, however, is whether Shakespeare could have employed his pen merely to "witch up" existing plays. If it is disturbing to think that he did, it would be incredible if he did not. That the thought should be disturbing is a reflection not only of how much he has been set apart from the rest in his theater world, but of how little is generally known about that world itself. Most of all, it shows how much Shakespeare is usually judged by purely modern standards—and not by Oxfordians alone.

Shakespeare, the Sole Begetter?

Drama is the most ancient of the literary arts of which we have major remains and it was in ancient Greece that three of the four supreme tragic poets flourished. The fourth, the modern favorite, Shakespeare, rekindled the flame of Aeschylus, Euripides and Sophocles, and to the primary hues of Attic Greek added the rainbow colors of Renaissance English that make his flame the most brilliant and warming of all. The Greeks looked upon drama as an art, just as we do, and rewarded their great playwrights, as we do. Certainly it is reasonable to suppose that Elizabethan England, which nurtured what is perhaps the greatest dramatic outpouring of all, must also have recognized drama as an art—and Shakespeare as its supreme artist. Reasonable. But wrong.

The sudden flowering of Elizabethan theater is dated to about 1590. There had been public theaters for nearly 25 years at the time, to be sure, but hardly anything is known about their repertory or their management. When we do hear of acting companies in these early years it is usually in the accounts of provincial towns. Then, in the last decade of the century, images begin to emerge from the obscurity. For the first time we hear of professional playwrights—Christopher Marlowe, Robert Greene, Thomas Kyd and George Peele—and a steady flow of popular plays begins to issue from printing presses. But the most important thing to our perception of the emergence of a professional theater is the accounts begun in February 1592 by the first Bankside theater magnate, Philip Henslowe. Disorganized, incomplete and scant of detail though it is, *Henslowe's Diary* provides insight into the period when popular theater reached maturity. A major thing to be learned from it is that Elizabethan acting companies needed a large number of plays to fill their repertories, and how, in Henslowe's theaters at any rate, these needs were met.

One of the most striking things we find in the diary is that, whether a play was new or a revival, no matter how popular it might be, it did not run daily for years, months or weeks, as in modern theaters. In fact, a play would not even be performed on successive days and rarely above three times a month—most often only twice after it settled into a place in the repertory. When the players of Ferdinando Stanley, Lord Strange, inaugurated the remodeled Rose in February 1592, they put on fifteen different plays in their first seventeen dates. Among them was Marlowe's *Jew of Malta,* which would be the most oft-acted play at the Rose. But precisely how oft was it acted? Although first performed on February 26, 1592, and revived periodically until June 23, 1596, only 36 performances are recorded in this period, or about the same number of times a play will be performed in a month nowadays.[2]

All told, 280 plays are found in the Diary between 1592 and 1602. Clearly the Rose's patrons expected a lot of variety and satisfying this demand required some effort, complicated in the early years by the sudden deaths of the first "name" dramatists in short order. Greene, only 34 years of age, died in 1592 of a surfeit of pickled herring and Rhenish wine; Marlowe, at 29, was murdered in a tavern in 1593; and Kyd, imprisoned and tortured in the inquisition into Marlowe's "lewd libels" and "blasphemies," fell destitute and died in 1594, aged 36. Add to this the plague that shut the London theaters for much of 1592 and nearly all of 1593, and the young industry was in a chaotic state. According to the *Diary,* old plays were the backbone of the repertory at the Rose during these years.

We know this because Henslowe would write "ne" beside a play to indicate a new work or old plays newly revised. Of the fifteen Strange's plays mentioned above, only one was so noted—the play of "harey the vi," presumed to be one of Shakespeare's *Henry VI* plays. All told, only 23 of the 65 plays performed between 1592 and 1594 were marked "ne" by Henslowe. However, of the 34 plays introduced into the Admiral's repertoire in 1595–96, thirty were so marked. Where did they all come from?

Henslowe created something akin to the studio system of Hollywood in the 1930s, where not art but entertainment, not quality but quantity, were paramount. The pace was frantic. "Henslowe's accounts," Neil Carson found, "indicate that plays were normally finished in four to six weeks." These figures also reflect "the haste with which plays were rushed into production. In a great many cases, prerehearsal preparations took only about two weeks."[3]

But even as new plays were being added at a greater rate, plays a half-dozen years old and more were regularly played and some did better at the box office than new plays.[4] However, were these plays identical to the versions originally enacted years earlier? Probably not, for there was an evident effort to keep old plays viable by periodic revision. We have definite information about this in the later half of the 1590s, when Henslowe began itemizing payments to dramatists and noting what they were for, among which were fees for "additions" to, or the "mending" and "alteration" of old plays. Such work would be done by hacks and notable playwrights alike, as we learn from the record of the first famous Elizabethan tragedy, Thomas Kyd's *Spanish Tragedy*.

Usually dated to about 1586, Henslowe invariably called it after its leading character, "Jeronimo" (in a variety of spellings). It was periodically staged at the Rose by Strange's Men from March 14, 1592, to January 22, 1593. Between the latter date and its next recorded staging on January 7, 1597, the play was apparently revised, for Henslowe entered it as "ne" in his accounts. This version is probably the one that Pavier published in 1602, for in his text there is no hint of the style of the playwright whom Henslowe paid for "additions" on September 25, 1601, and for "new additions" only nine months later, and that was Ben Jonson.[5] He was by then an established author with three acclaimed plays that he had already put into print. Nevertheless, he obviously consented to take on this anonymous task. If Jonson would do it, there is no reason to suppose there was any stigma attached to dramatic revisionism.

In fact, many playwrights under Henslowe's umbrella were called on for such duty, including such other accomplished playwrights as Heywood and Thomas Dekker. However, revision was also assigned to hacks, without regard to the standing of the original author. Marlowe was Shakespeare's nearest rival as a tragic poet and the greatest of his tragedies is *Doctor Faustus*. But when additions to this play were called for in November 1602, the task was handed to two mutually undistinguished goosequillians, William Birde and Samuel Rowley.[6] Nor, for that matter, did a play have to be from an earlier generation of drama to require additions. In November 1599, Anthony Munday, Michael Drayton, Richard Hathway and Richard Wilson were given ten shillings on the occasion of the first performance of their play, *Sir John Oldcastle*. However, not three years later, Dekker was paid £2 10s for additions to the play. His fee suggests the emendations were considerable.[7]

Henslowe's accounts end in 1602 and there are, of course, no similar records for other theaters and their acting companies. Nevertheless, how common and well-known the practice was may be heard in the commendatory verses of one Nicholas Downey in the unacted play, *Sicily and Naples; or, The Fatal Union*, by Samuel Harding. In his search for the silver lining in the author's failure to get the play produced, Downey says that his friend's play will enjoy the rare distinction of being printed just as it was written;

> In it's unchang'd and native infancy
> Before some players brain new drenched in sack
> Does clap each term new fancies on its back.

The phrase "each term" is a reference to the thrice-yearly terms of the law courts.[8] Of course, this is as much an exaggeration as it must have been little comfort to Harding. On the other hand, the practice was so notorious that Shakerley Marmion put it to metaphorical use in *A Fine Companion*, where the elderly wooer Dotario enters onto the stage to the comment of the aptly named servant, Crotchet:

> Look you, here comes the old lecher! He looks as fresh as an old play new vampt. Pray see how trim he is, and how the authors have corrected him; how his tailor and his barber have set him forth; sure he has received another impression.[9]

One of the most revealing items in the casebook of dramaturgical revisionism is Thomas Dekker's reconstructive surgery on *Old Fortunatus,* which may shed light on the question of *Hamlet* and the *ur-Hamlet*. This play made its first appearance in Henslowe's accounts on February 3, 1596, and was performed five more times until May 26 of that year. When it is next heard from in November 1599, Henslowe made three payments to Dekker for revisions totaling £6. So successfully did he rework the old play that some scholars think that the original must have been his as well.[10] On the other hand, £6 was the going rate for a new play and it might be that just such a complete transformation is what was expected of Dekker—just as it appears to have been of Shakespeare regarding *King John, The Taming of the Shrew* and, notably, *Hamlet*. (*Old Fortunatus* holds more of interest, which will be discussed shortly.)

Putting aside matters of standard theatre practice and the work of merely mortal playwrights, it must be asked how cogent Cyr's observation about *Hamlet* is in the first place. Without the *ur-Hamlet* for comparison, we cannot make any judgment on Shakespeare's use of and alterations to his presumed source, other than hazard the guess that it was an improvement. There are firmer grounds for seeing the transformation Shakespeare could work on a play, one of which there can be no doubt about his significant borrowings. The play in question is the old *King Leir,* and the renowned scholar W. W. Greg found it every bit as distressing to discover the great dramatist borrowing from this antique as Cyr found Shakespeare's indebtedness to an *ur-Hamlet.*

In Greg's concise article on Shakespeare's debt to the old play, his discomfort was owed to a conviction that the old play must have been printed in 1605 to capitalize on the popularity of Shakespeare's play—though he couldn't quite get the facts to fit.[11] The earliest notice of *King Lear* is a performance at court on December 26, 1606, and internal evidence points to its composition late in 1605, months after *King Leir* was licensed in the

Stationers' Register. But if *Lear* was already being acted at the Globe when *Leir* was published, how can Shakespeare's "dependence" on the old play be explained, especially when it "is not confined to matters of structure and situation, but manifests itself in some degree in similarities of thought and expression"? Despite "some two score parallels between the plays," Greg cannot accept the master taking from an inferior other. Thus he concludes that, even if Shakespeare's source was, as he suspects, a prompt-book of *Leir* itself, "I do not for a moment suppose that any of these echoes were conscious." Greg with *Lear*, like Cyr with *Hamlet*, misses the point.

It is not the retentiveness of Shakespeare's subconscious, nor the extent of his indebtedness to the *Leir*, that is the issue. Rather, it is what he made of the likes of *Leir*, the *ur-Hamlet*, and all the crude materials from which he fashioned the greatest body of work in world literature. We can see this at work, in Greg's own words, in the scene where the chastened king begs forgiveness of Cordelia, the faithful daughter he rashly banished. Shakespeare, he comments, took this "affecting but clumsy scene" in *Leir* and "transmuted [it] in two magic touches in his own play." Of the Shakespearean metamorphosis in its entirety he found "the whole thing has been fused and transmuted in the alembic of his genius." Greg is so very close. Perhaps we can see his genius more clearly if we look upon it not as an alembic—a purifying vapor—but as alchemy, which transmutes baser materials into something infinitely rarer. After all, very few works of art can claim an immaculate conception, those of Shakespeare and his contemporaries not excluded. However, as George Steiner would say of them, though they "plundered freely wherever their eyes roamed . . . what they took, they took as conquerors, not borrowers. They mastered and transformed it to their own measure with the proud intent of surpassing what had gone before." [12]

After all, Shakespeare was guilty of nothing more than doing what was expected of the dramatists of his day, and that was providing plays to fill the playhouse. Indeed, nothing was sacred: Shakespeare's fellows felt as free to tamper with his writings as he did with those of others. In this regard, it is odd that Cyr should have chosen the phrase "witch it up" for his revampings, for that is literally what the King's Men did to *Macbeth* when they upped the number of witches in the play from three to four. At some time, the company borrowed Hecate from Thomas Middleton's failed play *The Witch*, as well as two of its songs, and transplanted them into act three, scene five, and act four, scene one of Shakespeare's play. Furthermore, they had additional dialogue written (possibly by Middleton himself) to witch up Hecate's part, and integrate her into the play. (To explain her late appearance, she scolds her sisters for not having called upon her earlier to "show the glory of our art.")

The Unkindest Cuts

Revision of another kind kindles doubts about Shakespeare's authorship of the plays: the cuts in many of the texts as they have come down to us. These cuts were made by his fellows to reduce the plays to a reasonable performance length—which, if the prologue to *Romeo and Juliet* is any guide, would be some "two hours' traffic of our stage." However, it is doubtful that the nearly 3,200-line text of that play, or others of similar length, could ever have been acted in that time. The longest of all, *Hamlet*, ran five hours when Maurice Evans put it on in all its 3,900-line glory. Its length did not faze the critic John Mason Brown, whose remarks are commended to our attention by Ogburn. Of this production Brown said:

> It emerges as a thrilling entity, a work of art in which the supreme artist who fathered it has his unimpeded sway. No hacks have dared to prune his script pretending they knew his business better than he did. . . . The so-called subsidiary characters . . . now explain themselves to theatregoers as in the past they have done only to readers.[13]

These observations, bolstered by the opinion of such as Algernon Charles Swinburne that Shakespeare did not write merely for the stage, but even more for the studious reader, send Ogburn off on discourse on the nature of Shakespeare's artistry, which leads him to the conclusion that he was "above all a novelist."

What sparked this revelation was Ogburn's discovery that, in addition to *Hamlet*'s prodigious length, other plays (eight, to be exact) run from 3,300 to 3,600 lines. For comparison, he calls attention to plays by others that are as much as one-third shorter; with the line counts quoted by Ogburn, they are: Marlowe's *Jew of Malta* (2,260), Fletcher's *Faithful Shepherdess* (2,557), John Webster's *Duchess of Malfi* (2,510), and Jonson's *Sejanus* (3,156). It is, as one might expect, a very selective sampling.

The inclusion of *The Jew of Malta* is especially misleading. It was entered with the Stationers in 1594 but no edition exists before the one published in 1633, which is probably owed to its recent revival at court. The text definitely shows the hand of another playwright and there is no question that it originated in the playhouse. It therefore came to the printer both hacked and pruned, and is not at all a reliable guide to the length of the play as it was originally written by Marlowe about 45 years earlier. On the other hand, the three other plays specifically mentioned were printed at their author's behest and may be assumed to reflect their original manuscript.

The Faithful Shepherdess is the only play Fletcher himself put into print and apparently he kept an eye to its length in performance in this instance.

However, by himself or in league with his collaborators, this was not always the case; for, as Humphrey Moseley wrote of the plays that were getting their first printing in his Beaumont and Fletcher Folio, "When these comedies and tragedies were presented on the stage, the actors omitted some scenes and passages (with the author's consent) as occasion led them." In addition to providing evidence that playwrights chronically wrote more than would be acted, Moseley tells us something even more important, which is that the actors would make cuts with the author's consent.

What was, in fact, the ideal length for a reasonable performance time in Renaissance theater? The figure given for Webster's *Duchess of Malfi,* 2,510 lines, is too low by more than 400 lines; but even this relatively moderate figure was too long, and the title page states that the quarto contains "diverse things printed that the length of the play would not bear in the presentment." Webster also had a hand in bringing two other of his plays to press—*The White Devil* and *The Devil's Law-Case*—and each exceeds 3,000 lines.

However, a play that narrowly exceeds 3,000 lines, such as *Sejanus,* is hardly typical of Ben Jonson. On the other end of the Jonsonian scale is *Every Man Out of His Humor,* and the title page of the 1600 quarto confirms that more was printed than had been acted. A mild understatement. In fact, the text runs to some 4,500 lines, but there has never been the shadow of a doubt that he conceived this work for the public stage. Furthermore, as Ogburn acknowledges, the average length of Jonson's printed plays is 3,500 lines; only two of Shakespeare's plays—the melodramatic *Richard III,* as well as lofty *Hamlet*—exceed the *average* length stated for Jonson's plays.

Ultimately, line counts and averages in regard to printed plays actually do not mean much when taken by themselves. The numerous explicit references to the published texts being more than what was acted makes it evident that Shakespeare was by no means alone in writing more than could be performed in "two hours' traffic" on his stage no less than ours. However, perhaps even in his own time he had a reputation for recklessly exceeding the limit, for it was said of him that he "had an excellent fantasy, brave notions, and gentle expressions, wherein he flowed with that facility that sometime it was necessary he should be stopped: *Sufflaminandus erat* [he had to be checked]." The author of these words happens to be Ben Jonson. *Mirare quis loquatur!* (Look who's talking!)

"Worth the Audience of Kings"

For further evidence that Shakespeare was no mere playhouse poet, Ogburn introduces the opinion of Professor Richard Levin that eighteen plays, virtually half of his canon, were written for performance either at court,

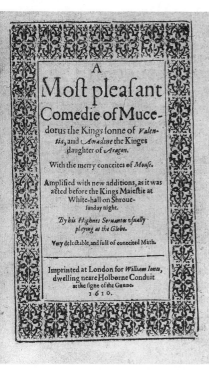

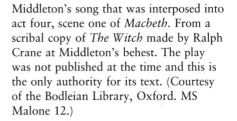

Middleton's song that was interposed into act four, scene one of *Macbeth*. From a scribal copy of *The Witch* made by Ralph Crane at Middleton's behest. The play was not published at the time and this is the only authority for its text. (Courtesy of the Bodleian Library, Oxford. MS Malone 12.)

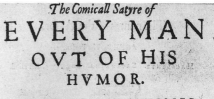

The Comicall Satyre of

EVERY MAN

OVT OF HIS

HVMOR.

AS IT WAS FIRST COMPOSED
by the AUTHOR B. I,

*Containing more than hath been Publickely Spo-
ken or Acted.*

VVith the seuerall Character of euery Person.

*Non aliena meo pressi pede \| * si propius stes
Te capient magis \| * & decies repetita placebunt.*

LONDON,

Printed for *William Holme*,and are to be sold at his Shop
at Sarjeants Inne gate in Fleetstreet.
1600. 2 3

Title page of *Every Man Out of His Humour* (1600). (Courtesy of The Huntington Library, San Marino, California. RB31191.)

A
Moſt pleaſant
Comedie of Muce-
dorus the Kings ſonne of *Valen-
tia*, and *Amadine* the Kinges
daughter of *Aragon*.

With the merry conceites of *Mouſe.*

Amplified with new additions, as it was
acted before the Kings Maieſtie at
White-hall on Shroue-
ſunday night.

*By his Highnes Seruants vſually
playing at the Globe.*

Very delectable,and full of conceited Mirth.

Imprinted at London for *William Iones*,
dwelling neare Holborne Conduit
at the ſigne of the Gunne.
1 6 1 0.

The title page of the third edition of *Mucedorus* (1610). (Courtesy of The Huntington Library, San Marino, California. RB62676.)

at the Inns of Court or the universities. Of course, the title pages of some plays say they were performed at court, to which we may add several others that are first mentioned in the Revels accounts. From contemporary sources we know that two plays were performed at the Inns of Court, and then there is the title page of the 1603 *Hamlet* that declares the play was acted at the universities of Cambridge and Oxford. But is this sufficient to consider these to have been specifically written for these venues?

Shakespeare's plays were indeed a fixture in court performances, but that is because his acting company was. The Chamberlain's Men performed a total of 32 times at court between their formation in 1594 and Queen Elizabeth's death in March 1603, an average of about three and a half times a year. She was not, however, quite the theater buff her successor James, and especially his wife Anne, were. In their first ten years as his servants, Shakespeare and his fellows played at court an average of about thirteen times a year—more than all the other London companies combined.[14] During this period, Shakespeare's plays made up the greatest part of the troupe's repertory, which also included many of his early plays. Given these circumstances, it is hardly surprising if there are speeches, passages, and scenes in some that might appear to have been written with an eye to performance at court, and an appealing case has been made that *The Merry Wives of Windsor* may have been written for the feast at Whitehall Palace on April 23, 1597, for the five newly elected Knights of the Garter—George Carey, Lord Hunsdon, the patron of Shakespeare's company among them. But if this is so, the quarto text has none of the features of a play written for the court and its title page says modestly that it was played "Both before her Majesty and elsewhere." Compare this with the quarto of Dekker's *Old Forunatus*.

Dekker, it may be remembered, received three payments from Henslowe in November 1599 for revising this old play, the last on the 30th "in full payment of his book of *Fortunatus*." However, on the very next day (which Henslowe recorded as the 31st), Dekker was given another pound for "altering" the play, and two more on December 12 for "the end of *Fortunatus* for the court"—half as much as he was paid for his reworking completed less than two weeks before.[15] Evidently the Admiral's Men were well pleased with Dekker's original labors insofar as they chose it as one of the two plays they would present at court (where it was enacted on December 27), but the amount he was paid for the new work suggests the alterations and additions were extensive. Equally evident from the immediate commission for renewed work, a play that was thought suitable for a playhouse audience had to be ornamented for its performance at court.

The court version apparently was a success, for on February 20, 1600, it was entered in the Stationers' Register as "*Old Fortunatus* in his new livery," and published with a title page that announced this was the play

"As it was played before the Queen's Majes
emphasize its regal lineage, the text was p
type, except for the stage directions, charac'
ken by the Spanish lord, Insultado (all in
speare quarto ever got such royal treatment

That the King's Men also revamped old piays ior peiioimaiice ai couit may be seen in *Mucedorus*, a popular comedy in the Chamberlain's/King's Men's repertoire that went through fourteen editions between the first in 1598 and 1642. (By way of comparison, the most editions of a Shakespeare play in the same period were the nine of *Henry IV, Part One*, which was also first published in 1598.) The third edition of 1610 announced that this quarto was "Amplified with new additions, as it was acted before the King's Majesty at Whitehall on Shrove Sunday night. By his Highness' Servants usually playing at the Globe." As there are previous editions of this play, unlike *Old Fortunatus*, the new text can be compared with the old, and it shows alterations and additions throughout. Furthermore, both plays have a prologue in praise of the sovereign, which is typical of plays fashioned for court performance. Once again, there is no such material in any Shakespeare quarto.

We know from Revels accounts that numerous Shakespeare plays were enacted at court and the frequency of the Chamberlain's/King's Men appearances at court during Shakespeare's active years suggests that most were presented before the monarch at one time or another. However, the title pages of only three quartos—*Love's Labor's Lost, The Merry Wives of Windsor* and *King Lear*—employ the popular cachet of a performance before the Queen's or King's Majesty by the time of its first printing.

The evidence that Shakespeare wrote plays specifically for performance at the Inns of Court is not any better. Two, *The Comedy of Errors* and *Twelfth Night*, are known to have been performed at Gray's Inn and the Middle Temple respectively, but there is nothing that suggests they were anything but recently penned popular comedies chosen to be played at the lawyers' Christmas revels. *Troilus and Cressida* is another matter altogether, a play with a curious contemporary history that deserves extra attention.

This play, it may be recalled, was printed in two states in 1609, the first entitled *The History of Troilus and Cressida*, the second *The Famous History of Troilus and Cressida*, to which an epistle to the reader was added that alleged it was a new play. In his study of the printing of these quartos, Philip Williams, Jr., found not only that both states were printed in the same press run, but that the "lower portion of the [second state] title-page contains standing type from the original title-page," from which he concludes that "the interval of time between the printing of the original title-page and the cancelling title-page was so short that the type from the orig-

THE
Hiſtorie of Troylus
and Creſſeida.

As it was acted by the Kings Maieſties
ſeruants at the Globe.

Written by William Shakeſpeare.

LONDON
Imprinted by *G.Eld* for *R. Bonian* and *H. Walley*, and
are to be ſold at the ſpred Eagle in Paules
Church-yeard, ouer againſt the
great North doore.
1609.

THE
Famous Hiſtorie of
Troylus *and* Creſſeid.

Excellently expreſſing the beginning
of their loues, with the conceited wooing
of *Pandarus* Prince of *Licia.*

Written by William Shakeſpeare.

LONDON
Imprinted by *G.Eld* for *R. Bonian* and *H. Walley*, and
are to be ſold at the ſpred Eagle in Paules
Church-yeard, ouer againſt the
great North doore.
1609.

The title pages of the 1609 quartos of *Troilus and Cressida*. (Courtesy of The Huntington Library, San Marino, California. RB59072; RB56669.)

inal title-page had not been distributed."[16] He does not consider it possible, however, that the type was not distributed because the altered title page and the accompanying epistle were planned before printing began, which would mean that the publishers, Richard Bonian and Henry Walley, intentionally had the quarto printed with two different title pages.

Williams speaks for many a Shakespearean scholar in believing it is "unlikely that the publishers, having gone to the trouble of and expense of the cancel as a part of the continuous printing of the quarto, would deliberately issue copies without that cancel." He therefore offers the explanation that "it is probable that in some copies, through accident or error, the cancel was not made," though he does acknowledge that the three surviving copies of the first state "suggest that . . . possibly a sizeable number of copies existed in this state."[17] (By comparison, only three copies of the 1604 *Hamlet* quarto and four of the 1605 are extant.) Such a large-scale accident, as well as the circulation of copies of the play with the original title page, seems especially odd after the publishers supposedly went to such lengths to correct the alleged misinformation.

Scholars incline toward Williams' belief that the circulation of the first state was an accident which—along with the second state epistle that claims the play was "never staled with the stage, never clapper-clawed with the palms of the vulgar," nor "sullied with the smoky breath of the multitude"—opens the door to vigorous speculation. Taking the epistle at its word (as most scholars do), the most popular explanation runs thusly: Bonian and Walley had reasonably assumed the play had been acted at the Globe. But before the printing of the quarto was completed, they learned they were mistaken and ordered a new title page be made up and an epistle added asserting the play's pristine past. And, according to the currently favored hypothesis, if *Troilus* had not been played at the Globe before its smoky-breathed multitude, it must then have been enacted before an elite audience—like the lawyers of one or another of the Inns of Court. Taking this one step further, the consensus is that it was for this audience the play was specifically written. Of this hypothesis, S. Schoenbaum comments that such judicious auditors "would suit this ratiocinative drama." But, he judiciously cautions, "However beguiling, this is, of course, mere speculation." [18] It is also speculation that leaves important questions unanswered.

For what reason did the publishers change the name of the play from *The History of Troilus and Cressida* (the name by which they entered it in the Stationers' Register) to *The Famous History of Troilus and Cressida?* Did they discover the title was wrong too? Then there is the reference on *The Famous History* title page to Pandarus as Prince of Licia. Whereas this is his title in Homer's *Iliad,* he is never so called in Shakespeare's play. But what is most remarkable is the epistle's "News" that it was a new play in 1609.

We know this play was originally licensed to James Roberts nearly six years earlier and all stylistic tests point to composition in about 1602. Whatever the source for the publishers' information that the play had not been acted at the Globe, they must have known this was not a new play. And is it indeed a fact that *Troilus* had not been performed at the Globe as late as 1609? Even if the play was originally written for a select audience, it was not privately commissioned from Shakespeare, for its 1603 entry to Roberts states that it was "acted by my Lord Chamberlain's Men." It would be without precedent for a theatrical company to put all its resources, including the talents of its playwright, into a play reserved for a private audience. To the contrary, the text of *Troilus* in the First Folio shows the influence of a promptbook made for public performance and even if we allow that it was originally written with a select audience in mind, it is highly doubtful that the players would have let it lie long before revising it for the Globe (see Afterwords, pp. 143–44). Ultimately, for all the effort to explain where *Troilus* was performed if not before the smoky-breathed multitude, it has gone unnoticed that the epistle does not hint that it was acted before any other audience either.

What makes all the speculation aroused by the epistle, no less the credence given to it, so remarkable is that, once past its startling news about the non-performance of the play, the rest of it turns out to be nothing more than a publisher's blurb. It dwells on the curative powers of Shakespeare's "comedies" (although the title page calls it a history and in the First Folio it is placed among the tragedies) that have powers to make "dull and heavywitted worldlings . . . better witted than they came, feeling an edge of wit set upon them more than they ever dreamed they had a brain to grind it on." All this wit is spent in urging the browser to buy the book, for surely he who does will "think your testern [six pence] well bestowed." Probably so. But to those who are inclined to buy the epistle, caveat emptor.

The title page of another quarto, the corrupt *Hamlet* of (1603), is the only concrete contemporary evidence connecting a Shakespeare play with the universities. It claims that the play was not only "divers times acted by his Highness' servants in the City of London," but "also in the two universities of Cambridge and Oxford." However, contemporary records show neither Cambridge nor Oxford were receptive to professional acting companies, especially not the universities.

As far as they were concerned, theatricals should be academic productions entirely and were thus disturbed by the increasing numbers of wandering players that came to their gates craving permission to put on common plays. In 1584, Oxford turned to its chancellor, Robert Dudley, Earl of Leicester, for relief. On the face of it, Leicester should have resisted such a prohibition, for he had been the patron of acting companies since 1559. His players would eventually be led by James Burbage, who built the Theatre in 1576 specifically for the company. Nevertheless, he did accede to the university's ban, stating that "the prohibition of common stage players [is] very requisite." It is probably not coincidental that a statute promulgated in the same year threatened "any Master, Bachelor, or Scholar above the age of eighteen" who so much as attended the performance of a play, "did so at the risk of imprisonment, while younger students were liable to 'open punishment' in St. Mary's Church." [19]

Unfortunately for the university, numerous acting companies had patents from noble patrons, whose patronage it might need from time to time. It was evidently thought unwise to risk antagonizing these lords by rudely turning away the actors who came in their name, wearing their livery and bearing their patents, and so the refusal to allow such a troupe to perform was usually accompanied by a stipend to leave. However, the officials seem to have viewed this as polite extortion and the record of such a payment was often accompanied by rude remarks in Latin. For instance, the first company known to have tried the prohibition happened to be Leicester's renewed troupe. When they were turned away from the university twenty shillings to the better, the payment was noted thusly in the accounts: "So-

lut[um] histrionibus Comitis Lecestriae ut cum suis ludis sine maiore Academiae molestia discederent" (The Earl of Leicester's players were told to take their plays and not bother the university again).[20] An unnamed company was given money and turned away with the notation *"ne ludos inhonestos exercerent infra Universitatum"* (to perform not their disgraceful plays in the university). Even the players of Queen Elizabeth were turned away, the first time in 1589/90 with the plea *"ut sine molestia ab Academia discederent"* (not to bother the academy again). But they came back three more times and each time were paid to leave.[21]

Cambridge University went to an even higher level to keep the players away from their gates. In July 1593 a letter was sent to Lord Burghley, renewing an earlier appeal to prohibit players from the university. On the 29th of the month the Privy Council acknowledging that, as "common players did ordinarily resort to the University, there to recite interludes and plays, some of them being of lewd example, and most of vanity," they therefore authorized the vice-chancellor and the heads of colleges "to take special order that thereafter there should be no plays or interludes of common players used or set forth, either in the University or in any other place within the compass of five miles."[22]

Despite King James's patent to his players, which did not exempt the universities from his command they be permitted to play "without any your lets, hindrances, or molestations," in 1604 he sent a letter to the chancellor and vice-chancellor "of our university of Cambridge," willing them to "wholly and altogether restrain, inhibit and forbid as well, all and all manner of unprofitable or idle games, plays or exercises" within five miles of the town and university—"especially bull-baiting, bear-baiting, common plays, public shows, interludes, comedies, and tragedies in the English tongue"—any manner of thing, in fact, that might attract the multitudes or "whereby the younger sort are or may be drawn or provoked to vain expense, loss of time or corruption of manners."[23]

Given this climate at the universities, it is hardly probable that the Chamberlain's/King's Men were ever welcomed at either, nor is there any record in the accounts of either university that notes a payment to this company, whether to play or to go away. The only mention of Shakespeare's company in Cambridge is of a single payment for a performance in the municipal accounts of 1595; they are not heard of at all in Oxford until 1604, the year after the *Hamlet* quarto that claimed the play had been performed there. Could there have been some oversight? Not at all likely. Queen Elizabeth's players, for example, are to be found nine times in Oxford's municipal records, four times in the university's.[24] In his study of players at the universities, F. S. Boas said of the possibility that the Chamberlain's/King's Men did, as the quarto claims, actually perform at Oxford:

[The] long succession of payments under different Vice-Chancellors proves that it was the settled policy of the University at this period to "buy off" the travelling companies. Hence it follows that neither *Hamlet* nor any other Shakespearean play can have been acted at Oxford during Elizabeth's reign with the consent of the academic authorities, much less under their auspices.[25]

These accounts stop abruptly in the year 1603–4, which would include the latest date for the performance of *Hamlet* stated in the quarto. Might the King's players have been shown special deference? The records do not say so, and point to the opposite; the last notice of a playing company in the university records happens to be of the troupe of his wife, Anne, in 1603/4, and as ever they were given forty shillings and told to depart *"sine strepitu"* (without causing a commotion). Clearly its exclusionary policy and the exasperated Latin in which it was expressed were in full vigor up to the moment the quarto was printed. After all, there is good reason to be wary of publisher's blurbs at any time, but especially with the likes of the "Bad Quarto" *Hamlet,* where the title page is unlikely to be any more authoritative than its mangled text.

For all the commotion and conjecture created in orthodox and heterodox circles alike by such as the second issue *Troilus and Cressida* and the 1603 *Hamlet,* on the whole, the sixteen quartos published between 1597 and 1622 place Shakespeare and his plays firmly in the public playhouses. In the first quarto editions, one makes no reference to the play being performed or who performed it; four mention the company that performed it only. Of the remaining eleven, only three, as noted above, say the play had been performed at court. In contrast, eight quartos (including the first issue of *Troilus*) state specifically that they were publicly played by either the Chamberlain's or King's Men (and the *Merry Wives* says that it had been acted "Both before her Majesty, and elsewhere"). Furthermore, there is contemporary record of five of the more demanding of his unpublished plays having been performed at the Globe: *Julius Caesar* (in the diary of Thomas Platter, September 21, 1599); *Macbeth, The Winter's Tale* and *Cymbeline* (Simon Forman's diary, 1610–11), and *Henry VIII* (three letters written after the Globe was razed by fire during a performance of the play). And, of course, the Chorus in *Henry V* addresses the spectator in the "wooden O"—the shape of the public playhouse and not the great hall of one or another of Queen Elizabeth's palaces.

In fact, toward the end of his career with the King's Men, Shakespeare was already giving place in the repertory of plays performed at court, especially to Beaumont and Fletcher (which will be discussed in detail in a later chapter). For that matter, in the later years of English Renaissance theater, he may not have been the darling of the select company at the Blackfriars either, if we may judge by the words of Leonard Digges. He may be remembered as the author of a poem to Shakespeare in the First Folio and some time before his death in 1635 he once again took pen in hand to pay homage to the popular dramatist. Addressing his comments to the actors he says:

> I do not wonder when you offer at
> Blackfriars, that you suffer: tis the fate
> Of richer veins, prime judgments that have fared
> The worse, with this deceased man compared.[26]

In plain language, Digges is saying that the fashionable fare the King's Men served up for the select audiences of their indoor theater was poor stuff in comparison to Shakespeare's, and so was the attendance at them. But let Shakespeare be played at the Globe, "The cockpit, galleries, boxes, all are full." If Digges can be taken at his word, it does appear that in his own age, Shakespeare was (with apologies) the caviar of the general.

Afterwords

"Hence Broker-Lackey"

Although the 1609 quarto is conjectured to be taken from Shakespeare's foul papers, the apparent sources of the First Folio text are the quarto in concert with a promptbook for a Globe performance. The most significant evidence for the latter source is the appearance of two similar colloquies between Pandarus and Troilus in act five in the folio, which may be seen in the Norton facsimile *First Folio of Shakespeare* (1968). As the play was not paginated in the folio, the numbers at the bottom of the page in the Norton facsimile are given.

Page 613, lines 3328–30 (would follow line 112 in scene three):

> *Pand.* Why, but heare you?
> *Troy.* Hence brother lackie; ignomie and shame
>   Pursue thy life, and live aye with thy name.

Page 615, lines 3569–71 (scene 10, lines 32–34):

> *Pand.* But heare you? heare you?
> *Troy.* Hence broker, lackie, ignomie, and shame
>   Pursue thy life, and live aye with thy name.

Lines 3328–30 are not in the quarto and suggest that the Globe text would have ended with Troilus' speech in scene ten—"Strike a free march to Troy! With comfort go; Hope of revenge shall hide our inward woe"— and the lines 3569–71, along with Pandarus' epilogue that follows, were omitted in the Globe version.[27]

⇥6⇤

The Dating of
Shakespeare's Plays

According to the Oxfordians, the traditional chronology of Shakespeare's plays—from 1589 at the earliest to 1614 at the latest—is
merely something tailored by scholars to suit the lifetime of the man they
presume to be the author and nothing more—a very strange accusation
when one considers that the Oxfordian chronology is tailored to suit the
lifetime of the Earl of Oxford (1550–1604). It is even stranger when one
sees which plays are challenged. One might expect that their particular
targets would be the dozen or so plays dated by Shakespearean scholars
to 1604 and later. But, aside from *King Lear* (1605) and *The Tempest*
(1611), most of the sustained challenges are to plays written before 1604.
Presumably, if earlier plays can be moved back ten or fifteen years, those
traditionally dated after 1604 must follow suit. And if it can be shown
that Shakespeareans are wrong about those, it must follow that they are
wrong about the others as well.

The touchstone for the Shakespearean chronology is the dozen plays
listed by Francis Meres in *Palladis Tamia*, which may be remembered also
as the book Ogburn believes to have been the instrument Oxford's friends
used to unveil his Shakespeare pseudonym. At the time of the publication
of *Palladis Tamia*, about September 1598, Meres credited the following
extant plays to Shakespeare: *The Two Gentlemen of Verona, The Comedy
of Errors, Love's Labor's Lost, A Midsummer Night's Dream, The Merchant of Venice, Richard II, Richard III, Henry IV, King John, Titus Andronicus,* and *Romeo and Juliet.*

The Taming of the Shrew almost certainly was written by this time but
it is not on Meres's list. He also missed the *Henry VI* plays, and we have
heard the appealing case that has been made for a 1597 date for *The
Merry Wives of Windsor*, the style of which belongs comfortably in this
period. The Oxfordians look hopefully on the fact that if he missed these

five, he may have missed more. Be that as it may, at least sixteen extant plays had been written by the time *Palladis Tamia* appeared. The traditional chronology adds another nine plays up to and including 1604, bringing the total that were written by the time of the Earl of Oxford's death to 25. It is, as mentioned, these plays that get most of the challenges, simply because the Oxfordians follow the lead of a most unorthodox orthodox scholar, A. S. Cairncross. The challenges prove to be highly selective.

In fact, the dating of many of the plays in Meres's catalogue is not questioned, and the greatest arguments are made for such plays as the two parts of *Henry IV, Henry V,* and *Hamlet*—the latter two names are found in *Henslowe's Diary,* the last of which was one of the seven plays acted during the brief coalition of the newly formed Lord Chamberlain's Men and the Lord Admiral's Men from June 5 to June 14, 1594. Rather than the *ur-Hamlet,* as Shakespeareans think, might not this have been an early version of Shakespeare's play, reflected in the Bad Quarto of 1603?

The Problem of Cairncross

The one thing that the *ur-Hamlet* and the 1603 quarto definitely have in common is that both have been considered ridiculous: the former in its own time, the latter in ours. The earliest reference to a play of *Hamlet* is in Thomas Nashe's dedicatory epistle to Robert Greene's *Menaphon* (1589). Here, the acid-witted Nashe addressed the "Gentlemen Students" of Oxford and Cambridge and at one point launches into an attack on those who borrow from Seneca for the stage and even have the audacity to attempt translations from the Latin. However, pointed references leave no doubt that his exemplar is Thomas Kyd, who presumed to leave his father's trade, and his own early calling, as a *noverint* (scrivener):

> It is common practice nowadays, amongst a sort of shifting companions, that run through every art and thrive by none, to leave the trade of *Noverint,* whereto they were born, and busy themselves with the endeavors of art, that could scarcely latinise their neck-verse if they should have need. Yet English Seneca read by candlelight yields many good sentences, as "blood is a beggar" and so forth; and if you entreat him fair on a frosty morning, he will afford you whole *Hamlets,* I should say handfuls of tragical speeches. . . . The sea exhaled by drops will in continuance be dry, and Seneca let blood line by line, and page by page, at length must needs die to our stage: which makes his famished followers to imitate the kid in Aesop, who enamored with the fox's newfangles, forsook all hopes of life to leap into a new occupation.

From the reference to *Hamlet* amidst the gibes at Kyd, scholars have drawn the inference that he was the author of this *ur-Hamlet.* Whether or not he was, there is no question that Nashe did not think much of its author, who was in his eyes little better than a cribber of "tragical speeches" from Seneca, whose ten tragedies were published in translation in 1581.

The next *Hamlet* allusion is by Thomas Lodge, who apparently thought no better of it than did Nashe. In *Wits Miserie* (1596), he described "Hate Virtue" as "a foul lubber, and looks as pale as the vizard [visage] of the ghost which cried so miserably at the Theatre like an oyster wife, Hamlet revenge." This seems a far cry from the play praised several years later by the erudite Gabriel Harvey: "The younger sort take much delight in Shakespeare's *Venus and Adonis;* but his *Lucrece,* and the tragedy of *Hamlet, Prince of Denmark,* have it in them to please the wiser sort."

Of one thing we can be certain: if we believe the 1603 text of *Hamlet* is an earlier state of Shakespeare's play, it would have taken witchcraft to transform it into the later version. A sample of its most famous speech—the "To be or not to be" soliloquy—will show why (parallel lines in the good version are in parentheses):

> To be, or not to be, aye there's the point, (1)
> To die, to sleep, is that all? Aye, all: (5)
> No, to sleep, to dream, aye marry there it goes, (9–10)
> For in that dream of death, when we awake, (11)
> And borne before an everlasting Judge, (none)
> From whence no passenger ever returned, (24–25)
> The undiscovered country, at whose sight (24)
> The happy smile, and the accursed damned. (none)

And so on. Quite apart from the shreds it makes of Shakespeare's poetry, it shreds sense as well. This quarto also picks scraps from several other plays, some unarguably not Shakespeare's, and in its entirety shows every sign of being a memorial reconstruction by actors who at some time had small roles in *Hamlet*.[1] Under any circumstances, it is surprising that the Oxfordian guardians of Shakespeare's unwavering excellence should wish to present this text as representative of his writing at any time in his career.

Ogburn's primary support for an early date for Shakespeare's *Hamlet* is the aforementioned A. S. Cairncross.[2] In *The Problem of Hamlet: A Solution,* Cairncross set himself the task of proving that the corrupt first quarto of *Hamlet* was a 1593 piracy of Shakespeare's play, which existed in its perfect form in 1588 or 1589. The essence of Cairncross speculation is that both Shakespeare and the pirate were members of the Queen's Men at that time and it was for this company that *Hamlet* was originally written.[3] Then, according to this scenario, in 1591 both switched allegiance to

Pembroke's Men—although there is no record of a Pembroke company until late 1592.

It is a fact that this company did fall on hard times in the plague summer of 1593, which opens the way for Cairncross to speculate that, in the following winter, "some of the company must have attempted a fresh venture in the provinces." There is absolutely no evidence whatever to support this and he acknowledges that "No direct trace of them or Pembroke's company is again found until 1597." Undaunted he forges on, appointing Shakespeare's erstwhile fellow the role of reconstructing plays from memory for this supposed provincial tour, for which he would, of course, choose *Hamlet,* as well as the second and third parts of *Henry VI* and *The Taming of the Shrew.*

Cairncross is able to bring his tale to a firm conclusion for the last three, for the allegedly pirated *The Taming of a Shrew* (although Shakespeare's hand in it is doubtful) and the two parts of *Henry VI,* which "fell into the publisher's hands in 1594 and 1595" were indeed published in those years. However, without the unlimited palette of unsubstantiated speculation at his command, the *Hamlet* story comes to a wobbly end: "the fact that the *Hamlet* piracy was held over until 1603 is an accident of which we have no explanation."

In his quest for evidence to support his hypothesis, Cairncross imports a German version of *Hamlet—Der bestrafe Brudermord,* a mutilated play of which the earliest existing text is dated 1710.[4] However, despite its origins in the 1603 and 1604 *Hamlet* texts (especially the former), and despite the fact that no performance of the German play is heard of before 1626, he determined that it was written about 1590—a date that he finds "justified and confirmed" by the travels of four English players, Robert Browne, Richard Jones, Thomas Sackville, and John Bradstreet, in Germany and other European countries in 1592 (not, as he states, 1591).

Cairncross now confronts the next hurdle: if *Hamlet* already existed in its final form, why does *Der bestrafe Brudermord* so closely resemble the mangled 1603 quarto text? We are asked to believe that it is because these players arrived in Europe theatrically empty-handed. For, writes Cairncross, "The repertoire of the English actors would have to be prepared as soon as possible, to give them some plays at least to proceed with. Thus, Hamlet is likely to have been reproduced early in 1591, on the actors' arrival."[5] In other words, these actors planned a tour on the continent, applied for travel papers, but set sail without a playscript! In fact, according to Cairncross' source, E. K. Chambers' *The Elizabethan Stage,* the actors were well prepared and we do have knowledge of at least some of the plays they performed in Germany. On August 30, 1592, they "approached the Frankfurt magistrates for leave to play at the Autumn Fair, where they gave *Gammer Gurton's Needle* and some of Marlowe's plays." Back in

Frankfurt in August 1593, "they played scriptural dramas, including *Abraham and Lot* and *The Destruction of Sodom and Gomorrha*."[6]

Ultimately, the inference to be drawn from Cairncross' whole-cloth fabrication is that these touring English players in 1592 and the Pembroke pirate in 1593 independently garbled the play in ways so similar that the 1603 *Hamlet* could seem a source for *Der bestrafe Brudermord*. This, like the rest of his hypotheses, is implausible and his fanciful conjecture proves to offer no evidence for an earlier dating of *Hamlet*.

Cairncross proves to have been one who was unbothered by a hobgoblin of consistency. To make his case for an earlier date for *Hamlet*, he determined that it was necessary to give earlier dates to a number of other plays too. In his preface he says that this further speculation may "prove unfounded or misguided without invalidating the main thesis of this volume." But when he actually embarks on his revisionary dating of these others he said: "Either these plays must have been written before 1593, or the argument relating to the date of Q1 [the 1603 *Hamlet*] collapses."[7] This eludes the notice of the sharp-eyed Oxfordians, who are only too happy to have the surmise of an "orthodox scholar" to show there are real doubts about the traditional chronology. Does he do any better with these plays than with *Hamlet*? Let's begin with *Twelfth Night*.

This play is traditionally dated 1601, but Cairncross decides that the reference to a Malvolio who does "smile his face into more lines than are in the new map with the augmentation of the Indies," is not, as generally supposed, to the Edward Wright map dated to 1599 or 1600, sometimes found in copies of the second edition of Richard Hakluyt's *Principal Navigations, Voyages, Traffiques & Discoveries of the English Nation* (1598–1600). Rather, he asserts it is a reference to the "map or globe" by Emery Mollineux that was made for the Middle Temple in 1592. Surely Shakespeare knew the difference between a map and a globe, as must Ogburn, but this does not prevent the latter from passing along this information and the assumption Cairncross draws from it, to wit: the play was written in time to be performed at court on Twelfth Night, January 6, 1593.[8]

In an attempt to justify his ambiguous identification, Cairncross claims that a map by Mollineux based on his globe "in its earliest state" was included in the first edition of Hakluyt's *Principal Navigations* (1589). This map is, in fact, an anonymous copy of the *Typus Orbis Terrarum* in Ortelius' Atlas, dated 1570. Wright's map, on the other hand, was called "one of the treasures of cartographical collections" by R. V. Tooley in his standard work, *Maps and Map-makers*, and it happens to be "notably rich in rhumb lines, i.e. the lines of direction for sailing," to which Malvolio's smiling face is likened.[9] As for Cairncross' other attempt to link the Mollineux globe with the play—"It is perhaps not a mere coincidence that

Twelfth Night is first mentioned in [John] Manningham's *Diary* as performed at the Middle Temple"—he neglects to mention that the date of this entry is January 6, 1602, nine years to the day after his supposed court performance.

When it comes to those plays of Shakespeare's of which a seemingly earlier play on the subject was in print, Cairncross applies a chicken-or-egg principle and, for his purposes, invariably finds that the lesser play is a mere shell of a Shakespearean exemplar—a "loose piracy" written to cash in on the popularity of the master's work. Such is the relationship he alleges between the anonymous play, *The Famous Victories of Henry the Fifth,* and Shakespeare's plays of *Henry IV* and *Henry V,* traditionally dated to 1596–99, but which he argues had all been written for and staged by Queen Elizabeth's Men no later than 1588. If so, the quarto of *The Famous Victories,* entered with the Stationers in 1594 but not put into print until 1598, presents a problem: the title page states that this is the drama "as it was played by the Queen's Majesty's Players." Certainly this troupe, which already had Shakespeare's originals, would not have added a "loose piracy" of them to their repertory. Cairncross gets around this by telling us nothing more about what is on the title page than that the play is ascribed to (rather than "as it was played by") the Queen's Men on the title page and thus can he claim that this "ascription" means only that this company owned the original plays, of which the quarto was a pirated version. For, to his mind, "It is unlikely, indeed impossible, that the Queen's, the dominant company in 1587–8, should ever have acted a play of the quality of *The Famous Victories.*" [10]

Ogburn initially commends Cairncross' opinion that the Shakespeare trilogy belongs to an earlier date and only later takes issue with his idea that *The Famous Victories* is a piracy, for he believes the old play holds important clues that point to Oxford's authorship of *Henry V.*[11]

According to Ogburn's scenario, the 17th Earl of Oxford gave a prominent role in this play to his ancestor, the 11th Earl, well beyond his actual place in the annals of Henry V, and especially in the Battle of Agincourt. He supposedly had cause to regret this show of family pride, not only because it jeopardized his own anonymity, but because it may have provoked untimely titters when it was performed at court, something that the queen could not tolerate. Therefore, when he transformed this homely prose play into the two-part *Henry IV* and *Henry V,* so totally did he purge the 11th Earl that, Ogburn laments, he is not even to be found in the dramatis personae of the new *Henry V!*

First of all, it should be noted that it is a time-honored theatrical tradition that characters who do not appear in a play are not included in the dramatis personae. More importantly, as *The Famous Victories* was originally in the repertory of Elizabeth's own company, it would seem to have been a likely candidate for performance before the queen and her court. But it does not appear any effort was made to alter or suppress it. To the contrary, it survived with all the Oxford parts intact to be published some thirteen years or so after it was written. At the very least, it seems the earl's imagined fit of discretion came too late. In fact, the likely reason Number 11 disappeared from Shakespeare's drama is that, unlike the author of *The Famous Victories*, he had before him Rafael Holinshed's *Chronicle of England, Scotland, and Ireland* (1587), and thus did he restore Oxford's progenitor to his proper place in the reign of Henry V.

Such is the sort of evidence adduced to redate earlier plays. What is more important, of course, is whether more credible grounds for redating the plays of 1604 and later are offered. Let's see.

A Tale of Two—or Three—Lears

In 1594, Philip Henslowe recorded a performance of *King Leare* on April 6, and again on the 9th. Five weeks later, May 14, to be precise, a bookseller named Edward White entered *The Most Famous Chronicle of* LEIRE, *King of England, and his Three Daughters* in the Stationers' Register. Oxfordians are satisfied that this is Shakespeare's earliest version of the play. In fact, they believe that *King Lear* in particular is a prime example, in the words of Gordon Cyr, of how "woefully weak" scholarly dating is. "If you ask me," he said, "the Stratfordians decided on 1606 for 'King Lear' because they were looking around for a period in the Stratford man's life that was relatively unencumbered." [12] It will, then, be of particular interest to see just how strong the Oxfordian case is.

The controversialists' format is a familiar one. Once again, the dissent from the traditional dating of the orthodox Cairncross is proffered. Once again, he has failed to take the great leap into heresy but instead returned to the familiar scenario he used regarding the history plays vis-à-vis *The Famous Victories*. "In reality," Cairncross says of the relation between Shakespeare's play and the anonymous *King Leir*, "*Lear* was written first— that is some time earlier than 1594—and that *Leir* represents an attempt to reproduce its main plot." [13] As far as Ogburn is concerned, this does not go far enough: *King Lear* is Shakespeare's revision of his own earlier *King Leir*. Thus, it is actually Shakespeare's play that was entered to White and is the same *Lear* that is found in *Henslowe's Diary*. Before investigating this hypothesis, we should first straighten out the facts.

In the very same sentence in which Ogburn quotes Cairncross' statement that it is "generally accepted that *Leir* was written earlier than May 14, 1594, on which date it was entered on the Stationers' Register," he unaccountably shifts this entry to April, stating it was made two days *before* the performances of this play on the 6th and 9th at the Rose! In this matter, Cairncross is, for once, right. Furthermore, Ogburn goes on to say that the title of the play given in the Stationers' Register entry is *"King Leare,"* just as it is spelled in *Henslowe's Diary*. In fact, the work was licensed to White under the title *Leire, King of England*.[14] White, however, never published the play and it is therefore impossible to use it as proof of anything; nor do we know anything more about the *King Leare* in *Henslowe's Diary* other than it was apparently an old play when it was performed at the Rose by a joint company of the players of the queen and the Earl of Sussex.[15] The entry to White does raise problems when, in 1605, an old play of *Leir* was printed just before we first hear of Shakespeare's *Lear*.

On May 8 of that year, *The Tragical History of King Leir and His Three Daughters* was licensed to the printer Simon Stafford. Stafford immediately transferred it to John Wright, "Provided that Simon Stafford shall have the printing of the book," and he did indeed print this *Leir* for Wright in that year.[16] Cairncross propounds the view, still adhered to by many scholars, that Wright, who was apprenticed to White until 1602, "probably bought the right to print one edition." He supports this assumption with the observation that "the copyright of *Leir* remained throughout in the hands of White and his executors." And, in fact, it was among "all the estate of Mistress White" that was assigned to Edward Aldee on June 29, 1624, and is found once again in the assignment of Aldee's copyrights to Richard Oulton by the Stationers' Court on April 22, 1640. There is, however, no record of its ever having been published by anyone who held the copyright—unless John Wright did indeed buy a onetime right to publish from his old master. But did he?

Unfortunately, Cairncross did not show similar diligence in tracing the history of Wright's *Leir* in the Stationers' Register. Though it was not specifically named in the transfer of his copies to his brother Edward on June 27, 1646, it was unquestionably among them. (It is noted in this entry that the works listed were only "part of the copies which lately appertained to John Wright.") Thus, on April 4, 1655, this *Leir* is named among the numerous works Edward Wright assigned to William Gilbertson. Obviously, John Wright had an outright claim on the play he published. This is supported by the original 1605 entry to Stafford and Wright, which is unconditional and makes no mention of a transfer to these men by Edward White. As two stationers could not hold the copyright to the same work, the White and Wright works cannot have been one and the same.

Can Wright's have been Shakespeare's early version? For the very same reason that we know White's *Leire* was not Wright's *Leir*, we can be cer-

tain Shakespeare's play had no relation to Wright's; for there was no challenge by either of these men when Nathaniel Butter entered *M. William
Shak-speare: His True Chronicle Historie of the Life and Death of King
Lear and His Three Daughters,* on November 26, 1607. Butter retained
his copyright until May 21, 1639, when it was transferred to M. Flesher.
In fact, scholars believe that the reason Butter entered this play specifically
as Shakespeare's and printed his name prominently on the title page was
to distinguish *His True Chronicle History* of *Lear* from Wright's *Leir,*
published as *The True Chronicle History.* (The work entered to White was
also published with a similar title: *The Most Famous Chronicle History.*)

Which leaves the question of why the Lear story should have been so
suddenly popular. It may be remembered that this question was pondered
by the scholar W. W. Greg. Whereas he was reluctant to accuse Wright of
trying to capitalize on the success of Shakespeare's play by publishing the
old one, he was dubious about its title-page claim of recent performance:

> I find it very difficult to believe that this respectable but old-fashioned
> play, dating back in all probability to about 1590, had been "divers and
> sundry times lately acted" in 1605, especially if the playhouse manuscript
> had been for years in the hands of stationers.[17]

Reluctantly, he concludes "there is plenty of grounds for suspicion, and it
is at least plausible conjecture that it was the popularity of Shakespeare's
play that suggested the publication of the old *King Leir.*" Greg was apparently unaware of a contemporary event that might have made the old play
peculiarly up-to-date—and may explain why Shakespeare put his hand to
it at about the same time.

Brian Annesley had served Queen Elizabeth long and well, if with no
unusual distinction, and was rewarded with estates and preferments. In
1600 he made his will, settling the lion's share of his properties on the
youngest of his three daughters, who happened to be named Cordell.[18] In
1603 he became senile and in October of that year his eldest daughter
Grace, Lady Wildgosse, with the enthusiastic support of her husband, Sir
John, tried to gain control over both his affairs and his person, which
meant control of his properties as well. Cordell so vigorously opposed the
couple's designs that Sir Robert Cecil sent a commission to oversee the
dispute. This included Annesley's friend, Sir James Croft, who, as a result,
became the governor of his affairs.

Cordell sent a touching letter of thanks to Cecil, especially for protecting
her father against Wildgosse, who would have him "begged a lunatic, whose
many years of service to our late dread Sovereign Mistress and native country
deserved a better agnomination, than at last gasp to be recorded and reg-

istered a lunatic."[19] Annesley died on July 10, 1604, and was buried in the chancel of Lee Old Church, Kent (now part of Greater London). The inscription on the tomb of Annesley and his wife, Audrey, concluded:

> Cordell the youngest daughter at her own proper cost and charges, in further testimony of her dutiful love unto her father and mother, caused this monument to be erected, for the perpetual memory of their names, Against the ungrateful nature of oblivious time.

This real-life drama does bear a marked resemblance to the fable of the legendary King Leir, whose youngest daughter was named Cordeilla, as introduced into English literature in about 1135 by the Welsh bishop Geoffrey of Monmouth in his *Historia regium Britanniae*. Given the society's propensity for finding metaphors for contemporary topics in ancient figures and events, the old play of *King Leir* was ready-made for the story of Annesley and his daughters. However, the real-life story may have been of particular interest to Shakespeare.

The monument erected by Cordell holds two other intriguing bits of information. First, it tells us that Annesley "had served Queen Elizabeth as one of the Band of Gentlemen Pensioners to her Majesty: the space of 30 years"; second, by the time it was erected, Cordell was the wife of Sir William Harvey, whom she married on February 5, 1608. *

The Gentlemen Pensioners were originally organized to be the monarch's "nearest guard" in peace and companions in arms in war, but by the end of the Tudor Age they were a largely ceremonial unit. In the last decades of Elizabeth's reign, the captains of this band happen to have been the Lords Hunsdon, the same who were the patrons of Shakespeare's acting company. It is not out of the question that by this mutual association, the actors might have known, or at least known *of* Annesley and his daughters, making the events of 1603 and 1604 of some immediacy to them.

Sir William Harvey's marriage to Cordell was his second. His first wife was to the widow of the second Earl of Southampton and of Sir Thomas Heneage. The dowager countess is better known to us as the mother of the third earl, who was Shakespeare's patron and the leading candidate for the fair youth of his sonnets. Charlotte Stopes offered the possibility that Harvey had come upon the manuscript of the sonnets in the countess's effects and that he was Mr. W. H., "the onlie begetter" who gave them to

---

* The correct figure of Annesley's service, according to information provided to me by William J. Tighe from his dissertation on the Gentlemen Pensioners, is forty years, from 1563 to 1603. Also see Gyles Isham, "The Prototype of King Lear and His Daughters," *Notes and Queries*, vol. 199 (1954), 150.

Thomas Thorpe for publication in 1609. In his article on *Lear* and the Annesley case, Geoffrey Bullough called this "wild surmise" and cautions that "There is no evidence that Shakespeare ever knew Harvey or Cordell Annesley."[20] This is true, as far as Shakespeare's possible personal associations are concerned. Be that as it may, the Annesley saga in itself is quite sufficient to explain the burst of interest in the Lear story in 1605.

Under any circumstances, John Wright may be acquitted of any attempt to capitalize on the success of Shakespeare's *Lear,* for the evidence suggests a date of composition some months after the old play was published. One piece of this evidence in particular has been the focus of Oxfordian efforts to debunk a 1605/6 date for *Lear:* the reference to the "late eclipses" in act one, scene two. In the words of Gordon Cyr, Shakespearean scholars

> make a big to-do over the fact that in 1605 there was supposedly a total eclipse, such as Gloucester seems to describe to Edmund when he speaks of "these late eclipses in the sun and moon." This question is discussed in Captain Hubert H. Holland's book "Shakespeare Through Oxford Glasses." He found that in fact there was no total eclipse in 1605—unless Shakespeare happened to be in Borneo at the time.[21]

I am indebted to Geoff Chester, a staff member of the Albert Einstein Planetarium at the National Air and Space Museum, for the information that there was indeed a partial eclipse of the moon at 3:45 in the morning of September 17, 1605 (on the Old Style English calendar), as well as a total solar eclipse on the longitude of England at 2 P.M. on October 2. Unless the sun shines in Borneo at ten o'clock at night, this eclipse definitely was not seen there.

The Winter's Tale and Tales of *The Tempest*

Of the twelve plays besides *King Lear* traditionally dated to the year of Oxford's death or later, Ogburn actually offers conjecture for an earlier date for only five, of which but three are subject to proof: *The Winter's Tale, The Tempest* and *Henry VIII*. The first of these, *The Winter's Tale,* is usually dated 1609 at the earliest, but Ogburn has nary a doubt that this is the very same work entered to Edward White on May 22, 1594.[22] His confidence rests solely on the coincidence that the Stationers' entry named the work *A Winter's Night's Pastime,* and when Shakespeare's play was presented at court on November 5, 1611, it was called *The Winter's Night's Tale* in the Revels account of the performance. Shaky grounds at best for so definite a conclusion. On the other hand, there are firm grounds for saying there is no relationship between them at all.

First of all, if White ever published this work, no copy is extant. We therefore have no idea what was in it or even if it was a play at all. Secondly, *The Winter's Tale* is one of the sixteen plays listed as not previously entered to other stationers in the First Folio entry in the Stationers' Register of November 8, 1623. Therefore, it cannot be the work entered nearly twenty years earlier. Finally, in Sir Henry Herbert's Revels account book, we find the following on August 19, 1623:

> For the King's players. An old play called *Winter's Tale*, formerly allowed of by Sir George Buck, and likewise by me on Mr. Heminges his word that there was nothing profane added or reformed, though the allowed book was missing, and therefore I returned it without a fee.[23]

As this tells us that the play was originally licensed by Buck, and as it was not until October 1610 that he gained the office of the Master of the Revels and thus the power to license plays for performance, it is evident that *The Winter's Tale* was not written before that year.

The first item of evidence that purports to date *The Tempest* before the traditional 1611 date concerns Shakespeare's model for Prospero's island. Some few past scholars have suggested Bermuda because the shipwreck in the play may owe its inspiration to an account of a shipwreck on that island in 1609. Ogburn offers in its stead Cuttyhunk, an island between Cape Cod and Martha's Vineyard, Massachusetts, based on a talk given in 1902 by Edward Everett Hale, entitled "Miranda was a Massachusetts Girl."[24] The occasion for the talk was the 300th anniversary of the discovery of the island by Bartholomew Gosnold, and here we discover its attraction to Ogburn. Gosnold's expedition was supposedly financed by the Earl of Southampton, whom he would like to believe had an intimate association with Oxford. Best of all, take away 300 years from 1902 and we arrive at 1602, when Oxford was yet among the living and could then have been the author of *The Tempest*. To make this hypothesis all the more appealing, Hale imagined Southampton entertaining captain and crew upon their return, and the playwright taking notes of their adventures. Alas, there are flaws in this fable—regardless of who the playwright might be.

First of all, any attempt to identify Prospero's island with any actual piece of real estate is frustrated, for it is many islands at once. Thus, when the Milanese lord Adrian declares, "The air breathes upon us here most sweetly," a debate erupts about its properties:

> *Sebastian.* As if it had lungs, and rotten ones.
> *Antonio.* Or as 'twere perfumed by a fen.

The Stationers' Register entry to William Jaggard and Edward Blount of previously unpublished plays, November 8, 1623. *The Winter's Tale* is the last of the plays grouped under "Comedyes." (Courtesy of The Worshipful Company of Stationers and Newspaper Makers)

Gonzalo. Here is everything advantageous to life.
Antonio. True, save means to live.
Sebastian. Of that there's none, or little.
Gonzalo. How lush and lusty the grass looks! How green!
Antonio. The ground indeed is tawny.
Sebastian. With an eye of green in't.

But in the very next scene, Caliban promises Stephano and Trinculo the bounty of an island lush indeed: "I'll show thee the best springs; I'll pluck thee berries; I'll fish for thee and get thee wood enough." Clearly, Prospero's domain existed nowhere but in the mind of the author.

Fictional though the island may be, modern scholars agree that the ship carrying the King of Naples home from Tunis traversed the Mediterranean Sea and is therefore where the island is located. We have the word on this of Ariel, Prospero's apprentice who drove the king and his party to the shores of the island, when he reassures his master of the safety of the other ships:

> for the rest o' th' fleet—
> Which I dispersed—they all have met again
> And are upon the Mediterranean flote
> Bound sadly home for Naples.

Lastly, it is doubtful Southampton was doing very much entertaining in 1602, for that was very much discouraged in his residence at the time—the Tower of London, where he was imprisoned ever since his participation in the Earl of Essex's insurrection in February 1601, and where he would remain until April 1603, when he was pardoned by King James. For the very same reason, we can be sure he did not have the means to finance any such expedition. He had been attainted and thus the queen seized all of his properties and deprived him of his title and income to boot. The totality of this seizure was duly noted in the Southampton municipal Court Leet Book, where we read, "Our most serene lady Queen Elizabeth, now holds the lands and tenements of Henry, late Earl of Southampton, who has been proven guilty of high treason committed by himself and by Robert, Earl of Essex." His name was stricken from the rolls of the city's Free Suitors and the queen named in his place.[25]

All this speculation was set in motion by the shipwreck that begins the play and Ariel's mention of the "still-vex'd Bermoothes." This coincidence has led Shakespeareans to think that it was the notoriety surrounding the wreck of the Virginian Council ship Sea-Venture, which attracted wide attention in 1610, that influenced The Tempest. Judge Minos D. Miller, Jr., purporting to provide "specific evidence and documented answers" to this, offers in its stead the wreck of the Edward Bonaventure in 1593, a ship that was supposedly purchased by the Earl of Oxford in the early 1580s and in which he feels the earl might have maintained a sentimental "continuing interest."[26]

Actually, there is only one reference to connect Oxford with this ship. In 1581, the famed navigator and explorer Sir Martin Frobisher was seeking support for a new expedition to the Orient, and it is in a letter from him to the Earl of Leicester (October 1, 1581) that we hear that Oxford "bears me in hand he will buy the Edward Bonaventure," but neither he nor Frobisher were able to meet the asking price. Within weeks of Frobisher's letter, Leicester, as the leading figure in organizing this ultimately ill-fated venture, appears himself to have purchased this ship for the expedition.[27]

Contrary to Miller's belief that it is not known whether the Edward Bonaventure was the ship Oxford (supposedly) "outfitted and commanded" against the Spanish Armada, it is definitely known it was not. The ship had been purchased by the merchant venturer Thomas Cordell of the Levant (or Turkey) Company, and was one of the seven ships of its

A contemporary painting of the Earl of Southampton in the Tower of London. The dates of his confinement—February 8, 1600 (that is, 1601), to April 1603—are on the wall. The earl's defiant spirit is reflected in the motto "In Vinculus Invictus" (Victorious though in chains). The cat was the earl's pet, which is said to have scoured London for his master before finding his Tower cell. (Courtesy of His Grace the Duke of Buccleuch and Queensberry, KT, Boughton House, Northamptonshire.)

squadron in the Spanish War. In this fleet it was commanded by James Lancaster, who was also its captain on the ship's final voyage, which we are led to believe ended with its wreck in Bermuda and thus may have been the real inspiration for the real author of *The Tempest*.[28]

Miller asserts that "Two accounts of the shipwreck of the *Edward Bonaventure* at Bermuda were printed and reported by Hakluyt," but quickly amends this to "the account of Edmund Barker of the last days of the *Edward Bonaventure*, and of Henry May of the shipwreck on Bermuda in 1593"—especially May's, from which "one sees that Shakespeare's *Tempest* draws almost word for word."

Perhaps Miller qualified his statement because, whereas May did set to sea on the *Edward Bonaventure*, his account makes it unmistakably clear that he was not on this ship when he was involved in a shipwreck. Rather, he had been put aboard a French ship on August 12, 1593, and it was this vessel that was wrecked off Bermuda. The cause definitely had nothing to do with weather. In fact, the crew demanded wine in reward for safely navigating the southward course around Bermuda and, as May relates,

after they had their wine, careless of their charge which they took in hand, being as it were drunken, through their negligence a number of good men were cast away. . . . We made account at the first that we were cast away hard by the shore, being high cliffs, but we found ourselves seven leagues off: but with our boat and a raft which we had made & towed at our boat's stern, we were saved, some 26 of us; among whom were no more English but myself.[29]

Apparently, the drunken sailors ran the ship aground and there is otherwise nothing in May's report that bears a resemblance to the shipwreck in *The Tempest*, no less supporting Miller's assertion that the play "draws almost word for word" on it.

As far as Barker's account is concerned, it does not offer a dramatic tale of "the last days of the *Edward Bonaventure*." Indeed, he cannot tell us of its last days at all because the ship was hijacked by five men and a boy of the crew while Barker and the rest of its complement were getting provisions on Mona Island, situated in the strait between Puerto Rico and the Dominican Republic. Its last days are to be found instead in Spanish reports, where we learn the undermanned ship ran aground off the southern coast of the Dominican, about 175 miles west of where the rest of its company had been marooned.[30]

For that matter, Miller is wrong in stating that, according to Shakespeareans, "the sole source available for Shakespeare to know of a shipwreck at Bermuda" was an account of the wreck of the *Sea-Venture* by Sylvester Jourdain in a tract entitled *A Discovery of the Barmudas, Otherwise Called the Ile of Divels*. In fact, the primary source for this, and more, is held to be a letter written by William Strachey, the secretary and recorder of the Virginia colony, which reflects the notoriety that surrounded the expedition commanded by Sir Thomas Gates and Sir George Somers sent to reorganize the colony in 1609.

En route they did indeed encounter a storm that damaged their ship near Bermuda. However, repairs were made and the voyage continued on to Virginia. In the following summer, he and Gates prepared a despatch on the colony to be carried to the Virginia patentees in England. Jourdain was in the party that sailed for England and upon landing he hurried into print his above-mentioned *Discovery of the Barmudas*. This perhaps contributed to the haste in which the Virginian Council published its *True Declaration of the Estate of the Colony of Virginia, with a Confutation of Such Scandalous Reports as Have Tended to the Disgrace of So Worthy an Enterprise*. This drew heavily on the report by Strachey and Gates and there is evidence of it in *The Tempest*. But it is instead a private letter by Strachey to an unidentified "excellent Lady" that scholars believe most strongly influenced many passages in the play.

Ogburn cites E. K. Chambers alone as a scholar who discerned parallels between this letter and *The Tempest*, noting that he did not give even one of them. However, if Ogburn had consulted the standard reference work, Geoffrey Bullough's *Narrative and Dramatic Sources of Shakespeare*, he would have found eight passages in the play that are cited as having striking parallels to Strachey, and in a footnote reference is made to the "exhaustive list" of such parallels assembled by R. R. Cawley.* This, in turn, has raised the question of how Shakespeare was privy to this letter, which was not published until 1625. Curiously, the Earl of Southampton was among the patentees in the Virginian Council, and so was the Earl of Pembroke. Or perhaps his source was another, closer to home: Sir Henry Rainsford of Clifford Chambers, two miles from Stratford-upon-Avon, who, like Shakespeare, was mentioned in the will of John Combe, Stratford's wealthiest citizen.

A more substantial question about the dating of *The Tempest* concerns the similarities between it and *Die Schöne Sidea* by the German playwright Jacob Ayrer, who died in 1605. Ogburn believes, predictably, the German play was inspired by Shakespeare's. However, in his *Shakespeare in Germany*, Albert Cohn supplies evidence that indicates Shakespeare's play was not Ayrer's source; nor was any English work:

> In all those cases in which we are acquainted with the sources from which Ayrer derived his plots, we see that he almost always retains the original names for his principal persons; and as it is highly improbable that these, for the most part purely German, names should have occurred in an English drama of the sixteenth century, we cannot place much confidence in the suggestion that any such work was the common source of the two plays in question.[31]

Given Ayrer's usual practice of retaining original names, if *Die Schöne Sidea* was drawn from direct acquaintance with *The Tempest* one wonders how Prospero was transformed into Ludolff, Ferdinand into Engelbrecht, and Miranda into Sidea. Thus, Cohn's conclusion that, "Ayrer appears rather to have worked after some German original, and this may have come to light in England in the form of some metamorphosis or the other."

Henry VIII, and the Problem of John Fletcher

The Oxfordian grounds for an early date for *Henry VIII* are threadbare: a "Henry VIII gown" and "a cardinal's gown" in an inventory of properties by Edward Alleyn among Henslowe's papers, allegedly dated to Shakespeare's early years. In fact, the inventory is undated and in Greg's edition of these documents he is able to place it no more exactly than "c. 1590–1600," but suggests that it may have been made at the same time as Henslowe's own inventory of 1598.[32] However, it would not be pushing the

---

* Geoffrey Bullough, *Narrative and Dramatic Sources of Shakespeare*, 8:240. Cawley's essay appeared in *Publications of the Modern Language Association*, vol. 41 (1926), 688–726.

upper limit of 1600 too far if these costumes had been made for the plays on Cardinal Wolsey, first mentioned on June 5, 1601, when Henslowe paid £1 to Henry Chettle "for writing the book" of one of them.[33]

What is especially incredible about such feeble evidence for an earlier date for *Henry VIII* is the incontrovertible evidence we have that it was a new play in 1613. For it was during a performance of this play on June 29, 1613, that the discharge of cannon aloft set fire to the Globe, which quickly burned to the ground. This was apparently the event of the cultural season and found its way into three surviving letters by gentlemen of fashion, two of which state specifically that *Henry VIII* (at this time called *All Is True*) was a new play at the time. The first was by Sir Henry Wotton to his nephew, Sir Edmund Bacon, on July 2:

> The King's players had a new play called *All is True*, representing some principal pieces of the reign of Henry 8, which was set forth with many extraordinary circumstances of pomp and majesty, even to the matting of the stage; the Knights of the Order with their Georges and Garter, the Guards with their embroidered coats, and the like: sufficient in truth within a while to make greatness very familiar, if not ridiculous. Now, King Henry making a masque at Cardinal Wolsey's house, and certain cannons being shot off at his entry, some of the paper, or other stuff wherewith one of them was stopped, did light on the thatch, where being thought at first but an idle smoke, and their eyes more attentive to the show, it kindled inwardly, and ran round like a train, consuming within less than an hour the whole house to the very grounds.[34]

Two days later one Henry Bluett, a London merchant, sent an account to his uncle, Richard Weeks of Somerset:

> On Tuesday last there was acted at the Globe a new play called *All is true*, which had been acted not passing 2 or 3 times before. There came many people to see it in so much that the house was very full and as the play was almost ended the house was fired [that is, set fire to] with shooting off a chamber which was stopped with tow, which was blown up into the thatch of the house and so burnt down to the ground.[35]

There is a conflict between the two letters as to when the fateful cannon shot was fired. The scene described by Wotton is the fourth in act one, and indeed there is a stage direction of "Drum and trumpet; chambers discharg'd" that heralds the arrival of the king and his entourage disguised as "great ambassadors to foreign princes." As there is no later direction for a cannon to be fired, Wotton is probably right. Nor, as a matter of interest, do they agree on the one injury. Bluett's was a hero, "scalded with the fire by adventuring to save a child which otherwise had been burnt." Wotton's merely saved his own life when his breeches caught fire, which "would perhaps have broiled him, if he had not by the benefit of a provident wit, put it out with bottle ale."

Henry VIII presents a greater problem to the Oxfordian argument, one which they understandably give very little attention. This play was the product of a collaboration between Shakespeare and John Fletcher, whose hand is found cumulatively in at least one-quarter of it.[36] Nor was this the only collaborative effort by these playwrights. The King's Men were paid for court performances of a play called *Cardenio* on May 20 and July 9, 1613. Though the play itself is not extant, it has an intriguing, if ultimately unsatisfying history linking the two dramatists.

We next hear of it in the Stationers' Register when, on September 9, 1653, Humphrey Moseley entered *"The History of Cardenio*, by Mr. Fletcher. & Shakespeare," among numerous other works. As Moseley was the publisher of the Beaumont and Fletcher Folio and several of their quartos, this entry reflects his apparent partiality for Fletcher. However, he is not known to have published it and once again the play disappears from view until 1710, when it was probably the subject of a letter by Charles Gildon in *The Tatler*. As an example of the "corruption of the stage," he cites the case of the refusal to produce "a valuable Jewel";

> I mean a play written by Beaumont and Fletcher, and the immortal Shake-spear, in the maturity of his judgment, a few years before he died. . . . There is infallible proof that the copy is genuine; yet this rarity, this noble piece of antiquity, cannot make its way to the stage, because a person that is concerned in it is a person, who of all persons, Mr. C[ibber] does not approve.[37]

Ultimately, three manuscripts of *Cardenio* wound up in the hands of Lewis Theobald, the editor of an early edition of Shakespeare's plays. One, he claimed, was in the handwriting of John Downes, the prompter of the Duke of York's players, managed by William D'Avenant and led by the most famous actor of his day, Thomas Betterton. Of the other manuscripts Theobald says no more than one he "was glad to purchase at a very good rate, which may not, perhaps, be quite so old as the former; but one of them is much more perfect and has fewer flaws and interruptions in the sense." Typical of worshippers of the Immortal Bard at the time, Theobald did not present these manuscripts for performance, but instead adapted them in a play entitled *Double Falsehood*, which premiered on December 13, 1727. Of its authorship, Theobald was content with second billing— "Written Originally by W. Shakespeare; And now Revised and Adapted to the Stage By Mr. Theobald"—relegating Fletcher to a mention in the

The entry of *Cardenio* to Humphrey Mosely in the Stationers' Register on September 9, 1653. (Courtesy of The Worshipful Company of Stationers and Newspaper Makers)

preface of printed editions: "my partiality for Shakespeare makes me wish that Every Thing which is good, or pleasing, in that other great poet [Fletcher], had been owing to *his* pen."[38]

The Theobald manuscripts have not come to light and he never sent any one of them to the press. Therefore, the best evidence we have of the time of their collaboration is that the play is based on the story of Cardenio in Cervantes' *Don Quixote*, which was not published in English until 1612. In his lengthy essay on *Cardenio,* John Freehafer observed that the resonances of the Spanish masterpiece in *Double Falsehood* are clearly owed to this earliest edition, which Theobald apparently did not have a copy of.[39] Taken with the court accounts, the Moseley entry and Gildon's reference to an unacted play by Fletcher and Shakespeare, it seems likely there was such a joint venture in *Cardenio.* Beyond this we cannot go.

Charlton Ogburn, somewhat more partial to Shakespeare than even Theobald, does not mention John Fletcher's association with *The Two Noble Kinsmen* at all.[40] In fact, in his only mention of this play, its title is reduced to lower case when we are told the kinsmen themselves, Palamon and Arcite, were also the eponymous characters of a play performed before Queen Elizabeth at Oxford in 1566. The import of this in Oxfordian lore is that the earl was awarded a master's degree at this time and Ogburn imagines that he was already so stagestruck that he could not possibly have passed up the chance to perform in it. We may infer that this would later flower in his authorship of *The Two Noble Kinsmen.*

Ogburn cautiously claims to hear nothing more than Shakespeare's unmistakable voice in this play. However, it is the voices of both men that are unmistakable and this is supported by contemporary evidence. Both the 1634 entry in the Stationers' Register and the title page of the quarto published in that year agree that it was written by "William Shakespeare and John Fletcher." As those who had a hand in only the revision of a play did not get equal billing with the original author, it is certain this play was a collaborative work. By ignoring Fletcher's part in this play, Ogburn spares himself the task of explaining Oxford's collaboration with him, an especially difficult union when one considers that Fletcher's play-writing career began two years after the earl's death.

Questions for a Chronology

Apart from the fact that the Oxfordians do not offer substantive evidence for an earlier date for any play, their effort at redating fails on several other counts. First of all, by the time of Oxford's death on June 4, 1604, specific contemporary evidence of one kind or another is found for 23 of the 25 plays written to that date according to the traditional chronology. However, in this same time, there is no authentic mention of even one of the other thirteen extant plays—especially odd when one considers that these are his most artistically accomplished works and include a dispro-portionate number of the plays on which his fame rests. It is hardly plau-sible that the acquisitive printers and booksellers, the same who attempted to or did actually put into print seventeen of these 25 plays between 1594 and 1604, should have made no effort in that same period to publish works that would have had the greatest appeal to the literati.

The second, and most important point, is that the traditional model—before and after June 4, 1604—is not merely a matter of putting a date on a given play. Rather, it is based on studies of Shakespeare's artistic devel-opment and the characteristics of language and style that suggest nearness of composition of one play to another, as well as authentic records of the play in contemporary sources. From this emerges a chronology—an order of the writing of each play, from first to last. Although there is no univer-sally agreed upon chronology, the substantive disagreements among schol-ars over the dating of plays usually concerns the ones of the first five or six years.

Under any circumstances, one does not need a linguistic slide rule to see that the plays named in *Palladis Tamia* are Shakespeare's earlier works, for only a small number display the command of language, characteriza-tion and the stage that distinguish his later works. Compare them with the plays written between 1598 and 1604—*Hamlet, Julius Caesar, Much Ado About Nothing, Henry V, Measure for Measure* among them—and the differences are evident. But in comparing these works with what came after them, the differences prove to be more than just in Shakespeare's development of his art.

Beginning with *Othello* in 1604, Shakespeare wrote a succession of plays that come under what is known as Jacobean tragedy. Anyone who has read or seen them—*Othello, Lear, Macbeth, Antony and Cleopatra, Cor-iolanus*—senses more at work than an artist at the height of his powers. These plays are vastly different in outlook from the 1590s drama that was attuned to the "optimistic temper of Elizabethan humanism [which] reflected the excitement of an age discovering new cultural, intellectual and artistic horizons." For with the fading of the long-reigning Elizabeth, this expansive spirit gave way to a more introspective age that ripened after the accession of King James. Robert Ornstein said of the tragedians who expressed the temper of this new time that they "do not so much lament the end of the Renaissance adventure of discovery as reckon its costs and darker consequences. Embodied in their plays is an awareness that familiar ways of life are vanishing and that traditional political and social ideals are losing their relevance to the contemporary scene."[41] We can no more shuffle Shakespeare's Jacobean drama into his Elizabethan work temperamentally than stylistically. This new age that lifted Shakespeare to his greatest heights was one that Oxford barely lived to see.

Ultimately, the Oxfordian attempt to undermine the traditional chronology falls apart because they really offer nothing in its place. Even if more substantive grounds were provided for earlier dates for such as *Hamlet, Henry V, Lear,* and the other half a dozen or so plays that the Oxfordians target, the whole amounts to nothing more than a willy-nilly redating of a smattering of plays. It leaves completely undone the task of establishing Oxford's development of style, vocabulary, and characterization in a logical order. In fact, the Oxfordians offer no chronology at all and the dating of the plays turns out to be an issue in which they prove to be especially, one might say woefully, weak.

⇥7⇤

Shakespeare's Reputation in the Seventeenth Century

S hakespeareans and Oxfordians agree that the author of the plays was a genius, perhaps the greatest genius ever. However, his own age was negligent in passing down information about this titanic figure, an omission that bothered generation upon generation of Shakespeareans not a whit. The first wave of idolators was all but entirely literary men, who were not distracted by either the modern standards of scholarship or the archival material we have today of both Shakespeare and the theater of his time. All the better to set their imaginary forces to work on his writings, augmented by a patchwork of fable and folklore, toward the creation of the Immortal Bard. When Shakespeare was finally admitted into college in the middle of the nineteenth century, scholars saw little reason to question the incredible figure that was passed down to them.

Those who doubt that the son of a glover from a Midlands market town could possibly have been the author of the plays observe, correctly, that there is scanty contemporaneous material about the man who wrote the plays and point to the absence of any explicit acknowledgment of the gentleman of Stratford-upon-Avon as the creator of those magnificent works in his hometown. Peter Jaszi wondered how it can be that

> No obituaries marked his death in 1616, no public mourning. No note whatsoever was taken of the passing of the man who, if the attribution is correct, would have been the greatest playwright and poet in the history of the English language.[1]

The man who "would have been the greatest playwright and poet in the history of the English language"? That is certainly what he was to become. But how was he seen by his contemporaries, in the theater and outside it? What was his reputation during the great age of English theater? And afterwards? These are the questions that are at the heart of the "Shakespeare mystery."

The Reputation of the Theater in Shakespeare's Day

To know what Elizabethans thought of Shakespeare, we must first know what they thought of his profession. It appears that, from the moment in 1576 that James Burbage opened the doors of the Theater in Shoreditch, north of the London city walls, it was a tremendous popular success, which may have been the impetus to his erection of a second playhouse nearby, the Curtain, in the next year. According to a contemporary writer, £2000 was paid in admissions to playing spaces in 1578, which meant that between a quarter and a half million people saw public performances in that year alone.[2] The lion's share undoubtedly went to Burbage's playhouses, the only known major facilities at the time. Unfortunately, their success also instigated an assault on theater that would continue for the next 65 years, when the Parliamentarians succeeded in banning public performances altogether.

The best known of the early attacks was a sermon preached from the cross in St. Paul's churchyard on November 3, 1577, by "T. W."—thought to be Thomas White. "Look but upon the common plays in London," he exhorted, "and see the multitude that flocketh to them: behold the sumptuous Theatre houses, a continual monument of London's prodigality and folly." Referring to a current outbreak of the plague, White went on to associate the disease and the theater in a syllogistic masterpiece. A disease, he declared, must be "cured in the cause," and as "the cause of plagues is sin, if you look to it well: and the cause of sin are plays: therefore, the cause of plagues are plays." He concluded with a short list of the sins "set agog" in the playhouses: "theft and whoredom, pride and prodigality, villainy and blasphemy," all on parade in "those schools of vice, dens of thieves, and theatres of all lewdness." However, opposition to the public stage and the flocking multitude was by no means limited to preachers.

A secular round was fired by George Whetstone in the dedication of his comedy, *The History of Promos and Cassandra* (1578). Whetstone had no quarrel with classical drama, but found the modern plays of all nations offensive for a variety of reasons—from the "lascivious" comedy of the Italian to the "too holy" German, who "presents on the common stage what preachers should pronounce in the pulpits." But, for total aesthetic failure, his countrymen were unrivaled:

> The Englishman in this quality is most vain, indiscreet and out of order;
> he first grounds his work on impossibilities; then in three hours runs he
> through the world, marries, gets children, makes children men, men to

conquer kingdoms, murder monsters, and bringeth gods from Heaven, and fetcheth devils from Hell.

There was evidently no satisfying Master Whetstone.

The most damaging assault, however, came from a renegade. Stephen Gosson had been a playwright himself, but in 1579 he wrote the *School of Abuse; Containing a Pleasant Invective against Poets, Pipers, Players, Jesters, and Such like Caterpillars of a Commonwealth*—a phrase that found its way into Shakespeare's *Richard II* where, in act two, scene three, Bolingbroke (the future Henry IV) speaks of

> Bushy, Bagot, and their complices,
> The caterpillars of the commonwealth,
> Which I have sworn to weed and pluck away.

Of the pamphlet itself and its popularity, William Ringler commented that it was "witty, forceful, and vigorous . . . read by gentlemen of pleasure for its style, as well as by more sober citizens for its moral teaching."

Gosson was moved by what went on in London's playhouses, both on and off the stage. On the stage the players seduced the spectator with "strange consorts of melody, to tickle the ear; costly apparel, to flatter the sight; effeminate gesture, to ravish the sense; and wanton speech, to whet desire to inordinate lust." This was matched by the young gallants in the audience who would seduce virtuous maidens, and the harlots who plied their trade in this "general market of bawdry." In 1580, London's government added its voice to the anti-theater forces and tried to enlist the aid of the Privy Council, asking that plays "be wholly stayed and forbidden as ungodly and perilous, as well at those places near our liberties, as within the jurisdiction of this city."

This revulsion, of course, reflects opinion of the theater before the dawn of the Golden Age. How the opinion of the enlightened must have changed when the plays of Shakespeare graced the stage and Jonson was crafting his brilliant comedies! In fact, in the year 1612, when Shakespeare had written virtually all of his masterpieces and Jonson nearly all of the plays that he would publish to establish himself as a literary artist, Sir Thomas Bodley, the founder of the Bodleian Library at Oxford University, gave voice to the continuing low regard of drama held by men of discrimination.

In 1609 Bodley made an agreement with the Stationers Company by which a copy of every published work entered with the guild would be sent to his library. But on January 1, 1612, he wrote a stern letter to Thomas James, the keeper of the library, cautioning him against cataloguing all of the "London books":

There are many idle books & riff raffs among them, which shall never come into the Library, & I fear me that little which you have done already, will raise a scandal upon it, when it shall be given out, by such as would disgrace it, that I have made up a number with almanacs, plays & proclamations: of which I will have none but such as are singular.

Two weeks later he wrote James again, informing him that he "can see no good reason to alter my opinion." Whereas 34 years earlier George Whetstone found all modern plays deficient, Bodley singled out English plays for contempt:

Haply some plays may be worth the keeping: but hardly one in forty. For it is not alike in English plays & others of other nations: because they are esteemed for learning the languages, & many of them compiled by men of great fame for wisdom & learning, which is seldom or never seen among us.

Bodley brought this letter to a rousing conclusion: "the more I think upon it, the more it doth distaste me that such kind of books should be vouchsafed a room in so noble a Library." He took consolation in the knowledge that if he erred in his harsh judgment, "I think I shall err with infinite others."[3]

Bodley died in the next year and we can only wonder if he would have approved of the violation of his principles in 1616, when *The Workes of Benjamin Jonson* was admitted into his library. Would Jonson, with his "adherence to neo-classical principles [and] his more faithful adaptation of classical models," have been in Bodley's estimation that one in forty worthy of being in "so noble a Library"?[4] Perhaps he might have taken into account that Jonson, in addition to his plays, included his poetry and royal masques that truly entitled his folio to be called his *Works*. One wit did not. Ignoring the poems and masques, he homed in on Jonson's plays— and his ego:

> *To Mr. Ben. Johnson demanding the*
> *reason why he call'd his plays works.*
> Pray tell me, Ben, where doth the mystery lurk,
> What others call a play, you call a work.
>
> *Thus answer'd by a friend in Mr.*
> *Johnson's defence.*
> The author's friend thus for the author says,
> Ben's plays are works, when others' works are plays.[5]

But then, even Ben would concede that, at least among pagan gods, his works might be confused with mere plays. Thus, in his "Execration Upon Vulcan," written after the fire that consumed his library in 1623, he took the god to task for devouring his books and scholarly writings, but acknowledged that Vulcan could say,

> There were some pieces of as base allay,
> And as false stamp there; parcels of a Play,
> Fitter to see the fire-light, than the day.[6]

Jasper Mayne would have needed no pagan god to consign his comedy, *The City Match*, to the flames—it was an office he was prepared to do himself. Written for presentation by the King's players, before Charles I and his wife, Queen Henrietta, the monarch rewarded its author with embarrassing approbation. The epistle "To the Reader" of the 1639 quarto says that Mayne was "so adverse from raising fame from the stage, that at the presentment, he was one of the severest spectators there; nor ever showed other sign whereby it might be known to be his, but his liberty to despise it." The prologue spoken upon its performance at the Blackfriars theater tells the tale of Mayne's public humiliation:

> He's one whose unbought Muse did never fear,
> An empty second day, or a thin share;
> But can make th'actors, though you come not twice,
> No losers, since we act now at the King's price;
> Who hath made this play public, and the same
> Power that makes laws, redeem'd this from the flame.
> For th'author builds no fame, nor doth aspire
> To praise from we that he condemn'd to th'fire.

If a man of serious literary pretensions thought public performance of a play—even one written for court and commended by the king—so degrading, those with a taste for reading serious literature cannot be expected to have held plays written for the common stage of much value.

That plays remained at the nadir of literary endeavor is made evident in the preface to a book published when all the great works of that now-legendary epoch in theater history had been written. In 1655, John Cotgrave, as "a part of my recreation in these much distracted times," gathered nearly 1,700 quotations from plays and published them as *The English Treasury of Wit and Language*. In his epistle to the reader, he sets out an argument against "the more serious heads" who would "disdain me for my subject." The "dramatic poem" had, he declared, been lately too much slighted, not only by such whose talent falls short of understanding, but by many who have had a tolerable portion of wit; who, through a stiff and obstinate prejudice, have (in neglecting things of this nature) lost the benefit of many rich and useful observations, not duly considering, or believing, that the framers of them were the most fluent and redundant wits that this age (or I think any other) ever knew, and many of them so able scholars and linguists; as they have culled the choicest flowers out of the greater number of Greek, Latin, Italian, Spanish, and French authors (poets especially) to embellish and enrich the English scene withal, besides almost a prodigious accruement of their own luxuriant fancies.

Five years after Cotgrave wrote these words, a new age of drama was born and, coincidentally, something resembling literary criticism. Plays and those who wrote them, past and present, would be given serious attention. There was nothing like it during the English Renaissance; given the conventions of that age, we probably would not have a much better idea of precisely how the contemporaries of these dramatists valued them, even if the guardians of literary decorum had not held plays in contempt. As it is, our knowledge of contemporary opinion depends on the chance survival of letters of gossipy men about town, the writings of an assortment of lesser or greater literary figures (mostly the former), and those associated with the theater itself. During Shakespeare's lifetime, even this haphazard mechanism was not yet in full swing. The surest source of praise for the playwright, the commendatory verses in an edition of a play he was himself involved in the publication of, was never tapped by Shakespeare. On the other hand, in terms of what we can expect to hear from the Renaissance Englishman, we can seek for Shakespeare's standing among the other playwrights of the time. What do they have to tell us?

The Reputation of Shakespeare in His Own Day

It has been observed that Queen Elizabeth was the first English monarch to lend her name to an age. But, in the popular mind, the Elizabethan Age is the Age of Shakespeare. His name arrests our eye as no other. It is as wonderful to find it on, say, a certificate naming him as a tax defaulter, as to find it on the king's patent to the players. But, as we have seen, it is because we only have notice of the man who was Shakespeare on such as that certificate that Oxfordians believe there is a suspicious silence about the author of the plays. Presumably the clerk who made up the certificate knew this was the name of the famous playwright and, if this was he indeed, the minion should be expected to have noted that, if not made a marginal note of all of his plays he had seen. Farfetched? Not too. For there are parallels to this in the thinking of traditional scholars.

For instance, there is the case of Sir Humphrey Mildmay, who often frequented the playhouses in the decade before the civil wars and noted his attendance in a diary. He rarely gave more than the name of the play he saw and the admission price. When moved to comment on a play, his remarks were limited to such as "a base play," or "a pretty and merry comedy."[7] Of one visit Mildmay said nothing more than, "this afternoon I spent at a play with good company," from which the scholar F. J. Furnivall was able to glean very important information. As Sir Humphrey neglected to say what play he saw, Furnivall decided that it was "probably not one of Shakspere's, or it would have overpowered the recollection of 'good company.'" In fact, there is only one entry of a Shakespeare play in his diary: "not far from home all day; at the Blackfriars & a play this day called the *Moor of Venice [Othello]*".[8] As we can see, Mildmay was so overpowered that he remembered to name the play (as he did in most cases), but not overpowered enough to name the author or to say whether he thought it "a base play" or, perhaps, a pretty and merry tragedy. Just another day at the theater for Sir Humphrey Mildmay.

In fact, the theater buff of the day was not inclined to opinion at all. When the eccentric Dr. Simon Forman attended performances of *Macbeth*, *Cymbeline* and *The Winter's Tale* in 1610 and 1611, he gave lengthy digests of the plays but nary a word of praise, not even a clue as to whether he enjoyed them. Once again, the author's name was not deemed worth a mention. Which brings us to the most important question of all: just how often do we hear praise of Shakespeare the playwright?

During his lifetime, the name William Shakespeare appeared on the title page of thirteen quartos—including *Hamlet* and *King Lear; most, if not all, of his 39 plays had been publicly acted by then. Shakespeare's contemporaries surely did not have to know the identity of the author of the plays to praise the name attached to them. But, much of what there is is directed to the author of the narrative poems *Venus and Adonis* and *The Rape of Lucrece*. In fact, after Francis Meres gave prominent attention to him in *Palladis Tamia* in 1598, there are only six references to Shakespeare's quality as a playwright until his death in 1616. The earliest of these is also the most interesting; first, because it comes from William Camden, one of the most respected minds of the age and, second, because of what becomes of it at the hands of Charlton Ogburn.

In *Remains Concerning Britain* (1605), Camden compared contemporary writers to the great poets of earlier ages, bravely numbering dramatists among them:

These may suffice for some poetical descriptions of our ancient poets; if I would come to our time, what a world could I present to you out of Sir Philip Sidney, Ed[mund] Spenser, Samuel Daniel, Hugh Holland, Ben Jonson, Th[omas] Campion, Mich[ael] Drayton, George Chapman, John Marston, William Shakespeare, and other most pregnant wits of these our times, whom succeeding ages may justly admire.[9]

Ogburn finds it remarkable that Camden should have put Shakespeare in such company in 1605 but, upon the publication of his *Britannia* only two years later, the only residents of Stratford-upon-Avon mentioned are the fourteenth-century Archbishop of Canterbury, John de Stratford, and Hugh Clopton, the sixteenth-century Mayor of London who built the famous bridge over the River Avon.[10]

Contrary to the impression given by Ogburn, *Britannia* was not a new work in 1607. In fact, five editions of *Britannia* were published before the one of 1607. Furthermore, its title in full makes it plain Camden's purpose was a work of serious antiquarian scholarship and not a guide to the habitats of contemporary literary figures. First published in 1586 and written entirely in Latin, *Britannia, sive florentissimorum regnorum Angliae, Scotiae, Hiberniae et insularum adjacentium ex intima antiquitate chorographica Descriptio* (A description of features, to the earliest times of the powerful kings, of England, Scotland, Ireland, and the adjacent islands) was primarily concerned with the history and ancient structures of Britain's towns and cities, gathered in his perambulations throughout the English countryside.

It is noteworthy that, in all the editions of *Britannia,* he ignored the "pretty house of brick and timber" (as it was described more than forty years earlier by the antiquarian John Leland), which was built and occupied by the same Hugh Clopton whose bridge Camden praised. Known as New Place, this was the house Shakespeare bought in 1597. It was, incidentally, built just across the lane from the Guild Chapel—one of the very rare fraternal chantries that was not made within the fabric of a church, as were those of even the wealthiest guilds in England's greatest towns. It must have been a great pride of Stratford and it also owed a great deal to Clopton's gifts. But Camden took no notice of it either. Put into perspective, there hardly seems anything mysterious about the absence of Shakespeare in *Britannia.*

Furthermore, like *Britannia,* the complete title of what is commonly called *Remains concerning Britain* is revealing; it is *Remains of a Greater Work, concerning Britain, the Inhabitants Thereof, Their Languages, Names, Surnames, Impress, Wise Speeches, Poesie, and Epitaphs.* The "Greater Work" is, of course, *Britannia,* and Camden devised the *Remains* as a sort of supplement to it; a collection of material that was not appropriate to his antiquarian masterpiece—including recognition of his nation's preeminent figures in literature, past and present, of which Shakespeare is but one. In this, Camden's is typical of allusions to Shakespeare in contemporary works.

In fact, of the other five instances in which he is praised, it is noteworthy that in three we find Shakespeare's solitary genius in crowded company. Such is the case in the next allusion to Shakespeare the dramatist in Edmund Bolton's *Concerning Historical Language and Style* (1610), in which he took note of "the books also out of which we gather the most warrantable English are not many to my remembrance . . . among the chief, or rather the chief, are in my opinion these"; and when he arrives at the playwrights, they are the works of "Shakespeare, Mr. Francis Beaumont, & innumerable other writers for the stage; and press tenderly to be used in this argument."

In the dedication to *The White Devil* (1612), John Webster graciously acknowledged his peers, but surprisingly crowds his predecessor in Jacobean tragedy with two authors notable for lighter works:

> Detraction is the sworn friend to ignorance: For mine own part I have ever truly cherished my good opinion of other men's worthy labors, especially of that full and heightened style of master Chapman; the labored and understanding works of master Jonson; the no less worthy composures of the both worthily excellent Master Beaumont & Master Fletcher; and lastly (without wrong last to be named) the right happy and copious industry of M. Shake-speare, M. Dekker, & M. Heywood, wishing that I may be read by their light.

Webster is exclusive in comparison to Edmund Howes. In his continuation of John Stow's *Chronicle of England* (1614), Howes named Shakespeare as but one of eleven dramatists in a list of 27 literary figures who are "Our modern, and present excellent poets, which worthily flourish in their own works."

Shakespeare does have an epigram of his own in Thomas Freeman's *Runne, and a Great Cast* (1614); and in the next year Francis Beaumont is presumed to be the F. B. who wrote a verse-letter to Ben Jonson, saying:

> here I would let slip
> (If I had any in me) scholarship,
> And from all learning keep these lines as clear
> As Shakespeare's best are, which our heirs shall hear
> Preachers apt to their auditors to show
> How far sometimes a mortal man may go
> By the dim light of nature.[11]

These are all. However appalling it may be to us, Shakespeare's immediate contemporaries give little indication that they thought of him as the greatest playwright of his own time, no less of all time. After all, when Francis Meres singled out Shakespeare for praise in 1598 it was because he was then the "only Shake-scene" in the country—the only active playwright of the moment with a significant body of work that was identifiably his own. But as the playwrights then at the beginning of their careers developed in the next decade, and as other talented dramatists swelled their ranks, Shakespeare took his place among them in the critical view. In no small measure he was put in that place by the aggressively self-promoting Ben Jonson.

Shakespeare epitomized Elizabethan drama in all its exuberant variety. But that drama was dying with its age and the new wave of dramatists were not to be bound to the past. They were poised to go in a new direction and Jonson was there to point the way. His plays provided, in the words of Richard Dutton, "a recipe for a kind of realism, a kind of theatrical experience in which the members of the audience are not taken imaginatively *out* of themselves but are engaged by the truthfulness of the play." Perhaps in the way of driving home the contrast between his new drama and the old, Jonson introduced his 1616 folio with a pointedly altered version of the comedy *Every Man in His Humour*. When he originally wrote the play in 1598, it was set in Florence, in keeping with the Italianate fashion of the time. However, when he remade it into the version that appears in his folio, its setting was moved to London, its characters and their idiom unmistakably, contemporarily English.

But he was not content to let the reader draw his own conclusions. He prefaced the folio text with a verse that declared his was a superior brand of play, and he left little doubt of whose it was superior to. Not that he denied the talents of the old-fashioned dramatic poet—including "some such / As art, and nature have not bettered much." But convention dictated that he "purchase your delight at such a rate, / As, for it, he himself must justly hate." Among the examples of such drama we find the plays that,

> with three rusty swords,
> And help of some few foot-and-half-foot words,
> Fight over York and Lancaster's long jars:
> And in the tiring-house bring wounds to scars.
> He rather prays you will be pleased to see
> One such, today, as other plays should be.
> Where neither Chorus wafts you o'er the seas;
> Nor creaking throne comes down, the boys to please;
> Nor nimble squib is seen, to make afeared
> The gentlewomen; nor rolled bullet heard

> To say, it thunders; nor tempestuous drum
> Rumbles, to tell you the storm doth come.[12]

The *Henry VI* plays, *Henry V, Cymbeline* and *The Tempest,* too, in one fell swoop!

As Shakespeare had Hamlet criticize the old style of acting—"O, it offends me to the soul, to hear a robustious periwig-pated fellow tear a passion to tatters"—Jonson was offended to the soul by the playwright who wrote the passion to begin with, offering in its stead,

> deeds, and language, such as men do use:
> And persons such as Comedy would choose,
> When she would show an image of the times,
> And sport with human follies, not with crimes.

Jonson, we know, satisfied the keeper of the Bodleian Library that he was worthy of its founder's vision; his folio was admitted into the Bodleian and listed in the library catalogue of 1620, the only plays in its collection besides Robert Daborne's, *A Christian Turn'd Turk* and Heywood's *The Four Prentices of London.*[13] Nothing of Shakespeare's was yet recognized among the "one in forty" worth keeping, nor would he be until Jonson's lead was followed and he too appeared in folio.

Ultimately, to literary England, 1616 was notable not as the year it buried Shakespeare, but raised Jonson. This was done in the most conspicuous way by King James, who awarded him an annuity of 100 marks, by which he effectively became Britain's first poet laureate. What is more, he did indeed succeed in becoming the examplar for the serious dramatic poet, as he was to Shakerley Marmion. In his elegy to Jonson, Marmion defined this model:

> For whils't that he in colors, full and true,
> Men's natures, fancies, and their humors drew
> In method, order, matter, sense, and grace,
> Fitting each person to his time and place;
> Knowing to move, to slack, or to make haste,
> Binding the middle with the first and last;
> He fram'd all minds, and did all passions stir,
> And with a bridle guide the theatre.[14]

Jonson would be saluted as the England's premier dramatic artist for all of the seventeenth century.

Some idea of what the cognoscenti considered admirable in sentiment and expression in drama is to be found in John Cotgrave's *English Treasury of*

Wit and Language mentioned above. At first glance, it would seem Shakespeare had at last come into his own: the 147 quotations from his plays are nearly half-again as many as from any other's. However, these were taken from 26 plays.* Jonson is represented by 111 quotes, but they are taken from only eleven plays; Chapman is also represented by 111 quotes from ten, while a mere four plays yielded 104 quotes by Webster. However, Cotgrave's laurel for quotability goes overwhelmingly to Fulke Greville, Baron Brooke—63 from his *Alaham*, 47 from *Mustapha*. Greville wrote what has come to be known as closet drama and he left his personal recipe for concocting such plays, which he concluded by deferring to his idol, Sir Philip Sidney, in the matter of stage plays:

> For my own part, I found my creeping genius more fixed upon the Images of Life than the Images of Wit . . . ordering matter and form together for the use of life, I have made those tragedies no plays for the stage; be it known, it was no part of my purpose to write for them, against whom so many good and great spirits have already written.[15]

The next plays that Cotgrave found most quotable were John Webster's tragedies, *The Duchess of Malfi* (46), and *The White Devil* (36), followed by Jonson's *Catiline* (33), and *Sejanus* (28). In fact, Shakespeare does not show up on this chart until number fifteen—*Hamlet*, as might be expected—however, Cotgrave could find only eighteen passages to commend. The other three of his famous tragedies, *King Lear, Macbeth* and *Othello*, taken together yielded only sixteen quotes—as many as John Ford's *Broken Heart* or Sir John Suckling's *Brennoralt* alone. Clearly, indication of Shakespeare's overpowering position in literature is not to be found here. Nor will it be found in the age that was ushered in when Charles II reclaimed the throne in 1660.

Shakespeare in the Restoration

King Charles returned to England on May 25, and not three months later issued patents to Thomas Killigrew and Sir William D'Avenant to form acting companies, under the patronage of the king and his son James, Duke of York, respectively. However, especially for the first several years, the reborn theater had to depend on the plays written before the civil wars and it is no coincidence that they should have turned principally to Shake-

---

* See Gerald Eades Bentley, "John Cotgrave's *English Treasury of Wit and Language* and the Elizabethan Drama," 186–203. Bentley includes seven quotes from *The Puritan* "because the manuscript notes usually say 'Shakespears Puritan.' " These have been omitted here because the play is not recognized as part of the Shakespeare canon.

speare, Jonson, and Beaumont and Fletcher. This may not have been a reaffirmation of their earlier reputation as the "Triumvirate of Wit" alone—they were also the only dramatists whose works were conveniently available in collections.

Killigrew apparently laid claim to all the works that had been in the stock of the old King's company, but in December 1660, D'Avenant was granted exclusive rights to eleven plays, eight of which were by Shakespeare. This turned out to be a stroke of luck for the old dramatist, for Sir William was an innovator. The diarist Samuel Pepys would soon write of the downcast state of the King's players after a visit to their playhouse:

> In this afternoon I went to the theatre, and there I saw *Claracilla* (the first time I ever saw it), well acted. But strange to see this house, that used to be so thronged, now empty since the opera begun; and so will continue for a while, I believe.[16]

The "opera" (more akin to Gilbert and Sullivan than the Italian kind) was one of the great attractions D'Avenant had to offer; Shakespeare was the other, after a fashion—D'Avenant's fashion.

Sir William came by his affinity for Shakespeare naturally—very naturally, if we may believe the gossip-monger John Aubrey, who claimed that he in his cups "declared that he writ with the very spirit that Shakespear [did], and was contented enough to be thought his son." Indeed, his father, John Davenant (William Frenchified the name), abandoned London, as well as the family calling of merchant tailor, to set up shop in Oxford as a vintner. It was in his tavern that Shakespeare is supposed to have been an overnight guest on his journeys to and from Stratford on many occasions. Whether or not Aubrey's report is reliable, whatever the circumstances of D'Avenant's birth may have been, he came by his theatrical standing legitimately.

He succeeded Ben Jonson as poet laureate in 1637 and soon showed a flair for theatrical innovation, which was fulfilled in the playhouse in Lincoln's Inn Fields that was opened for his company in June 1661. The most notable manifestation of D'Avenant's genius was the introduction of movable scenery to a public playhouse. But he also had the good fortune to get the services of the young Thomas Betterton, who was quickly recognized as the greatest actor in Restoration theater, a position he held until his death in 1710. In no role did he shine more brightly than Hamlet.

Pepys saw his first *Hamlet* on August 24, 1661, and confided to his diary that it was "done with scenes [that is, scenery] very well, but above all, Betterton did the Prince's parts beyond imagination." Betterton's genius never failed him, even when, though in his seventies, he gave his last-known performance of the young Dane on September 20, 1709. "Had you

Thomas Betterton as Hamlet. (Courtesy of the Folger Shakespeare Library)

been tonight at the playhouse," Sir Richard Steele wrote of the occasion in the *Tatler*, "you had seen the force of action in perfection." For, despite his age, the "admired Mr. Betterton acted youth, and by the prevalent power of proper manner, gesture, and voice, appeared throughout the whole drama a young man of great expectation, vivacity and enterprise."

Shakespeare's play, however, did not age quite so well. Just three months after Pepys told his diary of his pleasure, John Evelyn told his something quite different: "November 26.—I saw *Hamlet Prince of Denmark* played, but now the old plays beg[i]n to disgust this refined age, since his Majesty being so long abroad." After all, the play had been created for another kind of theater and a contemporary, Richard Flecknoe, celebrated the innovations of Restoration stage, but lamented its effect on plays, old and new alike. In *Love's Kingdom* (1664), he wrote that, in comparison to the bare Elizabethan stage, ours now for cost and ornament are arrived to the height of magnificence. But that which makes our stage better makes our plays the worse perhaps, they striving now to make them more for sight than hearing; whence the solid joy of the interior is lost, and that benefit which men formerly derived from plays, from which they seldom or never went away but far better and wiser than they came.

Shakespeare fared especially badly on the scenic stage, for his plays were oblivious to the classical unities of time, place and action. Indeed, the virtually unadorned Globe stage allowed him to ask the spectator to "Piece out our imperfections with your thoughts." This was asking too much of the Restoration theatergoer, who wanted nothing left to the imagination. Many of Shakespeare's plays demanded that scenes be frequently carried from here to there and back, and trying to give a physical form to all of this jumping about laid bare Shakespeare's episodic structure, his lack of unity. The need for regular scene changes in his plays, observed Gary Taylor, "served as an inescapable irritant, waving in front of the spectators' noses an aspect of Shakespeare they disliked."[17] D'Avenant had the remedy to his this: he would mold Shakespeare to suit his theater and contemporary tastes.

Shakespeare Reformed

Whether or not D'Avenant did actually boast he "writ with the very spirit that Shakespear [did]," he rewrit Shakespeare for the very spirit of his time. He apparently agreed with Evelyn about *Hamlet* and set about improving it. Of the result, the scholar Hazelton Spencer commented: "the exigencies of the theatre do not fully account for the maltreatment of the Shakespearean line in these Restoration stage versions." He summarized these changes and why they had been made thusly: "Two principle aims seem to have governed the editor of this text: he sought to make it clearer and also more elegant. To the Restoration, Shakespeare was frequently both obscure and crude."[18] *Hamlet,* however, fared comparatively well. With a very few of exceptions, the plays that were not rewritten entirely are not known to have been produced at all.

D'Avenant made a hash out of *Measure for Measure* and *Much Ado About Nothing,* which emerged as *The Law Against Lovers,* and transformed *Macbeth* into a version of his opera ("the Witches," Spencer noted, "lose their mysterious flavor—they become vaudevillians"). Some time before 1670, D'Avenant enlisted John Dryden, Shakespeare's most outspoken admirer in the Restoration period, to alter *The Tempest.* In his preface to the printed edition of this version, Dryden generously (perhaps gladly) gave the credit for the most strenuous changes to D'Avenant.

D'Avenant died before he could inflict anymore improvements, but he had set a fashion. Dryden followed him not only as poet laureate, but in reforming Shakespeare. In fact, he reformed entirely *Antony and Cleopatra* into *All for Love*—no mean alteration but a completely original play "Written in Imitation of Shakespeare's Style," which was acted in preference to Shakespeare's. He also made an entry among the Restoration alterations with his version of *Troilus and Cressida*, subtitled *Truth Found Too Late*. What the modern may find most curious are his remarks on Shakespeare in the preface. He begins well enough, favorably comparing him to the Greek tragic poet Aeschylus. In fact, he finds his countryman superior in every way but one: in the age of Aeschylus "the Greek tongue was arrived to its full perfection," whereas English still lacked a "perfect grammar" in Dryden's time. This did not prevent Dryden from finding contemporary English superior to Shakespeare's. Indeed,

> the tongue in general is so much refined since Shakespeare's time, that many of his words, and more of his phrases, are scarce intelligible. And of those which we understand, some are ungrammatical, others coarse; and his whole style is pestered with figurative expressions, that it is as affected as it is obscure.

So much for the beauties of Shakespeare's language. Of his artistry Dryden allowed that "there appeared in some places of it, the admirable genius of the author," but on the whole it was necessary "to remove that heap of rubbish, under which many excellent thoughts lay wholly buried." To accomplish this he "new modeled the plot; threw out many unnecessary persons [and] improved those characters which were begun and left unfinished."

When Dryden converted to Roman Catholicism and wrote in praise of the soon-to-be deposed King James II, he was deprived of the office of laureate, which was passed to Thomas Shadwell—still another Shakespeare adapter. In 1674, he had added music to the D'Avenant-Dryden *Tempest* and thus turned it into a full-blown Restoration opera. Like Dryden, he tried a solo adaptation, selecting *Timon of Athens* as his victim. The most interesting feature of this work for these purposes is the quarto title-page declaration that at his hands *Timon* had been "Made Into a Play." That there can be no question this was Shadwell's personal opinion, in his dedication to the Duke of Buckingham he wrote:

> I am now to present your grace with this History of *Timon*, which you were pleased to tell me you liked, and it is the more worthy of you since it has the inimitable hand of Shakespeare in it, which never made more masterly strokes than in this. Yet, I can truly say, I have made it into a Play.

Opening scene of the operatic *Tempest*. This engraving from Nicholas Rowe's 1709 edition of Shakespeare's plays depicts the stage set of *The Tempest* as adapted by D'Avenant and Dryden, to which music was added by Thomas Shadwell in 1674. An edition of this version was printed in that year which described the scene in detail:

> a thick Cloudy sky, a very Rocky Coast, and a Tempestuous Sea in perpetual Agitation. This Tempest (supposed to be raised by Magick) has many dreadful Objects in it, as several Spirits in horrid shapes flying down amongst the Sailers, then rising and crossing in the Air.

(Courtesy of the Folger Shakespeare Library)

The title page of the D'Avenant–Dryden *Macbeth* (1674). (Courtesy of the Folger Shakespeare Library)

MACBETH,
A
TRAGÆDY.
With all the
ALTERATIONS,
AMENDMENTS,
ADDITIONS,
AND
NEW SONGS.

As it's now Acted at the Dukes Theatre.

First Edition.

LONDON;
Printed for P. Chetwin, and are to be Sold by most Booksellers, 1674.

It is left to our imaginations to know what it was looked upon as being before Shadwell turned himself loose on it.

Shadwell's successor as poet laureate, Nahum Tate, had three adaptations to his credit: *Richard II, Coriolanus* and, the most notorious of all Restoration adaptations, *King Lear.* Tate especially disliked unhappy heroes and unhappy endings and he was determined that this play "conclude in a success to the innocent distressed persons." The alternative was too terrible to contemplate: "Otherwise I must have encumbered the stage with dead bodies, which makes many tragedies conclude with unseasonable jests." To prevent this catastrophe, Tate had the

> good fortune to light on one expedient to rectify what was wanting in the regularity and probability of the tale, which was to run through the whole [play], a love betwixt Edgar and Cordelia, that never chang'd word with each other in the original.

In the end, the noble Duke of Albany delivers all of the kingdom (save his well-earned marriage portion) to Lear, who in turn consigns it to Cordelia. For himself he wishes nothing more than a cool cell where he may retire with Gloucester and happily live away what ever-after they have left to live. Thus could Edgar triumphantly conclude the play with the reassuring observation "That Truth and Virtue shall at last succeed"—a cheerful alternative to his gloomy speech and the dead march that ends Shakespeare's *Lear.*

Shakespeare's Edgar lamented, "the worst is not, / So long as we can say, 'This is the worst.' " When it comes to Restoration adaptations, we can say Tate's *Lear* is *the* worst. Not that others didn't try; they just were not left plays so high to bring so low. But they were industrious. The adaptations by Tate and the three other poets laureate account for damage wrought upon only eleven plays. Eleven more were maimed and deformed by others of lesser standing. Another eight are not known to have been acted at all. In stark contrast, William van Lennep's survey of the plays on the Restoration stage revealed that 120 old plays entered the repertoire in a "relatively unaltered state." [19]

In Praise of Shakespeare

To be sure, Shakespeare was praised both before and after the civil wars. Prominent in this chorus of acclaim were Ben Jonson and John Dryden, the outstanding figures in literature of their respective eras. However, both tempered their praise of Shakespeare the artist with criticism of his art.

In Jonson's case, this could have a comical affect. He divulged his private opinion of Shakespeare's work in a note entitled *De Shakespeare nostrati,* published after his death in *Timber; or, Discoveries Made upon Men and Matter* (1641). Here kudos and condemnation tumble out together; Shakespeare indeed, "had an excellent fantasy; brave notions, and gentle expressions: wherein he flowed with that facility, that sometime[s] it was necessary he should be stopped." But, with an almost visible shrug of the shoulders, Jonson allowed that "he redeemed his vices with his virtues. There was ever more in him to be praised then to be pardoned."[20]

Similarly, in his essay *Of Dramatic Poesy* (1668), Dryden held that Shakespeare "of all modern, and perhaps ancient poets, had the largest and most comprehensive soul," and at the height of his power, "All the images of nature were still present in him . . . when he describes anything, you more than see it, you feel it too." On the other hand, "He is many times flat, insipid; his comic wit degenerating into clenches, his serious swelling into bombast." Nevertheless, he concludes of Shakespeare, "he is always great when some great occasion is presented to him." In contrast, Dryden here declared Jonson to have been "the greatest man of the last age," and held him to be "the most learned and judicious writer which any theatre ever had."[21] By and large, most in that century agreed.

In his study of the reputations of Shakespeare and Jonson in their own century, Gerald Eades Bentley found that,

> Not only was Jonson mentioned oftener, quoted oftener, and praised oftener, but his individual plays and poems were named more frequently than Shakespeare's though his canon is smaller.

Indeed, according to his tally of allusions to the works of both authors, six of Jonson's plays (as well as his masques and poems) outnumber Shakespeare's earliest entry, *The Tempest,* which probably owes no little part of its position to allusions to the D'Avenant-Dryden-Shadwell version.[22] Needless to say, Bentley's figures have not gone unchallenged by loyal Shakespeareans—not without some cause.

Bentley and his critics used the words reputation and popularity interchangeably. As in Cotgrave's compilation of quotations, Jonson's tragedies, *Catiline* and *Sejanus,* are far better represented than any play of Shakespeare's in Bentley's computations, but neither was well received in the playhouse. (In his dedication to *Sejanus,* Jonson wrote that the play "suffered no less violence here, than the subject of it did from the rage of the people of Rome.")[23] However, in his comedies, Jonson was most often able to alloy his stagecraft with his principles of literary decorum, pleasing the grounding and the judicious alike. Add to this his standing in court and among the scholarly, his skill in creating the image of a literary artist and casting himself as that very image, and it should be recognized that he earned his reputation in his century. But this is not to say he was its most popular playwright.

Bentley did indeed discard such as the number of the editions of the plays of the two dramatists in compiling his statistics. In the *Shakespeare Quarterly*, David L. Frost noted that, from 1594 to 1700, there were 89 printings of 23 Shakespeare quartos (an average of 3.87 per play), compared to only 22 of thirteen Jonson plays (an average of 1.69). Furthermore, there were four printings of the Shakespeare folio to the three comprehensive Jonson collections. Frost endorses W. W. Greg's reasonable observation that "writers might praise and quote Jonson; it was Shakespeare that people read."[24]

More to the point, it was Shakespeare that they preferred to see. This is clearly heard in the commendatory verses by Leonard Digges that were affixed to the 1640 edition of Shakespeare's poems. Digges, who may be remembered as having written verses for the First Folio, died in 1635, but left behind a lengthy poem, half of which is given over to the drawing power of Shakespeare's plays in the theater, using the artful Jonson's for comparison:

> So have I seen, when Caesar would appear,
> And on the stage, at half-sword parley were,
> Brutus and Cassius: oh how the audience
> Were ravish'd, with what wonder they went thence;
> When some new day they would not brook a line,
> Of tedious (though well laboured) *Catiline*,
> *Sejanus* too was irksome; they priz'd more
> Honest Iago, or the jealous Moor.
> And though the Fox *[Volpone]* and subtle *Alchemist*,
> Long intermitted could not quite be missed,
> Though these have shamed all the ancients, and might raise,
> Their author's merit with a crown of bays.[25]

Dryden apparently knew of Shakespeare's greater popularity among the general run of theatergoers in the earlier time, remarking that "however others are now generally preferred before him, yet the age wherein he lived, which had contemporaries with him Fletcher and Jonson, never equalled them to him in their esteem."[26]

Perhaps, at least in relation to Jonson, things may not have been all that different in Dryden's own time. Aphra Behn, the first woman to have made a living from her writings, prefaced the edition of her play *The Dutch Lover* (1673) with an outspoken, no-nonsense epistle, which even pokes fun at the effusive style of address that was then the fashion, "Good, Sweet, Honey, Sugar-Candied Reader" (adding wryly, "Which I think is more than anyone has called you yet"). Eventually, she trained her sights on those who worshiped learned Ben by contrasting the pleasures of Jonson and Shakespeare in performance:

> I have seen a man, the most severe of Jonson's sect, sit with his hat removed, less than a hair's breadth from one sullen posture for almost three hours at *The Alchemist;* who at that excellent play of *Harry the Fourth* (which yet I hope is far enough from farce) hath very hardly kept his doublet whole; but affectation hath always had a greater share both in the action and discourse of men than truth and judgment have.[27]

Her choice of a play is important, for *Henry IV* was one of those that had not been altered and it was, therefore, unadorned Shakespeare that the devout Jonsonian was enjoying.

Indeed, for all the praise heaped upon Jonson, it would seem that he was already in the grip of what T. S. Eliot, in writing of him, called a "conspiracy of approval": "damned by the praise that quenches all desire to read the book . . . afflicted by the imputation of virtues which excite the least pleasure." Its effects were marked by the last two decades of the seventeenth century, when Bentley found the Shakespearean allusions caught up with and passed Jonson's. But even then, Bentley notes, Jonson was "still called great more often than Shakespeare."[28]

However, drawing the battle lines so exclusively between Shakespeare and Jonson does not give a complete picture of the standing of English Renaissance dramatists in either half of that century—especially not when it is painted without Beaumont and Fletcher, the "Gemini" of drama who, with Shakespeare and Jonson, were dubbed the "Triumvirate of Wit" by Sir John Denham, himself a playwright. In fact, when Shakespeare, Jonson, or both, were saluted as the standard of dramatic excellence, Beaumont and Fletcher were usually in their company.

They were a "Gemini" indeed. Contemporaries most often mentioned them in one breath, publishers most often put both names on the title page of a quarto, although Beaumont is present in only thirteen of the more than fifty works of "Beaumont and Fletcher" that have survived. Their happiest collaboration was *Philaster,* which was a great success for the King's Men about 1609 and put them in demand with this elite troupe. Thus, in the Revels Account for 1611–12, there is the first record of the King's players performing one of their plays at court, *A King and No King,* played on December 26, 1611. Just one year later they would account for four of the plays set before the king. However, the repertory was still dominated by Shakespeare, who was represented by seven. This was to be reversed entirely in the next decade.

For many years the records do not name the plays presented at court, just the number. But in those years that are complete, there is no question that Beaumont and Fletcher had become the overwhelming favorites. Like their debut season ten years earlier, the 1621–22 season was a spare one and the King's Men put on only six plays; four were by the pair—none were Shakespeare's. In the far more productive 1630–31 season, they accounted for ten of the twenty plays—Shakespeare only one. In all, from 1615 to the last court performance before the civil wars on January 6, 1642, of the 114 plays at court identified by name, 41 were by Beaumont and Fletcher, only fifteen by Shakespeare, Jonson a mere seven.[29] Of course, we do not have any similar records for this period of the King's Men's public performances at the Globe and Blackfriars. There is reason to believe that Shakespeare held his own against them no less than Jonson on the popular stage of the earlier era. But this was definitely not the case in the four decades after the Restoration.

The Restoration stage was not as "popular" as the one Shakespeare wrote for. There was no pit, like the Globe's, where the groundlings could see a play for a penny. The scenery and orchestra introduced by D'Avenant were costly and made it necessary to set the price of admission above what the Restoration apprentice or student could afford. Besides, it was a theater designed to appeal to a more uniformly "better sort"—and Beaumont and Fletcher were most appealing to them. Although Dryden had made Shakespeare and Jonson the mighty opposites of theatrical style, he gave Beaumont and Fletcher the broad middle ground. Of the pair, Dryden declared, "I am apt to believe the English language in them arrived to its highest perfection." However, the most important claim that he makes for them is that "Their plays are now the most pleasant and frequent entertainments of the stage; two of theirs being acted through the year for one of Shakespeare's or Jonson's."[30] This is borne out by performance records.

William van Lennep, in his introduction to a collection of performance records from 1660 to 1700, found that "whereas half of the works in the Beaumont-Fletcher canon came into the repertory in the opening years of the Restoration, the plays of Shakespeare appeared a few at a time, with some of these soon discarded."[31] At least 39 of their plays were acted and, what is more remarkable, most were produced without alterations for most of this period. Only seven of Jonson's plays are known to have been performed in London, but these too were largely as he had written them. Only in Shakespeare's case did Restoration theater managers consider it necessary to alter his plays massively for them to be palatable to their audiences.

Further testimony to the strength of Beaumont and Fletcher throughout the entire seventeenth century is to be found in the quarto editions of their plays. As we have seen, Shakespeare was published in 89 editions of 23 plays between 1594 and 1700. The King's Men had greater success in keeping Beaumont and Fletcher from the press and only sixteen of their plays were printed before the closing of the theaters in 1642. Most were very popular, all but one running to multiple editions (the exception happens to be *The Two Noble Kinsmen,* the play Fletcher wrote with Shakespeare). After the Restoration, two more, taken from the 1647 folio, were published in quarto. In all, there were 71 editions of eighteen plays by 1700—an average of 3.94 per play, slightly better than Shakespeare's 3.87.

Even more impressive, eleven of their sixteen previously published plays were reprinted during the Restoration era without alterations, compared to only two virtually unaltered Shakespeare plays, *Othello* and *Henry IV, Part One.* Two other plays by Shakespeare were printed during the Restoration from folio texts, *Julius Caesar* and *Macbeth.* The latter is particularly interesting. In the first edition of 1673, its author was definitely not the attraction and Shakespeare is mentioned nowhere in the book. Although the text was virtually the same as the folio's, its publisher, William Cademan, wanted the buyer to think this was the version "Acted at the Duke's Theatre," and it did have three songs from D'Avenant's production. For their part, the acting company would not permit this scanty text with its inelegant language to pass for their spectacular and in the next year their text—"With all the Alteration, Amendments, Additions, and New Songs"—was published. The original author goes unnoticed still.

William Shakespeare has been for so long placed so high above his contemporaries—indeed, so high above all who ever put pen to paper—that the notion he could ever have been viewed as anything but an Ossa amongst warts seems impossible for us to imagine—and accept—today. However, in the Golden Age he *was* but one in the Triumvirate of Wit; the playwright who brought drama to its highest pitch before the wave of neoclassicism set in.

Furthermore, the Restoration was clearly anything but a restoration as far as Shakespeare was concerned. He had the good fortune early on to fall into the hands of the most successful theater-man of the day, what today we would call a showman, and he did keep the Shakespeare name before the public. But the criticism of him as a literary artist intensified, while the plays that pleased audiences before the civil wars had to be, for the most part, completely refashioned to please the Restoration theatergoer. At best, the Restoration praised Shakespeare and buried him. His apotheosis would have to wait until well into the next century. This would be a "sea change" indeed—"Nothing of him that doth fade," but was instead turned "Into something rich and strange." What the the last four decades of the 1600s did to Shakespeare's plays, the last four decades of the 1700s would do to the author himself.

⇁ 8 ⇽

The Bard before Bardolatry

A t the dawn of the eighteenth century, the possibility that Shakespeare would be the brightest star in its twilight seemed remote indeed. How the man who created by the "mere Light of Nature" exploded into a supernova is critical to the authorship controversy. Ironically, this transformation may be owed to nothing so much as the state of the early quarto and folio texts. One can only wonder how his reputation would stand if his plays had survived in texts as well edited as Jonson's. Or if the First Folio, like the 1647 Beaumont and Fletcher Folio, had consisted of only unpublished plays of which there were no maimed or deformed quartos for comparison. For it was correcting the real and perceived flaws in his texts in what became the pursuit of the "perfect edition of the plays of Shakespeare" that began the nearly total reversal in his critical standing.

These editorial tasks were not taken on by obscure academic scholars, but by some of the leading literary figures of the day. He would be freed from the strictures of Aristotle, only to be bound over to many masters—his genius resting with successive editors, each possessed of the unique insight into the true meaning his predecessors lacked utterly; what a contemporary writer said of one could be said of many: "A professed critic has a right to declare that his author wrote whatever he thinks he should have written, with as much positiveness as if he had been at his elbow."[1] This comment reflects the rivalries between competing editors, which delighted both the literary world and the reading public. The literary folk, however, would eventually put aside their differences to unite against a common foe—the actors—which turned into a more general rivalry between the scholars and the actors, and their respective partisans.

Of course these editors did not create the perfect edition—that is yet to be done. But their efforts did serve to focus attention on the actual texts (rather than the ersatz versions presented on the stage), and by this intense

The Infant Shakespeare Attended by Nature and the Passions. *This engraving made after the painting by George Romney was commissioned for a London shrine of the Cult of Shakespeare, James Boydell's Shakespeare Gallery, where more than 150 pictures depicting characters and scenes from the plays were exhibited between 1789 and 1804. (Courtesy of the Folger Shakespeare Library)*

study discovered and publicized beauties that overwhelmed the faults. In the process, the flaws of the author began to undergo a transformation as well: the man who was said to have worked by the "mere Light of Nature" at the beginning of the century, would be depicted at its end as one for whom at birth Nature withdrew her veil to reveal her countenance "in complaisance to her favorite child." This was a reflection of the newest rivalry—for the perfect edition of Shakespeare no longer, but for the perfect Shakespeare.

The Editions of Rowe and Pope

Shakespeare's transformation was begun innocently enough by Jacob Tonson. He specialized in publishing collections of famous writers, from those of antiquity to such Restoration favorites as the playwrights William Congreve, Thomas Otway, and the multi-faceted Dryden. In 1709 the additions to his catalogue were Mathew Prior, Sir John Denham, Sir John Suckling and William Shakespeare.[2] Since Shakespeare wrote plays, Tonson apparently reasoned that a proper editor should be a playwright himself. Accordingly, he dipped into the depleted ranks of current dramatists and chose Nicholas Rowe who, as one might expect, approached his editorial chores like a dramatist. He began with the basics, listing the dramatis personae for each play and dividing it into acts and scenes. In addition, in the current fashion, he gave each scene a location ("A Street," "A Palace," "A Prison," and so on), regularized the names of the characters in speech prefixes and added stage directions that were missing. However, when it came to editing the texts themselves, Rowe had barely a clue.

In his dedication to the Duke of Somerset, Rowe spoke with justified modesty about his textual accomplishments:

> I have taken some care to redeem him from the injuries of former impressions. I must not pretend to have restored this work to the exactness of the author's original manuscripts. Those are lost, or, at least, are gone beyond any inquiry I could make; so that there was nothing left but to compare the several editions, and give the true reading as well as I could from thence. This I have endeavoured to do pretty carefully, and rendered very many places intelligible that were not so before.

In this last aim he did succeed from time to time. For instance, when Ross tells Macbeth of how Duncan received news of his victories in act one, scene three, the folios had it, "as thick as tale / Can post with post." Rowe emended this to, "As thick as hail / Came post with post"—a reading that is still accepted. On the other hand, Rowe's principal source for the texts was the very worst of the folios—the fourth of 1685. If he had access to

The frontispiece in volume 1 of Nicholas Rowe's 1709 edition of *The Works of Mr. William Shakespear*. The cameo picture is after the "Chandos painting" of Shakespeare. (Courtesy of the Folger Shakespeare Library)

any of the individual editions printed during Shakespeare's lifetime they are not in evidence (though D'Avenant's *Hamlet* is).

Rowe's most notable achievement was his effort to assemble some sort of life for Shakespeare, for which he relied heavily on Thomas Betterton, whose "veneration for Shakespeare" had set him wandering in Warwickshire, there "to gather up what remains he could of a name for which he had so great value." Alas, he did not venerate Shakespeare so much that he did not feel obliged to reiterate his hero's disregard of dramatic decorum; to him is owed the remark that he "lived under a kind of mere Light of Nature . . . in a state of almost universal license and ignorance." *

At long last, someone wearied of the neo-classical stick that Shakespeare had been beaten with for decades. This was Charles Gildon. In 1710, he edited a collection of Shakespeare's poetry, but expended comparatively little of his commentary on the poems. Instead, he prefaced the book with

---

* The quotations from the prefaces of Shakespeare's editors in this chapter are taken from the first editions. Some of these are in Beverley Warner, ed., *Famous Introductions to Shakespeare's Plays*, but several are from later editions that may not have passages identical to those quoted here.

an "Essay on the Art, Rise, and Progress of the Stage," in which he responded to Shakespeare's axiomatic disregard for Aristotle by saying, in effect, if Shakespeare broke his rules, a new set of rules were needed. And he just happened to have at hand a replacement for Aristotle's Rules of Unity: Gildon's "Rules of Art, that the reader may be able to distinguish [Shakespeare's] errors from his perfections, now too much and too unjustly confounded by the foolish bigotry of his blind and partial adorers." And, for the first time, a note of privileged knowledge creeps in, for his "Rules of Art indeed are not for any man to whom Nature has not given a genius, without which it is impossible to observe, or indeed perfectly to understand them." Gildon was apparently the lonely possessor of Nature's bounty in this respect. The modern critic was born.

Once he got the poems out of the way, Gildon returned to his favorite topic in his "Remarks on the Plays of Shakespear," critical accounts of individual plays, many of which are followed by "examples of his beauties"—those "fine things . . . as to topics and descriptions, and moral reflections." Nonetheless, on the whole, Rowe's edition was well received in the contentious literary world of the day and a second edition was printed in 1714. Gildon, however, pointed toward the future.

It took a while for someone to pick up on his cue and realize its implications: that the plays could be viewed primarily as literary works that happened to have been written for the stage. Alexander Pope, the greatest poet of the day, was ideal to expound this point of view. In fact, he took it a step further: everything that was wrong with the plays was owed to their theatrical origins. Thus began the division of Shakespeare into two camps: Shakespeare for the reader versus Shakespeare for the spectator.

On the face of it, Pope's proposal for a new edition of the plays seemed promising enough. In 1721, he advertised through Tonson for "old editions of single plays," and did succeed in amassing some two dozen of them.[3] Unfortunately, as one might expect, he approached his editorial chores like a poet. His edition was published in 1725 and in it the texts of the plays came out as so much filler between passages of poetic merit. These were marked for the reader's attention with inverted commas in the margin and, in those instances "where the beauty lay not in particulars but in the whole, a star is prefixed to the scene." Perhaps indicative of Pope's taste, Shakespeare's most quotable play by modern lights, *Hamlet*, is especially deficient in these adornments. His famous soliloquies are unmarked; only Claudius' soliloquy—"O, my offense is rank, it smells to heaven"—had the fine poetic sentiment that appealed to Pope's refined poetic judgment. On the whole, Shakespeare's beauties were more than offset by the many passages that Pope determined needed his ministrations and others so beyond redemption that they were removed from their place in the play in question and dropped to the bottom of the page. For, though Shakespeare had "great excellencies," Pope commented, "he has almost as great defects."

How was one to explain this inconsistency? Shakespeare's ability to be sublime and ridiculous, learned and ignorant? Pope struck close to the truth: the fault lay not in the author but in his profession. Shakespeare was, after all, a player and thus, "our author's faults are less to be ascribed to his wrong judgment as a poet, than his right judgment as a player." His fellow players, on the other hand, did not have the saving grace of being poets at all, especially not "his first editors," Heminges and Condell. They must be the parties responsible for the "arbitrary additions, expunctions, transpositions of scenes and lines, confusion of characters and persons, wrong application of speeches [and] corruptions of innumerable passages."

What the players didn't leave in shambles was ruined by the publishers. "Many blunders and illiteracies," Pope decided, must be due to "the first publishers of his works." Errors of such "gross kind" as he discovered could hardly have been the work of the author, nor "any man who had the least tincture of a school, or the least conversation with such as had." Curiously, the example he lighted upon to illustrate these "palpable blunders" was the anachronism of "Hector's quoting Aristotle" in act two, scene two of *Troilus and Cressida,* where Hector slights Paris and Troilus with the comment that their arguments are

> not much
> Unlike young men whom Aristotle thought
> Unfit to hear moral philosophy.

Hector, of course, lived centuries before Aristotle. Curiously, Dryden in his adaptation of the same play, also wished to remove the onus from Shakespeare for the condition of the printed text, though his villains were the actors: "so lamely is it left to us that it is not divided into acts; which fault I ascribe to the actors who printed it after Shakespear's death; and that too so carelessly that a more uncorrect copy I never saw."

It so happens that *Troilus and Cressida* was a bad choice for exonerating the author of ignorance and carelessness. Dryden seems to refer to a folio text, which modern editors believe was made from a promptbook that may have been emended by Shakespeare himself, while the source of the text in the 1609 quarto, which Pope had a copy of, appears to be Shakespeare's foul papers. Thus, the texts for which his two admirers are determined to acquit him of any blame are from the author's own hand.

196 · SHAKESPEARE, IN FACT

Theobald versus Pope—and Vice Versa

Pope's slight to *Troilus and Cressida* added ammunition to the attack of Lewis Theobald on his edition. Theobald was himself working on discovering "the true reading of Shakespeare," which was published in the year after Pope's edition as *Shakespeare Restored*. In the introduction, he avowed his high opinion of Pope's "genius and excellencies," but mercilessly laid bare his failings as an editor. The critical work itself was devoted to *Hamlet* and, that his "emendations may stand in a fairer light," Theobald felt "obliged" to contrast them with Pope's. However, in an appendix he took aim at Pope's more egregious notions. He had great fun with Pope's idea that the corrupt line on the dying Falstaff in *Henry V*—"His nose was as sharp as a pen, and a table of green fields"—was an extreme example of the damage Shakespeare's fellows had done. Pope supposed that the latter clause was a prompter's note for the company's property man, who he imagined was named Greenfield, to bring on a table at that point. Theobald suggested that this was actually a reference to the Lord's Prayer and emended the line to read "[he] babbled of green fields"—an emendation that has been accepted.

However, he especially tweaked Pope for his objection to Hector's mention of Aristotle: "To shelter our author from such an absurdity," Theobald observed, "the editor has expunged the name of Aristotle and substituted in its place, 'graver sages.'" In a classic of literary one-upsmanship, he rejoined:

> If the poet must be fettered down strictly to the chronology of things, it is every whit as absurd for Hector to talk of philosophy as for him to talk of Aristotle. We have sufficient proofs that Pythagoras was the first who invented the word philosophy . . . and he was near 600 years after the date of Hector.

Simply, Pope was made to look foolish and he was duty-bound to reply. He did so brilliantly.

Theobald became the chief target of his satire *The Dunciad*. This was first published as an unadorned poem in 1728, but in the next year Pope issued his full-blown "Variorum" edition, mocking Theobald in both form and content. He wastes no time, beginning by conjuring how his antagonist would have glossed the satire's title:

> It may be well disputed whether *[Dunciad]* be a right reading. Ought it not rather to be spelled *Dunceiad*, as the etymology evidently demands? That accurate and punctual man of letters, the Restorer of Shakespeare, constantly observes the preservation of this very letter *e* in spelling the

The frontispiece of Pope's "Variorum" *Dunciad* (1729). (Courtesy of the Folger Shakespeare Library)

name of his beloved author, and not like the common careless editors, with the omission of one, nay sometimes of two *ee*'s (as Shak'spear), which is utterly unpardonable.[4]

Pope, however, had already issued a second edition of Shakespeare's plays in which he grumpily acknowledged adopting Theobald's emendations, at least "as many of 'em as are judged of any the least advantage to the poet: the whole amounting to about twenty-five words." In fact, it was more like a hundred, according to Theobald's accounting. Declaring Pope as the editor of Shakespeare to be "absolute unequal to that task," Theobald promised volumes of emendations like those in *Shakespeare Restored* that would confirm it.[5]

The hyperactive world of literary London was not about to let Pope and Theobald have all the fun. Now the Shakespeare wars were joined by the master satirist Jonathan Swift. In the person of "Dean Jonathan," Swift wrote a *Parody on the 4th Chapter of Genesis* (1729), in which we hear that "the town had respect unto Theobald and his Shakespeare. . . . But unto Pope and his Shakespeare the town had not respect; and Pope was very wroth, and his countenance fell." Indeed, quite apart from the superiority of his commentary, Theobald was also popular, and thus when "Pope rose up privately against Theobald, and cast stones and filth at him, and evil entreated him. . . . the thing *[The Dunciad]* pleased not the town."

Perhaps emboldened by the acclaim for his book and the sympathy of the literary community, Theobald abandoned his plan to issue more volumes of emendations in favor of an edition of his own of Shakespeare's works, which was published early in 1734 (though dated 1733 according to the Old Style calendar). Now it was the turn of William Warburton to wax wroth—an odd condition for a divine who would rise to the bishopric of Gloucester.

It seems that Theobald, like his predecessors, welcomed the critical suggestions of other scholars and Warburton was especially profuse. Theobald acknowledged Warburton in about 250 of the 1,355 notes in his edition while praising "the indefatigable zeal and industry of my most ingenious and ever-respected friend, the Reverend Mr. William Warburton" in his introduction. Nevertheless, the cleric was displeased. It is not clear precisely what had incensed him. Was it that Theobald did not adopt all of his readings; or that his help in the edition's preface was not acknowledged (though forewarned it would not be)? Whatever it was, the editor was excommunicated from Warburton's good graces.[6]

This experience with Theobald did not diminish his zeal for spreading the Gospel of Shakespeare according to Warburton. Thus, when the retired parliamentarian Sir Thomas Hanmer devoted his golden years to the attempt "to restore the sense and purity" of Shakespeare, Warburton was happy to exchange notes with him. However, at some time Warburton decided to put out an edition of his own and he was infuriated to learn that Hanmer intended to publish a rival edition in Oxford. Thus Warburton prefaced his edition with an assault on both Theobald and Hanmer (though both were by then dead):

> The one was recommended to me as a poor man, the other as a poor critic, and to each of them, at different times, I communicated a great number of observations which they managed, as they saw fit, to the relief of their several distresses.

Their greatest sin, however, was that they contrived to publish editions that, despite Warburton's mighty contributions, "left their author in ten times a worse condition than they found him." Warburton goes on at some length in this fashion to arrive at the conclusion that "They separately possessed those two qualities which, more than any other, have contributed to bring the art of criticism into disrepute, Dullness of Apprehension and Extravagance of Conjecture." The reception given Warburton's edition suggests that his contemporaries felt he was as generously endowed with those two qualities as Theobald and Hanmer put together.

The most notable critique gained popularity as *The Canons of Criticism* (1748), written by Thomas Edwards. Although specifically aimed at Warburton, it applies not only to the work of earlier editors, but to those in the generations to come. There has been no shortage of editors who have followed Canon II, the editor's "right to alter any passage he does not understand," as well as its kin, Canon IV: "Where he does not like an expression, and yet cannot mend it, he may abuse his author for it"; or Canon V, "he may condemn it as a foolish interpolation." On he went, a full twenty canons, to which more were added in later editions.

Johnson, Garrick, and Stratford I: c 1745

With all the commotion in the literary community at the time, an event that would radically alter the course of Shakespearean criticism and, ultimately, the reputation of the poet might have escaped general notice, though it did catch Warburton's eye. Having dismissed lesser writings on Shakespeare as "absolutely below serious notice," he did reserve praise for "some critical notes on *Macbeth*, given as a specimen of a projected edition, and written, as appears, by a man of parts and genius." This man was Dr. Samuel Johnson.

The work mentioned, *Miscellaneous Observations on the Tragedy of Macbeth* (1745), included a sheet folded into the back of the book that announced his "Proposals for Printing a New Edition of the Plays of William Shakespear," illustrated by a specimen from *Macbeth*. Preparations were far enough along that the format, paper and type had been selected, a price agreed upon, and subscriptions invited. The printer was to be his friend Edward Cave, famed as the publisher of *The Gentleman's Magazine*, who was immediately warned that he would do no such thing in a letter from Jacob Tonson III (April 11, 1745):

> Sir, I have seen a proposal of yours for printing an edition of Shakespear, which I own much surprised me; but I suppose you are misled by the edition lately printed at Oxford [Hanmer's], and that you think it is a copy that anyone has a right to; if so, you are very much mistaken . . . I doubt not I can show you such a title as will satisfy you, not only as to the original copy, but likewise to all the emendations to this time.[7]

The copyright law did indeed allow publishers to claim the works of dead authors as their exclusive property and the Tonsons had staked out Shakespeare for their own. Johnson's project was abandoned for the time being.

For all the critical sound and fury, the most important influence on Shakespeare's reputation was the actor David Garrick. Curiously, he had been introduced to London by Johnson and Cave. Garrick was a student of Johnson's short-lived Edial academy in Lichfield, and when Johnson closed its doors and set off for London on March 2, 1737, young David was at

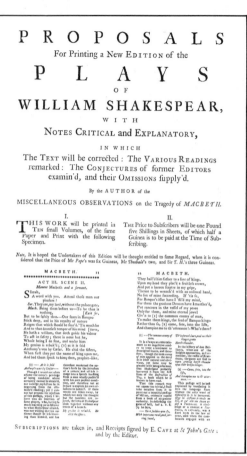

Samuel Johnson's proposals for a new edition of Shakespeare (1745). (Courtesy of the Folger Shakespeare Library)

The playbill of John Ward's benefit performance of *Othello* to raise money for the restoration of the *Shakespeare Monument*. The notations are in the hand of Reverend Joseph Greene. (Courtesy of the Folger Shakespeare Library) his side. Garrick at first went into partnership with his brother as a wine merchant, but his real interest lay in the stage. Johnson encouraged his pupil's yearning, persuading Cave to allow the young man to put on a performance in his shop in the great room above the arch of St. John's Gate. Thus did Garrick make his London debut in what had been the entranceway to the Revels Office in Shakespeare's lifetime.

London was quite ready for Garrick. After Betterton's death, Shakespeare's histories and tragedies maintained their popularity as a sort of antidote to the modern comedies, but a successor to the great tragedian who dominated the stage for a half-century had not been found. However, on October 19, 1741, Garrick appeared on the public stage as Richard III to great applause. The next day he wrote his brother to announce he was a wine merchant no more. His fame continued to grow and in 1747 he became a partner in the Drury Lane Theatre, where he would star in seventeen roles from Shakespeare. He thus consolidated his special relationship with the author in the public mind, and in his own, which would lead to his signal contribution to the Shakespeare saga. But that was well in the future and Shakespeare's hometown, Stratford-upon-Avon, which would be its staging ground, had already staged an event that was a portent of things to come.

According to Oxfordians, Shakespeare's birthplace was indifferent to its famous son until that day when Garrick "came to town and pointed out that a gold mine lay at hand."[8] This not only gets it precisely backwards (Garrick, we shall see, was merely a vein that it tapped), but Stratford first celebrated its famous son 23 years before the Coming of Garrick.

In May 1746, a company of strolling players came to the town and John Ward, "the Master of these Wanderers," prevailed upon the mayor to allow him to turn the town hall into a theater. Their run was extended into September and the actors, to thank Stratford for its hospitality, proposed to act a Shakespeare play, the profits of which "should be solely appropriated . . . to the repairing [of] the original monument of the poet," in Stratford's Holy Trinity Church.[9] At least that is what the Reverend Joseph Greene, the curate and schoolmaster of Stratford-upon-Avon, told his brother Richard, though he himself is credited with originating the idea. Whether or not he did, he most certainly was active in preparing the program, down to writing the prologue to the performance that was spoken by Ward. The play chosen was *Othello*, which was performed on September 9. Greene thought the benefit netted sixteen or seventeen pounds, though the actual figure is given at £12 10s. With these proceeds, the Oxfordians suppose the statue was altered to turn a grasping commodities speculator into an inspired poet.[10]

Their evidence for this is the engraving of the monument in William

Dugdale's *Antiquities of Warwickshire Illustrated,* published in 1656, which does depict a monument almost completely different from the one we know. Why, the figure even seems to be clutching an overstuffed pillow (or is it a sack of grain?—with tassles?), rather than the now familiar figure with a pen in its right hand, its left resting on a sheet of paper. On still another hand, it should be noted that this is by no means the only example of an illustration in *Antiquities* that has fooled moderns into believing major changes had been made to a monument. Aside from the one in question, the most notable is the superb latten gilt effigy on the tomb of Richard Beauchamp, Earl of Warwick, in the Church of St. Mary in Warwick. Comparing Dugdale to the present effigy, it would seem that its supplicating hands were moved and the earl was given a new head in the wholesale restoration of his chapel, begun in 1674. But, thanks to Dugdale himself, we know that no such changes were made.

The restoration was Dugdale's brainchild and he administered the trust until his death in 1686, when he was succeeded by his son, Sir John. They left behind a very thorough set of detailed accounts and pertinent documents. For instance, from early in John's incumbency there is an itemized account of payments for work on the tomb, down to such details as "a new wing to the griffin [at the effigy's foot] & a new tail & claws & coronet to the crest" at the head of the effigy.[11] But there is no record of new work on the effigy itself and there is no evidence anywhere else that alterations were made to the figure. Furthermore, there are similar disparities in many another monument depicted in his volume, including the Clopton and Carew tombs in the Stratford church. On the whole, the illustrations in *The Antiquities of Warwickshire* are most definitely not to be relied upon.[12]

Dugdale's errors in *Antiquities* are typical of the errors, whether of carelessness or license, common to the time. In the latter case, in very much the same way editors felt free to alter old plays, artists changed the features of their subjects to suit their aesthetic standards. And it must be said that Shakespeare's features, especially as they appear in the folio engraving and the Stratford bust, were a prime candidate for such cosmetology. One example of this may be found in Pope's 1725 edition of Shakespeare, which also happens to shed light on whether there were, in fact, changes made to the Shakespeare monument.

The most popular portrait of Shakespeare, reputedly handed down from D'Avenant to Betterton, is known as the Chandos portrait.[13] It had already gained this stature in 1709, when it was used as the model for the poet's likeness in the frontispiece of Rowe's edition (see illustration). It reappeared in a different setting in Pope's Shakespeare. George Vertue was enchanted by the Chandos portrait and when he was commissioned to provide a drawing of the Stratford monument for Pope, he took the liberty

George Vertue's engraving in Pope's edition of Shakespeare's plays (1725). (Courtesy of the British Library)

In a modern photograph. (Courtesy Records Office Shakespeare Birthplace Trust Stratford-upon-Avon)

of substituting the Chandos head for the one on the monument. At the same time, he coincidentally gives evidence that the Dugdale engraving is wrong, for in every other respect, Vertue's illustration depicts the monument we see today. Its columns are not, as in Dugdale, topped by lions' heads; the putti of Labor and Rest sit comfortably on the top of the monument rather than balanced precariously on its edge. Most of all, except for its face, the figure too is the same, one hand holding a pen, the other resting on a sheet of paper.

But was the face altered from the cadaverous image in Dugdale to the puffy-faced figure in the present monument? In the Reverend Greene's chatty letters to his brother Richard, he leaves little doubt that it was not. Richard was by profession an apothecary, but he had set up a museum of sorts and asked Joseph for some Shakespeare items for it. The prime piece he had to offer was a mold of the face on the monument. In a letter to Richard dated October 30, 1773, he tells how and when the mold was made:

> In the year 1748, the original monument of Shakespear in the chancel of Stratford church was repaired & beautified. As I previously considered that when that work should be finished, no money or favor would procure what I wanted, namely a mold from the carved face of the poet, I, therefore, with a confederate, about a month before the intended reparation, took a good mold in plaster of Paris from the carving, which I now have by me, & if you will promise I shall have one plaster cast from it . . . the mold shall become yours.[14]

As the ever-wary Oxfordians are likely to seize on Greene's reference to the "original" monument, let it be noted that he used the word to distinguish it from the fanciful statue of the poet placed in Westminster Abbey in 1740. In fact, he wrote a letter in 1759 to Edward Cave, which was published in the June issue of *The Gentleman's Magazine,* discussing the merits of the two likenesses. The letter is endorsed: "Conjectures in defense of the Original Monument of Shakespeare, in the Collegiate church of Stratford upon Avon, Warwickshire."[15]

Greene had previously had a mask made for James West of Alscot, who wanted to have a marble bust of Shakespeare made by the sculptor Michael Rysbrack. He apparently contacted Greene for a likeness of Shakespeare and was sent one of the masks in return. In a letter to West of January 16, 1758, Greene gave details about the making of the mold for it:

> If Mr. Rysbrack carves your Shakespeare from the mask he had of me, I am very sure it answers exactly to our original bust. For Heath the Carver & I took it down from the chancel wall & laid it exactly in a horizontal

posture before we made the cast, which we executed with much care, so that no slipping of the materials could occasion the unnatural distance in the face which he mentions.[16]

Evidently Rysbrack was put off by the features of the bust and the sculpture he completed in 1760 shows a pensive Shakespeare that bears little resemblance to the face in the monument and none whatsoever to the Dugdale illustration.

There was, however, no sculptor involved in the monument's restoration. The only name connected with this work is John Hall of Bristol, who was not a theatrical manager, as Ogburn's source (probably confusing him with John Ward) erroneously states. He was, rather, a limner, by definition one who embellishes objects with gold and colors. However, we learn that West had Hall make a painting of the monument in its prerestoration state, which has been assumed, incorrectly, to be the same now in the Shakespeare Birthplace Trust; it appears instead to be the one Greene commissioned of Edward Grubb (see Afterwords, pp. 217–18).[17] Identical to the existing monument, it is additional evidence that nothing more was done to the monument in 1748 beyond necessary repairs and the renewal of its coloring. Which brings us to a little-noted climactic year in the apotheosis of Shakespeare.

Johnson, Garrick, and Stratford II: 1756

The most significant harbinger of things to come was the agreement between Samuel Johnson and the Tonsons for the publication of a new edition of Shakespeare, announced to the public in a pamphlet, *Proposals for Printing, by Subscription, the Dramatic Works of William Shakespeare.* This edition would be a work of scientific criticism and in the *Proposals* Johnson described his methods. His chief innovations were to be:

It will exhibit all the observable varieties of all copies that can be found, that, if the reader is not satisfied with the editor's determination, he may have the means of choosing better for himself;

This editor will endeavor to read the books which the author read, to trace his knowledge to its source and compare his copies with their originals;

that by comparing the works of Shakespeare with those of writers who lived at the same time, immediately preceded or immediately followed, he shall be able to ascertain his ambiguities, disentangle his intricacies, and recover the meaning of words now lost in the darkness of antiquity.[18]

The Michael Rysbrack bust of Shakespeare, made for Joseph West of Alscot. (Courtesy of Birmingham Museum & Art Gallery)

The "Hall painting" of the Shakespeare monument. (Courtesy Records Office, Shakespeare Birthplace Trust Stratford-upon-Avon)

He also unilaterally proclaimed a new spirit in Shakespeare criticism. Whereas "former editors have affected to slight their predecessors," Johnson the editor would admit "all that is valuable . . . from every commentator, that posterity may consider it as including all the rest, and exhibiting whatever is hitherto known of the great father of the English drama."

"The great father of the English drama" merely? Shakespeare was more than that to David Garrick. Shakespeare was to him a beneficent god. His blessings helped him to a villa in Hampton and, accordingly, Garrick erected a Temple of Shakespeare on his estate, which too was finished in 1756. Finished, but not complete. A proper temple needed an image of its deity, and so Garrick commissioned a life-size statue of Shakespeare from Louis-François Roubiliac, the most popular sculptor of the day. It was installed in the temple in 1758 and "a dozen chairs were provided for its admirers, who might be served tea under its very shadow."[19]

However, the idol had a flaw: there were blue veins in the marble used for the head and when Garrick saw this he masked his dismay with a witticism, exclaiming, "What, was Shakespeare marked with mulberries?" This was an allusion to the third and most unexpected of the great events. Garrick was referring to the Shakespearean version of the True Cross: the Martyred Mulberry—a tree that the citizens of Stratford believed Shakespeare had planted in the garden of New Place with his own hands. Alas, the property had been conveyed in 1756 to the Reverend Francis Gastrell, who was strangely indifferent to holy objects. Complaining that the tree caused the house to be dark and damp, Gastrell cut it down to a storm of protest. In retrospect, it seems all a part of a divine plan.

Curiously, Gastrell, like Johnson and Garrick, had Lichfield connections; he was a canon of the city, as well as being the vicar of Frodsham in Cheshire. He was also connected to another of Lichfield by marriage. This was his brother-in-law, Gilbert Walmesley, who happens to have given Garrick his start in show business. When Garrick was a lad of eleven, Walmesley allowed him to set up a stage in his home in Lichfield Cathedral Close, where the boy put on a performance of George Farquhar's *The Recruiting Officer*. But it was Gastrell who would, albeit inadvertently, lay the way for Garrick to play eventually on his greatest stage of all—the town of Stratford.

The wood from the mulberry was purchased by one Thomas Sharpe, who fashioned it into all sorts of sacred objects—toothpick cases, tobacco stoppers, inkstands and the like. For all this, in 1762, some six years after the event, Garrick purchased four pieces, sufficient to make an elaborately carved armchair. After a time, people began to wonder whether all this could come from one tree and the suspicion was heard that Sharpe's "curious toys and useful articles" were not all from the True Mulberry. Deeply wounded, Sharpe denied the charge, concluding: "I do hereby declare and take my solemn oath, upon the four Evangelists, in the presence of Almighty God, that I never worked, sold, or substituted any other wood than what came from, and was part of, the said tree."[20] It was the great demand for Sharpe's trinkets that may have alerted Stratford to the Shakespearean gold mine and, accordingly, it was to the mulberry that the town turned for the mother lode.

Stratford needed a new town hall but had only £200 of the £678 for its construction. The town fathers, with enterprise rare for the time, came up with a money-raising scheme that would take advantage of its famous native through his surrogate, David Garrick—if only he could be enticed into make some gift for the new building, it might encourage further donations. At the end of November 1767, Francis Wheler, the steward of the Stratford Court of Record, then in London, wrote the town clerk, William Hunt, with a frankly worded plan that built to a climax:

> And in order to flatter Mr. Garrick into some such handsome present, I have been thinking it would not be at all amiss if the Corporation were to propose to make Mr. Garrick an Honorary Burgess of Stratford and to present him therewith in a box made of Shakespear's mulberry tree.

Garrick took the bait, hook, line, and sinker. He promised the town a bust of Shakespeare for the niche in the north front of the new town hall and, into the bargain, a portrait of himself (in a pose similar to the one of the Shakespeare statue in Westminster Abbey) with his arm wrapped around a bust of Shakespeare (the painting was destroyed in a fire).

Accordingly, on October 11, 1768, Garrick was "unanimously elected an Honorary Burgess . . . [the] copy of his said freedom of the said Borough should be presented to him in a small, neat chest constructed from a mulberry tree planted by Shakespeare himself." The chest and the document were sent to Garrick on May 3, 1769, and on the 8th he wrote to the corporation thanking them for the freedom, "sent to me in such an elegant and *inestimable* Box." In fact, so delighted was he with the honor that he decided to make still another gift to Stratford. Three days later, the following notice appeared in the *Public Advertiser:* "We hear that . . . a Jubilee in honor and to the memory of Shakespeare will be appointed at Stratford the beginning of September next."[21] In his final performance at Drury Lane before the theater closed for the summer, Garrick bade farewell to his audience until its September re-opening—

> Unless we meet at Shakespeare's jubilee,
> On Avon's banks, where flowers eternal blow;
> Like its full stream our gratitude shall flow.

The Shakespeare statue by Roubiliac made for Garrick's Shakespeare Temple. (Courtesy of the British Museum)

The mulberry chest presented to David Garrick. The back panel of the chest, based on the famous contemporary painting of Garrick as King Lear, by Benjamin Wilson (c. 1760). (Courtesy of the British Museum)

Johnson, Garrick, and Stratford III: c 1765

This call for a pilgrimage to the place of the poet's nativity also turned out to be a call to arms for London's literary community. Shakespeare's proper interpreter, as far as they were concerned, was not the actor, but the scholar, for "No ephemeral stage work could rival the eternal values of written commentary."[22] It was the culmination of a sentiment that had been forty years in the making.

It will be remembered that Alexander Pope laid nearly all the faults he found in Shakespeare's plays to the fact that the author was, in the first place, a player, that he wrote for the "judgments of that body of men whereof he was a member," and the "innumerable errors" in the printed works were owing to "one source, the ignorance of the players, both as his actors and as his editors." In other words, Shakespeare had to be rescued from his origins, a point of view that rapidly gained adherents. Thus, when Theobald dedicated *Shakespeare Restored* to John Rich, he would chasten him for holding that opinion, noting that Rich was one who had "gone a great way . . . towards banishing [Shakespeare] the benefit of the stage and confining us to read him in the closet." (Theobald was not using *closet* in any modern sense but, as in Gertrude's closet in *Hamlet*, a private chamber.) A "Strolling Player," identified as John Roberts, rose to the defense of his profession in *An Answer to Mr. Pope's Preface to Shakespeare* (1729), with the pointed observation that it is "as utterly unreasonable to call Shakespeare's judgment in question as an author because he was an actor, as to degrade Mr. Pope's capacity as a poet because he is Pope the Editor."

Theobald and Roberts were voices in the literary wilderness. The justification for textual criticism was the failure of preceding editors and commentators to repair the damage that was done to them in the playhouse. Even Johnson in his Proposals felt obliged to regret that Shakespeare placed his plays "in hands so likely to injure them," especially by passing them along to stage scribes who were "little qualified for their task . . . at a time when the lower ranks of the people were universally illiterate." Johnson did not renew these criticisms in his edition. Rather, he in effect affirmed Ben Jonson's declaration that Shakespeare was "not of an age, but for all time," for he had by then begun "to assume the dignity of an ancient, and claim the privilege of an established fame and prescriptive generation." Like the great dramatists of Greek and Roman antiquity, Shakespeare could be best seen by the light of literary scholarship. To do this, the works themselves had to be cast in a new light.

How was Shakespeare to take up residence with Aeschylus and Sophocles, Plautus and Terence, if he had not played by their rules? Pope had advanced the opinion that "To judge . . . Shakespeare by Aristotle's rules is like trying a man by the laws of one country who acted under those of another." But the belief persisted that this failure alone disqualified him from consideration as an artist. Johnson's was the reasoned and reasonable voice that emancipated Shakespeare from the ancient strictures, declaring that they were supported by reasoning "so specious that it is received as true, even by those who in daily experience feel it to be false."[23] He celebrated the "general nature" and individuality of his characters: "his scenes are occupied only by men . . . even where the agency is supernatural, the dialogue is level with life." This became his fulcrum to free Shakespeare from "judgments upon narrow principals." Were his "Romans not sufficiently Roman," his kings "not completely royal"? Indeed they were not! For Romans were men, just as kings are men, and they therefore partake "of good and evil, joy and sorrow, mingled with endless variety of proportion and innumerable modes of combination."

The spell broken, others rose to free Shakespeare, for once and all, from the neoclassical precepts: "for ignoring the ancients, for violating decorum by resorting to tragicomedy and supernatural characters, and for using puns and blank verse."[24] Johnson provided a framework for viewing these as the workings of a conscious artist, for proclaiming Shakespeare's genius rather than apologizing for it. On the other hand, he received mixed reviews as an editor. It was, unfortunately, deserved.

Although his Proposal had promised that his edition would be available "on or before Christmas 1757," it wasn't actually completed and at the booksellers until October 1765. The nine years between the proposal and the edition were largely spent not in study, but procrastination, and he failed to deliver on the exacting editorial goals he had promised. One critic was George Steevens, who issued a leaflet plainly titled "To the Public," on February 1, 1766. However, he did not take Johnson to task for his own failures in judgment, but because he was too selective in getting the thoughts of others to illuminate texts. "There is scarce a reader of Shakespeare," Steevens declared, who had not come upon something that "may have escaped the researches of the most industrious commentator." What is more, the merit of these submissions should not be left to the judgment of one man, but "subjected to other eyes and other opinions." Nor did he bow to the prejudice against actors. He announced that Garrick had consented to be one of the judges, and he was "no less desirous to see him attempt to transmit some part of that knowledge of Shakespeare to posterity." However, Steevens would not prove so liberal when Garrick unveiled his plans for the Shakespeare Jubilee at Stratford, and he is thought to be the anonymous voice that led the chorus of derision.

In formulating the jubilee, Garrick assumed that, very much as at Drury Lane, it would be his show. As far as literary critics were concerned, this was tantamount to declaring that, very much as at Drury Lane, Shakespeare was Garrick's personal preserve.[25] In their attempt to steal the show, the literary attack went beyond the question of who was truly best qualified to proclaim Shakespeare's greatness. Not even the town that sent him forth into the world was spared.

It was quite enough that Stratford was the Shakespearean Bethlehem— what right had it to be its Jerusalem as well? It was in London that he had flourished; it was the seat of his fame, and its literary lights were now making him shine brighter and truer than ever before. Stratford must be reduced to the Bohemia of *The Winter's Tale,* a consort of rude sheep-shearers at the ready to fleece the woolly-heads who would flock to the festival. Garrick was cast as a sort of Autolycus, luring the unsuspecting whose pockets would be picked clean. A popular mock pastoral presented a chorus of tipsy Stratford burgesses electing Garrick the steward of this festival of knavery:

> Come, brothers of Stratford, these flocks let us shear,
> Which bright as if washed by our Avon appear!
> The coolest are they who from fleeces are free,
> And who are such trimmers, such trimmers as we?
>   Sing tantara, shear all, shear all.[26]

Perhaps the literary men were unaware that Shakespeare's father had himself traded in wool. At any rate, the welfare of the unwary was not their real concern.

Garrick had been formally elected the Steward of the Jubilee, an honor that the literary community felt should have been conferred upon Johnson. But it was really much more than a matter of choosing between two men. It was, instead, a question of who were best qualified to carry Shakespeare's torch, to whose wisdom his fame was to be entrusted. This was heard explicitly in the *Public Advertiser* two weeks before the event:

If this Jubilee is meant to be a serious meeting in honor of the greatest poet born in any nation, or in an age, *why were not literary men* placed at the head of it? . . . Are men of learning the most insufficient preservers of the reputation of a poet? Shakespeare, 'tis true, wrote chiefly for the stage, but does it follow from thence that he is entitled only to histrionic honors?[27]

Indeed, the theater had kept his name alive for 150 years, thank you. But now he was being elevated to a higher plane; the torch should be passed to a new generation, and a new kind, of Shakespearean; the theatrical Shakespeare and the scholarly Shakespeare formally parted company.

Garrick tried to mollify the literati through an anonymous letter in *The Gentleman's Magazine*. Whereas newspaper accounts spoke only of "the pageantry . . . solely calculated for *the million,* who are capable of receiving pleasure through the medium of the senses only," the writer revealed that "our great Roscius" was preparing "a dish of *Caviari . . .* for such intellectual spirits who are susceptible of more abstracted and refined intelligence."[28] For the first day of the jubilee, Garrick was cooking up "a curious discrimination of [Shakespeare's] tragic from his comic powers, and probably ascertain the long contested problem, 'Whether Melopomene [the Muse of tragedy] or Thalia [the Muse of comedy] derives most honor from the labors of the Avon bard.'" The second day's banquet was "An examination of the Poet's versification . . . a discussion of the harmony of his numbers, the knowledge of the rhythms, which he exercised in so eminent degree, and the wonderful attention which he gave to the variations of his pauses." The conclusion of this "intellectual feast," as well as the lighter fare offered to the gourmands, was to be nothing less than "the apotheosis of Shakespeare."

This Garrick achieved—probably beyond his most extravagant expectations. The literati sullenly stayed away from the jubilee, but the mighty and the meek descended upon the little town of some 2,300 citizens. Opinion was sharply divided as to whether the affair was, as Johnson's biographer, James Boswell, called it, "the most remarkable event since the establishment of the theatre in western Europe," or the "farcical fiasco" that characterized anti-jubilee sentiment. In its wake, the worst fears of the literary Shakespeareans were not quite realized: the festival did not deliver Shakespearean criticism to "a Fraternity of Tradesmen." But this phrase may have masked their real concern. Just when they were transforming the poet into a subject worthy of serious scholarship, Garrick was threatening to turn him into an object of pagan worship whose high priest was an actor. In this instance, their fears were well founded.

Jopson's Coventry Mercury, published in that city eighteen miles from Stratford, was traditionally indifferent to theater, but from the inception of the event it was alive with jubilee news. Poems and reviews of books about the festival preceded the event; after it, Garrick's Jubilee revue at the theater in distant Drury Lane was newsworthy, as was any local who had seen it. Shakespeare fever became a contagion. "Sweet Willy-O" was celebrated in song and verse; the plays took on their now-familiar form as books of quotations; his dramatis personae were pillaged for pen names for the authors of letters and articles in popular journals, and their impersonations showed up at costume balls and theater parties. Worse yet, Garrick was acclaimed as the "Best Commentator on Great Shakespeare's Text"; it was he who revealed Shakespeare in all his perfection and thus "scorched the eyes of all be-doctored Bats."[29] A wall was built between the play-

The cover of *The Gentleman's Magazine* for August 1769. Garrick's letter is the fifth item. The magazine's offices were in the room over the archway in this illustration, and it was here Garrick showed his mettle as an actor some thirty years earlier.

BELOW: A ticket for the Stratford Jubilee, September 6 and 7, 1769. The ticket is signed by Garrick's brother George. (Courtesy of the Folger Shakespeare Library)

house poet and the literary artist and, at the same time, between the actor and the scholar. Their last common ground—the preference for adaptations—would soon be erased too.

The Scholars' Shakespeare versus the Actors' Shakespeare

For all the exertions of Johnson and those who followed him to redeem Shakespeare's texts from the earlier eighteenth-century editors, there was not at first any great desire to see the theatrical adaptations swept out entirely. By 1786, 31 plays had been transformed in a total of seventy altered versions.[30] Glory of England though he had become, allowed the inscrutability of genius though he was, there were times Shakespeare was hard to take. Even Johnson owned to a preference for Tate's conclusion to *King Lear,* in which Cordelia "has always retired with victory and felicity," whereas Shakespeare "suffered the virtue of Cordelia to perish in a just cause, contrary to the natural ideas of justice, to the hope of the reader and, what is yet more strange, to the faith of the chronicles" (that is, Geoffrey of Monmouth's twelfth-century *Historia Britonum*).[31] Garrick, for his part, had restored some of Shakespeare's original to the Tate play, but if the *Lear* "as performed at the theatre in Drury Lane" in Bell's acting edition of Shakespeare (1773) is faithful to it, he added just so much of the original that his version, "by judiciously blending Tate and Shakespeare, is made more nervous than that of the Laureate [Tate]."[32] More nervous, but not too nervous: Garrick kept Tate's happy ending, to the great relief of his audiences.

Inevitably, the outpouring of critical works and commentary accustomed the fragile sensibilities of the late eighteenth century to the shocking sexuality, violence and cruelty of Shakespeare in the raw. There were some early criticisms of adaptation, to be sure, but the concerted effort to rid Shakespeare of the pollution of lesser pens began in earnest, according to R. W. Babcock, in 1784. This took the form of attacks on individual adaptations, but it began the movement that rid the stage of virtually all the altered versions during the nineteenth century. But even in its original garb, Shakespeare in performance paled beside Shakespeare in the study.

As early as 1769, Johnson declared that "Many of Shakespeare's plays are the worse for being acted, *Macbeth,* for instance," and he later voiced his doubt that Garrick had "ever examined one of his plays from the first scene to the last."[33] On the page, Shakespeare allowed the reader to pause and reflect, to relish beauties and allow his mind to roam free. On the stage, even if the original text was used, Shakespeare was bounded by the abilities of the actors, the fashion of the day, and the restrictions of time that required entire scenes to be cut and some characters to disappear altogether.

216 · Shakespeare, in Fact

For that matter, if the democracy of the theater allowed the masses to join in the celebration of Shakespeare, literary criticism proved to be no less egalitarian. In his leaflet "To the Public," Steevens said that "a perfect edition of the plays of Shakespeare requires at once the assistance of the antiquary, the historian, the grammarian, and the poet." But he also issued a call to any in the great variety of readers who were "able to illustrate, from his profession, or track of reading, what may have escaped the researches of the most industrious commentator." Many were ready to answer that call and their ruminations were frequently to be found in the periodicals of the day. Even if this rarely shed light on the texts, it did serve to focus a great deal of attention on them by a great many. What they found was, after all, quite wonderful.

What would Shakespeare's reputation have been if he had survived in perfect texts? From the modern point of view, the probable guess would be that, without the impediments and confusion that exists to some degree in nearly all of his texts, his genius would have been immediately recognized by discerning readers. On the other hand, we know the text of *Troilus and Cressida* is, with near certainty, the author's original but, as we have seen, it was the object of critical derision and went unperformed for nearly 250 years. *King Lear,* meanwhile, was simply unbearable in the original; *Timon of Athens* had to be made into a play, *Macbeth* into an opera. The possibility exists that perfect Shakespeare might have joined the plays of Jonson, Beaumont and Fletcher as period pieces—admirable, but wearisome to modern tastes.

As for the adaptations, if his contemporaries were not subjected to such indignities, neither were they regularly altered to keep them in step with current tastes and fashions. Though critics may have continued to admire his colleagues, their works became irrelevant to changing times and ultimately all but dropped from view. Furthermore, in Betterton and Garrick, Shakespeare had the good fortune to be represented on the stage by the two greatest and most beloved actors of their times, which also served to keep Shakespeare always in public view. But then, he helped himself considerably by creating great tragic figures, by providing serious heroes that were scarcely found in the works of other playwrights, while his comedies offered characters whose foibles were not narrowly bounded by any one class or any one age.

Of one thing we may be certain: if there had been perfect texts, there would not have been a Pope or a Theobald and the lively literary set-to they ignited. Nor would there have been a Warburton exercising his "right to declare that his author wrote whatever he thinks he ought to have written," thereby setting off another round of enthusiastic counter-criticism. Very much as the theatrical adaptations kept Shakespeare before a wider public, this energetic debate kept him an active figure in eighteenth-century literary life as well. From all this disputation emerged an affirmation of the truth of Ben Jonson's comment that "he redeemed his vices with virtues," and that, after all, "there was ever more in him to be praised than pardoned." At the same time, we may also see the truth of Samuel Johnson's observation:

> Yet it must be at last confessed that, as we owe everything to him, he owes something to us; that, if much of his praise is paid by perception and judgment, much is likewise given by custom and veneration. We fix our eyes upon his graces and turn them from his deformities, and endure in him what we should in another loath or despise.[34]

By this measure, Shakespeare is deeply indebted to the generations since. But all in account, we are still his debtors. When we discover his genius, we may also feel we discover our own; in celebrating Shakespeare, he allows us to celebrate ourselves. Many do indeed owe him everything.

Afterwords

A Painting of the Shakespeare Monument before Its Restoration?

M. H. Spielmann in his article, "Shakespeare's Portraiture," includes a picture of a painting of the Shakespeare monument. In his text he says that on the back of the painting is a label with an inscription by the avid Shakespearean archivist and collector, James Orchard Halliwell-Phillips, which reads:

> This old painting of the monumental effigy of Shakespeare is of great curiosity, being the one painted by Hall *before he recoloured the bust in* 1748. The letters proving this are in the possession of Richard Greene, Esq., F. S. A., who presented them some years ago in *Fraser's Magazine*. I purchased the picture of Mr. Greene, who is the lineal descendant of the Rev. Joseph Greene of Stratford, the owner of the painting of about 1770. J. O. Halliwell.[35]

This painting was in the possession of the Earl of Warwick at the time of Spielmann's writing, but it was deposited by the present earl with the Shakespeare Birthplace Trust in Stratford-upon-Avon in 1972. With the always thorough and generous assistance of Robert Bearman, senior archivist of the Trust, I have discovered that it is not the painting done by Hall, the limner who restored the monument, described in Joseph Greene's correspondence.

In a letter to his brother Richard (probably the grandfather of the Richard Greene mentioned on the label affixed to the painting), dated February 28, 1787, the Reverend Greene wrote:

> About 40 years ago, an ingenious limner from Bristol, of the name of Hall, being at Stratford on a visit to an acquaintance, Mr. West the elder, if I mistake not, employ'd him to copy the Original Monument of Shakespeare in the chancel of Straford church, with its several architectural decorations, such as its columns, entablatures, &c. . . . This little painting of our great Bard in his Monument, which is executed only on pasteboard, seem'd in length of time to be disregarded by Mr. West; for after it had been toss'd about & injured, not having any frame or guard for it, the old Gentleman, (ignorant I had one painted by Mr. Grubb of Stratford), without [my] asking for it, gave it to me, & I have for a considerable time had it in my possession. I have often had thoughts of sending it to you, could I have guess'd it would be worth your acceptance; but having lately considered it is not so far damaged as to prevent Mr. Stringer's easily setting it to rights, I will send it to you as a small gift, there being nothing wanting but the apex, or top part of the monument, which was a human skull, now worn away with the pasteboard.[36]

My inquiry of Dr. Bearman revealed that the painting illustrated in Spielmann's article is the one now at the Trust, that it does include the top of the monument, and is on canvas, not pasteboard. Clearly it is not the painting by Hall described by Greene. But then, what painting is it?

It should be noted that, although Halliwell-Phillips says that this is the painting of the "effigy" before its restoration in 1748, he also identifies Reverend Greene as "the owner of the painting of about 1770." This may explain the parenthetical mention in Greene's letter to a painting he had made by "Mr. Grubb." Grubb has been identified as Edward Grubb, a stone mason and carver who added portrait painting to his repertoire.[37] He was born about 1740 and would then have been eight years old at the time the bust was restored—it seems safe to say that Master Grubb did not do this painting at that time. On the other hand, if this painting was done in 1770, as the label says, this might mean that Greene had had a copy made of the Hall painting by Grubb in that year. In any event, Halliwell-Phillips died in 1889, before any questions were raised about the bust. Considering the source of the painting, there is a strong likelihood that it does depict the bust before it was restored. If so, it merely confirms what is already evident: no changes were made to the Shakespeare monument.

⇢9⇠

The Claim for the Earl of Oxford

The great frustration of the Oxfordians is that academic Shakespeareans do not pay attention to their scholarship nor address their questions. It is also their great fortune. The questions raised about Shakespeare's "qualifications" to have been the author of the plays, and the doubts raised about the reliability and authenticity of the record of the man and his theatrical career, dominate the debate about the authorship. But just as the academic silence has allowed the focus to remain on Shakespeare, it has also allowed the Oxfordian assertions about their hero to go unchallenged. How good actually are Oxford's qualifications? How accurate is the Oxfordian version of the record of their man and his career?

Of Pen Names and the Cob of Avon

A joke in scholarly circles regarding the authorship question runs: the plays were written by someone named Shakespeare, but it was an entirely different person also named Shakespeare. Except it's no joke to the Oxfordians. William Shakespeare was a different person: Edward de Vere, the Earl of Oxford, who took that name as his pseudonym. But why William Shakespeare, of all names, for a pen name?

Oxfordians propose that he was influenced by the badge of one his lesser titles, Viscount Bulbeck, which purportedly depicts a lion shaking a spear. However, upon closer inspection of the Bulbeck badge, it turns out the lion has shaken it so vigorously that he did break his spear. Which may lead to an even more fabulous round of speculation about Oxford's ambitions. Consider that the earl secretly embraced Catholicism for a time; consider that Adrian IV (1154–59), the only English pope, was named Nicholas Breakspear—the possibilities are boundless.

Another clue that is offered to explain why he should have chosen the

Shakespeare sobriquet is the "heroical address" to Oxford by the writer Gabriel Harvey, delivered in 1578 before the queen and court at Audley End, outside of Harvey's native Saffron Walden. His speech on "the combined utility and dignity of military affairs and of warlike exercises," praises loftily the earl's excellence in verse and prose, but beseeches him to "throw away the insignificant pen, throw away bloodless books, and writing that serve no useful purpose; now must the sword be brought into play, now is the time for thee to sharpen the spear and to handle great engines of war." And again: "Thine eyes flash fire, thy countenance shakes a spear; who would not swear that Achilles had come to life again?"[1] All this suggests not only a possible source for Oxford's pseudonym, but leads Ogburn to suggest that he might already have been known in theatrical circles by the name William Shakespeare.[2] This being the case, we are left to wonder why the name disappears from theatrical notice for at least fifteen years, as well as what the point is of having a pseudonym if the secret is so well-known that it may be so casually alluded to.

With this we have all the evidence that has been offered that allegedly associates Oxford with the name William Shakespeare.

On the other hand, in his commendatory verse in the First Folio, Leonard Digges identifies the author as the man buried in Holy Trinity Church in Stratford-upon-Avon:

> When that stone is rent,
> And time dissolves thy Stratford monument,
> Here we alive shall view thee still: this book,
> When brass and marble fade, shall make thee look
> Fresh to all ages.

And, in Ben Jonson's eulogy in the folio, it does appear that "Sweet swan of Avon" refers to the man identified with the market town on that river. As far as the Oxfordians are concerned, these first references definitely associating the playwright with Stratford are too little, too late. Besides, the River Avon is long and presumably there were swans everywhere on it—including Bilton in eastern Warwickshire, where the Veres held a manor. Here is where the Sweet swan actually had his nest according to Charles Wisner Barrell.[3]

The source for Barrell's facts is Dugdale's *Antiquities of Warwickshire Illustrated,* where he found that this "literary hideaway" was kept by the 17th Earl until "Towards the latter end" of Elizabeth's reign. The surviving records, summarized in the *Victoria History of the County of Warwick,* are somewhat more precise. Of its article on Bilton, Ogburn relays the information that, "In 1574 Edward, Earl of Oxford, leased it to John, Lord Darcye, and in 1580 he sold it to John Shuckburgh, who immediately leased it to Edward Cordell." Despite this straightforward language, Ogburn thinks it is not entirely clear as to precisely what was leased and sold.[4] If he had read on past the lease to Cordell his doubts would have been answered:

> John Shuckburgh died in 1599, having by deed of 8 November 1595 settled the manor on his sons Henry and Francis in tail male successively, with a jointure for Christian, the wife of Henry, who in 1599 was 35 years of age. Henry Shuckburgh in turn sold the manor to Edward Boughton (who already held the portion of Bilton that had belonged to Pipewell Abbey) in 1610.

As we can see, the complete record of the estate covering Oxford's lifetime gives no indication that he retained any part of Bilton. For that matter, there is nothing that ever places Oxford at Bilton physically, not before 1580, not after. It appears that the swan can be securely left by the Avon where it flows past Stratford.

Oxford as a Patron of Players

If, for the sake of argument, we grant that William Shakespeare may have been a pseudonym adopted to conceal the author of the plays and poems from the public, why should this name appear among those of common players as a "servant" of the Lord Chamberlain and King James? The Oxfordians believe that the answer lies in the earl's patronage of the arts—theatrical companies in particular, by which he assumes a position very like that of a modern producer-director. Thus, according to Peter Jaszi, in Hamlet's advice to the players we hear what, typically, "a theatrical patron of the day, such as Oxford, would have had to say to his player-employees."[5] Where he got this information about the backstage role of patrons is a mystery, for the contemporary record about the involvement of patrons in their companies is slight.

The significant exception is a letter preserved in the *State Papers Domestic,* dated June 30, 1599, which say the Earl of Derby was "busy penning comedies for the common players," presumably his own.[6] None of these plays have been identified. In fact, Jaszi goes well beyond what extant records tell us in calling the actors "player-employees." The playing companies of aristocrats would be used to enhance the status of their patrons by performing at court and at the manors of peers from time to time; but especially after 1572, this seems incidental to the main reason for patronage. In that year an act was passed that restricted the freedom of travel on England's highways. A bit of background is useful.

During the fifteenth century, the peers of England amassed hosts of "liveried servants," retainers who owed their allegiance to a nobleman rather than the king. These were the core of the private armies that were arrayed for and against the reigning monarch in the intermittent battles between the houses of York and Lancaster, known as the Wars of the Roses. Henry Tudor took advantage of these bands in wresting the crown from Richard III, in 1485. However, when he ascended the throne as Henry VII, the armies of nobles loyal to York continued to harass the new monarch and in the third year of his reign (1487–88), he issued an order against the maintenance of retainers. Compliance with this, and with other later decrees, was impermanent.

During Queen Elizabeth's reign, the divided loyalties were not between contending royal houses, but between the Church of England, represented by Elizabeth, and the Church of Rome, in the person of Mary, queen of Scots. Much of the nobility adhered to Catholicism and sought to supplant the English queen with the Scots'. An especially dangerous revolt, led by the Earls of Northumberland and Westmoreland, broke out in 1569 and was not quelled for three years. To discourage further uprisings, on January 3, 1572, Elizabeth renewed the statutes against "the unlawful retaining of multitude[s] of unordinary servants by liveries, badges, and other signs and tokens." This statute effectively limited a lord's retainers to household servants and lawyers.[7] The actors who were in service to a peer were not either and therefore could no longer wear his livery. Within six months, a new law was enacted that specifically affected players and other wandering entertainers.

At this time there was only one playhouse in London and players had to travel from town to town seeking spaces public and private to put on their plays. The act of June 29, 1572, demanded the punishment of persons above fourteen years of age without any means of support who traveled the highways of England. Players were brought specifically within its compass:

All and every person and persons being whole and mighty in body and able to labor, having not land or master, nor using any lawful merchandise, craft or mystery [trade or calling] whereby he or she might get his or her living; and all fencers, bear-wards [bear wardens], common players in interludes, and minstrels, not belonging to any baron of this realm or towards any other honorable personage of greater degree . . . shall be taken, adjudged and deemed rogues, vagabonds and sturdy beggars.[8]

It cannot have been long after that James Burbage and five of his fellows wrote to the Earl of Leicester to request protection for themselves, his "humble servants and daily orators," desiring your honor that (as you have been always our good lord and master) you will now vouchsafe to retain us at this present as your household servants and daily waiters, not that we mean to crave any further stipend or benefit at your lordship's hands but our liveries as we have had, and also your honor's license to certify that we are your household servants when we shall have occasion to travel among our friends as we do usually once a year, and as other noblemen's players do and have done in time past; whereby we may enjoy our faculty in your lordship's name as we have done heretofore.

Apparently, Leicester not only acceded to their request, but on May 10, 1574, secured a patent from Queen Elizabeth for them "to use, exercise and occupy the art and faculty of playing . . . throughout our Realm of England."[9]

The actors' message suggests that Leicester may have given them some direct payment ("any *further* stipend") for their maintenance. Leicester, however, appears to have considered players essential to his status. Burbage and company were likely to have taken part in his fabled entertainment of the queen at his castle of Kenilworth in July 1575. Ten years later, players were in his retinue when he led the English force that assisted the Low Countries in their revolt against Spain.

Players in Leicester's service have a relatively full history from 1559 until his death in 1588. This was rarely the case with other nobles—including Oxford. We do not hear of a company under his name until 1580, when the players of Leicester's brother Ambrose, Earl of Warwick, transferred their allegiance to Oxford. The record of this troupe under Oxford is somewhat confused. They were definitely in London in the spring of 1580 and in June of that year were refused permission to play at Cambridge University. However, when we next hear of a company bearing his name, in the records of Norwich for 1580–81, they are called "the Earl of Oxenford's lads," and at Bristol in September 1581, the company consisted of nine boys and a man.[10] Nothing is heard of the adult players until 1583, when several of his players were taken into the above-mentioned troupe that was created for Queen Elizabeth out of the best players of the existing companies. However, Oxford quickly took advantage of an ongoing dispute over the lease to the first Blackfriars playhouse.

Its owner, Sir William More, had been trying to evict two companies of boy actors, the Children of the Chapel and the Children of Paul's. Oxford bought a "sub-sublease" to the playhouse and made a gift of it to John Lyly, his secretary famed as the author of *Euphues*. Only Paul's boys came under Oxford's patronage for certain, and they appeared at court in the 1583–84 holiday season, where they performed Lyly's comedy, *Sapho and*

Phao. Lyly was also named as the payee for "the Earl of Oxford his servants."*

Since Oxfordians find hidden meaning in coincidental connections, however tenuous, the subsequent history of the Blackfriars property is most interesting. More did not relent in his efforts to evict the boys and Oxford seems to have lost interest. Thus did Lyly sell the lease in 1584 to (of all people) Lord Hunsdon, who already had the lease of the mansion house a.:d garden. When the leases on both properties terminated in 1590 and 1591, More refused to renew them. It is curious to note that when in 1596 James Burbage leased the same properties originally rented by Oxford, Hunsdon wrote to More to say that he,

> understanding that you have already parted with part of your house to some that means to make a playhouse in it; and also hearing that you mean to let or sell your other house, which once I had also, these are heartily to pray and desire you that I may have it at your hand.[11]

We can well imagine what Oxfordians would have made of a letter from the earl asking to lease a house near the premises just acquired for his company of actors.

It appears that Lyly ended more than the tenancy at Blackfriars when he transferred the lease. In the Christmas season of 1583–84, "the Children of the Earl of Oxford," performed at court on "St. John the Evangelist's Day . . . at night" (December 27). But Henry Evans, the manager of the Children of the Chapel, was now the payee and the play they put

---

* Irwin Smith in *Shakespeare's Blackfriars Playhouse* accepts the common belief that both of Lyly's plays were performed by a combined Chapel-Paul's company under Oxford's patronage, presumably based on the title pages of the 1584 editions of the plays, which state that they were "played before the Queen's Majesty . . . by her Majesty's Children and the Boys of Paul's," *Sapho and Phao* on Shrove Tuesday, *Campaspe* on "twelve day at night." Attention is invited to the Chamber Account for the court performances:

> To the master of the children of her majesty's Chapel for two plays, one upon twelveday at night and other on Candlemas Day at night, £15 paid 29 March 1584. And to the Earl of Oxford his servants for two plays, one upon New Year's Day at night, the other on Shrove Tuesday at night, paid to John Lyly, 25 November 1584, £20 in all. [David Cook and Frank Percy Wilson, eds., *Dramatic Records in the Declared Accounts of the Treasurer of the Chamber, 1558–1642*, vol. 6, *Malone Society Collections*, 22, 23.]

The performance of *Campaspe* on Twelfth Day night, it does then appear, was given by the Children of the Chapel, which seems to have remained a separate entity, the title pages notwithstanding. Furthermore, of the six other court comedies written by Lyly, the title pages of four state that they were played by the Children of Paul's only. Sorting this out will be left to some industrious scholar with a firsthand interest, which is beyond the scope of this book.

on, *Agamemnon and Ulysses,* was not by Lyly. It does seem their theatrical partnership had already come to an end. Furthermore, after this performance, nothing more is heard of Oxford's boy company. Lyly and the boys were the high-water mark of his theatrical patronage; no acting company of his would ever appear at court again.

In the 1585–86 records of Norwich, a new, presumably adult company of players under Oxford's protection is found, and in 1586–87 it is noted in Ipswich. In an anonymous letter to Sir Francis Walsingham, dated January 25, 1587, the writer complains about the playbills of acting companies that call the citizens of London to performances daily, "whereat the wicked faction of Rome laugheth for joy, while the godly weep for sorrow." Oxford's Men were among the offenders.[12] The next notices of this troupe are in the accounts of York in June 1587 and Maidstone in 1589–90. After this date no players under Oxford's name are heard from until 1600 when, on October 23, an anonymous play, *The Weakest Goeth to the Wall,* was entered with the Stationers. Published before the year was out, the title page identified it as having been performed by Oxford's players. On July 3, 1601, *The History of George Scanderbarge* was entered as a play of Oxford's Men. But there is no notice of the company itself until March 31, 1602, when the Privy Council notified the Lord Mayor of London that his company had joined with the Earl of Worcester's and allowed them to play at the Boar's Head Inn.[13]

The above constitutes the entire history of Oxford's theatrical patronage. For a man as passionately committed to theater as Oxfordians portray him as having been, it is a very spotty, undistinguished record. Ever hopeful, they nevertheless wonder if that is really all there was.

The Lord *Great* Chamberlain's Men?

Ogburn and Miller try to portray the Lord Chamberlains of the Household, Henry Carey, Lord Hunsdon, and his son George, as undeserving of being the patrons of so fabled an acting company as Shakespeare's. They wonder on what grounds scholars have anointed them as patrons of this troupe in the first place. Might they not have been the players of a greater lord, Edward de Vere, who happened to be the Lord *Great* Chamberlain of England!

An example of the Shakespearean assumption cited by Ogburn is E. K. Chambers' statement, "On October 8 [1594] Lord Hunsdon was negotiating with the Lord Mayor [of London] for the use by 'my nowe companie' of the Cross Keys inn for the winter season." Ogburn apparently assumes the writer was identified in it as the Lord Chamberlain and we may imply that Chambers arbitrarily decided that this must refer to Hunsdon.[14] Let's look at the letter itself.

The quotation in question appears on page 63 in volume one of Chambers' *William Shakespeare: A Study of Facts and Problems,* and a footnote directs the reader's attention to volume four, page 316 of his *Elizabethan Stage.* Had Ogburn given his attention to it, he would have found a transcript of the letter and that its author is nowhere identified as the Lord Chamberlain. Rather, this letter "To my honorable good friend, Sir Richard Martin, Knight, Lord Mayor of the City of London," is signed simply "H[enry] Hounsdon."

So Hunsdon had an acting company, but was it *the* Lord Chamberlain's company that was named in the March 1595 Chamber Account? Ruth Loyd Miller constructs an elaborate scenario to prove it was not. In it, the entry of a payment in a formal state document becomes an "ante-dated voucher" for an overdue payment and Oxford, as "the directing head of the Lord Chamberlain's Players had been one of those who had personally protested to the Queen over the delay his men had experienced in receiving their dues from the Treasurer of the Chamber." [15] The very next dramatic entry in the Chamber accounts shows that this story is groundless, the very next dramatic entry in the Chamber accounts is; it reads:

> To John Heminges and George Bryan, servants to the late Lord Chamberlain and now servants to the Lord Hunsdon, upon the Council's warrant, dated at Whitehall 25 December 1596, for five interludes or plays showed by them before her majesty. [16]

The payees, Heminges and Bryan, were unquestionably fellows in the same company as Kemp, Shakespeare and Burbage. The "late Lord Chamberlain" who had been their patron can only have been Henry, Lord Hunsdon, who had died the preceding July 23. Although his son George assumed his title, the Chamberlain's office was given to William Brooke, Lord Cobham. Thus, George Carey bore no distinction except Lord Hunsdon at this time, and thus were the players but "servants to the Lord Hunsdon" when this entry was made.

Miller's imagination was no less active in conjuring a story to explain Oxford's connection with the grant of red cloth at the time of King James's triumphal procession in March 1604. Noting Oxford's need to be properly attended in performing his duties in the ceremonies, "would it not be reasonable," she asks,

> to suppose that when Lord Oxford needed extra servants to assist with special duties relating to the Office of Ewrie, particularly during the coronation festivities, he would call on those ready at hand—men from his companies of actors? [17]

First of all, had Shakespeare and his fellows ever been in Oxford's service, at the time of the triumphal procession they had been servants to King James for ten months and according to the account book, it was as the king's servants, that they received the cloth. However, what is most remarkable is that she cites Ernest Law's *Shakespeare as a Groom of the Chamber* as one of her sources. This little book contains information that makes it certain these players had no connection with the Earl of Oxford.

The material that informs much of Miller's argument is found on pages 7 to 12 of Law's book. On page 10, a pamphlet celebrating the procession, *Time Triumphant,* by one Gilbert Dugdale, is quoted. In recounting that time when "heaven and earth [applauded] the Triumph of King James," the monarch's virtues shone especially in raising the estates of his gentry and peers. But, in further testimony to James's magnanimity, he "to the mean gave grace, as taking to him the late Lord Chamberlain's Servants, now the King's actors." Dugdale's pamphlet was rushed into print to capitalize on the event and entered in the Stationers' Register on March 27. The "late Lord Chamberlain" could only refer to George, Lord Hunsdon, who died on September 8, 1603. Oxford survived James's triumph by two months.

But might not the word *late* be taken to mean *lately,* as in formerly? The very next items in the pamphlet show it could not. Dugdale goes on: "the Queen taking to her the Earl of Worcester's servants that are now her actors, the Prince, their son Henry, Prince of Wales full of hope, took to him the Earl of Nottingham his servants, who are now his actors." As we can see, the word *late* does not precede either the Earl of Worcester or the Earl of Nottingham. A safe guess would be that Dugdale omitted it because they were among the living—which Lord Chamberlain George Carey was not.

The printed plays also give evidence that the patrons of the famous company were the Hunsdons. On the title page of *The Weakest Goeth to the Wall,* the actors that performed the play are identified as the servants of the "Earl of Oxenford, Lord Great Chamberlain of England," while fifteen published plays between 1597 and 1602—ten by Shakespeare—identify the players simply as the Lord Chamberlain's.* Could the full name of Oxford's office, as well as his title, have been omitted so frequently? The printed plays of the troupe of the Hunsdons' cousin, Charles Howard, the Lord High Admiral, show this is highly unlikely.

Four quartos of that company's plays were published before 1596 and in three of the four their patron was identified by the full name of his

---

*This includes the addition of the Lord Chamberlain's company to the title pages of the second quartos of *Titus Andronicus* (1600), and *Romeo and Juliet* (1599).

position, Lord High Admiral; only once as just the Lord Admiral. However, an interesting change takes place after their patron was created Earl of Nottingham on October 22, 1596. Of the nine quartos published after that date, he is called the "Earl of Nottingham, Lord High Admiral" in eight; in the ninth he is referred to as Lord High Admiral only. Thus, in twelve of the thirteen quartos, Howard's position was fully rendered as Lord High Admiral; only once after he was elevated was his title, Earl of Nottingham, omitted. In light of this, it is not plausible that Oxford's title should have been omitted, and his office shortened to Lord Chamberlain, in each and every quarto of the plays ascribed simply to the players of the Lord Chamberlain.

Finally, for all their sleuthing for hidden clues, the Oxfordians missed the clear evidence of the players' patron in the first edition of *Romeo and Juliet*. This quarto, dated 1597, identifies the company that played it as the "Lord of Hunsdon his servants." This indicates that it was printed before George Carey succeeded to the position of Lord Chamberlain upon the death of its previous holder, Lord Cobham, in March of that year. The play, we know, is Shakespeare's. The company, we can be sure, was that of the future Lord Chamberlain, just as it was certainly his father's.

The Oxfordians have clearly failed completely to show not only that the earl was the patron of this company, but that he had any connection whatsoever with this troupe virtually synonymous with Shakespeare.

The Case of the Missing 9th Earl

What "circumstantial evidence" is there in the plays themselves to suggest that the Earl of Oxford was their author? The evidence presented in one history play, *Henry V*, was unsupported, but the Oxfordians have another at hand. When the Earl of Burford was asked at the Washington moot "if he could bring any special insight to the authorship question," he replied, in the words of James Lardner,

> that having studied the family history he found it curious that the ninth earl of Oxford—"perhaps the most conspicuous person in the reign of Richard II"—was omitted from the Shakespeare play concerning that monarch. "The ninth earl created a whole revolt in England at the time," Vere said. "Richard had made him Marquis of Dublin and the Duke of Ireland, and there was a lot of jealousy." [18]

Another case of Oxfordian habeas corpus: as with *Henry V*, nothing proves Oxford guilty of writing the plays so much as an absent ancestor. However, Burford would have been better served if he studied the history of the play instead of the history of his family. For if he had, he would have

Lord Hunsdon's letter to the Lord Mayor of London, October 8, 1594. (Courtesy of Corporation of London Records Office. *Remembrancia II*, item 33.)

LEFT: The title page of the 1597 edition of *Romeo and Juliet*. (Courtesy of the Folger Shakespeare Library)

RIGHT: Henry Carey, Lord Hunsdon. Reproduced from *The Court of Queen Elizabeth* (1814), a version of Sir Robert Naunton's *Fragmenta Regalia*.

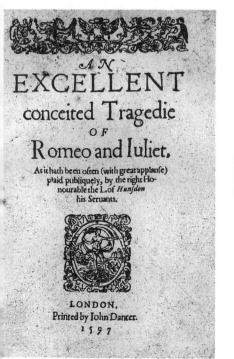

discovered that Shakespeare's audience might have been familiar with his ancestor and the events leading up to Shakespeare's *Richard II* from an earlier anonymous play that has been called both *Thomas of Woodstock*, the name by which it is commonly known, as well as *The First Part of Richard II*.

The episodic structure of *Woodstock* is typical of the early English history plays, such as the *Henry VI* trilogy. It jumps forward and backward in time to tell its tale, covering the years of Richard's reign from 1382 to 1397, leading up to the murder of the king's uncle, Thomas of Woodstock, Duke of Gloucester, in Calais.[19] This will be recognized as a major issue in the opening scenes of *Richard II*, where Gloucester's widow accuses the king of ordering his death, and is thus the most dangerous accusation hurled by Henry Bolingbroke at Thomas Mowbray, Duke of Norfolk, who was governor of Calais when Woodstock was murdered there.

The relationship of *Woodstock* to *Richard II* was summed up thusly by A. P. Rossiter: "the events of *Woodstock*, assumed to be known, have the most important bearing on the moral structure of Shakespeare's play; on the character of Richard, the mechanism of his fall, and the essential rights and wrongs behind the quarrel."[20] The Duke of Ireland is mentioned in this play, to be sure, but he is already dead at the outset and apparently made the most vivid impression on his wife:

> My husband Ireland—that unloving lord
> (God pardon his amiss, he now is dead),
> King Richard was the cause he left my bed.

Considering the king's turbulent relations with certain of his uncles and their adherents during so much of his reign, Burford's ancestor hardly merits the significant place either in Shakespeare's play or in history that he believes he should. The author of *Woodstock* thought so, too.

The Other Lord Chamberlain

In fact, whereas there are no real grounds to connect Oxford with *Richard II*, the circumstantial evidence that links it to Shakespeare's patron, the 1st Lord Hunsdon, is remarkable. It is also worth our attention because, contrary to the Oxfordian picture of him, we may find Hunsdon one of the more appealing figures in Elizabeth's court; an honorable, unpretentious man, in sharp contrast to the giddy, self-obsessed lords who buzzed about her—of which Oxford was for some time in the first rank.

Hunsdon's connection with the play began with the marriage of Thomas Mowbray's daughter Margaret, to Sir Robert Howard. From this inconspicuous alliance would issue a family that had "a roll of honours never equalled by any other English house in ancient or modern times."[21] When the Mowbray line was extinguished upon the death of Anne, the wife of Edward IV's son Richard, Duke of York, the younger of the "Little Princes," Richard III re-created the Norfolk dukedom for Margaret's son John Howard. The title was lost along with his life when he fought for the king at Bosworth Field, but was regained by his son Thomas (the Earl of Surrey in *Richard III*), after his victory over the Scots at Flodden Field. This was not his only good service to Henry VIII. His daughter Mary was the king's paramour, but her sister, Anne Boleyn, became his wife and the mother of the future Queen Elizabeth. Mary settled for a marriage to William Carey; Henry, Lord Hunsdon, was the product of this union. Thus was Hunsdon, by his Mowbray and Howard ancestry, a blood relation of seven figures in Shakespeare's plays, not including the "cameo role" of his first cousin, Elizabeth, in *Henry VIII*.

Lord Henry served his cousin faithfully throughout her reign. His most famous service was as Lord Warden of the East Marches toward Scotland, especially in the suppression of the rebellion of 1569, in which Thomas Percy, 7th Earl of Northumberland, played such an overwhelming role. When the chronicler of the Percys, Edward DeFonblanque, comes to this episode, he gives a most attractive portrait of Hunsdon: "He was a brave soldier, whose honourable and straightforward character forms a pleasing contrast to that of too many of Elizabeth's agents."[22] He later offers a stark example of that contrast in the queen's demands of retribution against the supporters of Northumberland:

> Lord Hunsdon, whose instincts (when deference to the harder nature of his royal cousin did not warp them,) were ever humane and generous, pleaded more than once for mercy to these "pore simple creatures"; but this was not to be, and the scenes which ensued were hardly surpassed in barbarity, though necessarily more limited in extent, by those enacted under the authority of the Duke of Alva in the Low Countries.[23]

At last, he pleaded for leniency toward the earl himself, to no avail. Thus, when ordered by William Cecil, Lord Burghley, to bring him to York for execution, Hunsdon replied that "My charge is but in this town and the East Wardenry . . . and surely I will rather suffer some imprisonment than do it," concluding:

> Therefore, my Lord, as ever I may think ye bear me any good will, or that Her Majesty hath any consideration of me, let some other be appointed to receive him of me either at Alnwick or Newcastle.[24]

Hunsdon would be spared having to accompany Northumberland to his execution in York.

The path of this unfortunate family again crossed his in June 1585, when Henry, the 8th Earl, was found dead in the Tower of London, where he had been imprisoned for adhering to the same cause as his elder brother, the 7th Earl. A bailiff attendant upon the earl testified that he had committed suicide with a dagger, but Hundson deposed to the contrary. He was present on the morning after Northumberland's death and stated that a surgeon removed three bullets that had made a massive wound in his chest.

These latter-day Percys were the descendants of the same family that played an important part in the overthrow of Richard II and in Shakespeare's play on the event. His *Richard II* also happens to be one of the earliest plays that he wrote in his association with Hunsdon's company. What is thought to be the earliest reference to this drama is in a letter from Sir Edward Hoby to Burghley's son, Sir Robert Cecil, endorsed December 7, 1595: "I am bold to know whether Tuesday may be more in your grace to visit poor Cannon Row [Hoby's home near Westminster Abbey] where, as late as it shall please you, a gate for your supper shall be open, and K. Richard present himself for your view."[25] Hoby, incidentally, was the husband of Lord Hunsdon's daughter Margaret. If Cecil accepted this invitation there is no record of what he thought of the play at the time, but in the treason trial of the Earl of Essex he made an apparent reference to its popularity with the earl and his cohorts (the Earl of Southampton among them). As such, *Richard II* was put on at the Globe on February 7, 1601, at the behest of his loyalists, perhaps with the idea that it would arouse popular support for Essex's cause. The deputation that paid for this performance happens to have been led by Sir Charles and Sir Jocelyn Percy, the sons of the 8th Earl of Northumberland.

Hunsdon personally was a straightforward man with a fondness for colorful language. Writing after 1632, Sir Robert Naunton said of him:

> As he lived in a ruffling time so he loved sword and buckler men, and such as our fathers were wont to call men of their hands, of which sort he had many brave gentlemen that followed him yet not taken for a popular and dangerous person.[26]

As one might suspect, this was not a man who would wish the company of the queen's fawning courtiers and their ambitious rivalries. He chose a curious metaphor to explain his desire to avoid his cousin's court: "I never was one of Richard II's men." *

---

* See Agnes Strickland, *Lives of the Queens of England*, 3:540. Hunsdon was not the first to make this comparison with Richard II's men. In 1578, Sir Francis Knollys wrote:

> For who will persist in giving of safe counsel if her Majesty will persist in misliking of safe counsel? Nay, who will not rather shrinkingly (that I may say no worse) play the parts of King Richard the Second's men, than enter into the odious office of crossing of her Majesty's will? [Thomas Wright, *Queen Elizabeth and Her Times: A Series of Original Letters*, 2 vols. (London: H. Colburn, 1838), 2:75.]

He was, however, eventually brought into court life as the Lord Chamberlain of the Royal Household, among the duties of which office were court entertainments, including supervision of the Office of the Revels. There is no record of how the players formerly in Lord Strange's service (with the addition of Shakespeare) came under Hunsdon's patronage, but the possibility presents itself it was done with the intention of bringing this established and accomplished troupe under the purview of the Crown. In light of Ogburn's illusory Herbert theatrical hegemony in the 1620s, it is noteworthy that Elizabethan theater was "hedged about" with Howards when this company came into Hunsdon's service.[27] The other major acting company was under the patronage of another of the queen's cousins, Charles Howard, Earl of Nottingham, while all the Masters of the Revels until 1623 were connected to the Howards by marriage—Edmund Tilney, George Buck and John Astley.

As for Shakespeare's association with Hunsdon, one may conjure the image of the playwright (with the urging of the rest of the company perhaps) seeking to ingratiate himself in his patron's regard by writing *Richard II* to reflect Hunsdon's discontent with Elizabeth's court. Or might he have done this at Hunsdon's bidding? In fact, there is only one certain conclusion to be drawn: in the small world of the Elizabethan aristocracy coincidental associations abound. If only one chooses his facts carefully, one might say selectively, the chances are excellent that they can be made to support any desired conclusion.

The Counterfeit Presentment

Oxfordians like to think they have their most powerful case for Oxford's authorship in those plays where they discern biographical details of the earl's life. For instance, is not the story of Bertram in *All's Well That Ends Well* uncannily close to Oxford's? In J. Thomas Looney's rendition, Bertram is, like Oxford:

A young lord of ancient lineage, of which he is himself proud, having lost a father for whom he entertained a strong affection, is brought to court by his mother and left there as a royal ward, to be brought up under royal supervision. As he grows up he asks for military service and to be allowed to travel, but is repeatedly refused or put off. At last he goes away without permission. Before leaving he had been married to a young woman with whom he had been brought up, and who had herself been most active in bringing about the marriage. Matrimonial troubles, of which the most outstanding feature is a refusal of cohabitation, are associated with both his stay abroad and his return home.[28]

Looney's synopsis, not surprisingly, sticks somewhat closer to Oxford's life than Shakespeare's play; which, in turn, sticks quite a deal closer to its source: the ninth story in Day Three of Boccaccio's *Decameron*. Internal evidence indicates that Shakespeare used the translation by William Painter in his *Palace of Pleasure*, which was first published in 1566 and again nine years later.[29] We have been spared the suggestion that Oxford wrote the *Decameron* also.

It is a fact, however, that Oxford was a royal ward, though he was actually brought up under the supervision of William Cecil, Lord Burghley. According to the Oxfordians, he is impersonated in the part of Polonius in the play in which the earl is cast in the title role: *Hamlet*. According to the Oxfordians, Polonius is an unmistakable lampoon of the lord who was Queen Elizabeth's closest counselor. So satisfied are they that that's a fact, they go on to assert that such audacity in a common playwright would have resulted in the play being censored and its author punished. Instead, they note, it was given the royal seal of approval, signified by the royal arms on the first page of the 1604 *Hamlet* printed by James Roberts.[30]

A minor detail: the coat of arms in the quarto was no longer the royal arms when it was published. Upon the accession of King James in March 1603, the lion of the monarch's native Scotland and the harp of Ireland replaced the old arms of England and the "new" arms of France in two of the quarters of the royal arms. In fact, what appears in *Hamlet* is nothing more than a printer's decorative ornament known as a headpiece. This is confirmed by its appearance in later books. It was passed on to Jaggard when he bought out Roberts, and he made similar use of that ornament in the misdated quartos of 1619, where it is to be found in *Henry VI, Part Three, The Merchant of Venice, King Lear* and *Pericles*. Surely these were not printed with royal sanction. Furthermore, it is also found in the first English translation of the entire *Decameron,* which was duly entered to Jaggard on March 22, 1620, though the imprint of his son, Isaac, appears in the books. Although the work was licensed by the Bishop of London's secretary, the Register entry notes it was "recalled by [the Archbishop] of Canterbury's command." There is no doubt this ornamental headpiece was not a royal cachet.

But then, it is doubtful anyone would have recognized Burghley in the buffoonish counselor in *Hamlet* in the first place. His relationship with Elizabeth has been called "one of the most remarkable partnerships in English history." He was present at the queen's first council meeting in November 1558 and, until his death forty years later, guided her through one of the most dangerous periods in that nation's history. He was rewarded with one of only ten new peerages that were created during the queen's 44-year reign and was one of only two new peers who did not already possess ancestral claims or blood relationship to the queen. He

Letter from the Earl of Oxford to Lord Burghley, July 13, 1576. The earl warns Burghley that he "should not urge further" for the Countess of Oxford at court, declaring "for always I have and will still prefer mine own content before others." (Courtesy of the Marquess of Salisbury) was alone in being raised to the peerage "exclusively on the grounds of political and administrative services to the Crown." [31]

About all that can be said for the Oxfordian conjecture is that it would be entirely consistent with Oxford's character to so abuse Burghley. After all, the earl taxed the counselor for failing to rescue him from the financial straits he got himself into, as well as for not getting him the preferments he sought. But this pales beside the misery he visited on Burghley by marrying his daughter Anne. Abroad in Italy, Oxford joyfully greeted the news of the birth of his first child in July 1575. By the time he returned from his Grand Tour in April 1576, he was convinced the girl was not his. He would allow his wife to come to court, provided that she did not come when he was present, "nor at any time have speech with me." It would be six years before they were reconciled but, despite the birth of two more daughters thereafter, the relationship remained an uneasy one. On May 5, 1587, Burghley wrote to Sir Francis Walsingham of the state of Oxford's household:

> No enemy I have can envy me this match; for thereby neither honour nor land nor goods shall come to their children; for whom, being three already to be kept and a fourth likely to follow, I am only at charge even with sundry families in sundry places for their sustenance. But if their father was of that good nature as to be thankful for the same I would be less grieved with the burden.

Certainly Burghley's daughter was not Oxford's Ophelia—anymore than Oxford was a bereaved Hamlet when his wife died. Instead of leaping into his beloved's grave in an extravagance of grief, upon her death in June 1588, Oxford is not named among those who attended the funeral. [32]

It comes as no surprise that those who would see Burghley in Polonius should see Oxford in Hamlet. It would be a surprise, however, if Oxford's contemporaries saw the earl in Ophelia's description of the prince:

> The courtier's, soldier's, scholar's, eye, tongue, sword,
> The expectancy and rose of the fair state,
> The glass of fashion and the mould of form,
> The observ'd of all observers.

The only substantial biography of Oxford is by B. M. Ward, written with the declared purpose of rescuing the earl from his reputation as "an eccentric of doubtful character and boorish manners." [33] Ward did indeed quite thoroughly comb archival records relating to Oxford specifically and, on the face of it, his biography seems authoritative. Unfortunately, in his determination to rehabilitate his subject, he did not do his research on events surrounding the earl's public life quite as thoroughly.

The Courtier

Let's look first at Oxford the courtier. As in other aspects of his life, he got off to a promising start. In a tournament in May 1571, Oxford was awarded a tablet of diamonds and on the occasion it was reported, "There is no man of life and agility in every respect in the Court but the Earl of Oxford." In June 1572, he bore the Sword of State in a procession of Knights of the Garter and in August was the governor of a "castle" in a mock battle for Elizabeth's entertainment at Warwick. In a letter in May 1573, Gilbert Talbot told his father, the Earl of Shrewsbury, "My Lord of Oxford is lately grown into great credit, for the Queen's Majesty delighteth more in his personage and his dancing and his valiantness than any other." But here we also have a foreshadowing of his undoing; for "If it were not for his fickle head," Talbot went on, "he would pass any of them shortly."[34] Oxford lost little time in confirming Talbot's observation about his headstrong nature.

In early July 1574, Oxford suddenly left England. As if it were not bad enough that he departed the country without the queen's permission, his ultimate destination was reported to be Brussels, the headquarters of the Earl of Westmoreland and other expatriate English Catholics. It seems that he had some contact with them before he was persuaded to return to England about two weeks later. Assured that he rebuffed the advances of the rebels, the queen shortly restored him to her favor, but the "desire of travel [was] not yet quenched in him." This time with royal leave, in January 1575 Oxford left for fifteen months on the continent, principally in Italy. He returned to England a confirmed Catholic.

Not long after he arrived in April 1576, he secretly joined with Lord Henry Howard, Francis Southwell and Charles Arundel, in a pact to advance Catholicism in England. His break with them was dramatic. "A few days before Christmas," 1580, in the presence of the French ambassador, Michel de Castelnau, Seigneur de la Mauvissière, he revealed his cohorts to the queen and asked forgiveness for joining with them. Ward determined that Oxford acted purely out of patriotism. "Lord Oxford had opened [the queen's] eyes" to the Catholic danger, he declares, and takes issue with the traditional historical view that the anti-Catholic measures of 1581 were instigated by such as the activities of the Jesuits Robert Parsons and Edmund Campion. For, though they had been in England "as far back as April 1580," it was not till Lord Oxford's disclosures in December and the Proclamation in January, that Campion was apprehended and sentenced to death. These dates make it clear that it must have been Lord Oxford's dramatic interview that induced the Queen to take the first decided step against her Catholic subjects—a step that Burghley, Walsingham, and the House of Commons had vainly urged upon her over and over again in the past.[35]

In fact, Parsons and Campion, who had actually arrived in England in June 1580, were hunted since they left London in July. As early as August 1580, Parsons wrote, "We are encountering many dangers . . . because the enemy have a special hatred for us who are the first to come as precursors and they are planning every sort of evil for us."[36] In a November letter crammed with tales of the persecution and punishment of English Catholics, he said of his forays into London, "though I have many places in London where I can stay, yet in none of them do I remain beyond two days, owing to the extremely careful searches that have been made to capture me." This same letter reports that Burghley took the occasion of the swearing in of the Lord Mayor of London to complain "publicly in very grave terms of the Pope and the Jesuits, who, he said, had conspired against the English state."[37] Contrary to the impression left by Ward, Campion was not captured close upon Oxford's Christmas presentation but in July 1581; nor would he be tried and executed for another four months.

After all, what was the startling revelation that led Ward to assert Oxford galvanized the queen into action? The only account we have is a letter from Mauvissière to his king, Henry III, and the only charge he relates was that his erstwhile friends "conspired against the State by having made profession of the Catholic faith." Much else of what the letter says the queen told the French ambassador and the French ambassador told his king may be written off as diplomatic posturing. However, there is no reason to doubt the truth of his statement that Elizabeth declared she already knew Howard, Southwell and Arundel to be Catholics and that it was with "great regret . . . that she was obliged to place [Howard and Southwell] under restraint" as a result of Oxford's disclosures. After all, it was no secret that much of the gentry and even more of the aristocracy professed Catholicism. Francis Bacon probably stated her feelings toward her Catholic subjects with a good degree of accuracy:

Her Majesty, not liking to make windows into men's hearts and secret thoughts, except the abundance of them did overflow into overt and express acts or affirmations, tempered her law so as it restraineth only manifest disobedience, in impugning and impeaching advisedly and manifestly her Majesty's supreme power, and maintaining and extolling a foreign jurisdiction.[38]

As for the January Proclamation cited by Ward to justify his rather optimistic interpretation of the earl's behavior, it concerned the "revocation of students from beyond the seas and against the retaining of Jesuits." One might wonder what this has to do with the courtiers and Ward has an explanation at the ready: Oxford is credited with "showing up the Catholic conspirators and their Jesuit accomplices."[39] In fact, according to Mauvissière, the only mention of a Jesuit was of the one "who had celebrated the Mass about four years ago at which they [Oxford and his comrades] were reconciled to the Roman Church."

Oxford's confederates, as Ward says, did undoubtedly favor the marriage between Elizabeth and Francis, Duke of Anjou. But then, so did Elizabeth. The undersized, pockmarked duke may have been the only man she had seriously wished to marry. It was not until 1582 that the Protestant faction prevailed and marriage negotiations were ended. Upon their last meeting in that year, Elizabeth escorted the duke to Canterbury, where she bade him farewell with verses of her own composition, concluding:

> Some gentler passions slide into my mind,
>   For I am soft, and made of melting snow;
> Or be more cruel, Love, and so be kind,
>   Let me or float, or sink, be high or low;
> Or let me live with some more sweet content;
>   Or die, and so forget what love e'er meant.

At last, for all the far-reaching effects on national policy that were supposedly set in motion by Oxford's revelations, it should be recognized that none of the men whom he specifically accused were formally charged with anything. Understandably, Ward and his successors would wish to put the earl's behavior in the most flattering light, but the facts point to a less-flattering explanation for it: apprehensive of the danger to himself in the gathering storm of anti-Catholic sentiment, Oxford felt it politic to protest his loyalty and give proof of it by betraying his friends.

Though Oxford's disclosure placed Elizabeth in an uncomfortable position in regard to Catholics in the aristocracy, he seems to have remained in her good graces and on January 22, 1581, won the prize in the tournament that celebrated Philip Howard's succession to the earldom of Arundel. In two months' time he would be deep in Elizabeth's displeasure.

There was little that moved her to outrage more than couplings, whether or not sanctified by marriage, which she did not sanction. The most notorious incident was the disgrace of the Earl of Leicester when his secret marriage to Lettice Knollys, the widow of Walter Devereux, Earl of Essex, was revealed. However, a dalliance with a woman in her household was the gravest offense. This is amply demonstrated by her actions when Shakespeare's patron, the Earl of Southampton, got Elizabeth Vernon, one of the queen's Maids of Honor, pregnant. Abroad at the time news reached him of her pregnancy, Southampton sneaked into England, married her, and promptly fled back to the continent. When the secret marriage was revealed, the queen ordered Southampton's return and, in the meanwhile, "commanded that there shall be provided for the novissima countess the sweetest and best appointed lodging in the Fleet [prison]." When Southampton at last mustered the courage to return, he was given a lesser lodging in the same prison.[40]

Oxford was not so honorable. His dalliance was with Anne Vavasour, a Gentlewoman of the Bedchamber, as we learn in a letter to the earl of Huntingdon of March 23, 1581:

> On Tuesday at night Anne Vavasour was brought to bed of a son in the maiden's chamber. The E[arl] of Oxford is avowed to be the father, who hath withdrawn himself with intent, as it is thought, to pass the seas. The ports are laid for him and therefore if he have any such determination it is not likely he will escape.
>
> The gentlewoman the selfsame night she was delivered was conveyed out of the house and the next day committed to the Tower. Others that have been found any ways party to the cause have also been committed.[41]

Oxford, in his wonted fashion, abandoned the woman, thereby creating more rancorous feelings, which culminated in a duel with the woman's uncle, Thomas Knyvet, a Gentleman of the Privy Chamber, in 1582.

In the meanwhile, his former Catholic compatriots countered his revelations about them with some of their own—including such tidbits as this from Sir Henry Howard:

> Railing at Francis Southwell for commending the Queen's singing one night at Hampton Court, and protesting by the blood of God that she had the worst voice and did everything with the worst grace that ever woman did, and that he was never [so] non-plussed but when he came to speak of her.[42]

The queen apparently had her fill of Oxford's genius for turmoil and he was at last banished from her presence for two years; he would not be formally restored to her favor until June 1583. This seems an appropriate time to ask just how high in her favor he had ever gotten.

Beginning with his continental escapade in 1574, he displayed no capacity for governing himself, and this is reflected in his career at court, which has been succinctly summed up by Steven W. May:

He ascended briefly if at all to the heights of favoritism sustained by such fellow courtiers as Leicester, Hatton, and Ralegh. In further contrast with these men it is noteworthy that [Elizabeth] never appointed Oxford to a position of trust or sole responsibility. . . . He was never entrusted with a diplomatic mission, entertainment of foreign dignitaries, nor office at court or in the government at large. His sole distinction in affairs of the realm was his hereditary post as Lord Great Chamberlain, an office with very real if ceremonial duties, which traditionally included his presence at court during the five great feasts of the year, specific functions at a coronation or the creation of peers, attendance upon the soverign on processions to Parliament, and jurisdiction over Westminster Hall at the time of a coronation, trial of peers, "or any public solemnity."[43]

The Soldier

It is probable that Oxford the soldier snuffed any flickering hopes of Oxford the courtier. He can be certainly placed in a military situation only twice. The first time was in 1570, when he served under Thomas Radcliffe, Earl of Sussex, during the Northern rebellion. Oxford's service came during the devastating campaign led by Sussex against Scotland in April and May 1570. He is not mentioned in any of the reports of the campaign and in what capacity he served is not known. The second was his appointment as governor of Harwich during the Spanish War eighteen years later.

In between there is a confused episode, one in which Ward labors to elevate the earl's status in affairs of state. The matter in question is whether Oxford had a command in the Low Countries War against Spain in 1585. That he had is the only possible interpretation to Ward's mind of a letter from Oxford to Burghley on June 25 of that year. It speaks of a "suit" by which he declared he was "almost at a point to taste that good which Her Majesty shall determine." This was a prelude to a request for money, for he was "disfurnished and unprovided to follow Her Majesty, as I perceive she will look for, I most earnestly desire your Lordship you will lend me £200 till Her Majesty performeth her promise."[44] We hear nothing more specific about the nature of the queen's promise.

Ward assumes that it must have had to do with the provisional force that had been sent to assist the so-called United Provinces under the command of Sir John Norris, pending the outcome of negotiations for a formal English presence in the Low Countries. For when next we hear of Oxford, a party of his men land at Flushing in the Low Countries on August 28 and, by September 3, the earl himself was in the Netherlands, where instructions were issued for the victualing of Oxford and his retinue, as well as Norris and his officers. There is no further mention of the earl until October 14, when a ship carrying his goods was captured by the Spanish.

By October 21, he was back in England. Ward thinks this was the culmination of "a scheme [that] had been set afoot by Leicester and his party to supersede him." Supersede him as what?

Ward bases his surmise that Oxford had an important command in Norris' army on "a letter from Lord Burghley to Lord Oxford found on board. This letter appointed him to the command of the Horse." Leicester, presumably, had this countermanded and, sure enough, no sooner had Oxford departed for England than the queen signed Leicester's commission as the commander of the English forces; in November Sir Philip Sidney— "with the rank of General of the Horse"—assumed his post as the governor of Flushing. Ward may be credited with making chaos out of confusion.

First of all, the document in question, a letter from one Thomas Doyley to the Earl of Leicester, is principally an account of the detention of himself and the others aboard the ship by the Spanish. They were held for ransom—not because they were declared to be enemies—but

because enemy's goods were found in our ship, namely, the Earl of Oxford's, which they proved by letters of my Lord Treasurer's to him, wherein he wrote of her Majesty's grant of the commanding of the horsemen, which letter one of the Earl of Oxford's chamber brought over in our boat, with his money, apparel, wine, and venison, etc.[45]

Doyley appears to be relating the contents of Burghley's letter according to his Spanish captors and, thus, we cannot be certain just what was meant by the reference to "grant of the commanding of the horsemen." The military position of General of the Horse was awarded, with the monarch's consent, by the commanding general (Leicester in this case), and it was a foregone conclusion that the post in this campaign would go, not to Sidney, but to Leicester's stepson, the Earl of Essex, which it did in fact. Could it be then that Oxford was offered the post of Master of the Horse? Positively not! Master of the Horse was the third highest office in the royal household after the Lord Steward and Lord Chamberlain, and the holder of that office happens to have been Leicester. His appointment is said to have been the first act of Elizabeth's reign and he held on to it until his death in 1588, when it passed to Essex.[46] The meaning of the reference to the "commanding of the horsemen" remains in doubt; but there is no doubt that Oxford was not formally considered for an important position, whether in the Low Countries or at home.

What of the impression left by Ward that Leicester used his standing with the queen to snatch Oxford's glory for himself? Leicester was, in fact, the chief advocate of English intervention in the Low Countries and led the delegation from the United Provinces in state from Lambeth to Nonsuch Palace, where the treaty of alliance was concluded on August 20. It specified the appointment of "some person of respect and quality" to be the English Governor-General and, as Roy Strong remarked, "It is not surprising that even the official documents offer no alternative candidates [to Leicester] for the post."[47] Leicester's position as the commander of the English force was evidently secure before Oxford ever left England. Furthermore, there is no mention whatsoever of Oxford in these, or any official English papers regarding the Low Countries, any more than there is any record of his having taken part in military actions. Under any circumstances, precisely what Oxford was doing in the Low Countries in the first place is uncertain.

We do, on the other hand, have a good record of Oxford's activities during the war against the Spanish Armada in 1588—good enough to show that Ward's account is a hopeful fiction. Citing Camden as his source, he says that Oxford "fitted out a ship at his own expense" and "took part in the fighting during the early days of the encounter" with the Armada. This he assumes from a letter from Leicester to Walsingham from the English camp at Tilbury on July 28, 1588—

My Lord of Oxford . . . returned again yesterday by me, with Captain Huntly as his company. It seemed only his voyage was to have gone to my Lord Admiral; and at his return [from] thither he went yesternight for his armour and furniture. If he come I would know from you what I should do. I trust he be free to go to the enemy, for he seems most willing to hazard his life in this quarrel.

—from which Ward deduces that "his ship had been put out of action."[48] Indeed, it was a fierce fight, attested to by a stanza in some verses by a "J. L." in a book entitled, *An Answer to the Untruths, Published and Printed in Spain, in Glory of Their Supposed Victory Achieved against Our English Navy* (1589):

> De Vere, whose fame and loyalty hath pierced
> The Tuscan clime, and through the Belgike lands
> By wingèd Fame for valour is rehearst,
> Like warlike Mars upon the hatches stands.
> His tuskèd Boar 'gan foam for inward ire,
>   While Pallas filled his breast with warlike fire.

Ward declares that this "graphic description of the Earl . . . conveys the impression that the ballad was written by someone who actually saw Oxford standing in full armour on the deck of his ship," and supposes that J.

L. was none other than Oxford's faithful servant, John Lyly. In fact, these verses were appended to a book written by an anonymous "Spanish Gentleman; who came hither out of the Low Countries." Written in Spanish, J. L. was the translator, and we find his name in full in his dedication to Lord Admiral Howard, and it turns out to be James Lea, who seems to have added his verses to improve upon those of the author. There is no reason to believe he was an eyewitness to this event—or that there was any such event to witness, for that matter. Leicester's letter of the 28th, says that Oxford had just gone to fetch his armor the previous day, which would presumably include his helmet surmounted by his crest of a "tuskèd Boar."

The reliability of all such panegyrics must be questioned. Camden's account of the peers who joined the fleet, cited by Ward, is contradicted by John Knox Laughton in his introduction to State Papers Relating to the Defeat of the Spanish Armada. Of Camden's lengthy roll of notable volunteers, only three are verified, and Laughton thinks it unlikely that the rest, Oxford among them, could have been in the fleet without being "once mentioned by [Lord Admiral] Howard, by Robert Cecil, by Seymour, or by any of the correspondents of Burghley and Walsyngham, or by these." However, he does accept the word of Robert Carey, Lord Hunsdon's son, that he was in the fleet at the battle of Gravesend, and thus concludes:

> It must therefore be admitted as possible that the others were also in the fleet, though—without corroborative testimony—it remains extremely improbable. That Ralegh had a command in the fleet and "led a squadron as rear-admiral" is virtually contradicted by the evidence now before us.[49]

Additional doubt is cast on Oxford's participation in the English fleet by a list of the 34 ships in service against the Armada, including their captains and officers, appended to Laughton's compilation. Neither Oxford nor the Captain Huntly named in Leicester's letter are among them.* Furthermore, ten tapestries were commissioned by the Lord Admiral to commemorate the victory over the armada (all perished in the fire that consumed the Palace of Westminster in 1834), each depicting an event in the sea war surrounded by a border of portraits of those who gave notable service, 22 in all. Again Oxford is not among them.

How then do we explain Leicester's remarks about Oxford? Putting aside

---

* See B. M. Ward, The Seventeenth Earl of Oxford, 1550–1604, from Contemporary Documents, 2:324–25. A complete list of all ships in the English and Spanish fleets—down to the twenty-ton Black Dog—is to be found in Philip Morant's "Account of the Spanish Invasion," in John Pine's The Tapestry Hangings of the House of Lords: Representing the Several Engagements between the English and Spanish Fleets (1739), pp. 9–11. A Captain Huntley is nowhere mentioned.

A tapestry commissioned by Lord Admiral Howard to commemorate the defeat of the Spanish Armada. This tapestry depicts the taking of the *San Lorenzo,* which foundered trying to escape the fireships, August 8, 1588. (Courtesy of the Folger Shakespeare Library)

Ward's romantic promptings, Oxford was among several gallants who belatedly wished to get in on the action and sought a commission in the English fleet. His request evidently was routed to the queen rather than the Lord Admiral—with calamitous results.

Returning to Ward's story: Oxford, his ship supposedly out of commission, made "application to the Commander-in-Chief for service with the land forces." If so, his wish was granted, for a post was promptly found for him: governor of the garrison in Harwich, in Essex. Just four days after his letter quoted above (August 1), Oxford was again the subject of a letter to the secretary from Leicester:

> I did, as her Majesty liked well of, deliver to my Lord of Oxford her gracious consent of his willingness to serve her. And for that he was content to serve her among the foremost as he seemed. She was pleased that he should have the government & all those that are appointed to attend that place, which should be two thousand men, a place of great trust and of great danger. My Lord seemed at the first to like well of it. Afterward he came to me and told me he thought the place of no service nor credit, and therefore he would to the court and understand her Majesty's further pleasure, to which I would not be against. But I must desire you, as I know her Majesty will also make him know, that it was of good grace to appoint that place to him, having no more experience than he hath, and

then to use the matter as you shall think good. For mine own part, being gladder to be rid of him than to have him, but only to have him contented, which now I find will be harder than I took it, and [he] denieth all his former offers he made to me rather than not to be seen to be employed at this time.[50]

Ward tries to put the best face on this: "After his experiences at sea Lord Oxford must have looked upon the offer of the command of a Naval Base as somewhat of the nature of anti-climax." This atop missing "the dramatic episode of the fire-ships"! (The fireship assault was, in fact, launched a week later, beginning about midnight, August 8.) So may be excused his "restlessness amounting almost to insubordination." Oxford, he supposes, might have shared a favorite Shakespeare quotation with Horatio Nelson in these circumstances: "if it be a sin to covet honour, I am the most offending soul alive."

It seems odd that the 38-year-old Oxford, supposedly a seasoned veteran of battle and fresh from a great fight at sea, should have been given the command of the small Harwich garrison as commensurate to one "having no more experience than he hath." At any rate, if we can judge by Leicester's letter, it does seem that his contemporaries did not look upon Oxford as the Second Coming of Henry V, but rather in the way the Constable of France viewed the boastful Dauphin in that same play:

> *Duke of Orleans.* I know him to be valiant.
> *Constable.* I was told that by one that knows him better than you.
> *Orleans.* What's he?
> *Constable.* Marry, he told me so himself, and he said he car'd not who knew it.

Refusing the command of Harwich as a position "of no service nor credit" could be seen as the action of a man who did not covet honor, but glory.

Whatever his motivations may have been, it seems highly unlikely that the queen would have been quite so sensitive as Ward to Oxford's emotional state at that moment of great national peril. His rejection of the command may well have been viewed as insubordination outright. One might go so far as to call it dereliction of duty. Whatever words one chooses for Oxford's behavior, Leicester thought further on it and added a postscript to his August 1 letter to Walsingham to make it clear he wanted to hear nothing more of this unstable man: "I am glad I am rid of my Lord Oxford, seeing he refuseth this, and I pray you let me not be pressed anymore for him, what suit soever he make." * The evidence suggests that the queen was of the same mind.

---

* This postscript, not printed by Ward, is taken from a facsimile of Leicester's letter.

A thanksgiving service for the victory over Spain was celebrated in November at St. Paul's. In keeping with his position as Lord Great Chamberlain, Oxford rode before Elizabeth in the procession. He all but disappears from court thereafter. The Oxfordians would have it that this was a voluntary retirement, probably to devote his remaining years to his literary endeavors. A greater likelihood is that his refusal of the Harwich command was the last straw; Elizabeth had at last reached the end of her patience with the ungovernably fickle head of the Earl of Oxford. Evidence of this will be presented shortly.

As for Oxford the soldier, despite the heroic efforts of his supporters to portray him as a veritable Hotspur, the fact is that he is known to have bloodied his sword against none but his own countrymen. An entry in Burghley's journal on July 23, 1567, records:

> Thomas Brinknell, an under-cook, was hurt by the Earl of Oxford at Cecil House, whereof he died, and by a verdict of *felo de se* [putting an end to his own life], with running upon a point of a fence sword of the said Earl.[51]

And in March of 1582 came the aforementioned duel with Thomas Knyvet in which both were hurt, "my Lord of Oxford more dangerously."

The Scholar

Oxford the scholar fares considerably better than the courtier or soldier. He was well tutored in Burghley's household and did matriculate at Cambridge (though it is likely the master's degrees that he was awarded by that university in 1564 and by Oxford University in 1566 were honorary).[52] But the question is whether the author of Shakespeare's plays was indeed a scholar?

If Shakespeare was a scholar, it is a fact that eluded the scholarly for centuries. Tom Bethell thinks this can all be blamed on Ben Jonson who, in

> his prefatory poem in the First Folio (1623), misleadingly told readers that Shakespeare had "small Latin and less Greek." Jonson also spread the idea that Shakespeare was nature's child, who "wanted art." This falsely implied that Shakespeare's poetry was the spontaneous, untutored babbling of a provincial.[53]

Clearly, Jonson had duped all the learned figures of his time and, even after his reputation as the arbiter of taste faded, generations of scholars could not resist finding other blunders in the works of this babbling provincial. Even today, we are still in his thrall.

For instance, he is blamed, this time by Minos Miller, for leading astray scholars, and even a Supreme Court Justice (William Brennan), when he criticized Shakespeare for giving a seacoast to Bohemia, a region in land-locked Czechoslavakia, in *The Winter's Tale*. In fact, we learn that Jonson was the ignoramus, unaware that Bohemia did, after a fashion, have a seacoast at one distant time. According to a note in the *Monthly Magazine* (January 1, 1811), proffered by Miller:

> In the year 1270 the provinces of Stiria and Carniola were dependent on the crown of Bohemia. Rudolf, who became King of the Romans in 1273, took those provinces from Ottocar, the King of Bohemia, and attached them to the possessions of the house of Austria. The dependencies of a large empire are often denominated from the seat of government; so that a vessel sailing to Aquileia or Trieste, might, in the middle of the thirteenth century, be correctly described as bound for Bohemia. The shipwreck, in The Winter's Tale, is no breach of geography.[54]

There is no doubt that such rarified knowledge could not have been known to any but a rare scholar of cosmography and history, as Shakespeare and, apparently, Ben Jonson were not. To hazard a guess, it is very doubtful that Oxford would have known about it either.

On the other hand, Jonson was evidently also ignorant of Robert Greene's prose romance *Pandosto, The Triumph of Time*, just as Miller is evidently unaware that this was Shakespeare's primary source for *The Winter's Tale*. And in *Pandosto* we find the episode of its young hero caught in a three-day tempest at sea:

> But upon the fourth day about ten of the clock, the wind began to cease, the sea to wax calm, and the sky to be clear, and the mariners descried the coast of Bohemia, shooting off their ordnance for joy that they had escaped such a fearful tempest.[55]

There is no reason to suppose that Shakespeare gave Bohemia a seacoast for any other reason than it was in *Pandosto* and useful to his story.

Nor is this the only instance of jumbled geography in Shakespeare. In his edition of *The Comedy of Errors*, R. A. Foakes tries to untangle its locations. For instance, Shakespeare places Epidamnum (Durazzo in modern Albania) between Corinth and Epidaurus, although it is actually northwest of both. Foakes offers sources that might explain the error but, as he commented earlier, "There is no reason to expect geographical accuracy . . . of a playwright who elsewhere gave Bohemia a sea-coast and made a port of Milan."[56]

The Oxfordians have plucked other things from other plays that, to them, seem strange coming from a man of Shakespeare's background. As with the examples above, there is rarely anything that cannot be readily accounted for in contemporary works—his errors included—just as there is rarely anything that has not been explained in modern editions and critical studies. Impressive though they may seem when argued one by one, taken in the whole they are actually widely scattered, a minute fraction of all the allusions that argue the author was someone with a grammar school education, as will be shown in the next chapter.

The Glass of Fashion

Oxford's tour of Italy, alluded to earlier, looms large in the arguments for his authorship. Numerous plays that predominate in the first decade of Shakespeare's production are set in Italy, and according to the Oxfordians, the author's knowledge of Italian topography displays an intimacy that could only come from firsthand experience. Indeed, didn't that scrupulous orthodox scholar E. K. Chambers remark that Shakespeare "seems to have been remarkably successful in giving a local colouring and atmosphere" to these plays, and even "shows familiarity with some minute points of local topography."[57] And then (as Foakes noted) there's Milan, 75 miles inland from the Gulf of Genoa, which becomes a seaport in *The Two Gentlemen of Verona*.

Indeed, Oxford returned from his sojourn so immersed in Italian culture that he appeared in the image of the Italian courtier—and not a little of the couturier, as we hear from the chronicler John Stow:

Milliners or Haberdashers had not any gloves embroidered, or trimmed with gold or silk, neither gold nor embroided girdles and hangers, neither could they make any costly wash or perfume; until about the fourteenth or fifteenth year of [the reign of] the Queen the right honourable Edward de Vere, Earl of Oxford, came from Italy, and brought with him gloves, sweet bags, a perfumed leather jerkin, and other pleasant things. And that year the Queen had a pair of perfumed gloves trimmed only with four tufts, or roses, of coloured silk; the Queen took such pleasure in these gloves that she was pictured with those gloves upon her hands, and for many years after it was called the Earl of Oxford's perfume.[58]

Skipping past earlier manifestations of the Italian Renaissance in England—among them such trifles as the tomb of Henry VII in Westminster Abbey executed by Pietro Torrigiani and the terra-cotta roundels commissioned of Giovanni da Maiano by Cardinal Wolsey for Hampton Court Palace—Ogburn surmises that, by coming home Italianate in dress and tastes (and even in sense of smell), Oxford had imported the Italian Renaissance into England![59]

Alas, not everyone seems to have had Ogbburn's discriminating discernment of the earl's signal contribution to English culture. In April 1580, about a year and a half after the supposedly admiring Gabriel Harvey praised Oxford at Audley End, he wrote three letters to the poet Edmund Spenser with "some Precepts of our English reformed Versifying," to which he added a poem entitled *Speculum Tuscanismi* (The mirror of Tuscanism), an evident lampoon of the earl that reads in part:

> For life Magnificoes, not a beck but glorious in show,
>   In deed most frivolous, not a look but Tuscanish always.
>   His cringing side neck, eyes glancing, physnomy smirking,
>   With forefinger kiss, and brace embrace to the footward.
>
>   .   .   .   .   .
>
> Delicate in speech, quaint in array: conceited in all points,
>   In Courtly guiles a passing singular odd man,
>   For Gallants a brave mirror, a Primrose of Honour,
>   A Diamond for nonce, a fellow peerless in England.[60]

To Harvey's embarrassment, the letters and poem were printed. In 1592, he gave a glimpse of the aftermath: "[Lyly] would needs forsooth very courtly persuade the Earl of Oxford that some in those Letters, and namely the Mirrour of Tuscanismo, was palpably intended against him, whose noble Lordship I protest I never meant to dishonour with the least prejudicial word of my tongue or pen." This disclaimer is disingenuous.

A draft of a "dialogue in Cambridge between Master GH and his company," written a few months later, was preserved in Harvey's "Letterbook." Following 23 lines quoted from *Speculum Tuscanismi,* the discourse continues, "Now tell me . . . if this be not a noble verse and politique lesson . . . in effect containing the argument of his [Harvey's] courageous and warlike apostrophe to my lord of Oxenford in his fourth book of Gratulationum Valdinensium."[61] (*Gratulationes Valdinenses* is the name under which his addresses at Audley End were published.) Thus, Harvey not only identifies Oxford as the object of his satire, but casts doubt upon the sincerity of his earlier encomium on the earl. This might well include his exclamation that the earl "hast drunk deep draughts . . . of the Muses of France and Italy."[62] They are definitely not evident in his poetry.

The earl's only certain literary remains are sixteen poems, with another four that are possibly his. Perhaps we may give credence to Harvey's words at Audley End—"I have seen many Latin verses of thine, yea, even more English verses are extant"—and assume that what survives represents a small portion of his poetry. However, if it is also representative of it, he seems to have brought back everything from Italy but its innovations in literature.

There is no doubt that Oxford showed originality as a poet. In his *Elizabethan Courtier Poets,* Steven W. May, the foremost scholar of the genre, states that, whereas "[Sir Edward] Dyer has been considered the premier Elizabethan courtier poet, that is, the first to compose love lyrics there, the available evidence confers this distinction upon the earl of Oxford." He adds, "De Vere's eight poems in [*Paradise of Dainty Devices* (1576)] create a dramatic break with everything known to have been written at the Elizabethan court up to that time. . . . The diversity of Oxford's subjects, including his varied analyses of the lover's state, were practically as unknown to contemporary out-of-court writers as they were to courtiers."[63] Thus Oxford's themes. Of his style, however, he wrote elsewhere: "De Vere's sixteen canonical poems are the output of a competent, fairly experimental poet working in the established modes of mid-century lyric verse."[64] I am indebted to May for providing me with this concise assessment of Oxford's influences:

The "golden," essentially Italian influences injected into English verse during the 1580s by Sidney and his followers in and out of court changed the rhetoric and technical forms of lyric verse in ways not reflected in DeVere's known poetry: [the Earl of] Essex, [Sir John] Harington, Greville, and even Dyer, with many others, write some of their works, at least, in the new style, but I can't detect it in Oxford's work.[65]

This hardly sounds like the same man whose exuberant language has invigorated the English tongue for centuries and whose phrases are mouthed unknowingly by many who have only a nodding acquaintance with his works.

Similarly, it seems odd that the man at once dedicated to great literature and immersed in things Italian, as Oxford purportedly was, should have made that nation's presence felt in his writings in nothing more than a smattering of topographical features in a handful of plays. For, even though Shakespeare conformed to the contemporary fancy for Italian locales in some plays, elsewhere we hear distinct disdain for those who brought a taste for Italy to the English court, such as in *Richard II,* where the Duke of York grumbles about the courtly demand for the

> Report of fashions in proud Italy,
> Whose manners still our tardy apish nation
> Limps after in base imitation.

In fact, Richard's court followed the lead of its monarch, who aped the fashions of France; evidently, York's remark was intended as a commentary on the contemporary court. In this respect, it does not seem very plausible that the man who did so much to bring the fashions of proud Italy to Elizabeth's court, and suffered some ridicule for it, could have written those words.

In fact, Shakespeare need not have done any more to his so-called Italian plays than Ben Jonson did to *Every Man in His Humour* in order to plant them firmly in Elizabethan soil: change the names of the characters and locations to English ones and each play is right at home in contemporary England.

A Resident Dramatist in Queen Elizabeth's Court?

In 1586, Queen Elizabeth granted Oxford an annuity of £1,000. "What did he spend this money on? and what did he do in return for his £1,000 a year?" Ward wonders. "He certainly did none of the things we might have expected. He did not serve [the Queen] as a Minister, as a Privy Councillor, as an Ambassador, or as a Soldier." Which leaves only one possible explanation: it was Oxford's reward for being "instrumental, by means of his brain, his servants, and his purse in providing the Court with dramatic entertainment." He imagines Elizabeth "would very naturally be unwilling to allow so valuable a courtier to go bankrupt and be compelled to leave the Court for lack of means to maintain his position."[66]

The quality of these entertainments seems to be confirmed in *The Arte of English Poesie* (1589), which is attributed to the courtier George Puttenham. In it, the author proclaims that among the courtly playmakers,

> for Tragedy, the Lord of Buckhurst [Thomas Sackville] and Master Edward Ferrers for such doings as I have seen of theirs do deserve the highest price; The Earl of Oxford and Master [Richard] Edwards, of her Majesty's Chapel, for Comedy and Interlude.[67]

Nine years later, Puttenham's judgment is seconded by Francis Meres in *Palladis Tamia,* where Oxford heads the list of "the best for Comedy amongst us."

Puttenham's treatise on the state of the arts in Elizabeth's court is addressed to the queen herself, "being already, of any that I know in our time, the most excellent poet," he declares, not entirely in flattery. "Forsooth," he continues, "by your princely purse, favours and countenance, making in what manner ye list, the poor man rich, the lewd well-learned, the coward courageous, and vile both noble and valiant." Thus, on page 2. Alas, when we turn to page 16, we learn that her favor did not always shower upon either the sciences or the arts in her court, for:

it is hard to find in these days of noblemen and gentlemen any good mathematician, or excellent musician, or notable philosopher, or else a cunning poet; because we find so few great princes much delighted in these same studies. Now also of such among the nobility or gentry as be very well seen in many laudable sciences, and especially in making of poesie, it is so come to pass that they have no courage to write and if they have, yet are they loath to be a knowen of their skill. So as I know very many notable gentlemen in the court that have written commendably, and suppressed it again, or else suffered it to be published without their own names to it; as if it were a discredit for a gentleman to seem learned, and to show himself amorous of any good art.

And on page 49, Puttenham catalogues the "crew of courtly makers" in Elizabeth's time, men "who have written excellently well as it would appear if their doings could be found out and made public with the rest, of which number is first that noble gentleman, Edward Earl of Oxford." It is two pages later that we find Oxford sharing top billing with Richard Edwards for the "highest price" in comedy and interlude.

What happened to these plays of Oxford's? Why were they allowed to disappear from view? Or were they? Might William Shakespeare have been the second "front man" for Oxford—the first being none other than John Lyly, the most influential literary figure of his day?

Lyly made his mark in 1578 with his prose work *Euphues*. Although it lives on in the somewhat sullied word "euphuism," in its own time it was hailed as a "new English." Fifty-four years later, its fame was remembered by the editor of his eight court comedies, who commented that "that beauty in court which could not parley Euphuism was as little regarded as she which now there speaks not French." Lyly dedicated its 1580 sequel—*Euphues and His England*—to Oxford, about the same time he was welcomed into de Vere's household, where he was referred to as the earl's secretary. However, having his facile pen at hand was a distinct bonus to Oxford in 1583, when he wished to recover some of his former luster at court by putting on plays—specifically, those written by Lyly. Or so the world was allowed to think.

It all sounds strikingly familiar as Ward edges toward the conclusion that their author was actually the Earl of Oxford. For instance, in *Sapho and Phao* there is a suggestion that the author had knowledge of a ferry that ran to Sicily. Lyly, of course, had never been there—Oxford, of course, had. Then there are the verses "of the highest standard," that were not printed in the contemporary quarto editions of his comedies, but only in 1632 collection. "Personally," Ward offers, "I think [Lyly] did not publish them for the simple reason they were not his to publish."[68] Consider the quarto editions of the comedies themselves—*all* published anonymously, according to Ward. However, he does note, that Lyly's name is found in the Stationers' Register entry of *Sapho and Phao* on April 6, 1584, which shows "that this was not a piratical venture, and that Lyly himself was concerned in the publication." Thus, Ward concludes, that "these anonymous quartos only become comprehensible if we recognize that the plays were a collaboration, and that Lord Oxford, for personal reasons, preferred them to be brought out anonymously."

Merely a collaboration? He now ponders whether the Master of the Revels would have licensed this play with its "obvious allusions to the Queen's love affairs" had it been written by a mere professional playwright? "But if we substitute the Lord Great Chamberlain of England for the professional playwright all difficulties vanish." Finally, there is Gabriel Harvey's comment in 1593 that Lyly, "sometime [formerly, that is] the fiddlestick of Oxford, [was] now the very babble of London." Ward acknowledges that the reference to Oxford might be to the university—but if it is a double entendre, as he thinks it may be:

> Surely the interpretation is that Lyly was at one time the passive instrument employed by the Lord Oxford to play his tunes. Indeed, the more one thinks it over the more one is obliged to confess that Lyly recedes further into the background, and Lord Oxford appears in greater prominence.

Thus the evidence for Oxford's authorship of Lyly's plays, which sounds very much like a rehearsal for the Shakespeare-Oxford authorship. Does it play any better?

Actually, *Sapho and Phao* is the only play for which Ward makes a case for Oxford's authorship. However, all the internal evidence he can muster—reminiscent of Shakespeare the cosmographer—is the allusion to Sicily. It hardly seems remarkable that a playwright in the earl's household should have picked up this scrap from his employer. What then of the purported allegory on the thwarted French marriage in this play? In the first place, Elizabeth would not have gracefully suffered any allusion to that affair by Lyly—or Oxford. As early as 1566, her displeasure with theatrical editorializing had reached the point where Richard Edwards, the Master of her Chapel Children, protested in his play *Damon and Pithias*:

> Wherein, talking of courtly plays, we do protest this flat: We talk of Dionysius' court, we mean no court but that! Lo, this I speak for our defense, le[s]t by others we be shent. But worthy audience, we we you pray, take things as they be meant.

The queen soon after instructed the Master of the Revels to put an end to allusions to her affairs, whether of state or of the heart. "The Revels Office continued 'perusing and reforming' plays to please the queen until the very end of her reign," Lyly's most recent editor, Carter A. Daniel, has observed, "and no play that ran the risk of offending her would ever have been allowed to get as far as a performance at court."[69] This is but one of several reasons that he dismisses the alleged courtly commentary in Lyly's plays as "nonsense," the major reason being that the plays with their "timeless and universally applicable themes" stand on their own, making "the idea that he was only writing parlor games [seem] quite ridiculous."

In regard to the anonymous publication of the comedies, there is no more significance that can be attached to this than to any of the vast number of literary works published without attribution at this time. Furthermore, Lyly's name below that of the publisher Thomas Cadman in the Stationers' Register entry of *Sapho and Phao*, rather than suggesting his connivance in its publication, turns out to be meaningless. Ward could not have known that this would be exposed as one of the many aggravating forgeries of authors' names into the Stationers' Register by that bane of researchers, John Payne Collier.[70] But Ward should have known that not all of the court comedies were printed without attribution: *The Woman in the Moon* (1597) and *Love's Metamorphosis* (1601) do name Lyly as the author on the title page.

Under any circumstances, Lyly's employment in Oxford's household probably ended before the composition of at least five of the eight court comedies. Whereas Oxfordians like to think he remained in his service until 1590—when his playwriting career came to a supposedly inexplicable end—the latest certain date that he can be placed in the earl's employ is May 1587; insofar as Oxford was then living on his annuity, it is doubtful Lyly could have been kept on much past this date. In fact, the termination of his services is the likely reason that the last five of his eight court plays were written—he needed a source of income.

Only two of the court comedies, *Sapho and Phao* and *Campaspe* (also in 1584) were published during Lyly's association with the boy companies at Blackfriars under Oxford's patronage. They are, as well, the only two of his eight plays in which both the Children of the Chapel and Paul's Boys are jointly named as the acting company in the quartos. In regard to his other six comedies, published between 1591 and 1601, the title pages of four state that they were acted by the Children of Paul's only, and the earliest date of a court performance that corresponds to the dates given in the quartos is February 2, 1588, in *Endymion*. The boys would run afoul of the authorities some time in 1590 and were "dissolved," which is the most probable reason that Lyly's career as a dramatist came to so abrupt a halt.[71] After all, there are no grounds for associating Lyly's comedies with de Vere after 1584.

What is more, there is nothing that associates Lyly's literary talents with

Oxford's. The man who gave England a new way of speaking in *Euphues* also "inaugurated a new kind of drama," according to his scholar Leah Scragg, "one directed toward a highly sophisticated audience and designed, in his own words, 'to move inward delight, not outward lightness,' " for which he created dialogue "without parallel for its elegance and wit." [72] His vogue did not last long. Hastened to its end by the naturalistic style of the public stage, "his style was soon to be ridiculed as absurd and old-fashioned." But in his brief noonday he was an innovator.

It is impossible to imagine Lyly's style owed anything to Oxford, whose style was old-fashioned to begin with, no less that the earl might have had a major hand in these comedies. It is easier to imagine that de Vere, who did not lack for imagination where his talents and prowess were concerned, might have taken credit for Lyly's work. Consider that Puttenham went beyond the confines of the court to mingle the unnamed author of *Shepherd's Calendar* (Edmund Spenser) with Sir Philip Sidney and Sir Thomas Chaloner as the outstanding pastoral poets, but somehow took no notice of Lyly or his works although he was certainly visible at court, which Spenser was not. One can only wonder if at some time the plays of Oxford's boys became "Oxford's plays"—in Oxford's mind, anyway. This would explain Puttenham's otherwise inexplicable praise of Oxford, for the "highest price" for comedy should unquestionably be paid to Lyly.

The Thousand-Pound Annuity

Present-day Oxfordians are wary of Ward's hypothesis that the earl was the author of Lyly's plays (although it is not dismissed entirely). But they most enthusiastically embrace his hypothesis that the queen granted him a £1,000 annuity for "providing the Court with dramatic entertainment"—not under the cover of Lyly, but as William Shakespeare. There is, however, another, more prosaic reason why he would have been granted that munificent sum: he had ruined himself.

Sir George Buck, the Master of the Revels who is down in the Oxfordian books as a friend and admirer of the earl's, seems actually to have been "vouchsafed . . . his familiar acquaintance" on only one occasion and that for the apparent purpose of giving his version of the waste of his earldom. This meeting was recorded in Buck's *History of King Richard the Third* (1619) and he dutifully recounts Oxford's story that "certain rich and prosperous men desired to farm [collect fees from] a part of his earldom," for which Oxford would get £12,000, as well as use of his residences, parks, woods or forests (leaving one to wonder what the investors got). Furthermore, Buck passes along the comments of "some grave and discreet and honourable persons" who "[affirmed] that he was much more like to raise and to acquire an earldom than to decay and waste and lose an old earldom."[73]

Why did Buck report all this uncritically when all the evidence was to the contrary? His great-grandfather, it so happens, was executed for fighting in the cause of Richard III at Bosworth Field. Buck's family was rescued from ruin by Thomas Howard (the Earl of Surrey in *Richard III*), the son of Richard's most loyal noble, John Howard, the 1st Duke of Norfolk. As Buck wrote, but for Thomas his family would have "withered with the White Rose" (the badge of the Richard's family, the House of York). Sir George perhaps felt an obligation to set right the record of the king for whom his family and its benefactors had fought and died.

On the other side of the coin, the architect of Richard's defeat was Oxford's ancestor, the 13th Earl. And so it suited Buck's purposes to allow Edward to be seen as "a magnificent and a very learned and religious nobleman," whose ruin was none of his doing, but was rather "by the fate of the divine ordinance"—the sins of the 13th Earl visited upon the 17th as "a warning not to lift a finger . . . to destroy princes nor the children of princes and of heroical persons." Thus was the Oxford earldom "wasted and almost all dilapidated and spoiled, and the castles and manors pulled down." The angel of retribution, it turns out, was the 17th Earl himself.

Oxford's irresponsibility surfaces in his mid-twenties, when he financed his European travels in 1575–76 at a cost of at least £3,761, having left behind £6,000 in debts. When Burghley wrote to the earl of his complaining creditors, he replied, "let rather my creditors bear with me awhile, and take their days assured according to that order I left, [rather] than I so want in a strange country, unknowing yet what need I may have of money myself." He goes on to say that they will be paid with the profits from his lands, but he adds characteristically, "if I cannot pay them as I would, yet as I can I will, but preferring my own necessity before theirs" (March 17, 1575).[74] During the entire course of his continental tour, Burghley was beleaguered by his creditors on the one side and the earl's demands for more money and orders to lease or sell his estates on the other. Burghley was thanked for his good offices upon Oxford's return by having to defend himself against the earl's "cavillations," among them, "That he had not his money made over sea so speedily as he desired."[75]

Nevertheless, perhaps for his daughter's sake, Burghley continued to seek favor for Oxford. In March 1583, he wrote to that purpose to Vice-Chamberlain Sir Christopher Hatton; significantly he had to protest that the earl had only four servants rather than a retinue of fifteen or sixteen, and presses the case as one for his own relief, if not Oxford's:

When our son-in-law was in prosperity he was the cause of our adversity by his unkind usage of us and ours; and now that he is ruined and in adversity we are only made partakers thereof, and by no means, no, not by the bitter tears of my wife, can obtain a spark of favour for him.[76]

Evidently, well before 1586, Oxford was quite nearly, if not utterly, broke.

Perhaps he initially adjusted to the income provided by his annuity, but in 1590 we find the poet Thomas Churchyard, who had been employed by Oxford in palmier times, standing bond for rooms Oxford wished to lease at £25 quarterly from Juliana Penn, the mother-in-law of Burghley's private secretary, Michael Hicks. Predictably, Oxford did not pay his rent and was the recipient of an anguished letter from Mistress Penn over "The grief and sorrow I have taken for your unkind dealing." Despite this unhappy start, the lady tried to cajole the lord with a happy ending:

> If it please your lordship to show me your favor in this [suit?], I shall be much bound to your honor and you shall command me and my house or anything that is in it, whensoever it shall please you.[77]

The earl was apparently unmoved and, although she told him she "would be loathe to trouble [Churchyard] for your honor's sake," she eventually had to approach him to make good his bond, which elicited a wounded reply:

> Good Mistress Penn. I never deserved your displeasure, and have made her Majesty understand of my bond touching the earl, and for fear of arresting I lie in the sanctuary. For albeit you may favor me, yet I know I am in your danger, and am honest and true in all mine actions.

Nothing more is heard of this matter. But it is a reflection on Oxford's reputation that a bond should have been required for so small a sum in the first place, and that it would seem he could find no one of greater position as his surety.

Indeed, Ward would have it that little more is heard of the earl in any matter, asserting that "It is almost impossible to penetrate the obscurity surrounding" the last fifteen years of his life—just not so impenetrable that Ward cannot surmise that "There can be little doubt that literature, his main interest in life, occupied the greater part of his time."[78] As a matter of fact, those years are hardly so obscured that we cannot see that his pen and brain were busily at work, although literature was most definitely not their occupation.

His interests now turned to one money-making scheme after another, for which, somewhat more humbly than in former days, he wrote Burghley time and again. In May of 1591, it is a request to exchange his £1,000 annuity for a lump sum payment of £5,000; in the next year, a request for the import monopolies on oils, wools and fruits. In October 1593, he renews his plea for furthering his suit for those monopolies and, for good measure, adds the stewardship of the Forest of Essex.[79] In the spring of the next year a new scheme, this time to farm Her Majesty's tin—which seems to have been a persistent interest for the remainder of the decade.

On March 9, 1595, two documents were received by Burghley from Oxford containing a dense analysis on the stocks of and revenues to be had from tin. On the 20th of the month, came a letter from Oxford to Burghley that reveals that "this last year past I have been a suitor to Her Majesty that I might farm her tins, giving £3,000 a year more than she had made." If this is near the mark it means that during the period when the Lord Chamberlain's company was formed, Oxford's overriding interest was in tin. Over the next four weeks, seven more letters arrived—all on the subject of tin. One year later, tin is still the topic of his correspondence; again, in June 1599, just about the time when the Globe opened for business on Bankside, Oxford renewed his appeals, now to Sir Robert Cecil, Burghley having been relieved of the earl and lesser worldly burdens in the previous August.[80]

After some five years of effort, it apparently dawned on Oxford that he would not be successful in his scheme to farm tin and struck out in a new direction. In July 1600, he wrote Cecil to beg his good offices in obtaining the recently vacated governorship of the Isle of Jersey. The appointment went instead to Sir Walter Ralegh; ever hopeful, he writes again in February 1601 to ask Cecil's voice in his desire for the presidency of the Council of Wales.[81] He did not get that either.

It is noteworthy that, in the aforementioned letter of March 20, 1595, Oxford wrote: "I most earnestly and heartily desire your lordship to have a feeling of mine unfortunate estate, which, although it be far unfit to endure delays, yet have consumed four or five years." Here, in Oxford's own words, we have evidence he had been out of royal favor since 1590 at the latest.

This history of Oxford's fallen fortunes and his desperate attempts to improve it, show the speculation about the allegedly mysterious nature of his £1,000 annuity is unfounded. There is still more that puts the purpose of the stipend beyond doubt. First, the straightforward language of the Privy Seal Warrant of June 26, 1586, by which it was granted to him. The sum was to be "paid unto Our said Cousin," it says,

> at four term of the year by even proportions: and so to be continued unto him during Our pleasure, or until such time as he shall be by Us otherwise provided for to be in some manner relieved; at which time Our pleasure is that this payment of One Thousand Pounds yearly to Our said Cousin in manner above specified shall cease.[82]

Steven W. May summed up its intent precisely: "Its unusual form, an annuity paid in quarterly installments, shows that it was designed to solve an unusual problem, the preservation of a necessary state figure, whose irresponsibility precluded a grant which might be farmed out, commuted, or sold." [83]

Any lingering doubts are dispelled by two other documents. The first is an undated letter in 1604 from King James to "my little beagle," Robert Cecil, Viscount Cranborne. It is a thorough account of his interview with Edmund, Lord Sheffield, who declared that he had gone £10,000 in debt to fulfill his duties as President of the Council of North, for which he now sought a substantial annuity. James reported that he told Sheffield "he might have a taste of my favour for his further enabling in my service, I was contented to give him a pension for his life time of as great value as ever either the late queen or I ever gave to any subject, to wit £1,000." Sheffield, however, "reckoned that I had repaired the ruins of every nobleman's estate in England except his," and pressed for more. At last, he was told by the king:

Great Oxford when his state was whole ruined got no more of the late Queen; I myself bestow no more on Arabella my near cousin . . . but most of all myself, being heir to this crown, got but thrice as much, and I was sure, I said, he would not deny that I had been thrice more steadful to the State than ever he had been; and since he took example by other men's gifts I asked him what example would other men take of his gift being bestowed upon no greater person than a baron? [84]

Ogburn wonders if James called de Vere "Great Oxford" merely because of his "family name." [85] No: rather it was, as we can see, because of his title, asking Sheffield what others would make of it should he give a pension greater than an earl's to no greater than a baron.

The other document is the words of Oxford's second wife, Elizabeth, whom he had married in 1592. In a letter dated before August 20, 1604, she wrote to Cecil:

presuming his Majesty had referred the apportionment of an allowance for my own and my child's maintenance, unto yours and my Lord Northampton's consideration, I was very glad that the relief of this ruined estate, best knowen to your Lordships, rested in the favour of such persons, as both in honour, nature, and affection, would regard the desolate estate of my poor child and myself. . . . Your Lordship may truly inform his highness that the pension of a thousand pounds was not given by the late Queen to my Lord for his life, and then to determine, but to continue until she might raise his decay by some better provision. And as I hear his Majesty is most respective in performing of the late Queen's intentions,

Letter from Oxford's widow to Sir Robert Cecil regarding the earl's annuity. (Courtesy of the Marquess of Salisbury)

which makes me the more hopeful in my great distress, of his Majesty's favour. It hath been enjoyed but one year by his Majesty's gift, and it is all the relief I ever look for to sustain my miserable estate.[86]

This is clear testimony about the purpose of the annuity: Oxford's total ruin of his estate. Furthermore, the queen's actions, more so her inaction, in the more than sixteen years between her gift in June 1586 and her death in March 1603, put beyond doubt and question that she had no intention of making "some better provision" for him, or of employing his services to any greater extent than necessary. Clearly he had been eliminated from her good graces for once and all. What makes this all the more striking is that there is no great offense by Oxford on record that would explain this adamant behavior, which she usually sustained toward few but openly rebellious subjects. Rather, it does appear de Vere wore down her patience in installments, by word and by deed, over the course of years. We would certainly not expect her to have been so unyielding toward one who delighted her and her court with brilliant plays—if this was indeed Shakespeare.

In Regard to the Case for Oxford

Despite the impressive display of archival materials in Ward's biography of Oxford, his proclaimed determination to rehabilitate the earl's image too often led him to put the most optimistic interpretation on his place in events and in history, and to serve as his apologist when the traditional image of the earl threatened to break through. And, despite his announced intention to defer to literary critics in regard to Oxford's creative enterprises—discreetly consigning his own thoughts on the matter to "Interludes" between chapters—he does seem always to keep an eye to the chance his subject might indeed be the author of the famous plays. Before sending Oxford off to a retirement from the bustle of the court and the thrall of battle in favor of the life of a literary hermit, Ward prepared the way by giving the earl a prominent place in Elizabethan literature as a patron and poet, and appropriating for Oxford first the style and, at last, the works of the most influential literary figure in the 1580s, John Lyly. Where else could de Vere go in the 1590s but up?

There is no dispute that Oxford was not only a patron of literature, but actively encouraged literary men in the 1570s. He was instrumental in the publication of *Cardanus Comfort* (1573) and very probably did play an active role in the poetry anthology, *A Hundred Sundrie Flowres* (also 1573). The fortuitous circumstances of having Lyly in his service at a time when entertainments at court could enhance his standing with the queen resulted in two of the greatest court comedies in her reign.

On the other hand, there is reason for caution in assessing Oxford's contemporary standing as a poet. There are, at the utmost, twenty surviving poems by Oxford. How much of his entire output they represent, or how fully representative of his talent they are, cannot be known. But if his poetry was in fact so highly considered as contemporary sources suggest, it is surprising that so little of it should have survived. As Steven W. May noted,

> By the 1590s, the unwritten strictures forbidding aristocrats to publish their poetry met with increasingly frequent violations, and this process was accelerated by the publication of most of Sir Philip Sidney's poetry during the decade as a memorial to this national hero.[87]

The situation improved further upon the accession of James who, when he was King of Scotland only, had published a volume of poetry, *The Essays of a Prentice in the Divine Art of Poesie* (1584), as well as a translation of *The Furies* by G. de Saluste du Bartus under the title of *His Majesty's Poetical Exercises at Vacant Hours* (1586).

Finally, we are told that Oxford, in writing plays for the public stage in his mature years (perhaps even acting on them "for sport"), was thus willing to defy convention—though not so far as to put his name to them. And, as a young man he was so bold as to publish his own verse. Why did Oxford, or his supposed literary executors, make no effort to collect and publish his poetry and court comedy in the more relaxed climate of the 1590s? If we grant that Oxford might have refrained from publishing these works in life, why did not his purported literary executors do him this good office in death? Instead, we are told that the best tribute his devoted admirers could think of was to publish often-damaged versions of common plays nearly two decades after his death—and under the name of a "babbling provincial" at that.

The scarcity of Oxford's literary remains makes the preeminent position he is supposed to have occupied in his own lifetime suspect. Yet, in this small sample, his partisans are able to discern parallels between de Vere's poetry and Shakespeare's. The first to discover these similarities was Looney, whose source for Oxford's poetry was Alexander Grosart's edition (1872). Grosart vastly inflated the number of poems by de Vere, to which Looney added the songs from Lyly's plays and eleven works "arbitrarily selected" from *England's Helicon*.[88]

What is most significant about this inflation of Oxford's canon is the use partisans of his authorship have made of poems that are not his. Professor May's study of Oxford's poetry found that, among the poems Looney judged to be "the most crucial in the piecing together of the case" for Oxford's authorship, were verses definitely written by Robert Greene, Thomas Campion and Fulke Greville. "Later Oxfordians," he notes, "have fared no better at distinguishing the true Shakespearean ring from lines by other poets":

> This on-going confusion of Oxford's genuine verse with that of at least three other poets illustrates the wholesale failure of the basic Oxfordian methodology. . . . The comparisons set forth by Looney and elaborated upon by his successors fail in any way to connect Oxford with Shakespeare; they reveal instead that verses from a number of Elizabethan poets cannot be detected from the work of either Oxford or Shakespeare when the excerpts are placed in selective juxtaposition.

It will almost certainly be said that the preceding is a hostile view of the Earl of Oxford and we can be sure that this will not be the last word on Oxford's character and qualifications. However, what is really at issue here is not the earl himself, but what has been made of his life and writings to advance the cause of deposing William Shakespeare as the author of the most famous body of work in world literature. It does make evident that the scrutiny which has been lavished on Shakespeare and his scholars has been too rarely given to Oxford and his scholars.

⇥10⇤

Closing Arguments

The bard play-writing in his room,
The bard a humble clerk,
The bard, a lawyer, parson, groom,
The bard, deer-stalking after dark,
The bard a tradesman—and a Jew—
The bard a botanist—a beak—
The bard a skilled musician, too—
A sheriff and a surgeon, eke!

Thus did William S. Gilbert turn his wit on the fabulous, incredible creation that nineteenth-century "super-idolatry" made of Shakespeare. His rhyme was by no means inclusive at the time and he could not have foreseen all that was yet to come in this century. We can only imagine what barbs he'd hurl had he lived to see the Bard created an earl.

The closest thing to evidence of the Shakespeare of Gilbert's poem is the deer-poacher reference, popularized by Nicholas Rowe in the 1709 edition of his plays. The rest, owing in no small extent to the reader "able to illustrate, from his profession, or track of reading" summoned a century earlier by George Steevens, were adduced from the plays. Like the speculation that would cast him as a scholar, a soldier and a courtier, it treats the playwright as an isolated phenomenon, entire to himself, literally "not of an age, but for all time." Long since forgotten was the course for studying Shakespeare set out by Samuel Johnson, which was to discover the world in which he moved, "its modes of speech, and its cast of thought." He believed this must be done if the beauties in his works were not to be "lost with the objects to which they were united, as the figures vanish when the canvas is decayed." He could not have dreamed that this was also necessary if the man himself was not to be lost, at first behind many occupations and experiences far removed from the playhouses and, ultimately, removed entirely from the playhouses and into the court of England.

* * *

At the root of all the speculation, and the authorship controversy itself, is the desire to explain what caused this genius. The effort to find an explanation for every detail of that genius has proved a trap to Shakespearean and authorship controversialist alike. At last it must be recognized that it is impossible to find all the pieces, no less to form those scattered pieces we have to make a satisfactory picture of either the man or the artist. All we can do is try to place Shakespeare into the canvas of his age.

The many occupations mentioned in Gilbert's poem that Shakespeare allegedly had a hand in are how some suggest he spent his "lost years"— the period between the Stratford church record of the birth of his twins, Hamnet and Judith, around February 1, 1585, and Henslowe's entry of a performance of *Henry VI* seven years later. The Oxfordians will have none of this jack-of-too-many-trades. Rather, they scoff that the 20-year-old who was nothing more than a man with a family in a rural town, should suddenly reappear at 27 as an up-and-coming playwright. How odd, to lose sight of such a man for seven years!

How much odder, then, is the ten-year gap in the record of John Fletcher, Shakespeare's successor as the attached playwright of the King's Men? He was the son of Richard Fletcher, Queen Elizabeth's chaplain, dean of Peterborough and, in succession, the Bishop of Bristol, Worcester, and London. John was not quite twelve when he entered Bene't College, Oxford, where he was a bible clerk. Unfortunately, his father remarried without the queen's consent and was humiliated for his effrontery. This, and a surfeit of tobacco, is said to have hastened his demise in 1596, when John was not yet seventeen. We hear that he and his seven siblings were then taken into the care of their learned uncle Dr. Giles Fletcher, but nothing more until 1606, when the 26-year-old man suddenly appears in the company of Francis Beaumont as a playwright. What transformed the son of a well-known divine into the author of profane literature? No one bothered to tell us.

Of all the English Renaissance dramatists none seems to have been more ideally positioned to leave a good biographical trail than the man who took up the playwriting chores from Fletcher, Philip Massinger. His father, Arthur, was the secretary of Henry Herbert, the 2nd Earl of Pembroke, and he, like the earl's younger son, was probably named for the Countess Mary's storied brother, Sir Philip Sidney. In dedicating his play *The Bondman* (1624) to Philip, Earl of Montgomery, Massinger recalled his father's association with his family:

> Many years he happily spent in the service of your honourable house, and died a servant to it; leaving his to be ever most glad and ready to be at the command of all such as derive themselves from his most honoured master, your lordship's most noble father.

It would seem that his connection with this family long associated with the arts and formally connected to the theater during nearly all of his career in it, would have made Massinger one of the best documented of dramatists. However, his editor, Philip Edwards, summed up the biographical record of the man thusly: "We know very little about his personal life, where he lived, whether he was married, whether he had children, whether he was a practicing Catholic." But then, he does not find this surprising, for, "Like most Tudor and Stuart dramatists, he lives almost exclusively in his plays." [1]

What, then, of Shakespeare's "lost years"? Modern scholars think the most likely explanation is the most obvious: at some time he made his way into one or another of the many playing troupes that, for want of a permanent home, toured the countryside and stopped at Stratford. [2] Or perhaps he got his start closer to home, thanks to a most unlikely benefactor—Sir Thomas Lucy.

Like many of status and position in Elizabethan England, Lucy was the patron of an acting troupe. Notice of the company is found in the accounts of Coventry for 1583–84, about the time that the Earl of Leicester lost the heart of his acting company to Queen Elizabeth's elite troupe. Nevertheless, by the time the earl departed for the Low Countries in 1585, he had players enough to leave behind a company that toured in England, while taking a select troupe with him to the continent—Will Kemp, George Bryan, and Thomas Pope, three men who were to become Shakespeare's fellows in the Chamberlain's company, among them.

Now, Lucy was on cordial terms with Leicester, who was deputized by the queen to confer knighthood on Sir Thomas in the great hall of his mansion of Charlecote, and over the years he was at the ready to serve the earl—from tracking down his enemy, Edward Arden of Park Hall (a relation of Shakespeare's), to offering the services of an aged archer named Burrell. Might it be that when Leicester needed players to revive his troupe, Lucy offered his actors—and might Shakespeare have been among them? For Lucy was also deeply involved in the affairs of Stratford, and perhaps the talents of this young townsmen had come to his attention. The reader is cautioned that this is sheer speculation, the sort of coincidence that too often ripens into evidence and hardens into fact. Perhaps less of a coincidence is that Leicester commended his picked players, including Kemp, Bryan and Pope, to King Frederick II of Denmark, where they then played before his court in Elsinore Castle. Elsinore Castle, curiously, is not mentioned in Shakespeare's sources for *Hamlet,* and we may wonder if this experience of his future fellows had something to do with his setting for this play. [3]

Another of the supposed mysteries posed by the Oxfordians is the absence of any known tribute to Shakespeare upon his death in 1616. There was no public mourning, no volumes of elegiac verse—not a word. By way of contrast, Beaumont, they point out, died 48 days before him and was buried in the company of Chaucer and Spenser in the Poet's Corner in Westminster Abbey. Can we believe Shakespeare's undoubtedly adoring contemporaries were content to leave his relics to a distant, dusty market town? Extraordinary indeed in the light of Shakespeare's current reputation. But this we know is not how he was regarded at the time and it is illuminating to consider the disposition of the remains of his King's Men successors, Fletcher and Massinger.

It should first be considered that the spot now known as Poet's Corner had not achieved that status in 1616. Spenser was placed there because he worshiped Chaucer, the man he called his master. There is no record of why Beaumont's remains were placed there, but it was not because it was a shrine set aside for Britain's literary gloried, nor was it yet when Ben Jonson died in 1637: he was buried, reputedly standing upright, beneath an eighteen-inch blue marble square in the north nave aisle of the abbey. On the other hand, it would seem only fitting that Fletcher should have been interred near his dear friend and collaborator, Beaumont. However, when he died in 1625, he was buried in an unmarked grave in St. Saviour's Church, the present Southwark Cathedral. Perhaps he was disposed of hugger-mugger because he is presumed to have died of the plague. This was not the case when Philip Massinger was unexpectedly found dead of natural causes in 1640, but not only was he deposited in this same church, but, as we learn from a poem by his admirer and probable patron, Sir Aston Cokayne,

> In the same grave Fletcher was buried here
> Lies the stage-poet Philip Massinger:
> Plays they did write together, were great friends,
> And now one grave includes them at their ends.[4]

That there may be no mistaking Cokayne's meaning, the epigram, which appeared in his *Chain of Golden Poems* (1658), is entitled "An Epitaph on Mr. John Fletcher, and Mr. Philip Massinger, Who Lie Buried Both in One Grave in St. Mary Overies Church in Southwark." The whereabouts of this grave has never been discovered.

If all this seems odd, consider the case of King James, the monarch who reigned over England when its tragic theater flourished. He was carried to Westminster Abbey with all due pomp and ceremony upon his death, but not only was no monument erected to him, the location of his remains was unknown until 1869, when they were discovered to have been placed with those of Henry VII and his queen, Elizabeth of York, in the vault below their monument in the abbey.[5] It does seem that, as a rule, the age of the Stuart kings had no great enthusiasm for honoring their great departed. Shakespeare was thus given the only monument that was proof against time's fell hand, as noted by Leonard Digges in his First Folio verses:

> Shakespeare, at length thy pious fellows give
> The world thy works: thy works, by which outlive
> Thy tomb thy name must. When that stone is rent,
> And time dissolves thy Stratford monument,
> Here we alive shall view thee still: this book,
> When brass and marble fade, shall make thee look
> Fresh to all ages.

This Shakespeare "memorial" was, of course, primarily a commercial venture. It is the only respect in which his age and ours are truly similar.

Stratford in Shakespeare's Day

In the attempt to dispose of the "Stratford man" it is not surprising that the Oxfordians should want to dispose of Stratford itself. Not only is it, in their reckoning, a place unworthy of his hallowed bones, but hardly the sort of place deserving of sending forth a Shakespeare into this world. Why, was it not, in the words of a since-reformed Oxfordian, "considered a rustic backwater by 16th-century Londoners"? Possibly. But then, it is possible that these same Londoners considered just about every town outside of London rustic backwaters, just as everyplace outside of London is called "provincial" to this very day. Precisely what did Shakespeare's contemporaries have to say about his hometown?

The only testimony I know of is in William Camden's *Britannia,* which was translated from the Latin by Philemon Holland in 1610. According to this edition, Camden said that Stratford was

> a proper little merchant town, beholden for all the beauty it hath to two men there bred and brought up, namely, John of Stratford, Archbishop of Canterbury; and Sir Hugh Clopton, Mayor of London, who over the Avon made a stone bridge supported with fourteen arches, not without exceeding great expenses.

Holland was a bit conservative in translating Camden's *"non inelegans"* to mean "proper," rather than (as it sounds), "not inelegant"—even having a certain amount of charm. In the meanwhile, he reminds us that, before Shakespeare, the town gave England one of its great prelate-statesmen in John de Stratford, whose tomb has been called perhaps the finest

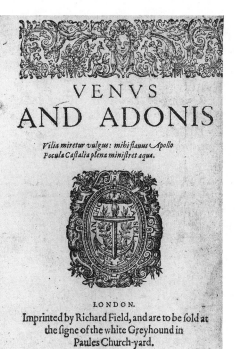

VENVS

AND ADONIS

Vilia miretur vulgus: mihi flauus ⌐Apollo
Pocula Caſtalia plena miniſtret aqua.

LONDON.
Imprinted by Richard Field, and are to be ſold at
the ſigne of the white Greyhound in
Paules Church-yard.
1 5 9 4.

The title page of *Venus and Adonis*,
printed by Richard Field. (Courtesy
of the Huntington Library, San
Marino, California. RB69260.)

stone monument in Canterbury Cathedral; as well as Mayor of London
Clopton who, in addition to endowing the bridge, also renewed portions
of the chapel of the Holy Cross, the fraternal guild that numbered among
its members the Duke of Clarence, the very same who was impersonated
in Shakespeare's *Henry VI* plays and in *Richard III*.

Nor were Stratford origins by any means a guarantee of illiteracy. Warwickshire, the county in which it is situated, accounts for a rather low
percentage of the young men who were apprenticed to London stationers
between 1563 and 1700, but through no fault of Stratford's. After the 31
from Coventry, the next highest number is the sixteen from Stratford, more
than twice as many as any other town in the county. Among the Stratford
apprentices was Richard Field, the son of a tanner, who was two years
older than Shakespeare. Field would take over the print shop of his master,
the respected printer Thomas Vautrollier, a specialist in classics and medical books. He would be the printer of the only literary works Shakespeare
would himself put into print, the narrative poems, *Venus and Adonis* and
The Rape of Lucrece. But this is, of course, merely an annoying coincidence as far as Oxfordians are concerned.

Paul Morgan, who made this study of the Warwickshire apprentices, comments that "A possible influence on the geographical distribution besides that of family connexions, was the presence of schools. Stationers' Company apprentices, from the nature of their trade, had to be literate."[6] He does note cautiously that there is no more certainty that these apprentices attended their local grammar school than there is that Shakespeare did his. But, by whatever means, Stratford clearly did produce literate folk. Indeed, the man for whom the preeminent institution of American literacy was named, John Harvard, was the product of the union of a Stratford butcher's daughter, Katherine Rogers, and a Southwark butcher's son. The coincidence of locales has inevitably fueled speculation that Shakespeare played the matchmaker—need it be said that there is no evidence for this? At any rate, the university took advantage of the happy coincidence to purchase the house built in 1596 by Katherine's father, Thomas. One of the domestic gems of Stratford, it is now known as Harvard House.

Shakespeare's Rarified Knowledge

Mere literacy cannot account for what Oxfordians perceive as knowledge that cannot have been found in books. For instance, the Earl of Burford has determined that there are "hundreds of 'in' jokes at the royal court" to be found in the plays—a sure sign that the author was one of the courtly in-crowd.[7] What is more, his plays are supposedly brimful with hints he had intimate knowledge of life at court. There is not a clue as to where Burford got his knowledge of what was in at court, but the best source that has come down to us, at least for the period from 1597 to 1627, are the letters of a commoner, John Chamberlain, who has been quoted in this book from time to time. Chamberlain's father, an alderman, sheriff of London, and a master of the Company of Ironmongers, died when his "tender, sickly, and weak" son was eleven, leaving the boy in the care of Thomas Gore, a grocer, and an inheritance that perhaps met his needs into adulthood.[8]

Nothing is known of him in the 25 years between the time he left Cambridge without having taken a degree and the beginning of his prodigious correspondence. When he reemerges, he has developed friendships in court circles, but his principal source of gossip was at St. Paul's Cathedral, where he went almost daily. The great church "was the heart of London," Norman Egbert McClure wrote in his introduction to the letters, and

here he heard the latest news, found books fresh from the press; here came courtier and serving-man, actor and alderman and apprentice; here the spectacle, the pageant of London life passed before him.

It has been conjectured Chamberlain was the model for Ben Jonson's "grave Master Ambler, news-master of Paul's," the "fine-paced gentleman" who walked the middle aisle of the cathedral. Whether or not this was he, it does appear this man from a modest background clearly found the means to gather the news of the day, both in court and out.

Indeed, one need not have gone so high on the social ladder as Chamberlain for such information, according to Shakespeare. In the scene of King Lear's reconciliation with Cordelia, he tells her of his wish for nothing but to live out his time with her,

> And pray, and sing, and tell old tales, and laugh
> At gilded butterflies, and hear poor rogues
> Talk of court news; and we'll talk with them too,
> Who loses and who wins; who's in who's out.

Even if the playhouse poet did not have the time to pass strolling the middle aisle of Paul's, he was often enough at court as a player to have picked up tidbits of its ways and manners and, perhaps, stock up his supply of the latest in-jokes. We cannot know for certain how poor rogues and common playwrights got their knowledge of what's "in" and who's out, any more than we can know how John Chamberlain ingratiated himself into court circles. Of one thing about our common playwright we can be certain: he cannot help but to have spent more time at court than the Earl of Oxford in the years after 1588, when de Vere is known to have been there hardly at all.

Another thing found in Shakespeare that is posed as being sacred to courtiers is his knowledge of falconry, the sport of hunting with hawks. To the contrary, Thomas Heywood was no courtier, but in his play *A Woman Kill'd with Kindness* (1607), the third scene of act one is given over to this sport and its terminology. Although Heywood "is primarily interested in the moral implications of a quarrel arising out of a foolishly excessive wager," G. Blakemore Evans notes of this scene, "he effectively catches something of the exhilaration and involvement experienced by true aficionados of the sport."[9] It is unlikely that Heywood was any more a true aficionado than Shakespeare, and his knowledge of technical hawking terms is traced to Gervase Markham's *The Gentlemans Academie*, a 1595 "reworking of the much earlier *Boke of St. Albans* (1486)." Shakespeare, however, might have had a personal reason for his interest in falcons, for it was the crest of the Shakespeare coat of arms. At any rate, a total of 79 different species of birds are named in his works. It has not been suggested that he kept an aviary.

*   *   *

What, then, of his use of legal terms? Shakespeare toys with these with the jaunty familiarity of an irreverent lawyer. The question of his legal knowledge has been most recently tackled by O. Hood Phillips, a jurist, legal scholar and educator, in *Shakespeare and the Lawyers*. In the chapter, "Did Shakespeare have a Legal Training?" he gathered and summarized the varying opinions that have been handed down. The most reliable assessment of the playwright's knowledge of law, in his opinion, is that of P. S. Clarkson and C. T. Warren,

> whose reading of Elizabethan drama revealed that about half of Shakespeare's fellows employed on the average more legalisms than he did, and some of them a great many more. Most of them also exceed Shakespeare in the detail and complexity of their legal problems and allusions, and with few exceptions display a degree of accuracy at least no lower than his.

Clarkson and Warren's verdict is that Shakespeare's references "must be explained on some grounds other than that he was a lawyer, or an apprentice, or a student of the law." What separates him from the others is his knack for making legal terms serve his drama, in the opinion of Justice Dunbar Plunket Barton. "Where Shakespeare's legal allusions surpassed those of his contemporaries," he said, ". . . was in their quality and their aptness rather than in their quantity or technicality." [10]

Then there is the matter of Shakespeare's French. Jonson did not say he had even less than small knowledge of that language. Yet, in *Henry V*, the French princess Katherine turns her English lesson into bawdy French. "Le foot," to the princess' ears, becomes *foutre* (fuck) and the *o* in *le count* vanishes. Where did Shakespeare get any French, no less enough to make such naughty puns?

Unlike Shakespeare's legalese, which is scattered throughout his plays, what is remarkable about his French is that he spent nearly all of it in this one play. In addition to Katherine's English lesson, there is the comic scene of the Boy translating the pleas of Monsieur le Fer for Pistol and the delightful wooing of Katherine by Harry in his broken French. If we insist upon the solitary bard—"play-writing in his room," but with no education in the tongue—this is puzzling. Not so, if we allow him his place in a theater company, where these scenes might have been worked up with the connivance of one of his fellows who did have a command of the tongue. Allow him a place in the contemporary theater and there is the possibility another dramatist was called in to provide this dialogue.

In the workaday realm of Elizabethan theater, no job was too small for the professional playwright. Thomas Dekker's services for the topical play,

The Late Murder in White Chapel; or, Keep the Widow Waking, were limited to "two sheets of paper containing the first act . . . and a speech in the last scene of the last act of the boy who had killed his mother." Neil Carson found "Dekker's contribution of that single speech" surprising, but goes on to note that, although this is "at odds with the picture of independent composition of acts, scenes, or plots often put forward" as the usual method of collaboration, it "corresponds quite closely with the one surviving example of a dramatic collaboration, the manuscript book of *Sir Thomas More"*—a play, coincidentally, for which Shakespeare seems to have performed a similar service.[11]

The above does not exhaust the catalogue of doubts Oxfordians have raised about what, in their estimation, a fellow of Shakespeare's status and background should or should not know. These allegedly rare tidbits are largely isolated and scattered throughout his plays; the explanation for the great many are to be found in critical studies or the notes in modern editions of the respective plays. In some cases the answers may be unsatisfactory because the materials for better are wanting; for a significant amount of the printed works and documents of Shakespeare's day are lost, and what has survived are imperfect materials that hold out little hope of perfect solutions.

Shakespeare's Classical Knowledge

Nothing so disqualifies Shakespeare to the Oxfordian mind than their conviction that his plays reveal a man who had a sound classical education. For instance, where did the grammar school boy who had "small Latin and less Greek," muster the competence in the latter tongue to have read the *Ajax* of Sophocles in the original? So he must have, for Sophocles had not yet been Englished and, in act one, scene one, of *Titus Andronicus,* we find:

> The Greeks upon advice did bury Ajax
> That slew himself; and wise Laertes' son,
> Did graciously plead for his funerals.

One possibility that has been offered as Shakespeare's source is Lambinus's Latin commentaries, widely read in the grammar schools of the day.[12] An even stronger possibility is that Shakespeare did not write this scene at all. It has long been recognized that the first act may be the work of another, usually thought to be George Peele. Sifting through the arguments, the Wells-Taylor *Textual Companion* concludes that, whereas "influence or imitation can account for the parallels with Peele . . . it is harder to explain why such parallels should concentrate so heavily in one part of the play." [13] All of which points to the likelihood that the first act was actually written by Peele. But, regardless of how Sophocles got into this play, one lone allusion in one of 38 plays is hardly compelling grounds for saying the author was a Greek scholar.

What about the *Menaechmi* of Plautus, the source for *The Comedy of Errors?* Shakespeare's play was certainly written no later than 1594, when it was performed in the Christmas revels at Gray's Inn, while the English translation of Plautus was not published until 1595. However, precisely when Shakespeare's play was written may shed light on his source. *Errors* is usually dated among his very first works, perhaps as early as 1589. Wells-Taylor makes a compelling case for a 1594 date for this play. The earlier dating, it argues, "has little to do with external or internal evidence"; rather, "it reflects a judgement that the play's classical and farcical character is uncharacteristic of Shakespeare's mature comedy, and a prejudice that Shakespeare should logically have moved from imitation of classical models to development of his own 'romantic' forms." Based primarily on stylistic evidence, as well as the doubt a five-year-old play would have been chosen for the Lawyers' revels, the *Textual Companion* suggests 1594 as a preferred date for this play. [14]

This conjecture, it should be noted, is offered without any reference to Shakespeare's sources, but it does open interesting possibilities in this respect. The translation of the *Menaechmi* by William Warner, although published in 1595, was entered with the Stationers on June 10, 1594. When it was at last issued, the printer addressed its readers, noting:

> The writer hereof (loving Readers) having diverse of this poet's comedies Englished, for the use and delight of his private friends, who in Plautus' own words are not able to understand them, I have prevailed so far with him as to let this one go farther abroad. [15]

In plain language, Warner followed the common practice of circulating copies of his work among friends, and it is possible that the patron of the Lord Chamberlain's Men was one of them. Warner's earlier works, a prose tale entitled *Pan His Syrinx or Pipe* (1585), and a long epic, *Albion's England* (1586), were printed under the patronage of Lord Chamberlain Hunsdon. It is therefore within the realm of probability that he was one of the private friends delighted by Warner's *Menaechmi*, which might explain why Shakespeare wrote his play at this time. Furthermore, it has been suggested that Shakespeare might have been influenced in choosing a title for the play by Warner's reference to "much pleasant error" in "The Argument" of his translation. [16]

Under any circumstances, Shakespeare had so thoroughly altered the

language and the plot of the *Menaechmi* that there is little more of Warner's translation found in it. For the same reason, it is impossible to trace
his source to any one Latin edition of the play, but it is not out of the
question that there was such an edition. Put in other words, what if Shakespeare *had* read Plautus in the original?

We should understand that what the Oxfordians are saying is not that
Shakespeare had, in Ben Jonson's words, "small Latin and less Greek,"
but instead that he really had none at all, whereas they hold the author
of the plays was well-tutored in those tongues. T. W. Baldwin disagrees.
In his exhaustive two volume study of Shakespeare's firsthand knowledge
of the classics he takes issue with John Churton Collins, the Oxfordians'
source for the playwright's mastery of the classics:

> I know of no evidence to justify the conviction of Collins that Shak-
> speare's "knowledge of the classics both of Greece and Rome was re-
> markably extensive." Remarkably extensive it may appear to us, but so
> far as I can find it was only that of a grammar school graduate who had
> an interest in the literary side of certain Latin classics.[17]

Baldwin succinctly summed up Shakespeare's classical knowledge and its
origins with the observation that "no miracles are required to account for
such knowledge and techniques from the classics as he exhibits. Stratford
grammar school will furnish all that is required."[18]

Shakespeare's contemporaries give not a hint of a suspicion that the playwright was a classical scholar. But, as we have seen, this may be blamed
on Ben Jonson's verdict on his command of Latin and Greek and his gullible contemporaries, as well as centuries of scholar, who pliantly deferred
to his opinion. Jonson's contemporaries, however, were not quite so intim-
idated as we are led to believe.

Leonard Digges was both a great admirer of Shakespeare and a sound
classical scholar, and we should expect him to fly to the dramatist's defense had his genius been slighted. In fact, he did just that in his commendatory poem that appeared in the 1640 edition of Shakespeare's poetry,
he sights Jonson's devotion and indebtedness to the classics. By comparison, of Shakespeare's classical training he wrote:

> Next, Nature only helped him, for look thorow
> This whole book, thou shalt find he doth not borrow,
> One phrase from Greeks, nor Latins imitate,
> Nor once from vulgar languages translate,
> Nor plagiary-like from others glean.

Unable to extol Shakespeare as a scholar, Digges chose to make a virtue of his natural talent. This sentiment is amplified in a famous anecdote involving a highly regarded scholar, the "ever memorable" John Hales.

Hales was elected a fellow of Merton College, Oxford, in 1605, appointed public lecturer in Greek in 1612, and subsequently held a fellowship at Eton. He seems no less qualified to proclaim Shakespeare's classical knowledge than to take on Jonson head-to-head on the subject. When the opportunity to do just that presented itself, the result was preserved thusly:

> In a conversation between Sir John Suckling, Sir William D'Avenant, Endymion Porter, Mr. Hales of Eton, and Ben Jonson, Sir John Suckling, who was a professed admirer of Shakespeare, had undertaken his defense against Ben Jonson with some warmth. Mr. Hales, who had sat still for some time, hearing Ben frequently reproaching him [Shakespeare] with the want of learning and ignorance of the Ancients, told him at last, "That if Mr. Shakespeare had not read the Ancients, he had likewise not stolen anything from 'em (a fault the other [Jonson] made no conscience of) and that if he would produce any one topic finely treated by any of them, he would undertake to show something upon the same subject at least as well written by Shakespeare.*

Hales clearly does not dispute Jonson's criticism of Shakespeare's lack of classical knowledge. Rather, like Digges, it is to him a virtue. Free of overt classical influences, Shakespeare could make the English language speak as eloquently as the ancient tongues.

We would not expect Shakespeare's eloquence to have escaped Oxfordian scrutiny and, of course, it has not. Specifically, they wonder where this provincial, even if he did have a grammar school education, got such a gigantic vocabulary. Thus, when Bethell reproached the poet John Milton for being one of those hoodwinked by Jonson into believing that a provincial Shakespeare spontaneously babbled "his native wood-notes wild," his weapon was the observation that "The well-educated Milton probably didn't realize that Shakespeare's vocabulary was twice his own." Shakespeare did indeed double the 8,000 words employed by Milton in his writings and, what is more, some number of these words are first found in his works and are thereby proclaimed as his inventions. For example, his use

---

*From C. M. Ingleby, Toulmin Smith, and F. J. Furnivall, *The Shakspere Allusion-Book: A Collection of Allusions to Shakspere from 1591 to 1700*, 1:373–74. This version of the anecdote is from Rowe's 1709 edition of Shakespeare. However, it was evidently a well-known story that was mentioned by Dryden (1668), Tate (1680), and Gildon (1694).

of *assassination* in *Macbeth* is the first known occurrence in English, and in *Love's Labor's Lost*, he transformed the word *plod* when he wrote:

> Small have continual plodders ever won,
> Save base authority from others' books.

But it should be noted, as is so often the case, he simply used words then in currency in a different sense. Many another of his neologisms are only the first examples of the use of a word in a particular sense, such as when Claudius tells Hamlet that his wish to return to Wittenberg is "most retrograde to our desire," which is the earliest recorded use of the astronomical phrase to mean "contrary." (It should not pass without comment that the modern who takes such liberties may be sent off to a dictionary to mend his ignorance.)

Shakespeare did unmistakably revel in the English language and its music. But he also had the practical need to make words to fit his verse and it is reasonable to suppose that in many cases necessity was indeed the mother of his invention. In this he was entirely a man of his time, for sixteenth-century England was indeed a "great feast of language." In regard to the samples above, the *Oxford English Dictionary* notes many coinages on *assassin* in this period, and *plod* meaning "laborious" had been introduced into the language in 1562. After all, Shakespeare's language, like his classical knowledge, are a reflection of the fact that he was a man of a very particular time in English history; in the words of Henri Fluchère:

> Shakespeare, though immortal, is not outside time: he is not a *lusus naturae*, a solitary giant, inventive and inspired, but someone who flourished between two precise dates—1590 and 1610. At any other moment of history he would not have been Shakespeare.[19]

As this suggests, it is in the glass of his age that we must look for him. Let's begin by recalling the Earl of Burford's great notion, to wit: "If you get Shakespeare wrong, you get the Elizabethan Age wrong." In fact, the earl has not only got it precisely backwards, but he has also made black of white. If we are to know Shakespeare, if we are to have a hope of finding an explanation for his genius—if we are not to get him wrong—we must begin by:

Getting the Elizabethan Age Right

The Elizabethan Age is but one period in the English Renaissance. Precisely what was this renaissance? Like the one on the European continent, it was a rebirth, a revival—specifically, as the *Oxford English Dictionary* defines it, "the great revival of art and letters, under the influence of classical models." The Renaissance came late, and fitfully, to England. The classicism of the Elizabethan era was not of the grave, didactic type, but rather, in the words of H. B. Lathrop, it turned to the classics "for variety and excitement, for color, for the enrichment of life, and not for its guidance and restraint." Not one of the Greek tragic poets, nor Aristophanes, the greatest of the comic poets, was translated into English. Even in their preference for the Roman writers, the Elizabethans did not choose the best. The "second-rate" Seneca alone had all of his tragedies put into English to become the model for Elizabethan tragic drama.[20] The classicism of the age was characterized by Hardin Craig thusly:

> In the study of the classicism of the Renaissance what we need to know is the ancient authors, not in their purified modern forms with archeological and textual addenda, but these authors plus their *spuria,* as printed and glossed in the sixteenth century and particularly as translated in the careless, anachronistic way of Elizabethan translators.

The Elizabethans, however, did not see themselves as careless and anachronistic. Rather, they had "made friends with the ancients and amplified their own society by admitting to it on equal terms the great men of old. Indeed, the literary intelligence of the Elizabethans is largely due to their hospitality."[21]

Quite clearly, Shakespeare and his colleagues did not view the ancients with the awe and mystique that attaches to them nowadays. What is more, as far as dramatists in particular were concerned, the comfort and familiarity of their contemporaries with the ancient tales was most useful. As the playhouse became the arena for treating matters of current interest, the distant times and nations served as a buffer between the playwright and a wary government. The companionable ancients offered a host of story lines that allowed the Renaissance dramatist to dress a topical issue in classical trappings. We have seen this device at work when Philip Massinger's original version of *Believe As You List* touched on events the Revels Office thought detrimental to England's peace treaty with Spain. With the help of Sir Walter Ralegh's *History of the World,* Plutarch and perhaps a few other classical sources, the "late & sad example" of King Sebastian of Portugal became the downfall of the second-century BC Syrian ruler, Antiochus the Great.

The literature and history of the ancients were but one source of plots for the stage. The chronicles of English history were especially popular for dramatization in the 1590s, while the romances of French, Spanish, Portugese and Italian writers were sought after by the book trade, some of which would supply the story line for English plays. In other words, the modern concept of originality did not exist for the English Renaissance author. Accordingly, there is no suggestion in any contemporary source that the dramatist who wrote a new play based on a tale already told in an earlier play, nor one who merely refashioned an old play, nor one who adapted a phrase from another, was guilty of either "plagiarism" or an artistic breach of any other kind. The miracle of Shakespeare is that he burst the literary confines of his age and its conventions to create timeless drama.

Nowhere do the Oxfordians get the Elizabethan Age more wrong than in posing Shakespeare's genius for language as an isolated phenomenon. Whereas the Renaissance in the continental nations had its greatest expression in paint, stone, and the sciences, the English Renaissance found its medium in words. Long before the great age of drama, English writers, indifferent to the purity of their tongue, snatched up words from other languages and adopted them as their own. They took words from Greek and Latin and Anglicized them and gave not a thought to a neat, orderly grammar. Inevitably, word-making became a fashion and the makers would demand credit for their innovations. Thus did George Puttenham proclaim his progeny, *scientific, idiom, methodical, savage,* and *audacious* (as well as *numerosity, implete* and *politien*). Although Thomas Nashe proposed *carminist* for "songwriter," he attacked the creators of "termagant ink-horn terms . . . hermaphrodite phrases, half-Latin, half-English."[22] So it was that by the time Shakespeare began writing for the stage, English had already developed into a language "of unsurpassed richness and beauty, which, however, defies all the rules."[23] But the late Elizabethans—and Shakespeare especially—were not to be outdone. "Shakespeare and his contemporaries," wrote the authors of *The Story of English,* "had experimented with the English language as no other writers before or since. There was an air of childish innocence in the ease with which they broke the rules and made the language sing." Shakespeare—*and* his contemporaries.

The special ear his age had for the harmonies of language is heard in the one work that is mentioned as the rival to his plays—the King James Bible. Lawrence Housman said of it that "Not Shakespeare nor Bacon nor any great figure in English literature has had so wide and deep an influence on the form of all the literary and political work." Nevertheless, there is little curiosity about the identity of its authors. Other Bibles in the vernacular preceded it, and its debt to the earlier versions is evident. The unique genius of its creators was to bring disparate forces together—"The Anglo-Saxon matches the Hebrew original in simplicity and directness; the Latin element brings sonority and stateliness"—to create a harmonious whole.[24] Yet, how many can name even one of those who performed this remarkable work?

Thomas Rogers's house, Stratford-upon-Avon. Now the Harvard House. (Courtesy Records Office, Shakespeare Birthplace Trust)

The title page of the King James Bible. (Courtesy of the Folger Shakespeare Library)

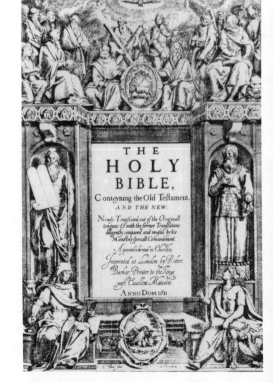

In fact, six companies of scholars, 49 men in all, gathered in Oxford, Westminster, and Cambridge to work on the James. That so many disparate hands could create this harmonious whole is "a miracle and a mystery" in the eyes of this Bible's scholar Olga Opfell, for "group writing seldom achieves great heights." No less miraculous, "Individual writings of the committeemen show no trace of the magnificent style" that suffuses the whole. Indeed, of the scholars who worked on it, the only name that is likely to be familiar except to scholars of the age is Lancelot Andrewes, the Bishop of Winchester who was King James's favorite preacher.* Opfell attributes their extraordinary achievement in no small part to the time in which they worked: "Whatever its glory, the King James Bible evolved in a special climate, a golden age of English literature, an influential period of English history."

It is difficult to measure just how much influence the popular stage had in this golden age of English literature. The literati broadcast their contempt for the products of the playhouses and we can only wonder how many might have slipped through their doorways to gather some "fire-new words" (as Shakespeare called them) from the stage, where words were all. There were few props; special effects were pretty much limited to such as a rolling cannonball, signifying thunder; lighting was provided by the sun, always an unreliable thing in England. Rather, it was words that turned day to night, called forth a russet dawn or a tempest, changed the stage from a castle to a city street, from a battlefield to a palace. But words did far more. They summoned forth the mighty and brought legends to life; carried the spectator to the embattled walls of Harfleur and the Forest of Arden. Most of all, they spanned the range of human emotions: "Witty dialogues, political discussions, machiavellian confessions, cries of despair or of vengeance, admissions of powerlessness or professions of faith were listened to with passionate interest."[25]

In amphitheaters that severally could hold between 1,500 and 3,000 spectators, it is unlikely that the dramatic companies could have thrived as they did if all but a few could understand, no less enjoy and appreciate, what they heard; just as it is doubtful that dramatists would have employed figures, events and images from ancient times up to their own if only a relative few in their audiences had the vaguest idea of what they were talking about. However, if the Oxfordians are believed, Shakespeare would have been wasting his golden words on the "unworthy scaffold," no less because of those who performed on it than those who beheld it.

---

* A complete list of the forty-nine translators is in Olga S. Opfell, *The King James Bible Translators,* pp. 135–37.

The Theater and Audiences of Shakespeare's Time

The players? A bad lot! What more proof do we need than that they presumed to be editors, cutting plays to ribbons and peddling the remains to printers, maybe passing off plays by inferior dramatists as Shakespeare's?[26] So little regard had they for great literature, can Shakespeare possibly have been done justice by such as these? As such criticisms trace their ancestry to Alexander Pope, it seems fitting to allow the "Strolling Player," John Roberts', *Answer to Mr Pope's Preface to Shakespear,* to speak for them:

> Why, what a tribe of wretched fellows these must be? . . . I wonder what they really did understand? They were wrong judges of poetry! They knew nothing of playing! They had no comfort of polite conversation! Nor had they any further taste of life or letters than what they could pick up over a pot of beer, with their unthinking brethren at the inns where they played, or in taking a sparing bottle of my Lord's wine, in the buttery, with his very learned steward.

Worse yet, women were played by boys! Why, according to Ogburn, the very thought that one day "I shall see / Some squeaking Cleopatra boy my greatness" was enough to drive the Queen of Egypt to embrace the asp. Can we believe that a mere boy could convincingly enact this magnificent and demanding role? Indeed, as there is no record of a public performance of *Antony and Cleopatra* in Shakespeare's time, this leads Ogburn to believe it was not written to be performed on the contemporary stage at all.[27] However, Lady Macbeth is a role at least as demanding on a "boy-actress," but we know that it was publicly played from Simon Forman's account of a performance of *Macbeth* at the Globe in his diary.[28] In fact, however much the idea of boys playing women's parts convincingly may strain Ogburn's, Shakespeare's contemporaries appear to feel they left little to the imagination.

Desdemona is with reasonable certainty a part that would have been played by a boy. In September 1610, Henry Jackson, a member of Corpus Christi College, Oxford, attended performances by the King's Men, "acted with enormous applause to full houses," in the town. In his critique set down in Latin, he commends the troupe for its tragedies, "acted with skill and decorum and in which some things, both speech and action, brought forth tears." But, of all in this distinguished company, he singled out the performance of Othello's wife,

> that famous Desdemona killed before us by her husband, although she always acted her whole part supremely well, yet when she was killed she

was even more moving, for when she fell back upon the bed she implored the pity of the spectators by her very face.[29]

Evidently the illusion created by a boy-actress was effective, for whether referring to the actor or the role, Jackson refers to the figure on the stage as "she" or "her."

It is doubtful anyone of the age was more critical than Ben Jonson, but he has left behind testimony to the excellence of the boys. In act two, scene eight, of *The Devil is an Ass* (1616), he tells of the cunning of the King's Men's Dick Robinson, who could play a woman's part so to the life that, according to Jonson, he in life went to a supper dressed as a lawyer's wife, and shocked the company by talking law, drinking to the assembled and talking bawdily. "O!" cries the character Ingine. "It would have burst your buttons, or not left you / A seam."[30]

Best of all are the ingenuous remarks of Thomas Coryate in writing of his travels in Italy, published as *Coryats Crudities* in 1611. The Italian playhouses he thought "very beggarly and base" compared to London's, nor did their actors compare with his countrymen "for apparel, shows and music." But, he comments with frank wonder, "Here I observed certain things I never saw before. For I saw women act . . . and they performed it with as good a grace, action, gesture and whatsoever convenient for a player, as ever I saw any masculine actor."[31] Coryate was obviously taken aback by his discovery that women could impersonate women as convincingly as the boy actors could.

That the boy-actress could hold his own against his female counterpart may be seen in the success of Edward Kynaston. He was born in 1643, the year after the drama was banned by the Commonwealth, and he could not have had the thorough training of the Renaissance boy actor, who was apprenticed to an adult actor. Nevertheless, even with the introduction of women on the Restoration stage, Kynaston's acting with D'Avenant's company won the praise of the finicky Pepys; and in 1708, the company's prompter, John Downes, reflecting on his long years in the theater, wrote that Kynaston in his youth "made a compleat female stage beauty, performing his parts so well . . . that it has since been disputable among the judicious, whether any woman that succeeded him so sensibly touched the audience as he."[32] At last, we can never know how truly the boy-actress captured the nuances of a woman and thus one can only wonder if a boy-Cleopatra could have done so badly as to have earned John Mason Brown's verdict against one woman who essayed the role, to wit: "Tallulah Bankhead barged down the Nile last night as Cleopatra and sank."

Nothing to the Oxfordian mind seems more improbable than that Shakespeare could have written for the spectators in the common playhouses.

Could the theatergoers at the Globe have savored fully, in the fleeting moment of performance, the depths and subtleties of his plays? Did the groundlings, the penny spectators who stood in the pit, understand one word of it? The very same whom Hamlet said "for the most part are capable of nothing but inexplicable dumbshows and noise"? (Curiously, he says this moments before a dumbshow is played, at his direction, before the court of Denmark.)

If the groundlings deserved their ill report at the time *Hamlet* was written, perhaps Shakespeare and his fellow dramatists effected a change in them, for we are given a different view by the time Thomas Dekker wrote his prologue to *If This Be Not a Good Play, the Devil Is in It* (1612). As Hamlet's criticism was actually aimed at actors who "split the ears of the groundlings," so Dekker attacked the playwrights who wrote of "ill-favored vices" only to "fill a house with fishwives." Instead, "Give me *That Man*," he cries, who does not pander to vulgar fashion—the dramatist who "[kills] the hearers' hearts," and ties

> His ear (with golden chains) to his melody:
> Can draw with Adamantine Pen, even creatures
> Forg'd out of the hammer, on tiptoe, to reach up,
> And (from rare silence) clap their brawny hands,
> T'applaud what their charmed soul scarce understands.

There likely was a time when the groundlings, used to a more steady diet of dumbshows and noise, could appreciate nothing else. If they had not reformed altogether by the time Dekker wrote this, apparently they were attentive enough and intelligent enough that they could be charmed by the music of an ingenious dramatist.

The groundlings were, of course, only one element in the multitudes who came to the Bankside playhouses. Evidence of the broad appeal of the drama is heard in the letter of a lawyer of Clifford's Inn named Philip Gawdy, who gleefully related the consequences when the Mayor of London and his council too strenuously executed the Privy Council's order to impress citizens for service in Flanders in 1602. The press gangs descended upon the playhouses and bowling alleys, rounding up 4,000 men, including not only gentlemen and servingmen, "but lawyers, clerks, country men that had law causes; aye, the Queen's men, knights, and as it was credibly reported one Earl." This impressment resulted in such an outcry that, Gawdy wrote, the Privy Council ordered no more gentlemen or servingmen were to be impressed (nor presumably knights or earls either). In relating this letter, the theater scholar Andrew Gurr comments that the lawyer may have overemphasized the number of gentry and nobility rounded up in the playhouses, but as for "the numbers involved—four thousand impressed from three amphitheatres and a few bowling alleys—seem accurate."[33]

However much Gawdy may have exaggerated, playhouse audiences were unquestionably drawn from all walks of life, and not England's alone. In 1607 or 1608, the Venetian ambassador Giorgio Gustinian, made up a party to see *Pericles* at the Globe. Among his guests were the French ambassador, his wife, and the secretary of the Florentine embassy. And, in 1610, an "entourage only slightly smaller" joined Prince Frederick Lewis of Württemberg to see a performance of *Othello* at the Globe.[34] However, it was a play involving an ambassador that gives us a clear picture of the diversity of the contemporary audience and its tastes.

Thomas Middleton struck upon an ingenious strategy to express broadly held anti-Spanish sentiment by having it played in *A Game at Chess,* which was licensed by the Master of the Revels on July 9, 1624. The King's Men were equal to his bold scheme, especially in the impersonation of Spain's ambassador to Britain, Gondomar, who was, according to "the news-master" John Chamberlain, "counterfeited . . . to the life, with all his graces and faces"—even to the replication of his apparel. The thinly veiled portrait of the ambassador so epitomized the play that Chamberlain did not call it by the title Middleton gave it, but rather "our famous play of Gondomar."[35] When the ambassador got wind of this he complained to King James, who promptly ordered a halt to performances, but not before it had an unprecedented run of nine successive dates. From Chamberlain we also hear that in that time the Globe was "frequented by all sorts of people, old and young, rich and poor, masters and servants, papists and puritans, wise men *et. ct.,* churchmen and statesmen . . . and a world besides." So varied a throng at a topical play nowadays is no more likely than that such a play would be given a major production in the first place—unless, perhaps, as a musical.

When we talk of the spectators who crowded the Globe and the other London theaters, we would do well to recall the observation of David Cressy that many in the Renaissance audience had, like Shakespeare and his fellow dramatists, grown up in "a period of unusual educational excitement and achievement," and, like Shakespeare, "part of his audience was uniquely well-educated." But credit is due all the playgoers, earl and groundling alike, for sustaining the most remarkable dramatic age in the history of the modern world.

The impetus to this theater may have been best defined by Alexis de Tocqueville in *Democracy in America,* in which he wrote of the competing forces of democracy and aristocracy, not as a theorist, but from firsthand experience. Of the singular place of drama in ages counterpoised between these poles of the social order he wrote, "When the yet untutored love of

The engraved title page of Middleton's *A Game at Chess*. (By permission of the British Library)

the pleasure of the mind begins to affect any class of the community, it is to the theater they turn." When this occurs, though the society itself may be aristocratic, a certain democracy reigns in the playhouse:

> It has always been in the theater that the learned and educated have had the greatest difficulty in making their tastes prevail over that of the people and preventing themselves from being carried away by them. The pit often lays down the law for the boxes.[36]

This is perhaps characteristic of English Renaissance theater to a greater degree than the theater of any other age. Its drama was not written, as nearly all drama since has been, for audiences narrowly defined by class or education, nor by social, cultural or political distinctions. The dainty set before the court might soon be set out at the "cockpit," and vice versa. The scope of its drama was breathtaking, embracing other ages and cultures and making them one with their own. The citizen who came to the playhouse to see a tragedy on one day might return on the next to see a comedy; perhaps this day it was the Rome of *Julius Caesar,* tomorrow it might be the Smithfield of *Bartholomew Fair.* They were gourmands at the ready to sample every emotion, theme or topic, every twist of a plot or turn of a phrase. They didn't demand the new and the novel only, but were apparently eager for revivals of the old drama (albeit with some mending).

Shakespeare was but one figure in this saga; his plays make up a tiny fraction of all those written in the half-century of Renaissance theater. By setting him above his time, we lose sight of the fact he was every bit as much a man of that time as Marlowe, Jonson, or Middleton. When we do this we cannot discover the nature of his genius, for then we do not ask why he holds center stage long after his colleagues have been relegated to the role of "Shakespeare's contemporaries."

Getting Shakespeare Right

The Oxfordian Shakespeare we have come to know is a literary artist first and foremost, only coincidentally a playwright. In fact, shorn of the constraints the theater imposed on his genius, we may see that "he was above all a novelist, and a novelist above all other novelists."[37] And it is a certainty that, in the proffered words of Algernon Swinburne, "Shakespeare never wrote merely for the stage." The evidence for this, he declares, comes from the author himself, specifically his *Hamlet,* where

> Scene by scene, line for line, stroke upon stroke, and touch after touch, he went over all the old laboured ground again; and not to ensure success in his own day, and fill his pockets with contemporary pence, but merely and wholly to make it worthy of himself and his future students.[38]

The very idea, indeed, that Shakespeare could have been (as the Oxfordians term it) a "mercenary," writing "for gain, not glory," is as entirely repugnant to Swinburne as it is beyond belief to the controversialists.

Swinburne is but one of the nineteenth-century critics who gave wing to Bardolatry and prove to be a bountiful source for Oxfordian quotations about Shakespeare's principally literary merit and the depredations of the stage upon it. Thus, William Hazlitt is quoted as saying, "We do not like to see our author's plays acted, and least of all, HAMLET." But in Hazlitt the Oxfordians have an uncertain ally.

He would give vent to such utterances when a particular performance, in this case Edmund Kean's, annoyed him. However, one of Kean's gestures in this very same performance also wrung the comment from him that "actors are the best commentators on the poets."[39] Under no circumstances did he share the views of such as Swinburne—or the Oxfordians—about Shakespeare the artist or his intended audience. To the contrary, in Hazlitt's view, Shakespeare

> wrote for the "great vulgar and the small," in his time, not for posterity. If Queen Elizabeth and the maids of honour laughed heartily at his worst jokes, and the catcalls in the gallery were silent at his best passages, he went home satisfied and slept the night well.[40]

What is more, although Hazlitt may have shared the shortcomings common to the critics of the day, he captured the unique qualities of Shakespeare's creations, and they all point to the stage.

Shakespeare's world was, by its very nature, one of many characters, many voices and many lives, for he was a player as well as a playwright. In the custom of the time, he would "double"—play two or three parts each day, creating several characters, voices and lives. There cannot have been a better school for the playwright, who, in the words of Gary Taylor, "had to perform all the parts in his head, momentarily recreating himself in the image of each."[41] Of Shakespeare's uncanny ability to do this Hazlitt wrote:

> That which, perhaps, more than any thing else distinguishes the dramatic production of Shakespeare from all others, is [his] wonderful truth and individuality of conception. Each of his characters is as much itself, and as absolutely independent of the rest, as well as of the author, as if they were living persons, not fictions of the mind.

On the whole, his plays, he concluded, are "expressions of passions, not descriptions of them. His characters are real beings of flesh and blood; they speak like men, not like authors."[42] This may be shrugged off as the lucky accident of his genius. Or we may recognize that it was because he approached his characters not as an author, but as an actor. What is more, his characters *were* "real beings of flesh and blood"—his fellow actors, whose voices, gestures and movements, he knew so thoroughly and so intimately. And for this we do have evidence from Shakespeare himself.

Scholars have duly noted that the characters in his earliest plays, written for various companies, do not have the individualized voices, the personal vocabularies, which contribute greatly to the illusion of each character being "absolutely independent of the rest" that is the hallmark of his mature art. It is little noticed how suddenly this individuation emerges after Shakespeare joined the Lord Chamberlain's Men in 1594. From the beginning of his affiliation with this company, each figure, great or small, takes on a personality of its own, and this may be owed to the stage persona of the particular actor who would play the part. This likelihood is reflected in an apparent theatrical in-joke in *Hamlet*, where Polonius replies to Hamlet's query about the part he played in a student theatrical by saying, "I did enact Julius Caesar. I was killed i'th' Capitol. Brutus killed me." Shakespeare's *Julius Caesar* had debuted in 1599, a year before *Hamlet*, and it is probable that the actor playing Polonius, thought to be John Heminges, had essayed the title role in *Caesar*, just as the actor playing Hamlet, Richard Burbage, played the role of Brutus. Thus would Polonius' reply amuse the playgoer who had seen the earlier play and would presage the similar outcome of the match of these two players in *Hamlet*.[43] It does then appear, if appearances are not deceiving, that Shakespeare created the role of Polonius with Heminges in mind—something it is extremely doubtful that a man who was anything but deeply, personally involved in this company would have, or could have, done.

Furthermore, the stage is important even to the beauties of his language, which threatened to exile his plays to the study to be treated as purely literary works. On the printed page, it is true, his words may be savored and (with the help of footnotes) yield meanings that can be missed in performance. The verse may be read as nothing but poetry (actors did so long enough); and, as Shakespeare matured, his prose became almost indistinguishable from his verse. (The speech that Richard Burton thought the most beautiful of all—Hamlet's "What a piece of work is a man"—is in prose.) However, the pleasures of Shakespeare in the study owe a debt to the fact his plays are, first and foremost, creations for the theater. He set words in verse not for poetic readings, but because the meter serves the function of cuing the actor to emphasis when reading a line. Yet, he did not tie his verse strictly to iambic pentameter for the scansion of the studious reader, but would shatter its rhythms for its dramatic effect on his auditors.

So Shakespeare was a player as well as a playwright: so were others of his day. Jonson and Heywood, for example, but one is rarely performed today, the other hardly ever. What has made Shakespeare the one who towers not only above his contemporaries, but over all who have written for the stage over the ages? Little more than half a century after Shakespeare died, John Dryden would write that he "of all modern, and perhaps ancient poets, had the largest and most comprehensive soul." Three hundred years later these words were echoed by a modern scholar, Robert Ornstein, who wrote that "his vision of life was so comprehensive that his art has never lost its relevance to the human situation."[44] Why of all the dramatists of his day was he so singularly touched by this genius?

Perhaps no small part of the reason is that Shakespeare was not of precisely the same day as Jonson, Heywood, and the rest. He began writing plays in the heady aftermath of the triumph over the Armada, and when the public theater was in the giddy days of its youth and enjoyed its greatest freedom. The drama in these years had little to do with psychology or, for that matter, artistic pretension. It borrowed freely and profusely from the ancients and admired its image in the classical glass. So thoroughly did these dramatists mine English history that the history play genre all but died out with the decade.

Shakespeare alone among the pioneers of this drama worked throughout this vital period and carried its art into the new century. He alone had gained mastery over comedy, history and tragedy, and he drew upon this experience when he embarked upon a more sophisticated drama for a new age. If we had only the twenty plays he wrote before 1601, his most memorable characters would have been Hamlet, Falstaff, perhaps Richard III, and it is doubtful that he would be regarded as the equal of Marlowe. However, the towering figures in his Jacobean tragedies—Othello, Macbeth, Lady Macbeth, Lear, and Cleopatra—owe an immeasurable debt to his grounding in the variety and spontaneity of the Elizabethan stage. Although they are drawn on a far grander scale than the characters in his Elizabethan drama, Shakespeare's Jacobean tragic figures retain the knack, in the words of Fluchère, to "speak as they would speak if faced with the same situations in which he placed them or with the characters he gave them." And this, he rightly says, "is the domain of *art*, not of the poet's *life*."[45]

Ultimately, when we seek Shakespeare's art and his audience, his own time would seem the best place to look, and it so happens that one of his contemporaries left us a picture quite different from Swinburne's. In 1604, a poet named Anthony Scoloker prefaced his only published work, *Daiphantus; or, The Passions of Love*, with an epistle on his epistle—specifically, how he wished his audience to receive it, and that was:

> It should be like the Never-too-well read Arcadia, where the prose and verse (matter and words) are like his mistress's eyes, one still excelling another and without co-rival; or to come home to the vulgar's element, like friendly Shakespeare's tragedies, where the comedian rides, when the tragedian stands on tiptoe. Faith it should please all, like Prince Hamlet.

Through the eyes of this contemporary we see that Shakespeare was viewed as a writer for the common class, in comparison to the richer tastes attracted to Sir Philip Sidney. Furthermore, dismaying though it might have been to Sidney's disciples and Shakespeare's earlier critics, it is a virtue in Scoloker's eyes that Shakespeare made himself friendly to his Globe audiences by tempering his tragedies with mirth. But it is his last sentence—"Faith it should please all, like Prince Hamlet"—that arrests the eye, for it brings to mind Shakespeare's own words.

Shakespeare wrote half a dozen plays after *Macbeth* that, though they have their admirers, are the least known to moderns and the least performed—except for *The Tempest*. This is the last play from his pen exclusively, and some critics hear in it an allegory on Shakespeare's theatrical career, a sort of farewell to the stage, with the poet in the role of the sorcerer Prospero. Cooler heads reject this utterly. Whichever side one falls on, Prospero's epilogue, be it for this one play or all of them, speaks no less to the poet's conjuring art than his own, and we hear the words:

> But release me from my bands
> With the help of your good hands:
> Gentle breath of yours my sails
> Must fill, or else my project fails,
> Which was to please.

We should bear these words in mind when we approach library shelves groaning with studies of his genius. For no scholarly tome has quite explained why each age turns to him to find its "form and pressure" when contemporary dramatists fail; why those who dwell in times far different from his own see themselves best reflected and their lives magnified in his words and characters. Is this owed entirely to the comprehensiveness of his soul and of his vision of life? Or is it owed to no less a degree to the inclusiveness of his drama? At last, we may see that Shakespeare's special genius is his ability to present his vision of life in a way that may be generally shared, understood and enjoyed. He succeeded uniquely in his project, "Which was to please."

That New Old-Time Orthodoxy

What the Oxfordians have put on trial is not only the traditional William Shakespeare but, to an even greater degree, the upholders of the tradition—the academic Shakespeareans, nearly all of whom have studiously refused to consider their evidence that purports to show that the record of the Stratford man is untrustworthy and that their Castle Hedingham man has the "qualifications" that the other man lacks. Although they profess to be pained by this indifference, they have enjoyed its benefits, not only insofar as their evidence has gone virtually unchallenged, but because their image of being gallant heretics has been unquestioningly accepted.

The Oxfordians are anything but heretics.

It is not a coincidence that they so often seek confirmation of their idea of Shakespeare's genius from the nineteenth-century literary critics, for it was in the "Idolatry Ad Astra" of that age that their omniscient superman was created. The great difference between the bygone idolators and the Oxfordians is that the former would have made him a jack-of-all-trades, whereas the latter think it can all be resolved in one trade—that of earl. Of course, this is nothing new either. In fact, the first candidate for the True Authorship honors was also an earl, Sir Francis Bacon, the Earl of Verulam (St. Albans). And there have been others, such as the Earl of Rutland, and Oxford's son-in-law, the Earl of Derby, amidst a host of aristocrats, not excluding a Queen of England. The logical conclusion to be drawn from this epidemic of Shakespeares is that a good number of the men and women in the upper echelons of Elizabethan life shared the cultural, social and political appetites of this very particular time in English history. What makes it such a remarkable time is that these appetites were also shared by the clerk, apprentice and student. The meeting place of this commonwealth of mind and spirit was the drama.

What the controversialists have never come close to explaining is where their particular candidate acquired the skills and the knowledge to have written so many of the most successful theatrical works in literary history. Whereas we are told that Shakespeare's perceived intellectual prowess could only have been gotten by hard study and harder experience, we are asked to believe that his unapproachable command of theater—the very thing that caused the director Peter Brook to write, "in the second half of the twentieth-century in England . . . we are faced with the infuriating fact that Shakespeare is still our model"—is nothing more than a happy accident of the author's genius.[46] Consider the words of the renowned theatre critic Brooks Atkinson who, writing in another context, said:

> Plays are infernally difficult to write. Ideas cannot be expressed vigorously in the theatre without some instinct for the stage—a sense of time, a sense of dramatic architecture, a sense of motion and emphasis, a knowledge of what actors can say or do, a feeling for the response of audiences. Some of these things can be learned by a study of craftsmanship or technique. A great deal more can be learned by acting or working backstage in the company of theatre people.[47]

In Shakespeare's day there were no schools of drama, no place to develop a command of dramatic craftsmanship and technique besides acting and working backstage in the company of theater people. And, to the best of our knowledge, no playwright was ever in better company.

When George Bernard Shaw called on the novelist Thomas Hardy to support his scheme for an English national theater as a memorial to Shakespeare, Hardy demurred out of his belief that the plays "would cease altogether to be acted some day, and be simply studied." This is the sad,

logical result of nineteenth century literary criticism and theatrical performance. It is therefore with particular cheer that one reads the following
words by a modern-day academic scholar, John Russell Brown: "Readers
and critics have become increasingly aware that the plays were written for
performance and reveal their true natures only in performance." He thus
wrote *Discovering Shakespeare* on the premise,

> that we should read and study the plays as if we were rehearsing them,
> and that we should then attempt to imagine performances. I have tried to
> show how every reader can use imagination and experience in the same
> way as an actor does, and how everyone can learn from what happens in
> a theatre during performance. So the texts of Shakespeare's plays can re-
> veal living images of life.[48]

This reflects the great transformation in Shakespearean studies over the
past two decades or so. Modern editions of the plays are giving growing
attention to the history of the performance of the respective play and the
stage may even influence what appears in footnotes. Most importantly,
thanks to the availability of Shakespeare on film and videotape, as well as
the ever-increasing number of permanent and traveling troupes, amateur
and professional, his plays in performance have become a part of the study
of them in colleges and universities.

But the happiest part of this transformation is something I have seen
with my own eyes in the course of more than six years of researching at
the Folger Shakespeare Library. Each succeeding springtime brings a larger
hoard of children from elementary through high school age who descend
on the library to enact scenes from his plays in its Elizabethan theater. The
delight on the faces of these boys and girls as they discover Shakespeare
by performing him themselves is a far cry from the benumbed expressions
of past students who were introduced to him by textbooks. This change is
welcomed by the academics who will inherit these youngsters. Thus did
Professor George Slover approve Shakespeare & Company's performance
programs for students with the comment, "The way for students to own
the texts is the way of the actor, not the scholar and critic."[49]

It is probably premature to say that Shakespeare will cease to be studied
some day, and be simply acted—not so long as there are academic journals
aplenty. But I will venture to say that these new approaches to his plays
bode the end of the authorship controversy. The young people who are
introduced to the author through his living drama are not likely to see
"friendly Shakespeare" in an aristocrat (and especially not in one so self-
obsessed as the Earl of Oxford). It would be poetic justice indeed if the
spear through the heart of the authorship controversy turns out to be the
joy of his plays discovered on such as the stage of a modern-day Elizabethan theater.

Notes

1. In the Court of Public Opinion

1. Quoted in Bentley Boyd, "A Rose Might Smell as Sweet by Another Name . . . ," *Chicago Tribune,* August 20, 1989.
2. James Lardner, "Onward and Upward with the Arts: The Authorship Question," *The New Yorker,* April 11, 1988, 100.
3. Ibid.
4. Giles E. Dawson, *Shakespeare Quarterly* vol. 4 (1953), 165. These comments appeared in his review of *This Star of England,* by Dorothy and Charlton Ogburn [Sr.]. The authors were the parents of Charlton Ogburn, the author of *The Mysterious William Shakespeare.*
5. Lardner, 89.
6. David Daniell, *"Coriolanus" in Europe* (London: Athlone Press, 1980), 56.
7. J. B. Leishman, ed., The *Three Parnassus Plays (1598–1601)* (London: Ivor Nicholson & Watson, 1949), in the First Part of *The Return from Parnassus,* lines 834–35.
8. Ibid., First Part of *The Return,* lines 1211–14.
9. John Davies, *The Complete Works,* Alexander B. Grosart, ed., 2 vols. (1878; Hildesheim: George Olms, 1969), in *The Scourge of Folly,* 2:58, 2:59–60, 2:53, 2:60–61.
10. Suetonius, "The Life of Terence," in Terence, *The Comedies,* trans. Betty Radice, rev. ed. (Harmondsworth: Penguin, 1976), 393.

2. Shakespeare of Stratford, His Record and Remains

1. Charlton Ogburn, *The Mysterious William Shakespeare* (New York: Dodd, Mead, 1984), 93.
2. Edgar Innis Fripp, ed., *Minutes and Accounts of the Corporations of Stratford-upon-Avon and Other Records, 1553–1620,* Vol. 2 (London: Oxford University Press, 1924), 49–61 passim.
3. David Thomas, *Shakespeare in the Public Records* (London: H. M. Stationery Office, 1985), 2.
4. Philip Henslowe, *Henslowe Papers, Being Documents Supplementary to Henslowe's Diary* (1907; Folcroft, PA: Folcroft, 1969), 2–4.
5. Philip Henslowe, *Henslowe's Diary,* W. W. Greg, ed., 2 vols. (1904; Folcroft, PA: Folcroft Library Editions, 1976), 2:278.
6. A. D. Wraight, *In Search of Christopher Marlowe* (New York: Vanguard Press, 1965). For the documents mentioned see: Birth Register, p. 4; Burial Register, p. 305; King's

School, p. 49; Cambridge University, pp. 53–100 passim, and 350–53; Privy Council, p. 88; Benchkin will, p. 229.

7. Ogburn, 95–98.
8. W. W. Greg, ed., *A Bibliography of the English Printed Drama to the Restoration,* 4 vols. (1939–59; Menston: Scolar, 1970), 1:230–31, 1:398–400.
9. Ibid., 1:272, 274.
10. Quoted in Don Oldenburg, "Beating Up on the Bard," *Washington Post,* December 18, 1990, B5.
11. Greg, 1:418.
12. R. B. McKerrow, *A Dictionary of Printers and Booksellers in England, Scotland and Ireland . . . 1557–1640* (1910. Reprint; New York: Burt Franklin, 1960, 278).
13. Greg, 1:271.
14. David Cressy, *Literacy and the Social Order* (Cambridge: Cambridge University Press, 1980), 58.
15. Ibid., 128–29.
16. David Cressy, ed., *Education in Tudor and Stuart England* (London: Edward Arnold, 1975), 112–13.
17. Ogburn, 123.
18. Robert Bearman, letter to the author, June 28, 1989.
19. Ogburn, 273–79.
20. James Lardner, "Onward and Upward with the Arts: The Authorship Question," *The New Yorker,* April 11, 1988, 103.
21. Lawrence Edward Tanner, *Westminster School: A History* (London: Country Life, 1934), 4.
22. David Riggs, *Ben Jonson: A Life* (Cambridge: Harvard University Press, 1989), 11.
23. G. F. Russell Barker and Alan H. Stenning, eds., *The Record of Old Westminsters,* 2 vols. (London: Chiswick, 1928), 1:vi; 1:v–vii.
24. William Drummond, *Ben Jonson's Conversations with William Drummond of Hawthornden,* Richard Ferrar Patterson, ed. (1923; New York: Haskell House, 1974), 23.
25. C. H. Herford, Percy Simpson, and Evelyn Simpson, *Ben Jonson,* 11 vols. (Oxford: Clarendon Press, 1925–51), 8:31.
26. Ibid., 1:3 fn 1.
27. Rosalind Miles, *Ben Jonson: His Craft and Art* (Savage, MD: Barnes & Noble, 1990), 5.
28. Drummond, 24.
29. Edgar Innis Fripp, ed., *Minutes and Accounts of the Corporation of Stratford-upon-Avon and Other Records, 1553–1620.* Vol. 1 (London: Oxford University Press, 1921), 33–34.
30. David Cressy, letter to the author, June 23, 1989.
31. Edgar Innis Fripp, ed., *Minutes and Accounts of the Corporation of Stratford-upon-Avon and Other Records, 1553–1620.* Vol. 3 (London: Oxford University Press, 1921), xiii.
32. Edgar Innis Fripp, *Shakespeare's Stratford* (1928; Freeport: Books for Libraries, 1979), 35.
33. Marcus Tullius Cicero, *The Letters to His Friends,* W. Gwynn Williams, trans., vol. 1 (London: W. Heinemann, 1943), 1:24, 1:25.
34. Cressy, *Literacy,* 169.
35. B. Roland Lewis, *The Shakespeare Documents; Facsimiles, Transliterations and Commentary,* 2 vols. (1940–41; Westport, CT: Greenwood Press, 1969), 1:280–86.
36. Lardner, 93.
37. Lewis: 2:509–11, for his extract.
38. Minos D. Miller, multiple letter, November 4, 1987.
39. Charles William Wallace, ed., *Advance Notes from Shakespeare, The Globe, and Blackfriars* (Stratford-upon-Avon: Shakespeare Head Press, 1909), 4, lines 40–43.
40. Anthony Richard Wagner, *Heralds of England: A History of the Office and College of Arms* (London: H. M. Stationery Office, 1967), 210.
41. Thomas, 33–34.

42. S. Schoenbaum, *William Shakespeare: Records and Images* (New York: Oxford University Press, 1981), 98.

43. Giles E. Dawson, "Shakespeare's Handwriting," *Shakespeare Survey* 42 (Cambridge: Cambridge University Press, 1990), 128.

44. Charles R. Forker, "Webster or Shakespeare? Style, Idiom, Vocabulary, and Spelling in the Additions to *Sir Thomas More*," *Shakespeare and Sir Thomas More: Essays on the Play and Its Shakespearean Interest* (New York: Cambridge University Press, 1989), 164, 153.

45. Charles Champlin, "Whomsomever Art Thou, Shaksper?" *Los Angeles Times*, January 12, 1984.

46. Henry Herbert, *The Dramatic Records of Sir Henry Herbert*, Joseph Quincy Adams, ed. (1917; New York: Benjamin Blom, 1964), 11.

47. William Sharp McKechnie, *Magna Carta: A Commentary on the Great Charter of King John*, 2d ed. (1914; New York: Burt Franklin, 1960), 165–68.

48. William Dodsworth, *An Historical Account of the . . . Cathedral Church of Sarum, or Salisbury* (Salisbury: Privately printed, 1914), 202.

49. James Clark Holt, *Magna Carta* (Cambridge: University Press, 1965), 247–48.

50. Godfrey R. C. Davis, *Magna Carta* (London: Trustees of the British Museum, 1963), 13.

51. Ogburn, 123.

52. Edmund Kerchever Chambers, "Dramatic Records: The Lord Chamberlain's Office," *Malone Society Collections*, vol. 2, part 3, W. W. Greg, gen. ed. (Oxford: Malone Society, 1931), 321.

53. Herford, 8:205; 8:202–12.

54. W. W. Greg, "The Bakings of Betsy," in *Collected Papers*, J. C. Maxwell, ed. (Oxford: Clarendon, 1966), 48–74.

55. *Western Manuscripts and Miniatures*, June 25, 1985. The catalogue is unpaginated. The description of the manuscript is found under item 50.

56. Ward Allen, *Translating the New Testament Epistles, 1604–1611* (Ann Arbor: University Microfilms International for Vanderbilt University Press, 1977), xxvii–xxviii; and Olga S. Opfell, *The King James Bible Translators* (Jefferson, NC: McFarland, 1982), 111.

57. Edward Arber, *A Transcript of the Registers of the Company of Stationers of London: 1554–1640 A.D.*, 5 vols. (1875–79; New York: P. Smith, 1950), 3:28.

58. Opfell, 101–4.

59. Ward Allen, ed., *Translating for King James; The only notes made by a translator of King James's Bible* (Nashville: Vanderbilt University Press, 1969), 112–13.

3. On the Paper Trail of the Player and the Playwright

1. Charlton Ogburn, *The Mysterious William Shakespeare* (New York: Dodd, Mead, 1984), 101.

2. Philip Henslowe, *Henslowe's Diary*, W. W. Greg, ed., 2 vols. (1904; Folcroft, PA: Folcroft Library Editions, 1976), 1:29.

3. Ibid., 1:72.

4. Ibid., 1:163.

5. Ibid., household: 1:3, 1:196–97, 1:199–200; Admiral's 1:126.

6. Ogburn, 102.

7. Giles E. Dawson, *Records of Plays & Players in Kent, 1450–1642, Malone Society Collections*, vol. 7 (Oxford: University Press, 1965), 18, 20, 17.

8. W. Kelly, *Notices Illustrative of the Drama . . . Extracted from the Chamberlains' Accounts and Other Manuscripts of the Borough of Leicester* (London: J. R. Smith, 1865), 82–85.

9. Dawson, xxvi.

10. David Cook and Frank Percy Wilson, eds., *Dramatic Records in the Declared Accounts of the Treasurer of the Chamber, 1558–1642*, vol. 6, *Malone Society Collections* (Oxford: The University Press, 1952), 29.

11. Ogburn, 65; 65–66.
12. Ibid., 65–66.
13. Charlotte Carmichael Stopes, *The Life of Henry, Third Earl of Southampton, Shakespeare's Patron* (Cambridge: The University Press, 1922), 112.
14. David Thomas, letter to the author, September 22, 1989.
15. David Thomas, letter to the author, August 21, 1989.
16. Cook, 31–32.
17. Desmond Bland, ed., *Gesta Grayorum. English Reprints Series* 22 (Liverpool: Liverpool University Press, 1968), 29, 29–33.
18. Ogburn, 65.
19. S. Schoenbaum, *William Shakespeare: A Compact Documentary Life*, rev. ed. (New York: Oxford University Press, 1987), 210.
20. B. Roland Lewis, *The Shakespeare Documentary: Facsimiles, Transliterations and Commentary*, 2 vols. (1940–41; Westport, CT: Greenwood Press, 1969), 2:508–9.
21. C. F. Tucker Brooke, *Shakespeare of Stratford. The Yale Shakespeare* (New Haven: Yale University Press, 1926), 31.
22. Lewis, 1:210–11, 1:208–16.
23. Ibid., 1:301, 1:299–306.
24. Lewis, 2:336–46.
25. Anthony Richard Wagner, *Heralds of England: A History of the Office and College of Arms* (London: H. M. Stationery Office, 1967), 211–12.
26. Ibid, 209–10.
27. MS. V.a.156, Folger Shakespeare Library.
28. College of Arms, London, MS. WZ. 276b.
29. Wagner, 204.
30. Edwin Nungezer, *A Dictionary of Actors* (1929; New York: AMS, 1971), 1451.
31. Ogburn, 30. See Lewis, 2:367–68.
32. John Thomas Looney, *"Shakespeare" Identified in Edward de Vere, Seventeenth Earl of Oxford, and the Poems of Edward de Vere*, Ruth Lloyd Miller, ed., 3d ed., 2 vols. (1920; Port Washington: Kennikat, 1975), 2:116.
33. David Thomas, *Shakespeare in the Public Records* (London: H. M. Stationery Office, 1985), 16.
34. Nungezer, 282.
35. Lewis, 2:520.
36. Ogburn, 101.
37. Henslowe, *Diary*, 1:13.
38. Ibid, 1:45.
39. *Dictionary of Literary Biography* 62; *Elizabethan Dramatists*, Fredson Bowers, ed. (Detroit: Gale, 1987), 82.
40. Robert Greene, *Robert Greene, M.A., Groats-Worth of Witte, Bought with a Million of Repentance/The Repentance of Robert Greene, 1592*, George B. Harrison, ed. (Edinburgh: University Press, 1966), 45–46.
41. Ogburn, 56–58.
42. Robert Greene, *Menaphon and A Margarite of America*, George B. Harrison, ed. (Oxford: Basil Blackwell, 1927), 4.
43. Tom Bethell, "The Case for Oxford/Reply to Matus," "Looking for Shakespeare," *Atlantic Monthly*, October 1991, 75, 78.
44. Henry Chettle, *Kind-Heart's Dream/A Mirror of Monsters* [by William Rankins] (New York: Johnson Reprint, 1972). The edition is unpaginated.
45. Ogburn, 122–23.
46. Gerald Eades Bentley, *The Profession of Dramatist in Shakespeare's Time, 1590–1642* (Princeton: Princeton University Press, 1971), 27.
47. W. W. Greg, ed., *English Literary Autographs, 1550–1650* (Oxford: Oxford University Press, 1925–32), facsimile XXII.
48. Richard Dutton, *Ben Jonson: To the First Folio* (Cambridge: Cambridge University Press, 1983), 11.
49. Bentley, 290.

50. Dutton, 12.
51. Charlton Hinman, *The Printing and Proof-Reading of the First Folio of Shakespeare*, 2 vols. (Oxford: Clarendon Press, 1963), 1:4.
52. For the study of *The Honest Man's Fortune*, see R. C. Bald, *Bibliographical Studies in the Beaumont and Fletcher Folio of 1647* (1937; Folcroft: Folcroft Library Editions, 1974) 53–57; for *The Humorous Lieutenant* and *The Woman's Prize*, see Hoy and Bowers in Francis Beaumont and John Fletcher, *The Dramatic Works in the Beaumont and Fletcher Canon*, Fredson Bowers, gen. ed., 7 vols. (Cambridge: Cambridge University Press, 1966–89), 5:291–96 and 4:3–9.
53. Bowers, introduction to *Beggars Bush*, in Beaumont and Fletcher, 3:227–30.
54. W. W. Greg, "Prompt Copies, Private Transcripts, and the 'Playhouse Scrivener,' " *Library*, 4th ser., vol. 6, 1925, 151–53. Also Hoy, introduction to *Bonduca*, in Beaumont and Fletcher, 4:151–52.
55. See Charles J. Sisson, "Introduction to *Believe as You List*," *The Seventeenth-Century Stage*, Gerald Eades Bentley, ed. (Chicago: University of Chicago Press, 1968) 170–95.
56. Sisson, 172–75.
57. Anthony G. Petti, *English Literary Hands from Chaucer to Dryden* (Cambridge: Harvard University Press, 1977), 1.
58. Ibid., 2.
59. Falconer Madan, et al., *The Original Bodleian Copy of the First Folio of Shakespeare (The Turbutt Shakespeare)* (Oxford: Clarendon Press, 1905), 5.
60. *A Catalogue of the Shakespeare Exhibition Held in the Bodleian Library* (Oxford: Bodleian Library, 1916), 14.
61. Wagner, 346–47.

4. The Publication of Shakespeare's Plays

1. James Lardner, "Onward and Upward with the Arts: The Authorship Question," *The New Yorker*, April 11, 1988, 102.
2. George Greenwood, *The Shakespeare Problem Restated* (1908; Westport, CT: Greenwood Press, 1970), 301, 298–306.
3. R. C. Bald, "Early Copyright Litigation and Bibliographical Interest," *The Papers of the Bibliographical Society of America*, vol. 36 (1942), 81.
4. Alfred W. Pollard, *Shakespeare's Fight with the Pirates and the Problems of the Transmission of His Text* (London: Alexander Moring, 1917), 34.
5. See Richard Beale Davis, "Early Editions of George Sandys' 'Ovid': The Circumstances of Production," *The Papers of the Bibliographical Society of America*, vol. 35 (1941), 255–76.
6. Gerard Eades Bentley, *The Profession of Dramatist in Shakespeare's Time, 1590–1642* (Princeton: Princeton University Press, 1971), 282–83.
7. Henry Herbert, *The Dramatic Records of Sir Henry Herbert*, Joseph Quincy Adams, ed. (1917; New York: Benjamin Blom, 1964), 64.
8. Edward Arber, *A Transcript of the Registers of the Company of Stationers of London: 1554–1640 A.D.*, 5 vols. (1875–79; New York: P. Smith, 1950), 2:496.
9. Philip Sidney, *Syr P. S. His Astrophel and Stella* (1591; Menston: Scolar, 1970), 79–80.
10. Arber, 1:155.
11. Bentley, 282.
12. Arber, 3:79.
13. Leo Kirschbaum, *Shakespeare and the Stationers* (Columbus: Ohio State University Press, 1955), 128, 127–30.
14. Philip Henslowe, *Henslowe's Diary*, W. W. Greg, ed., 2 vols. (1904; Folcroft, PA: Folcroft Library Editions, 1976), 1:113, 1:116–17, 1:119.
15. Arber, 3:158.
16. James Greenstreet, "The Whitefriars Theatre in the Time of Shakespere," *Transactions of the New Shakspere Society, 1887–1892*, ser. 1, no. 13 (1889), 276.
17. Bentley, 266, 266–67.

18. Ibid., 283–84.
19. Charlton Ogburn, *The Mysterious William Shakespeare* (New York: Dodd, Mead, 1984), 217.
20. Gerald Eades Bentley, *Shakespeare: A Biographical Handbook* (New Haven: Yale University Press, 1961), 184.
21. Ogburn, 3.
22. Ibid., 4, 196.
23. Tom Bethell, "The Case for Oxford/Reply to Matus," "Looking for Shakespeare," *Atlantic Monthly*, October 1991, 47.
24. Ogburn, 217–19.
25. Ibid., 218.
26. Pollard, 43–44.
27. Philip Henslowe, *Henslowe Papers, Being Documents Supplementary to Henslowe's Diary.* (1907: Folcroft, PA: Folcroft, 1969), 40.
28. W. W. Greg and Eleanor Boswell, eds., *Records of The Court of the Stationers' Company, 1576 to 1602* (London: The Bibliographical Society, 1930), 56.
29. Irwin Smith, *Shakespeare's Blackfriars Playhouse* (New York: New York University Press, 1964), 161.
30. Ibid., 471–75.
31. Ibid., 480–81.
32. Ibid., 95–96.
33. Arber, 3:37.
34. Ibid., 3:161.
35. See Stanley W. Wells and Gary Taylor, eds., *William Shakespeare: A Textual Companion* (Oxford: Clarendon Press, 1987), 396.; and Andrew S. Cairncross, "Shakespeare and the 'Staying Entries,' " *Shakespeare in the Southwest: Some New Directions*, T. J. Stafford, ed. (El Paso: University of Texas at El Paso, 1969), 80–92.
36. W. R. Streitberger, *Jacobean and Caroline Revels Accounts, 1603–1642*, vol. 13, *Malone Society Collections* (Oxford: Malone Society, 1986), xi.
37. Mark Eccles, "Sir George Buc, Master of the Revels," *Thomas Lodge and Other Elizabethans*, Charles J. Sisson, ed. (New York: Octagon, 1966), 463.
38. Streitberger, xiv.
39. Arber, 3:321, 3:333.
40. Ibid., 3:366, 3:378, 3:400.
41. Ogburn, 204–7.
42. H. P. Stopes, introduction, *Shakespeare's Troilus and Cressida: The First Quarto, 1609. Shakespeare-Quarto Facsimiles*, No. 13 (London: W. Griggs, n.d.), v, and Philip Williams, Jr., "The 'Second Issue' of Shakespeare's *Troilus and Cressida*, 1609," *Studies in Bibliography*, vol. 2 (1949–50), 30, 33.
43. Kirschbaum, 227.
44. Arber, 3:377.
45. William J. Neidig, "The Shakespeare Quartos of 1619," *Modern Philology*, vol. 8 (1910), 155–58.
46. Arber, 3:651.
47. William A. Jackson, ed., *Records of the Court of the Stationers' Company, 1602–1640*, (London: The Bibliographic Society, 1957).
48. Edmund Kerchever Chambers, "Dramatic Records: The Lord Chamberlain's Office," *Malone Society Collections*, vol. 2, part 3, W. W. Greg, gen. ed. (Oxford: Malone Society, 1931), 384.
49. Arber, 4:59.
50. John Chamberlain, *The Letters of John Chamberlain*, Norman Egbert McClure, ed., 2 vols. (1939; Westport, CT: Greenwood Press, 1979), 2:430.
51. F. P. Wilson, "The Jaggards and the First Folio of Shakespeare," *Times Literary Supplement*, November 5, 1925, 737.
52. Henri Estienne, *The Frankfort Book Fair: The Francofordiense Emporium of Henri Estienne*, James Westfall Thompson, ed. and trans. (1911; New York: B. Franklin, 1968), 82–83.

53. Charlton Hinman, *The Printing and Proof-Reading of the First Folio of Shakespeare*, 2 vols. (Oxford: Clarendon Press, 1963), 1:337–38, 1:342. The complete discussion of the chronology of the printing of the First Folio, pp. 1:334–65.
54. Ogburn, 225–27.
55. W. W. Greg, ed., *A Bibliography of the English Printed Drama to the Restoration*, 4 vols. (1939–59; Menston: Scolar, 1970), 1:346.
56. Ogburn, 227.
57. Gerald Eades Bentley, *The Profession of Player in Shakespeare's Time, 1590–1642* (Princeton: Princeton University Press, 1984), 125.
58. Cyrus Hoy, "The Shares of Fletcher and His Collaborators in the Beaumont and Fletcher Canon," *Studies in Bibliography*.
59. See Wells, 509–11 re *Lear;* 398–402 re *Hamlet.*
60. Bentley, *Profession of Dramatist*, 290.
61. Ogburn, 76–77, 83–84.
62. Chambers, 398.
63. Bentley, *Profession of Dramatist*. See the portions on Fletcher, 275–79, Massinger, 271–75, and Shirley, 266–71.

5. Questions about the Writing of the Plays

1. James Lardner, "Onward and Upward with the Arts: The Authorship Question," *The New Yorker*, April 11, 1988, 93.
2. Philip Henslowe, *Henslowe's Diary*, W. W. Greg, ed., 2 vols. (1904; Folcroft, PA: Folcroft Library Editions, 1976), 2:151.
3. Neil Carson, *A Companion to Henslowe's Diary* (Cambridge: Cambridge University Press, 1988), 59, 74.
4. Carson, 77.
5. Henslowe, 2:153.
6. Ibid., 2:168–69.
7. Ibid., 2:206.
8. Gerald Eades Bentley, *The Profession of Dramatist in Shakespeare's Time, 1590–1642* (Princeton: Princeton University Press, 1971), 239.
9. Ibid., 238–39.
10. Henslowe, 2:179; and Cyrus Hoy, *Introductions, Notes, and Commentaries to Texts in "The Dramatic Works of Thomas Dekker,"* Fredson Bowers, ed., vol. 1 (Cambridge: Cambridge University Press, 1980), 73.
11. See W. W. Greg, "The Date of *King Lear* and Shakespeare's Uses of Earlier Versions of the Story," *Library*. 4th ser., vol. 20 (1939–40).
12. George Steiner, *The Death of Tragedy* (New York: Hill and Wang, 1963), 42.
13. Charlton Ogburn, *The Mysterious William Shakespeare* (New York: Dodd, Mead, 1984), 84–85.
14. S. Schoenbaum, *William Shakespeare: A Compact Documentary Life*, rev. ed. (New York: Oxford University Press, 1987), 253.
15. Hoy, 71–72.
16. Philip Williams, Jr., "The 'Second Issue' of Shakespeare's *Troilus and Cressida*, 1609," *Studies in Bibliography*, vol. 2 (1949–50), 28.
17. Ibid., 31, 30.
18. Schoenbaum, 268. For studies regarding the second state quarto, also see Kenneth Muir, ed., introduction to *Troilus and Cressida* (Oxford: Clarendon Press, 1982), 8–9; and Stanley W. Wells and Gary Taylor, eds., *William Shakespeare: A Textual Companion* (Oxford: Clarendon Press, 1987), 123, 124. Regarding performance at the Inns of Court, see Wells, 438, note B.21.
19. F. S. Boas, *Shakespeare & The Universities* (Oxford: B. Blackwell, 1923), 19.
20. Ibid., 17.
21. Ibid., 18.

302 · NOTES

22. Charles Henry Cooper, *Annals of Cambridge*, 5 vols. (Cambridge: Warwick, 1842–53), 2: 520–21.
23. Ibid., 3:6–7.
24. Boas, 21.
25. Ibid., 18–19.
26. C. M. Ingleby, L. Toulmin Smith, and F. J. Furnivall, *The Shakspere Allusion-Book: A Collection of Allusions to Shakspere from 1591 to 1700*, 2 vols. (1932; Freeport: Books for Libraries, 1970), 1:456.
27. Muir, 8–9, 198.

6. The Dating of Shakespeare's Plays

1. See G. R. Hibbard, ed., *Hamlet. The Oxford Shakespeare* (Oxford: Clarendon, 1987), introduction, 71–84.
2. Charlton Ogburn, *The Mysterious William Shakespeare* (New York: Dodd, Mead, 1984), 387–88.
3. A. S. Cairncross, *The Problem of Hamlet: A Solution* (1936; Folcroft, PA: Folcroft Press, 1970), 87–98.
4. Ibid., 119–25.
5. Ibid., 125.
6. Edmund Kerchever Chambers, *The Elizabethan Stage*, 4 vols. (Oxford: Clarendon Press, 1923), 2:273–75.
7. Cairncross, ix, 129.
8. Ibid., 131; and Ogburn, 386.
9. Arthur Mayger Hind, *Engraving in England in the Sixteenth & Seventeenth Centuries*, vol. 1 (Cambridge: Cambridge University Press, 1952), 179, 181; and R. V. Tooley, *Maps and Map-makers*, 4th ed. (New York: Bonanza, 1970), 51.
10. Cairncross, 149.
11. Ogburn, 384, 425 fn 3.
12. James Lardner, "Onward and Upward with the Arts: The Authorship Question," *The New Yorker*, April 11, 1988, 93.
13. Cairncross, 157.
14. Ogburn, 384–85; and Edward Arber, *A Transcript of the Registers of the Company of Stationers of London: 1554–1640 A.D.*, 5 vols. (1875–79; New York: P. Smith, 1950), 2:649.
15. Philip Henslowe, *Henslowe's Diary*, W. W. Greg, ed., 2 vols. (1904; Folcroft, PA: Folcroft Library Editions, 1976), 2:162.
16. Cairncross, 158–59.
17. W. W. Greg, "The Date of *King Lear* and Shakespeare's Uses of Earlier Versions of the Story," *Library*. 4th ser., vol. 20 (1939–40), 382.
18. Geoffrey Bullough, "*King Lear* and the Annesley Case: A Reconsideration," in *Festschrift Rudolf Stamm* (Berne: Francke, 1969), 44.
19. Ibid., 46.
20. Ibid., 48.
21. Lardner, 92.
22. Ogburn, 386.
23. Henry Herbert, *The Dramatic Records of Sir Henry Herbert*, Joseph Quincy Adams, ed. (1917; New York: Benjamin Blom, 1964), 18.
24. Ogburn, 388–90.
25. Fossy John Cobb Hearnshaw and D. M. Hearnshaw, *Court Leet Records, AD 1578–1602*, vol. 1, pt. 2 (Southampton: H. M. Gilbert, 1906), 339, 357.
26. Minos D. Miller, multiple letter, November 4, 1987.
27. E. G. R. Taylor, *The Troublesome Voyage of Captain Edward Fenton, 1582–1583*, 2d ser., no. 113 (Cambridge: Hakluyt Society, 1959), 19, xxviii, 26.
28. Julian S. Corbett, *Papers Relating to the Navy During the Spanish War, 1585–1587*, ([London]: Navy Records Society, 1898), xx; and Kenneth R. Andrews, *English Priva-*

teering: English Privateering During the Spanish War, 1585–1603 (Cambridge: University Press, 1964), 210, 214–15.

29. Richard Hakluyt, *The Principal Navigations, Voyages, Traffiques & Discoveries of the English Nation*, 12 vols. (Glasgow: J. MacLehose, 1903–5), 10:200–1.

30. Hakluyt, 6:406; and Kenneth R. Andrews, *English Privateering Voyages to the West Indies, 1588–1595*, 2d ser., no. 111 (Cambridge: Hakluyt Society, 1959), 295–97.

31. Albert Cohn, *Shakespeare in Germany in the Sixteenth and Seventeenth Centuries* (1865; New York: Haskell House, 1971), lxx–lxxi.

32. Philip Henslowe, *Henslowe Papers, Being Documents Supplementary to Henslowe's Diary* (1907: Folcroft, PA: Folcroft, 1969), 52–53.

33. Philip Henslowe, *Henslowe's Diary*, W. W. Greg, ed., 2 vols (1904; Folcroft, PA: Folcroft, 1969), 2:218.

34. R. A. Foakes ed., *King Henry VIII. Arden Edition*. (London: Methuen, 1966), 180.

35. Maija Jansson Cole, "A New Account of the Burning of the Globe," *Shakespeare Quarterly*, vol. 32 (1981), 352.

36. Stanley W. Wells and Gary Taylor, eds., *William Shakespeare: A Textual Companion* (Oxford: Clarendon Press, 1987), 133–34.

37. John Freehafer, "*Cardenio*, by Shakespeare and Fletcher," *Publications of the Modern Language Association* 84 (1969), 502–3.

38. Ibid., 509.

39. Ibid., 501, 510.

40. Ogburn, 460.

41. Robert Ornstein, *The Moral Vision of Jacobean Tragedy* (Madison: University of Wisconsin, 1960), 24.

7. Shakespeare's Reputation in the Seventeenth Century

1. James Lardner, "Onward and Upward with the Arts: The Authorship Question," *The New Yorker*, April 11, 1988, 103.

2. William A. Ringler, *Stephen Gosson: A Biographical and Critical Study* (Princeton: Princeton University Press, 1942). This and following information on the reputation of theater in the years immediately after the opening of the Theatre is found in his excellent chapter, "The Attack on the Stage," 53–82.

3. Thomas Bodley, *Letters of Sir Thomas Bodley to Thomas James, First Keeper of the Bodleian Library* (Oxford: Clarendon Press, 1926), 219, 221–22.

4. Richard Dutton, *Ben Jonson: To the First Folio* (Cambridge: Cambridge University Press, 1983), 25.

5. C. H. Herford, Percy Simpson, and Evelyn Simpson, *Ben Jonson*, 11 vols. (Oxford: Clarendon Press, 1925–51), 9:13.

6. Herford, 8:204.

7. Philip Lee Ralph, *Sir Humphrey Mildmay: Royalist Gentleman* (New Brunswick: Rutgers University Press, 1947), 47.

8. C. M. Ingleby, Toulmin Smith, and F. J. Furnivall, *The Shakspere Allusion-Book: A Collection of Allusions to Shakspere from 1591 to 1700*, 2 vols. (1932; Freeport: Books for Libraries, 1970), 1:397.

9. Ibid., 1:127.

10. Charlton Ogburn, *The Mysterious William Shakespeare* (New York: Dodd, Mead, 1984), 112.

11. Ingleby, 1:213, 1:233, 1:243, and 1:245.

12. Herford, 3:303.

13. G. W. Wheeler, *The Earliest Catalogues of the Bodleian Library* (Oxford: University Press, 1928), 116.

14. *Dictionary of Literary Biography 58: Jacobean and Caroline Dramatists*, Fredson Bowers, ed. (Detroit: Gale, 1987), 131.

15. Fulke Greville, Baron Brooke, *Sir Fulke Greville's Life of Sir Philip Sidney*, introd. Nowell Smith (1907; Folcroft, PA: Folcroft Library Editions, 1977), 224.

16. Hazelton Spencer, *Shakespeare Improved: The Restoration Versions in Quarto and On the Stage* (Cambridge: Harvard University Press, 1927), 62.
17. Gary Taylor, *Reinventing Shakespeare: A Cultural History, from the Restoration to the Present* (New York: Weidenfeld & Nicolson, 1989), 16.
18. Spencer, 177, 178.
19. William van Lennep, in *The London Stage, 1660–1700*, vol. 1 of *The London Stage, 1660–1800*, cxxviii.
20. Ingleby, 1:348.
21. John Dryden, *On Dramatic Poesy, and Other Critical Essays*, George Watson, ed., 2 vols (New York: Dutton, 1962), 1:67, 1:31, 1:69.
22. Gerald Eades Bentley, *Shakespeare & Jonson: Their Reputations in the Seventeenth Century Compared*, 2 vols. (Chicago: University of Chicago Press, 1945), 1:107, 109.
23. Herford, 4:349.
24. David Frost, "Shakespeare in the Seventeenth Century," *Shakespeare Quarterly*, vol. 16 (1965), 82–83.
25. Ingleby, 1:455–57.
26. Dryden, 1:68.
27. Aphra Behn, *The Works of Aphra Behn*, Montague Summers, ed., 6 vols. (1915; New York: B. Blom, 19657), 1:224.
28. Bentley, 57–59.
29. Gerald Eades Bentley, *The Jacobean and Caroline Stage*, 7 vols. (Oxford: Clarendon Press, 1941–68), 1:94–100.
30. Dryden, 1:69.
31. Van Lennep in *The London Stage*, 1:cxxviii.

8. The Bard before Bardolatry

1. Thomas Edwards, *A Supplement to Mr. Warburton's Edition of Shakespeare, Being the Canons of Criticism* (1748; New York: AMS Press, 1972), 12.
2. Gary Taylor, *Reinventing Shakespeare: A Cultural History, from the Restoration to the Present* (New York: Weidenfeld & Nicolson, 1989), 69.
3. Arthur Sherbo, *The Birth of Shakespeare Studies: Commentators from Rowe (1709) to Boswell-Malone (1821)* (East Lansing: Colleagues Press, 1986), 2.
4. Alexander Pope, *The Dunciad Variorum, with the Prolegomania of Scriblerus*, introd. Robert Kilburn Root (1729; Princeton: Princeton University Press, 1929), x.
5. F. E. Halliday, *The Cult of Shakespeare* (New York: Thomas Yoseloff, 1960), 52–53.
6. Sherbo, 5–6; and Hugh C. Dick, introd. to Lewis Theobald, *Preface to the Works of Shakespeare* (Los Angeles: University of California, 1949), 4–5.
7. Karl Young, *Samuel Johnson on Shakespeare: One Aspect* (1923; Folcroft, PA: Folcroft Library Editions, 1977), 30.
8. Charles Champlin, "Whomsomever Art Thou, Shaksper?" *Los Angeles Times*, January 12, 1984.
9. Joseph Greene, *Correspondence of the Reverend Joseph Greene*, Levi Fox, ed. (London: H. M. Stationery Office, 1965), 57.
10. Charlton Ogburn, *The Mysterious William Shakespeare* (New York: Dodd, Mead, 1984), 211–13.
11. William Dugdale, *The Restoration of the Beauchamp Chapel at St. Mary's Collegiate Church, Warwick, 1674–1742* (Oxford: Roxburghe Club, 1956), 33, 42–43. The author was a descendant of the William Dugdale in question.
12. See M. H. Spielmann, "Shakespeare's Portraiture," in *Studies in the First Folio*, Israel Gollancz, ed. (1924; Folcroft, PA: Folcroft Library Editions, 1973), 14–21. The essay in its entirety provides a thorough, heavily illustrated study of early Shakespeare portraiture.
13. S. Schoenbaum, *William Shakespeare: Records and Images* (New York: Oxford University Press, 1981), 175–77.
14. Greene, 106–7.

15. Ibid., 172–73.
16. Ibid., 77–78.
17. Ibid., 145, 166.
18. Samuel Johnson, *Johnson's Proposals for His Edition of Shakespeare, 1756* (London: Oxford University Press, 1923), 6–7.
19. Hugh Tait, "Garrick, Shakespeare, and Wilkes," in *British Museum Quarterly*, vol. 24 (1961), 100–107.
20. Halliday, 64.
21. Tait, 101–3.
22. Martha Winburn England, *Garrick's Jubilee* (Columbus: Ohio State University Press, 1964), 20.
23. Beverley Warner, ed., *Famous Introductions to Shakespeare's Plays, by the Notable Editors of the Eighteenth Century* (1906; New York: Burt Franklin, 1968), 116–19, passim.
24. Robert Witbeck Babcock, *The Genesis of Shakespeare Idolatry, 1766–1799* (1931; New York: AMS Press, 1978), 3.
25. Martha Winburn England's fact-filled and entertaining *Garrick's Jubilee* cannot be bettered and I am indebted to this work, especially the chapters "What Was the Stratford Jubilee?" and "The Grass Roots of Bardolatry," for much of this portion on the Jubilee and its aftermath.
26. England, 22.
27. Ibid., 21.
28. In the August 1769 issue of *The Gentleman's Magazine*, 375.
29. England, 166, 171.
30. Babcock, 83.
31. Samuel Johnson, *Selections from Johnson on Shakespeare*, Bertrand H. Bronson and Jean M. O'Meara, eds. (New Haven: Yale University Press, 1986), 239, 240.
32. George C. D. Odell, *Shakespeare: From Betterton to Irving*, 2 vols. (1920; New York: Benjamin Blom, 1963), 1:377.
33. Babcock, 88.
34. Warner, 145.
35. Spielmann, 24.
36. Greene, 145–46.
37. Ibid., 146 fn 1.

9. The Claim for the Earl of Oxford

1. B. M. Ward, *The Seventeenth Earl of Oxford, 1550–1604, from Contemporary Documents* (London: John Murray, 1928), 157–58.
2. Charlton Ogburn, *The Mysterious William Shakespeare* (New York: Dodd, Mead, 1984), 597.
3. See Barrell's " 'Shake-speare's' Unknown Home on the River Avon Discovered" in John Thomas Looney, *"Shakespeare" Identified in Edward de Vere, Seventeenth Earl of Oxford, and the Poems of Edward de Vere*, Ruth Loyd Miller, ed. 3d ed., 2 vols. (1920; Port Washington: Kennikat, 1975), 2:355–69.
4. L. F. Salzman, *Victoria History of the County of Warwick*, vol. 6 (London: University of London Institute of Historical Research, 1951), 32; and Ogburn, 714.
5. James Lardner, "Onward and Upward with the Arts: The Authorship Question," *The New Yorker*, April 11, 1988, 101.
6. Edmund Kerchever Chambers, *The Elizabethan Stage*, 4 vols. (Oxford: Clarendon Press, 1923), 2:127.
7. J. Leeds Barroll, "The Social and Literary Context," *The Revels History of Drama in English*, vol. 3, 1576–1613 (London: Methuen, 1975), 5–9.
8. Chambers, 4:269–70.
9. Ibid., 2:86–88.
10. Ibid., 2:100.

11. Irwin Smith, *Shakespeare's Blackfriars Playhouse* (New York: New York University Press, 1964), 155–56, 162.
12. Chambers, 4:303–4.
13. Ibid., 4:334–45.
14. Ogburn, 732–34.
15. Looney, 2:132.
16. David Cook and Frank Percy Wilson, eds., *Dramatic Records in the Declared Accounts of the Treasurer of the Chamber, 1558–1642*, vol. 6, Malone Society Collections (Oxford: The University Press, 1962), 29.
17. Looney, 2:117.
18. Lardner, 88.
19. See A. P. Rossiter, *Woodstock, A Moral History* (London: Chatto & Windus, 1946), 21–23, for a scene-by-scene reconstruction of the events of this play.
20. A. P. Rossiter, "Unconformity in *Richard II*," in *Shakespeare: Richard II; A Casebook*, Nicholas Brooke, ed. (London: Macmillan, 1973), 223.
21. Granville Leveson-Gower, *The Howards of Effingham* (London: Roworth, 1888), 4.
22. Edward Barrington DeFonblanque, *Annals of the House of Percy*, 2 vols. (London: R. Clay & Sons, 1887), 2:55.
23. Ibid., 2:78–79.
24. Ibid., 2:117.
25. [Robert Cecil, Marquess of Salisbury], *Calendar of the Manuscripts of the Most Honourable, the Marquess of Salisbury*, 24 vols. (London: H. M. Stationery Office, 1883–1976), 5:487.
26. Robert Naunton, *Fragmenta Regalia, or Observations on Queen Elizabeth: Her Times and Favorites*, John S. Cerovski, ed. (Washington: Folger Shakespeare Library, 1985), 69, 70.
27. Ogburn, 217.
28. Quoted in Tom Bethell, "The Case for Oxford/Reply to Matus," "Looking for Shakespeare," *Atlantic Monthly*, October 1991, 58.
29. Geoffrey Bullough, *Narrative and Dramatic Sources of Shakespeare*, 8 vols. (New York: Columbia University Press, 1957–75), 2:376–77.
30. Ogburn, 11.
31. B. W. Beckingsale, *Burghley: Tudor Statesman, 1520–1598* (New York: St. Martin's Press, 1967), 270.
32. B. M. Ward, 285, 287.
33. Ibid., vii.
34. Ibid., 60, 395, 70–71, 78.
35. See pp. 206–14.
36. Ernest Edwin Reynolds, *Campion and Parsons: The Jesuit Mission of 1580–1* (London: Sheed and Ward, 1980), 84.
37. Robert Parsons, *The Letters and Memorials of Father Robert Persons, S. J.*, L. Hicks, ed., vol. 1, Catholic Record Society, vol. 39 (London: Catholic Record Society, 1942), 56–62.
38. Reynolds, 108–9.
39. Ibid., 97; and Ward, 214.
40. G. P. V. Akrigg, *Shakespeare and the Earl of Southampton* (Cambridge, MA: Harvard University Press, 1968), 72, 73.
41. [Reginald Rawdon Hastings], *Report on the Manuscripts of the Late Reginald Rawdon Hastings*, Francis Bickley, ed., 4 vols. (London: H. M. Stationery Office, 1928–47), 2:29–30.
42. Ward, 213.
43. Steve W. May, ed., *The Poems of Edward de Vere, Seventeenth Earl of Oxford and of Robert Devereux, Second Earl of Essex. Studies in Philology* 77 (1980), 7.
44. Ward, 251, 250–55.
45. Thomas Wright, *Queen Elizabeth and Her Times: A Series of Original Letters*, 2 vols. (London: H. Colburn, 1838), 2:267.
46. M. M. Reese, *The Royal Office of Master of the Horse* (London: Threshold, 1976), 154.
47. Roy C. Strong, *Leicester's Triumph* (Leiden: Sir Thomas Browne Institute, 1964), 25.

48. Ward, 289–90, 288–95.
49. John Knox Laughton, ed. *State Papers Relating to the Defeat of the Spanish Armada, Anno 1588.* 2 vols., 2nd ed. (1895; Aldershot: Navy Records Society, 1987), 1:1xxvi–1xxvii.
50. Ward, 292 (corrected).
51. William Murdin, ed., *A Collection of State Papers . . . Left by William Cecill, Lord Burghley*, vol. 2 (1759).
52. Conyers Read, *Lord Burghley and Queen Elizabeth* (New York: Knopf, 1960), 125.
53. Bethell, 50.
54. Minos D. Miller, multiple letter, November 4, 1987.
55. Bullough, 8:191.
56. R. A. Foakes, ed., in introduction to *The Comedy of Errors. Arden Edition* (London: Methuen, 1962), xxx.
57. Bethell, 50.
58. Ward, 129.
59. Ogburn, 44.
60. Ward, 189–90.
61. Virginia F. Stern, *Gabriel Harvey: His Life, Marginalia, and Library* (New York: Oxford University Press, 1979), 64–66.
62. Ward, 157.
63. Steven W. May, *The English Courtier Poets* (Columbia: University of Missouri Press, 1991), 52, 53.
64. May, *Poems of Edward de Vere*, 13.
65. Steven W. May, letter to the author, September 6, 1991.
66. Ward, 282.
67. George Puttenham, *The Arte of English Poesie* (1589; Amsterdam: Theatrum Orbis Terrarum, 1971), 51.
68. Ward, 275–79.
69. Carter A. Daniel, ed., introduction to *The Plays of John Lyly* (Lewisburg: Bucknell University Press, 1988), 14–19, 23.
70. Franklin Dickey, "The Old Man at Work: Forgeries in the Stationers' Register," *Shakespeare Quarterly*, vol. 11 (1960), 39–47.
71. Chambers, 2:18–19.
72. *Dictionary of Literary Biography 62; Elizabethan Dramatists*, Fredson Bowers, ed. (Detroit: Gale, 1987), 209.
73. George Buck, *The History of Richard the Third (1619)*, Arthur Noel Kincaid, ed. (London: Alan Sutton, 1979), 169–70.
74. Ward, 103.
75. Salisbury, 2:144–45.
76. Ward, 232.
77. Ibid., 301–3 (corrected).
78. Ibid., 348.
79. Ibid., 304–5, 308–11.
80. Salisbury, 5:136–37, 5:149–50, 6:97, 9:220.
81. Ward, 333–36.
82. Ibid., 257.
83. May, *Poems of Edward de Vere*, 8.
84. Salisbury, 16:395–98.
85. Ogburn, 766.
86. Salisbury, 16:258.
87. May, *Courtier Poets*, 158.
88. May, *Poems of Edward de Vere*, 10–12.

10. Closing Arguments

1. *Dictionary of Literary Biography 58; Jacobean and Caroline Dramatists*, Fredson Bowers, ed. (Detroit: Gale, 1987), 188.

2. S. Schoenbaum, *William Shakespeare: A Compact Documentary Life*, rev. ed. (New York: Oxford University Press, 1987), 115–17.
3. See Irvin Leigh Matus, *Shakespeare: The Living Record* (New York: St. Martin's, 1990), 11–14. Also see especially Erik Wikland, *Elizabethan Players in Sweden, 1591–92 &c.* 2d ed., rev. (Stockholm: Almqvist & Wiskell, 1971), 129–32.
4. Philip Massinger, *The Plays and Poems of Philip Massinger*, 5 vols., Philip Edwards and Colin Gibson, eds., (Oxford: Clarendon Press, 1976), 1:xx.
5. See Arthur Penrhyn Stanley, *Historical Memorials of Westminster Abbey*, 8th ed. (1896; London: John Murray, 1924), 499–526 for the fascinating story of his discovery.
6. Paul Morgan, *Warwickshire Apprentices in the Stationers' Company of London, 1563–1700. Dugdale Society Occasional Papers* 25 (Stratford-upon-Avon: Dugdale Society, 1978), 2–3.
7. Bentley Boyd, "A Rose Might Smell as Sweet by Another Name . . . ," *Chicago Tribune*, August 20, 1989.
8. John Chamberlain, *The Letters of John Chamberlain*, Norman Egbert McClure, ed., 2 vols. (1939; Westport, CT: Greenwood Press, 1979), 1:1–9.
9. G. Blakemore Evans, *Elizabethan–Jacobean Drama: The Theatre in Its Time* (New York: New Amsterdam, 1988), 157, 165–67.
10. O. Hood Phillips, *Shakespeare and the Lawyers* (London: Methuen, 1972), 191. The other works referred to are Clarkson and Warren, *Law of Property in Shakespeare and Elizabethan Drama* (1942; 1968), 285–86; and Barton, *Links between Shakespeare and the Law* (1929; 1971), 159.
11. Neil Carson, *A Companion to Henslowe's Diary* (Cambridge: Cambridge University Press, 1988), 58.
12. J. C. Maxwell, ed., *Titus Andronicus. Arden Edition* (London: Methuen, 1953), 22 fn.
13. Stanley W. Wells and Gary Taylor, eds., *William Shakespeare: A Textual Companion* (Oxford: Clarendon Press, 1987), 114–15.
14. Ibid., 116–17.
15. R. A. Foakes, ed., *The Comedy of Errors. Arden Edition* (London: Methuen, 1962), xxv.
16. Geoffrey Bullough, *Narrative and Dramatic Sources of Shakespeare*, 8 vols. (New York: Columbia University Press, 1957–75), 1:4.
17. T. W. Baldwin, *William Shakspere's Small Latine & Lesse Greeke*, 2 vols. (Urbana: University of Illinois Press, 1944), 2:675.
18. Ibid., 2:663.
19. Henri Fluchère, *Shakespeare and the Elizabethans*, Guy Hamilton, trans. (New York: Hill and Wang, 1956), 27.
20. H. S. Bennett, *English Books & Readers, 1558 to 1603* (Cambridge: Cambridge University Press, 1965), 251–52.
21. Hardin Craig, *The Enchanted Glass: The Elizabethan Mind in Literature* (1952; Westport, CT: Greenwood Press, 1975), 215, 213–14.
22. Joseph T. Shipley, *In Praise of English: The Growth & Use of Language* (New York: Times Books, 1977), 26.
23. Logan Pearsall Smith, quoted in Robert Crum, William Cran, and Robert MacNeil, *The Story of English* (New York: Viking, 1988), 96. The quotation following in the text is from page 128 of this book.
24. Olga S. Opfell, *The King James Bible Translators* (Jefferson, NC: McFarland, 1982), 132–33.
25. Fluchère, 21–22.
26. Tom Bethell, "The Case for Oxford/Reply to Matus," "Looking for Shakespeare," *Atlantic Monthly*, October 1991, 61.
27. Charlton Ogburn, *The Mysterious William Shakespeare* (New York: Dodd, Mead, 1984), 86.
28. Gamini Salgado, ed., *Eyewitnesses of Shakespeare: Firsthand Accounts of Performances, 1590–1890* (New York: Barnes & Noble, 1975), 31–32.
29. Ibid., 30.
30. C. H. Herford, Percy Simpson, and Evelyn Simpson, *Ben Jonson*, 11 vols. (Oxford: Clarendon Press, 1925–51), 6:208.

31. Michael Jamieson, "Shakespeare's Celibate Stage," in Gerald Eades Bentley, ed., *The Seventeenth-Century Stage* (Chicago: University of Chicago Press, 1968), 76–77.
32. See Philip H. Highfill, et al., *A Biographical Dictionary of Actors, Actresses . . . & Other Stage Personnel in London, 1660–1800,* vol. 9 (Carbondale: Southern Illinois University Press, 1984), 79–80; and Jamieson, 77–78.
33. Andrew Gurr, *Playgoing in Shakespeare's London* (Cambridge: Cambridge University Press, 1987), 66–67.
34. Ibid., 70.
35. Chamberlain, 2:577–78.
36. Alexis de Tocqueville, *Democracy in America*. J. P. Mayer, ed. George Lawrence, trans. (Garden City, NY: Doubleday, 1969), 489–490.
37. Ogburn, 87.
38. Ibid., 84, 77.
39. Jonathan Bate, *Shakespearean Constitutions: Politics, Theatre, Criticism, 1730–1830* (New York: Oxford University Press, 1989), 134–35.
40. William Hazlitt, *Lectures on the English Poets,* 3rd ed. (1841; New York: Russell & Russell, 1968), 106.
41. Gary Taylor, *Reinventing Shakespeare: A Cultural History, from the Restoration to the Present* (New York: Weidenfeld & Nicolson, 1989), 3.
42. Hazlitt, 94.
43. G. R. Hibbard, ed., *Hamlet. The Oxford Shakespeare* (Oxford: Clarendon, 1987), 3–4.
44. John Dryden, *On Dramatic Poesy, and Other Critical Essays,* George Watson, ed., 2 vols. (New York: Dutton, 1962), 1:67; and Robert Ornstein, *The Moral Vision of Jacobean Tragedy* (Madison: University of Wisconsin, 1960), 222–23.
45. Fluchère, 28.
46. Peter Brook, *The Empty Space* (New York: Atheneum, 1968), 95.
47. Brooks Atkinson, *Broadway Scrapbook* (New York: Theatre Arts, 1947), 145.
48. John Russell Brown, *Discovering Shakespeare* (London: Macmillan, 1981), 1.
49. Lawrence Malkin, "In Lenox They Are 'Dropping in' on the Bard of Avon," *Smithsonian,* November 1991, 136.

Bibliography

Books

Allen, Ward, ed. *Translating for King James; The only notes made by a translator of King James's Bible.* Nashville: Vanderbilt University Press, 1969.

Allen, Ward. *Translating the New Testament Epistles, 1604–1611.* Ann Arbor: University Microfilms International for Vanderbilt University Press, 1977.

Akrigg, G. P. V. *Shakespeare and the Earl of Southampton.* Cambridge, MA: Harvard University Press, 1968.

Andrews, Kenneth R. *English Privateering; English Privateering During the Spanish War, 1585–1603.* Cambridge: University Press, 1964.

Andrews, Kenneth R. *English Privateering Voyages to the West Indies, 1588–1595.* 2d ser., No. 111. Cambridge: Hakluyt Society, 1959.

Arber, Edward. *A Transcript of the Registers of the Company of Stationers of London: 1554–1640 A.D.* 5 vols. 1875–79. Reprint. New York: P. Smith, 1950.

Atkinson, Brooks. *Broadway Scrapbook.* New York: Theatre Arts, 1947.

Babcock, Robert Witbeck. *The Genesis of Shakespeare Idolatry, 1766–1799.* 1931. Reprint. New York: AMS Press, 1978.

Bald, R. C. *Bibliographical Studies in the Beaumont and Fletcher Folio of 1647.* 1937. Reprint. Folcroft, PA: Folcroft Library Editions, 1974.

Baldwin, T. W. *William Shakspere's Small Latine & Lesse Greeke.* 2 vols. Urbana: University of Illinois Press, 1944.

Barker, G. F. Russell, and Alan H. Stenning, eds. *The Record of Old Westminsters.* 2 vols. London: Chiswick, 1928.

Bate, Jonathan. *Shakespearean Constitutions: Politics, Theatre, Criticism, 1730–1830.* New York: Oxford University Press, 1989.

Beaumont, Francis, and John Fletcher. *The Dramatic Works in the Beaumont and Fletcher Canon.* Fredson Bowers, gen. ed. 7 vols. Cambridge: Cambridge University Press, 1966–89.

Beckingsale, B. W. *Burghley: Tudor Statesman, 1520–1598.* New York: St. Martin's Press, 1967.

Behn, Aphra. *The Works of Aphra Behn.* Montague Summers, ed. 6 vols. 1915. Reprint. New York: B. Blom, 1967.

Bennett, H. S. *English Books & Readers, 1558 to 1603.* Cambridge: Cambridge University Press, 1965.

Bentley, Gerald Eades. *The Jacobean and Caroline Stage.* 7 vols. Oxford: Clarendon Press, 1941–68.

Bentley, Gerald Eades. *The Profession of Dramatist in Shakespeare's Time, 1590–1642.* Princeton: Princeton University Press, 1971.

Bentley, Gerald Eades. *The Profession of Player in Shakespeare's Time, 1590–1642.* Princeton: Princeton University Press, 1984.

Bentley, Gerald Eades, ed. *The Seventeenth-Century Stage.* Chicago: University of Chicago Press, 1968.

Bentley, Gerald Eades. *Shakespeare: A Biographical Handbook.* New Haven: Yale University Press, 1961.

Bentley, Gerald Eades. *Shakespeare & Jonson: Their Reputations in the Seventeenth Century Compared.* 2 vols. Chicago: University of Chicago Press, 1945.

Bland, Desmond, ed. *Gesta Grayorum. English Reprints Series* 22. Liverpool: Liverpool University Press, 1968.

Blayney, Peter W. M. *The First Folio of Shakespeare.* Washington, DC: Folger Library, 1991.

Boas, F. S. *Shakespeare & the Universities.* Oxford: B. Blackwell, 1923.

Bodley, Thomas. *Letters of Sir Thomas Bodley to Thomas James, First Keeper of the Bodleian Library.* Oxford: Clarendon Press, 1926.

Brook, Peter. *The Empty Space.* New York: Atheneum, 1968.

Brooke, C. F. Tucker. *Shakespeare of Stratford. The Yale Shakespeare.* New Haven: Yale University Press, 1926.

Brown, John Russell. *Discovering Shakespeare.* London: Macmillan, 1981.

Buck, George. *The History of Richard the Third (1619).* Arthur Noel Kincaid, ed. London: Alan Sutton, 1979.

Bullough, Geoffrey. *Narrative and Dramatic Sources of Shakespeare.* 8 vols. New York: Columbia University Press, 1957–75.

Cairncross, A. S. *The Problem of Hamlet: A Solution.* 1936. Reprint. Folcroft, PA: Folcroft Press, 1970.

Carson, Neil. *A Companion to Henslowe's Diary.* Cambridge: Cambridge University Press, 1988.

A Catalogue of the Shakespeare Exhibition Held in the Bodleian Library. Oxford: Bodleian Library, 1916.

Chamberlain, John. *The Letters of John Chamberlain.* Norman Egbert McClure, ed. 2 vols. 1939. Reprint. Westport, CT: Greenwood Press, 1979.

Chambers, Edmund Kerchever. *The Elizabethan Stage.* 4 vols. Oxford: Clarendon Press, 1923.

Chambers, E. K. *William Shakespeare: A Study of Facts and Problems.* 2 vols. 1930. Reprint. New York: Oxford University Press, 1951.

Chettle, Henry. *Kind-Heart's Dream/A Mirror of Monsters* [by William Rankins]. New York: Johnson Reprint, 1972.

Cicero, Marcus Tullius. *The Letters to His Friends.* Vol. 1. W. Gwynn Williams, translator. London: W. Heinemann, 1943.

Cohn, Albert. *Shakespeare in Germany in the Sixteenth and Seventeenth Centuries.* 1865. Reprint. New York: Haskell House, 1971.

Cook, David, and Frank Percy Wilson, eds. *Dramatic Records in the Declared Accounts of the Treasurer of the Chamber, 1558–1642.* Vol. 6, *Malone Society Collections.* Oxford: The University Press, 1962.

Cooper, Charles Henry. *Annals of Cambridge*. 5 vols. Cambridge: Warwick, 1842–53.

Corbett, Julian S. *Papers Relating to the Navy During the Spanish War, 1585–1587*. [London]: Navy Records Society, 1898.

Coryate, Thomas. *Coryats Crudities*. London: Scolar, 1978.

Craig, Hardin. *The Enchanted Glass: The Elizabethan Mind in Literature*. 1952. Reprint. Westport, CT: Greenwood Press, 1975.

Cressy, David, ed. *Education in Tudor and Stuart England*. London: Edward Arnold, 1975.

Cressy, David. *Literacy and the Social Order*. Cambridge: Cambridge University Press, 1980.

Crum, Robert, William Cran, and Robert MacNeil. *The Story of English*. New York: Viking, 1988.

Daniel, Carter A., ed. *The Plays of John Lyly*. Lewisburg: Bucknell University Press, 1988.

Daniell, David. *"Coriolanus" in Europe*. London: Athlone Press, 1980.

Davies, John. *The Complete Works*. Alexander B. Grosart, ed. 2 vols. 1878. Reprint. Hildesheim: Georg Olms, 1969.

Davis, Godfrey R. C. *Magna Carta*. London: Trustees of the British Museum, 1963.

Dawson, Giles E. *Records of Plays & Players in Kent, 1450–1642. Malone Society Collections*. Vol. 7. Oxford: University Press, 1965.

DeFonblanque, Edward Barrington. *Annals of the House of Percy*. 2 vols. London: R. Clay & Sons, 1887.

Dictionary of Literary Biography 62; Elizabethan Dramatists. Fredson Bowers, ed. Detroit: Gale, 1987.

Dictionary of Literary Biography 58; Jacobean and Caroline Dramatists. Fredson Bowers, ed. Detroit: Gale, 1987.

Dodsworth, William. *An Historical Account of the . . . Cathedral Church of Sarum, or Salisbury*. Salisbury: Privately printed, 1814.

Drummond, William. *Ben Jonson's Conversations with William Drummond of Hawthornden*. Richard Ferrar Patterson, ed. 1923. Reprint. New York: Haskell House, 1974.

Dryden, John. *Dryden: The Dramatic Works*. 6 vols. Montague Summers, ed. 1932. Reprint. New York, Gordian Press, 1968.

Dryden, John. *On Dramatic Poesy, and Other Critical Essays*. George Watson, ed. 2 vols. New York: Dutton, 1962.

Dugdale, William. *The Restoration of the Beauchamp Chapel at St. Mary's Collegiate Church, Warwick, 1674–1742*. Oxford: Roxburghe Club, 1956.

Dutton, Richard. *Ben Jonson: To the First Folio*. Cambridge: Cambridge University Press, 1983.

Edwards, Thomas. *A Supplement to Mr. Warburton's Edition of Shakespeare, Being the Canons of Criticism*. 1748. Reprint. New York: AMS Press, 1972.

England, Martha Winburn. *Garrick's Jubilee*. Columbus: Ohio State University Press, 1964.

Estienne, Henri. *The Frankfort Book Fair: The Francofordiense Emporium of Henri Estienne*. James Westfall Thompson, ed. and trans. 1911. Reprint. New York: B. Franklin, 1968.

Evans, G. Blakemore. *Elizabethan-Jacobean Drama: The Theatre in Its Time*. New York: New Amsterdam, 1988.

Eyre, G. E. Briscoe, ed., and C. Robert Rivington, compiler. *A Transcript of the Registers of the Worshipful Company of Stationers, from 1640–1708 A.D*. 3 vols. 1913–14. Reprint. New York: P. Smith, 1950.

Fairfax-Lucy, Alice. *Charlecote and the Lucys.* 1958. Reprint. London: Victor Gollancz, 1990.

Fluchère, Henri. *Shakespeare and the Elizabethans.* Guy Hamilton, trans. New York: Hill and Wang, 1956.

Foakes, R. A., ed. *The Comedy of Errors. Arden Edition.* London: Methuen, 1962.

Foakes, R. A., and R. T. Rickert, eds. *Henslowe's Diary.* Cambridge: University Press, 1961.

Foakes, R. A., ed. *King Henry VIII. Arden Edition.* London: Methuen, 1966.

Fox, Levi. *The Early History of the King Edward VI School, Stratford-upon-Avon. Dugdale Society Occasional Papers 29.* Oxford: Dugdale Society, David Stanford, 1984.

Fripp, Edgar Innis. *Master Richard Quyny.* London: Oxford University Press, 1924.

Fripp, Edgar Innes. *Shakespeare's Stratford.* 1928. Reprint. Freeport: Books for Libraries, 1970.

Fripp, Edgar Innis, ed. *Minutes and Accounts of the Corporation of Stratford-upon-Avon and Other Records, 1553–1620.* Vol 1. (1553–1566); Vol. 2 (1566–1577); Vol. 3 (1577–1586). Vols. 1, 3, and 5 of *Publications of the Dugdale Society* (London: Oxford University Press, 1921, 1924, and 1926).

Greene, Joseph. *Correspondence of the Reverend Joseph Greene.* Levi Fox, ed. London: H. M. Stationery Office, 1965.

Greene, Robert. *Robert Greene, M. A., Groats-Worth of Witte, Bought with a Million of Repentance/The Repentance of Robert Greene, 1592.* George B. Harrison, ed. Edinburgh: University Press, 1966.

Greene, Robert. *Menaphon and A Margarite of America.* George B. Harrison, ed. Oxford: Basil Blackwell, 1927.

Greenwood, George. *The Shakespeare Problem Restated.* 1908. Reprint. Westport, CT: Greenwood Press, 1970.

Greg, W. W., ed. *A Bibliography of the English Printed Drama to the Restoration.* 4 vols. 1939–59. Reprint. Menston: Scolar, 1970.

Greg, W. W., ed. *English Literary Autographs, 1550–1650.* Oxford: Oxford University Press, 1925–32.

Greg, W. W., and Eleanor Boswell, eds. *Records of the Court of the Stationers' Company, 1576 to 1602.* London: The Bibliographical Society, 1930.

Greg, W. W. *Some Aspects and Problems of London Publishing Between 1550 and 1650.* Oxford: Clarendon, 1956.

Greville, Fulke, Baron Brooke. *Poems and Dramas of Fulke Greville, First Lord Brooke.* 2 vols. Geoffrey Bullough, ed. Edinburgh: Oliver and Boyd, 1939.

Greville, Fulke, Baron Brooke. *Sir Fulke Greville's Life of Sir Philip Sidney.* Introd. by Nowell Smith. 1907. Reprint. Folcroft: Folcroft Library Editions, 1977.

Gurr, Andrew. *Playgoing in Shakespeare's London.* Cambridge: Cambridge University Press, 1987.

Hakluyt, Richard. *The Principal Navigations, Voyages, Traffiques & Discoveries of the English Nation.* 12 vols. Glasgow: J. MacLehose, 1903–5.

Halliday, F. E. *The Cult of Shakespeare.* New York: Thomas Yoseloff, 1960.

[Hastings, Reginald Rawdon.] *Report on the Manuscripts of the Late Reginald Rawdon Hastings.* 4 vols. Francis Bickley, ed. London: H. M. Stationery Office, 1928–47.

Hazlitt, William. *Lectures on the English Poets.* 3rd edn. 1841. Reprint. New York: Russell & Russell, 1968.

Hearnshaw, Fossy John Cobb, and D. M. Hearnshaw. *Court Leet Records, AD 1578–1602.* Vol. 1, pt. 2. Southampton: H. M. Gilbert, 1906.

Heawood, Edward. *Watermarks, Mainly of the 17th and 18th Centuries.* Hilversum, Holland: Paper Publications Society, 1950.

Henslowe, Philip. *Henslowe's Diary.* W. W. Greg, ed. 2 vols. 1904. Reprint. Folcroft, PA: Folcroft Library Editions, 1976.

Henslowe, Philip. *Henslowe Papers, Being Documents Supplementary to Henslowe's Diary.* W. W. Greg, ed. 1907. Reprint. Folcroft, PA: Folcroft, 1969.

Herbert, Henry. *The Dramatic Records of Sir Henry Herbert.* Joseph Quincy Adams, ed. 1917. Reprint. New York: Benjamin Blom, 1964.

Herford, C. H., Percy Simpson, and Evelyn Simpson. *Ben Jonson.* 11 vols. Oxford: Clarendon Press, 1925–51.

Heywood, Thomas. *The English Traveller.* 1633. Reprint. Norwood, NJ: Theatrum Orbis Terrarum, 1973.

Heywood, Thomas. *If You Know Not Me, You Know Nobody.* Part 1. Madeleine Doran, ed. London: Malone Society, 1935.

Hibbard, G. R., ed. *Hamlet. The Oxford Shakespeare.* Oxford: Clarendon, 1987.

Highfill, Philip H., et al. *A Biographical Dictionary of Actors, Actresses . . . & Other Stage Personnel in London, 1660–1800.* Vol. 9. Carbondale: Southern Illinois University Press, 1984.

Hind, Arthur Mayger. *Engraving in England in the Sixteenth & Seventeenth Centuries.* Vol. 1. Cambridge: Cambridge University Press, 1952.

Hinman, Charlton. *The Printing and Proof-Reading of the First Folio of Shakespeare.* 2 vols. Oxford: Clarendon Press, 1963.

Holt, James Clarke. *Magna Carta.* Cambridge: University Press, 1965.

Howard-Hill, T. H. *Ralph Crane and Some Shakespeare First Folio Comedies.* Charlottesville: University Press of Virginia, 1972.

Hoy, Cyrus. *Introductions, Notes, and Commentaries to Texts in "The Dramatic Works of Thomas Dekker."* Vol. 1. Fredson Bowers, ed. Cambridge: Cambridge University Press, 1980.

Ingleby, C. M., L. Toulmin Smith, and F. J. Furnivall. *The Shakspere Allusion-Book: A Collection of Allusions to Shakspere from 1591 to 1700.* 2 vols. 1932. Reprint. Freeport: Books for Libraries, 1970.

Jackson, William A., ed. *Records of the Court of the Stationers' Company, 1602–1640.* London: The Bibliographical Society, 1957.

Johnson, Samuel. *Johnson's Proposals for His Edition of Shakespeare, 1756.* London: Oxford University Press, 1923.

Johnson, Samuel. *Selections from Johnson on Shakespeare.* Bertrand H. Bronson and Jean M. O'Meara, eds. New Haven: Yale University Press, 1986.

Kelly, W. *Notices Illustrative of the Drama . . . Extracted from the Chamberlains' Accounts and Other Manuscripts of the Borough of Leicester.* London: J. R. Smith, 1865.

Kendall, Alan. *Robert Dudley, Earl of Leicester.* London: Cassell, 1980.

Kirschbaum, Leo. *Shakespeare and the Stationers.* Columbus: Ohio State University Press, 1955.

Laughton, John Knox, ed. *State Papers Relating to the Defeat of the Spanish Armada, Anno 1588.* 2 vols. 2nd ed. 1895. Reprint. Aldershot: Navy Records Society, 1987.

Law, Ernest. *Shakespeare as a Groom of the Chamber.* London: G. Bell, 1910.

Leishman, J. B., ed. *The Three Parnassus Plays (1598–1601).* London: Ivor Nicholson & Watson, 1949.

Leveson-Gower, Granville. *The Howards of Effingham.* London: Roworth, 1888.

Lewis, B. Roland. *The Shakespeare Documents; Facsimiles, Transliterations and Commentary.* 2 vols. 1940–41. Reprint. Westport, CT: Greenwood Press, 1969.

The London Stage, 1660–1800: A Calendar of Plays, Entertainments & After-pieces. 5 vols. in 11. Carbondale: Southern Illinois University Press, 1960–68.

Looney, John Thomas. *"Shakespeare" Identified in Edward de Vere, Seventeenth Earl of Oxford, and the Poems of Edward de Vere.* Ruth Loyd Miller, ed. 3d ed., 2 vols. 1920. Reprint. Port Washington: Kennikat, 1975.

Lyle, J. V., ed. *Acts of the Privy Council of England, 1617–1619.* London: H. M. Stationery Office, 1929.

Madan, Falconer, et al. *The Original Bodleian Copy of the First Folio of Shakespeare (The Turbutt Shakespeare).* Oxford: Clarendon Press, 1905.

Massinger, Philip. *Believe As You List: A Tragedy.* T. Crofton Croker, ed. London: Percy Society, 1849.

Massinger, Philip. *The Plays and Poems of Philip Massinger.* Philip Edwards and Colin Gibson, eds. 5 vols. Oxford: Clarendon Press, 1976.

Matus, Irvin Leigh. *Shakespeare: The Living Record.* New York: St. Martin's, 1990.

Maxwell, J. C., ed. *Titus Andronicus. Arden Edition.* London: Methuen, 1953.

May, Steven W. *The English Courtier Poets.* Columbia: University of Missouri Press, 1991.

May, Steven W. ed. *The Poems of Edward de Vere, Seventeenth Earl of Oxford and of Robert Devereux, Second Earl of Essex. Studies in Philology 77,* 1980.

McKechnie, William Sharp. *Magna Carta: A Commentary on the Great Charter of King John.* 2d ed. 1914. Reprint. New York: Burt Franklin, 1960.

McKerrow, R. B., and others. *A Dictionary of Printers and Booksellers in England, Scotland and Ireland . . . 1557–1640.* 1910. Reprint. London: Bibliographic Society, 1968.

McKerrow, R. B. *Printers' & Publishers' Devices in England and Scotland, 1485–1640.* London: Bibliographic Society, 1913.

Meres, Francis. *Palladis Tamia: Wits Treasury.* 1598. Reprint. New York: Garland, 1973.

Middleton, Thomas. *A Game at Chess.* T. H. Howard-Hill, ed. Oxford: Malone Society, 1990.

Miles, Rosalind. *Ben Jonson: His Craft and Art.* Savage, MD: Barnes & Noble, 1990.

Morgan, Paul. *Warwickshire Apprentices in the Stationers' Company of London, 1563–1700. Dugdale Society Occasional Papers 25.* Stratford-upon-Avon: Dugdale Society, 1978.

Muir, Kenneth, ed. *Troilus and Cressida.* Oxford: Clarendon Press, 1982.

Murdin, William, ed. *A Collection of State Papers . . . Left by William Cecill, Lord Burghley.* Vol. 2. 1759.

Naunton, Robert. *Fragmenta Regalia, or Observations on Queen Elizabeth: Her Times and Favorites.* John S. Cerovski, ed. Washington: Folger Shakespeare Library, 1985.

Nungezer, Edwin. *A Dictionary of Actors.* 1929. Reprint. New York: AMS, 1971.

Odell, George C. D. *Shakespeare: From Betterton to Irving.* 2 vols. 1920. Reprint. New York: Benjamin Blom, 1963.

Ogburn, Charlton. *The Mysterious William Shakespeare.* New York: Dodd, Mead, 1984.

Opfell, Olga S. *The King James Bible Translators.* Jefferson, NC: McFarland, 1982.

Ornstein, Robert. *The Moral Vision of Jacobean Tragedy.* Madison: University of Wisconsin, 1960.

Oxford English Dictionary. J. A. Simpson and E. S. C. Weiner, eds. 2nd ed. 12 vols. Oxford: Clarendon Press, 1989.

Parsons, Robert. *The Letters and Memorials of Father Robert Persons, S. J.* L. Hicks, ed. Vol. 1. *Catholic Record Society.* Vol. 39. London: Catholic Record Society, 1942.

Petti, Anthony G. *English Literary Hands from Chaucer to Dryden.* Cambridge: Harvard University Press, 1977.

Phillips, O. Hood. *Shakespeare and the Lawyers.* London: Methuen, 1972.

Pine, John. *The Tapestry Hangings of the House of Lords: Representing the Several Engagements Between the English and Spanish Fleets.* 1739.

Pollard, Alfred W. *Shakespeare Folios and Quartos.* 1909. Reprint. New York: Cooper Square, 1970.

Pollard, Alfred W. *Shakespeare's Fight with the Pirates and the Problems of the Transmission of His Text.* London: Alexander Moring, 1917.

Pollard, Alfred William, G. R. Redgrave, et al. *A Short-Title Catalogue to Books Printed in England, Scotland, & Ireland.* 2 vols. 2nd ed., rev. and enl. London: Bibliographical Society, 1976–86.

Pope, Alexander. *The Dunciad Variorum, With the Prolegomania of Scriblerus.* Introduction by Robert Kilburn Root. 1729. Reprint. Princeton: Princeton University Press, 1929.

Puttenham, George. *The Arte of English Poesie.* 1589. Reprint. Amsterdam: Theatrum Orbis Terrarum, 1971.

Ralph, Philip Lee. *Sir Humphrey Mildmay: Royalist Gentleman.* New Brunswick: Rutgers University Press, 1947.

Read, Conyers. *Lord Burghley and Queen Elizabeth.* New York: Knopf, 1960.

Rees, Joan. *Samuel Daniel: A Critical and Biographical Study.* Liverpool: Liverpool University Press, 1964.

Reese, M. M. *The Royal Office of Master of the Horse.* London: Threshold, 1976.

Reynolds, Ernest Edwin. *Campion and Parsons: The Jesuit Mission of 1580–1* London: Sheed and Ward, 1980.

Riggs, David. *Ben Jonson: A Life.* Cambridge: Harvard University Press, 1989.

Ringler, William A. *Stephen Gosson: A Biographical and Critical Study.* Princeton: Princeton University Press, 1942.

Roberts, John. *An Answer to Mr. Pope's Preface to Shakespeare.* 1729.

Rossiter, A. P. *Woodstock, A Moral History.* London: Chatto & Windus, 1946.

Salgado, Gamini, ed. *Eyewitnesses of Shakespeare: Firsthand Accounts of Performances, 1590–1890.* New York: Barnes & Noble, 1975.

[Salisbury, Robert Cecil, Marquess of.] *Calendar of the Manuscripts of the Most Honourable, the Marquess of Salisbury.* 24 vols. London: H. M. Stationery Office, 1883–1976.

Salzman, L. F. *Victoria History of the County of Warwick.* Vol. 6. London: University of London Institute of Historical Research, 1951.

Schoenbaum, S. *Shakespeare's Lives: New Edition.* Oxford: Clarendon Press, 1991.

Schoenbaum, S. *William Shakespeare: A Compact Documentary Life.* Rev. ed. New York: Oxford University Press, 1987.

Schoenbaum, S. *William Shakespeare: Records and Images.* New York: Oxford University Press, 1981.

Shadwell, Thomas. *The Complete Works of Thomas Shadwell.* Montague Summers, ed. 5 vols. 1927. Reprint. New York: B. Blom, 1968.

Sherbo, Arthur. *The Birth of Shakespeare Studies; Commentators from Rowe (1709) to Boswell-Malone (1821).* East Lansing: Colleagues Press, 1986.

Shipley, Joseph T. *In Praise of English: The Growth & Use of Language.* New York: Times Books, 1977.

Sidney, Philip. *Syr P. S. His Astrophel and Stella.* 1591. Reprint. Menston: Scolar, 1970.

Smith, Irwin. *Shakespeare's Blackfriars Playhouse.* New York: New York University Press, 1964.

Spencer, Hazelton. *Shakespeare Improved: The Restoration Versions in Quarto and On the Stage.* Cambridge: Harvard University Press, 1927.

Stanley, Arthur Penrhyn. *Historical Memorials of Westminster Abbey.* 8th ed. 1896. Reprint. London: John Murray, 1924.

Steiner, George. *The Death of Tragedy.* New York: Hill and Wang, 1963.

Stern, Virginia F. *Gabriel Harvey: His Life, Marginalia, and Library.* New York: Oxford University Press, 1979.

Stopes, Charlotte Carmichael. *The Life of Henry, Third Earl of Southampton, Shakespeare's Patron.* Cambridge: The University Press, 1922.

Stopes, H. P. Introduction to *Shakespeare's Troilus and Cressida: The First Quarto, 1609. Shakespeare-Quarto Facsimiles,* No. 13. London: W. Griggs, n.d.

Streitberger, W. R. *Jacobean and Caroline Revels Accounts, 1603–1642.* Vol. 13, *Malone Society Collections.* Oxford: Malone Society, 1986.

Strickland, Agnes. *Lives of the Queens of England.* Rev. ed. 6 vols. London: George Bell & Sons, 1888–92.

Strong, Roy C. *Leicester's Triumph.* Leiden: Sir Thomas Browne Institute, 1964.

Swift, Jonathan. *Dean Jonathan's Parody on the 4th Chap. of Genesis.* 1729.

Tanner, Lawrence Edward. *Westminster School: A History.* London: Country Life, 1934.

Taylor, E. G. R. *The Troublesome Voyage of Captain Edward Fenton, 1582–1583.* 2d ser., No. 113. Cambridge: Hakluyt Society, 1959.

Taylor, Gary. *Reinventing Shakespeare: A Cultural History, from the Restoration to the Present.* New York: Weidenfeld & Nicolson, 1989.

Terence, *The Comedies.* Translated by Betty Radice. Rev. ed. Harmondsworth: Penguin, 1976.

Theobald, Lewis. *Preface to the Works of Shakespeare (1734).* Introduction by Hugh G. Dick. Los Angeles: University of California, 1949.

Theobald, Lewis. *Shakespeare Restored.* 1726. Reprint. New York, AMS Press, 1970.

Thomas, David. *Shakespeare in the Public Records.* London: H. M. Stationery Office, 1985.

Tocqueville, Alexis de *Democracy in America.* J. P. Mayer, ed. George Lawrence, trans. Garden City, NY: Doubleday, 1969.

Tooley, R. V. *Maps and Map-makers.* 4th ed. New York: Bonanza, 1970.

Wagner, Anthony Richard. *Heralds of England: A History of the Office and College of Arms.* London: H. M. Stationery Office, 1967.

Wallace, Charles William, ed. *Advance Sheets from Shakespeare, The Globe, and Blackfriars.* Stratford-upon-Avon: Shakespeare Head Press, 1909.

Ward, B. M. *The Seventeenth Earl of Oxford, 1550–1604, From Contemporary Documents.* London: John Murray, 1928.

Warner, Beverley, ed. *Famous Introductions to Shakespeare's Plays, by the Notable Editors of the Eighteenth Century.* 1906. Reprint. New York: Burt Franklin, 1968.

[Webster, Paul Francis.] *The Library of Paul Francis Webster.* Sotheby's, April 24, 1985.

Wells, Stanley W., and Gary Taylor, eds. *William Shakespeare: A Textual Companion*. Oxford: Clarendon Press, 1987.
Western Manuscripts and Miniatures [auction catalogue]. Sotheby's, June 25, 1985.
Wheeler, G. W. *The Earliest Catalogues of the Bodleian Library*. Oxford: University Press, 1928.
Wikland, Erik. *Elizabethan Players in Sweden, 1591–92 &c.* 2d ed., rev. Stockholm: Almqvist & Wiskell, 1971.
Wraight, A. D. *In Search of Christopher Marlowe*. New York: Vanguard Press, 1965.
Wright, Thomas. *Queen Elizabeth and Her Times: A Series of Original Letters*. 2 vols. London: H. Colburn, 1838.
Young, Karl. *Samuel Johnson on Shakespeare: One Aspect*. 1923. Reprint. Folcroft, PA: Folcroft Library Editions, 1977.

Articles in Collections, Journals and Periodicals

Bald, R. C. "Early Copyright Litigation and Biliographical Interest." *The Papers of the Bibliographical Society of America*, vol. 36 (1942), 81–96.
Barroll, J. Leeds, "The Social and Literary Context." In *The Revels History of Drama in English*. Vol. 3, 1576–1613. London: Methuen, 1975, 1–94.
Bentley, Gerald Eades, "John Cotgrave's *English Treasury of Wit and Language* and the Elizabethan Drama," *Studies in Philology*. Vol. 40 (1943), 186–203.
Bethell, Tom, "The Case for Oxford/Reply to Matus," "Looking for Shakespeare," *Atlantic Monthly*, October 1991, 45–61/74–8.
Boyd, Bentley, "A Rose Might Smell as Sweet by Another Name . . . ," *Chicago Tribune*, Aug. 20, 1989.
Bullough, Geoffrey, "*King Lear* and the Annesley Case: A Reconsideration." In *Festschrift Rudolf Stamm*. Berne: Francke, 1969, 43–49.
Cairncross, Andrew S., "Shakespeare and the 'Staying Entries.' " In *Shakespeare in the Southwest: Some New Directions*. T. J. Stafford, ed. El Paso: University of Texas at El Paso, 1969, 80–92.
Chambers, Edmund Kerchever, "Dramatic Records: The Lord Chamberlain's Office." In *Malone Society Collections*, vol. 2, part 3. W. W. Greg, gen. ed. Oxford: Malone Society, 1931, 321–416.
Champlin, Charles, "The Great Shakespeare Mystery Caper," *Town Hall Journal* [Pasadena, CA], August 22, 1989.
Champlin, Charles, "Whomsomever Art Thou, Shaksper?" *Los Angeles Times*, January 12, 1984.
Cole, Maija Jansson, "A New Account of the Burning of the Globe," *Shakespeare Quarterly*, vol. 32 (1981), 352.
Davis, Richard Beale, "Early Editions of George Sandys's 'Ovid': The Circumstances of Production." In *The Papers of the Bibliographical Society of America*, vol. 35 (1941), 255–76.
Dawson, Giles E., review of *This Star of England*, by Dorothy and Charlton Ogburn, *Shakespeare Quarterly* 4 (1953), 165–70.
Dawson, Giles E., "Shakespeare's Handwriting." In *Shakespeare Survey* 42. Cambridge: Cambridge University Press, 1990, 119–128.
Dickey, Franklin, "The Old Man at Work: Forgeries in the Stationers' Register," *Shakespeare Quarterly* 11 (1960), 39–47.
Eccles, Mark, "Sir George Buc, Master of the Revels." In *Thomas Lodge and Other Elizabethans*. Charles J. Sisson, ed. New York; Octagon, 1966, 409–506.

Forker, Charles R., "Webster or Shakespeare? Style, Idiom, Vocabulary, and Spelling in the Additions to *Sir Thomas More.*" In *Shakespeare and Sir Thomas More: Essays on the Play and Its Shakespearian Interest.* New York: Cambridge University Press, 1989, 151–70.

Freehafer, John, "*Cardenio,* by Shakespeare and Fletcher," *Publications of the Modern Language Association* 84 (1969), 501–13.

Frost, David, "Shakespeare in the Seventeenth Century," *Shakespeare Quarterly,* vol. 16 (1965), 81–89.

Garrick, David, Anonymous letter, *Gentleman's Magazine,* August 1769, 375.

Greenstreet, James, "The Whitefrairs Theatre in the Time of Shakspere," *Transactions of the New Shakspere Society, 1887–1892,* ser. 1, no. 13 (1889), 269–84.

Greg, W. W., "The Date of *King Lear* and Shakespeare's Use of Earlier Versions of the Story," *Library,* 4th ser., vol. 20 (1939–40), 377–400.

Greg, W. W., "The Bakings of Betsy." In *Collected Papers,* J. C. Maxwell, ed. Oxford: Clarendon, 1966, 48–74.

Greg, W. W., "Prompt Copies, Private Transcripts, and the 'Playhouse Scrivener,' " *Library,* 4th ser., vol. 6 (1925), 148–56.

Hoy, Cyrus, "The Shares of Fletcher and His Collaborators in the Beaumont and Fletcher Canon," *Studies in Bibliography,* vols. 8–15 (1956–62).

Hume, Robert D., "Securing a Repertory: Plays on the London Stage 1660–5." In *Poetry and Drama, 1570–1700: Essays in Honour of Harold F. Brooks.* Antony Coleman and Antony Hammond, eds. New York: Methuen, 1981, 156–71.

Isham, Gyles, "The Prototype of King Lear and His Daughters," *Notes and Queries,* vol. 199 (1954), 150–51.

Jackson, William A., "Edward Gwynn," *Library,* 4th ser., vol. 15 (1934–35), 92–96.

Jamieson, Michael, "Shakespeare's Celibate Stage," *The Seventeenth-Century Stage* (see entry under Bentley above), 70–93.

Lardner, James, "Onward and Upward with the Arts: The Authorship Question," *The New Yorker,* April 11, 1988, 87–106.

Malkin, Lawrence, "In Lenox they are 'dropping in' on the Bard of Avon," *Smithsonian* (November 1991), 134–45.

Matus, Irvin, "The Case for Shakespeare/Reply to Bethell," "Looking for Shakespeare," *Atlantic Monthly,* October 1991, 64–72/79–82.

Miller, Michael, "Computer Test Authenticates Shakespeare," *Washington Post,* April 21, 1990: C3.

Neidig, William J., "The Shakespeare Quartos of 1619," *Modern Philology,* vol. 8 (1910), 145–63.

Oldenburg, Don, "Beating Up on the Bard," *Washington Post,* December 18, 1990:B5.

Rossiter, A. P., "Unconformity in *Richard II.*" In *Shakespeare: Richard II; A Casebook.* Nicholas Brooke, ed. London: Macmillan, 1973.

Sisson, Charles J., "Introduction to *Believe As You List.*" In *The Seventeenth-Century Stage* (see entry under Bentley above), 170–95.

Spielmann, M. H., "Shakespeare's Portraiture." In *Studies in the First Folio.* Israel Gollancz, ed. 1924. Reprint. Folcroft, PA: Folcroft Library Editions, 1973, 1–52.

Tait, Hugh, "Garrick, Shakespeare, and Wilkes," *British Museum Quarterly,* vol. 24 (1961), 100–107.

Willard, Oliver M., "Jaggard's *Catalogue of English Books*," *Stanford Studies in Language and Literature* (1941), 152–72.
Williams, Philip, Jr., "The 'Second Issue' of Shakespeare's *Troilus and Cressida*, 1609," *Studies in Bibliography*, vol. 2 (1949–50), 25–33.
Wilson, F. P., "The Jaggards and the First Folio of Shakespeare," *Times Literary Supplement*, November 5, 1925, 737.
Wilson, F. P., "Ralph Crane, Scrivener to the King's Players." In *The Seventeenth-Century Stage* (see entry under Bentley above), 137–55

Letters and Manuscripts

Bearman, Robert, Letter to the author, June 28, 1989.
Brooke, Ralph, "Attack on Dethick." c. 1596–1600. MS. V.a.156, Folger Shakespeare Library, Washington, DC.
[Brooke, Ralph], "A note of some coats & Crests lately come to my hands Given by Willm Dethick . . ." c. 1700. MS. V.a.350, Folger Shakespeare Library, Washington, DC.
Cressy, David, Letter to the author, June 23, 1989.
Dethick, William, and William Camden, "The answer of Garter and Clarenceaux Kings of Arms to a Libellous Scroll against certain Arms supposed to be wrongly given." March 21, 1602. Ashmolean MS. 846, folio 50. Ashmolean Library, Oxford; and, College of Arms, London, MS WZ. 276b.
May, Steven W., Letter to the author. September 6, 1991.
Miller, Minos D., Multiple letter. November 4, 1987.
Thomas, David, Letter to the author. August 21, 1989.
Thomas, David, Letter to the author. September 22, 1989.

Index